Mr. Mob

ALSO BY MICHAEL NEWTON
AND FROM MCFARLAND

*The Ku Klux Klan: History, Organization,
Language, Influence and Activities of America's
Most Notorious Secret Society* (2007)

The FBI and the KKK: A Critical History
(2005; paperback 2009)

*Encyclopedia of Cryptozoology: A Global Guide to
Hidden Animals and Their Pursuers* (2005)

The FBI Encyclopedia (2003)

Mr. Mob

The Life and Crimes of Moe Dalitz

MICHAEL NEWTON

McFarland & Company, Inc., Publishers
Jefferson, North Carolina, and London

LIBRARY OF CONGRESS CATALOGUING-IN-PUBLICATION DATA

Newton, Michael, 1951–
Mr. Mob: the life and crimes of Moe Dalitz /
Michael Newton.
p.   cm.
Includes bibliographical references and index.

ISBN 978-0-7864-3516-6
softcover : 50# alkaline paper ∞

1. Dalitz, Morris.
2. Gangsters — United States — Biography.
I. Title.
HV6248.D223N49   2009   364.1092 — dc22 [B]   2009009230

British Library cataloguing data are available

On the cover: Moe Dalitz in Los Angeles, 1951
(AP Photo); pistol barrel tip ©2009 Shutterstock

Manufactured in the United States of America

*McFarland & Company, Inc., Publishers
Box 611, Jefferson, North Carolina 28640
www.mcfarlandpub.com*

For Toni Clark Drago

Acknowledgments

I owe special thanks for assistance in preparation of this work to Toni Clark Drago, David Frasier at Indiana University, and Heather Newton. Others who rendered valuable aid include, alphabetically: John Adams, U.S. District Court, Western New York; Karin Anderson, *Las Vegas Sun*; Chris Aprato, InfoNow Librarian, Los Angeles; Richard Bails Jr., U.S. District Court, Eastern Michigan; Donna Bath, Clerk of White Pine County, Nevada; Bentley Historical Library: Nancy Bartlett, Mary Jo Pugh, John Wimsatt; William Bible, Nevada Resort Association; Sharon Bidwell, *Louisville Courier-Journal*; Doris Blechman, *Detroit Free Press*; Bloomfield Township (Michigan) Public Library; *Boston Globe* library; Mary Braney, Massachusetts State Library; Shelley J. Burleson, Lyndon B. Johnson Library; James Casey, Western Reserve Historical Society; E. Censnis, Boston Public Library; Elizabeth Clemens, Walter P. Reuther Library; *Cleveland Jewish News:* Ted Ganger, Philip Slomovitz; Major Ronald Courtney, Department of the Army; Joyce Cox, Nevada State Library and Archives; Cuyahoga County Public Library: Gary Claxton, Barbara Musselman; Alice Dalligan, Detroit Public Library; Deanna DeMatteo, Las Vegas Strip Historical Site; Michael Elliott, Akron Public Library; Larry Engelman; Professor Sidney Fine, University of Michigan; Rabbi Irwin Groner, Congregation Shaarey Zedek; Norman Grutman; Mary Hanel, Kern County (California) Library System; Betty Havlena, *Detroit News*; Leland Hilligoss, St. Louis Public Library; Barbara Ickes, Free Library of Philadelphia; Mitch Ison, Clark County (Nevada) Public Library; Pat Kendel, *Cleveland Plain Dealer*; Harold Konigsburg; Rhoda Kruse, San Diego Public Library; Shelley Lavey, *Detroit Free Press*; Marcus Miller, Akron Police Department; Irwin Molasky; New York Public Library; Marilyn Nichols, Cleveland Public Library; Art O'Hara, Great Lakes Historical Society; Ohio Historical Society: Gary Arnold, Conrad Weitzel; Virgil Peterson; Warner Pflug, Walter P. Reuther Library; Rod Poteete; Holly Reed, National Archives; Robert Rockaway, Tel Aviv University; Bette Roth, Jewish Historical Society of Michigan; Jean Rudloff, Kentucky Department of Libraries & Archives; Rorie Sherman, *Penthouse*; Charles Sherrill, Western Reserve Historical Society; Becky Smith, Deputy Clerk, Kenton County, Kentucky; Charlene Smith, Kentucky Historical Society; Barbara Soper, Buffalo and Erie County Public Library; Charles South, National Archives; Rabbi Malcolm Stern, American Jewish Archives; Rep. William Thomas; John Thurman, California State Assembly; Elmer Turner, Cleveland Public Library; Wallace Turner, *New York Times*; University of Nevada, Las Vegas Special Collections: Su Kim Chung, Kathy War; U.S. Department of Commerce; Lester Velie, *Reader's Digest*; and Larry Weyhrich, Illinois State Library.

Table of Contents

Preface

The Mob. The Syndicate. The Mafia.

By any name, we know it well — or, do we?

Histories aplenty have been published, mapping every step of gangland evolution from the 1840s to the present. Countless mobsters are immortalized in popular biographies. A few, like Al Capone and Lucky Luciano, captivate platoons of rival authors, each of whom promotes his chosen subject as the wisest and most ruthless gangster of all time.

In fact, by definition, organized crime is a collaborative effort, typically involving dozens (even hundreds) of participants. No individual, however cruel or canny, owns sole credit for the founding and perpetuation of a criminal empire.

And yet, some stand out from the pack.

America's most secretive and most successful gangster never spent a night in jail, or even went to trial, despite a life of crime that spanned three-quarters of a century. He spun a web of myth and mock-respectability around himself so dense that even now, two decades after his demise, most journalists mistake the legend for reality.

Moe Dalitz was a pioneering architect of syndicated crime in the United States. From prohibition to the Reagan years, no other individual was present at so many pivotal events in gangland history. It is impossible to fully understand the modern Mob without first knowing Dalitz, his career, and the publicity campaign that cunningly transformed him from a thug to a revered philanthropist.

Moe's saga holds a vital lesson for American society today, when ethnic gangs thrive on the drug trade of our second prohibition and political corruption spawns new scandals on a weekly basis. Dalitz may be gone, but the conspiracy he helped to organize still thrives, despite the empty hype surrounding "wars on crime." Historians — and all Americans — ignore his lesson at their peril.

My research on Dalitz spans three decades, including eight years in Las Vegas, where Moe spent the last half of his life. In 1982–83, I traveled some 10,000 miles in search of Moe's beginnings and the roots of the cartel he personified. In the process, I interviewed and corresponded with attorneys, journalists and government officials, local law enforcement officers and federal agents. I collected records from the courts of seven states, along with transcripts of investigations carried out by Congress, the New York state legislature, the Illinois Racing Board, and California's state attorney general. Contacts in the NYPD's Intelligence Division rendered valuable service, as did San Diego's grand jury and the Chicago Crime Commission.

1

The mighty Federal Bureau of Investigation never laid a glove on Dalitz, though its agents shadowed him and tapped his telephones for decades. Following Moe's death, I filed a request for his dossier under the Freedom of Information Act. Bureau headquarters stalled for ten years, then released 2,700 pages of declassified material. While frequently inaccurate, redundant, and heavily censored, the FBI's file remains a gold mine of information on Dalitz, his times, and the syndicate he built from scratch with others like himself, who saw the promise of America and made it theirs.

1

Promised Land

The mysteries surrounding Moe Dalitz begin at least a quarter-century before his birth, with the arrival of his parents in America. Moe's father set the tone for his lifelong evasion of authority, employing varied names and birth dates as he moved from one state to another, changing his profession and identity as easily as other men changed clothes. He was a natural chameleon who handed down that talent — or compulsion — to his sons.

To understand that instinct for concealment, we must go back even further into history and track the movement of a people driven from their homes and their professions by a wave of hatred so intense that it was bound to mark their offspring. Persecution breeds resilience, schooling its survivors in the art of subterfuge, and no race in the past 150 years has learned that lesson better than the Jews of Eastern Europe.

* * *

The road begins in fourteenth-century Poland, where King Casimir the Great welcomed Jewish refugees driven from their homes in other parts of Europe. Widely and irrationally blamed for causing the Black Death in 1348, Jewish artisans and tradesmen were a boon to Poland's backward agricultural economy, soon comprising the bulk of a small "middle class" between nobles and serfs. Casimir broadened his empire by conquest, annexing present-day Ukraine in 1349, while a royal marriage merged Lithuania with Poland in 1386. For the most part, Polish Jews enjoyed a peaceful life.

That changed in 1654, when Russian invaders seized Minsk and Vilna. Thirteen years later, the Treaty of Andreuszowo divided Ukraine along the Dnieper River, with Russia claiming the eastern sector. Poland became a Russian "protectorate" in 1717, followed by Czarina Catherine the Great's appointment of a puppet-king in 1764. Eight years later, the first partition of Poland gave Vitebsk to Russia, while Austria claimed Galicia and Prussia seized West Prussia. A second partition, in 1793, gave Russia the districts of Podolia, eastern Volhynia and most of modern Belarus, while Prussia absorbed Greater Poland. Finally, in 1795, Russia devoured Curonia, Lithuania, western Belarus and western Volyhina; Prussia claimed the lands north and west of Warsaw, while Austria annexed territory south and east of that city. Poland officially ceased to exist for the next 123 years.

Those changes spelled disaster for Polish Jews. In an age when revolution toppled royalty in North America and France, Russia remained a feudal society in thrall to its Czar and the Eastern Orthodox Church. Formerly banned from Russia by royal edict, 750,000 Jews became unwilling subjects of the Czar. They were the ultimate outsiders, condemned from church pulpits as "Christ-killers," branded by their faith, their garb and their achievements as a breed apart.

In a nation whose population was 88 percent rural, 95 percent of Jews were urban dwellers. They owned 39 percent of Russia's factories, controlling 25 to 50 percent of the dairy, leather, lumber, soap, textile and tobacco industries. While only 5 percent of Russian Jews were gainfully employed, they represented 11 percent of all factory workers and 36 percent of all merchants. Since Russia had no public schools, Jews supported their own system of universal male education. Comprising less than 2 percent of Russia's population, Jews filed more than 50 percent of all university applications.

Some 95 percent of Russian Jews were confined within the Pale of Settlement, created to contain them in 1791, spanning the area of modern Poland, Belarus, Latvia, Lithuania and Ukraine, confining Jews who could not cross its boundaries without special permission from the Czar. By 1820 the Pale's captive Jewish population had increased to 4.9 million.

Jewish life within the Pale was highly formalized, with *shtetl* (village) dwellers pledged to obey 613 *mitzvot* (commandments) governing all aspects of life. The Talmudic rules dictated everything from methods of putting on shoes in the morning and slaughtering chickens to techniques for singing the Torah. Family was the core of *shtetl* life, which in turn mirrored God's sacred covenant with Israel. The *mitzvot* left little room for individuality inside the Pale, where gentiles were increasingly abusive toward their Jewish neighbors.

That abuse mirrored official policy, dictated from St. Petersburg. Alexander I was the first Czar to codify anti–Semitism with his Statute Concerning the Organization of the Jews in 1804. Pursuing the dual ends of assimilation and eradication of the *shtetl*, Alexander opened public schools to Jews for the first time, then decreed in January 1807 that no Jews were allowed to own or work in any inn or tavern. Since inn-keeping and liquor sales were two leading sources of income for Jews in the Pale, Alexander's decree struck at the heart of their economic life.

For all of Alexander's faults, Czar Nicholas I made his father seem liberal. His thirty years in power spawned more than 600 anti–Jewish decrees, ranging from village expulsions to state censorship of Hebrew and Yiddish books. His Cantonist Decrees of 1827 forced Jews to serve thirty-one years in the Russian army, beginning with forced conversion to Christianity at age twelve. On the civilian front, all Jews in Kiev were expelled from their homes in 1843. In 1844 the crown established special schools for Jews, to bring them "nearer to the Christians and to uproot their harmful beliefs which are influenced by the Talmud."

Czar Alexander II was moderate by comparison. He abandoned the cantonment system, reduced compulsory military service to six years, opened some high schools and universities to Jews, and relaxed the domicile restrictions for selected groups. Those Jews allowed outside the Pale included master artisans and skilled mechanics, university students, and merchants of the first guild. In 1861 Alexander liberated 47 million serfs from bondage to the land. A year later, Polish Jews were granted rights nearly equal to those of gentiles.

Still, there was a downside to Alexander's regime. Masters who lost their serfs in 1861 were compensated, while the serfs were simply cut adrift, left homeless. Two years later, Jews who joined in the Polish rebellion were exiled to die in Siberia. Russia's first pogroms — organized massacres of Jews — occurred in 1871, with tacit approval from local officials. That mayhem reinforced an age-old lesson in the usefulness of bribes. When violence threatened, ready cash often spelled the difference between life and death.

Whatever optimism Jews experienced during the reign of Alexander II was dashed with his assassination on March 1, 1881. Successor Alexander III sought to crush every trace of rebellion within his domain, aided by vigilantes of a "Holy Brotherhood" who staged more than 200 pogroms by year's end. Authorities ignored the rioting or actively joined in, while royal investigators blamed "Jewish exploitation" for the outbreaks. Christian leaders cheered the carnage, with the Holy Synod's procurator-general predicting of Russia's Jews that "one-third will die out, one-third will emigrate, and one-third will disappear without a trace" via conversion.

For the first time in more than a century, Jewish emigration was officially encouraged. On January 16, 1882, Russia's minister of the interior declared the nation's western borders "open for Jews" leaving the country. Those who missed the point were encouraged to flee by new legislation. Alexander's "May Laws" of 1882 barred Jews from owning real estate or engaging in commerce on Christian holidays. Travel within the Pale was also strictly limited: Jews could not move from one town to another, and a town that changed its name could legally expel Jews registered to live under the old name. New "percentage rules" of 1886–87 restricted Jewish high school and university enrollment to 10 percent within the Pale, 5 percent outside it, or 3 percent in Moscow and Kiev.

A key aspect of Alexander's legacy would be the wholesale exodus of Jews from Russia. Most fled first into Galicia, then a part of Austria on Russia's western border. Massed at Brody, they prepared to travel farther, seeking freedom. Millions of them would forsake Europe entirely, for a gamble in America.

* * *

Russian Jews were not the first to reach U.S. shores in the nineteenth century. A trickle of 7,500 arrived between 1820 and 1870, followed by 40,000 more in the 1870s, but nearly all of those were German Jews, many of them Reformists who shared little in common with their Orthodox brethren from Eastern Europe. In 1880, 90 percent of the world's Jewish population (some 7.7 million) remained in Europe, half that number in the former Polish provinces. That balance shifted after Alexander III assumed the Russian throne, with 1.8 million Jews fleeing westward between 1881 and 1900.

Upon arrival in America, 64 percent disembarked at New York City, 10 percent at Philadelphia, and 6 percent (some 66,000) at Boston. No matter where they landed, they faced a grim reception. Anti-Semitism in America had grown after the Civil War, exemplified by a proposed amendment to the Constitution declaring America a "Christian nation." Congress defeated that attempt to codify prejudice in 1874, but an American Protective Association was created to oppose "undesirable" immigrants in 1887, joined in 1894 by the Boston-based Immigration Restriction League.

New arrivals met no warmer welcome from their Jewish predecessors in America, who often resented Polish-Russian immigrants for their strict orthodoxy and their empty purses. As in Russia, eastern Jews were easily identified by their black clothing, beards, and bodies wasted by privation in their homeland or on the Atlantic crossing, described by author George Price as "a kind of hell that cleanses a man of his sins before coming to the land of Columbus."

Resistance was particularly stiff in Boston, where immigrants faced the combined opposition of old-stock patrician families and German Jews who had preceded them. Names "of Jewish complexion" appeared in Boston archives from 1634 onward, but the city's first recognized synagogue surfaced 210 years later. As in other cities, Boston's Jewish community was roughly divided between "German" and "Russian" Jews, the latter broadly regarded as any who arrived after 1880. In June 1882, when 415 Jews arrived from London, the local Hebrew Emigrant Aid Society refused to accept them, sending them on to New York.

And still they came. Boston received 14,600 immigrants between 1890 and 1895, 6,000

Millions of Eastern European Jews sought refuge in the United States (Library of Congress).

Boston's Jewish quarter, 1899 (Library of Congress).

of them Jews. They occupied the North End first, displacing Irish immigrants, later expanding into Chelsea, then across the Mystic River into Dorchester. Those neighborhoods became their ghettos, on a par for squalor with New York's Lower East Side. Anti-Semitic rioting erupted in Fall River, Massachusetts, when 600 Jews arrived in January 1892. Later that year, mothers in the North End were asked to stop their children begging on the streets.

In time, that life produced in some an attitude of bitter cynicism. On the streets of Boston — as in Moscow, Minsk, New York, Cleveland, Detroit — survival of the fittest was the rule.

* * *

Enter a man of mystery. His name was Barnet Dalitz, also called Bernard, Barney, and sometimes Benjamin. He gave his father's name as Alter on some documents, Morris on others. We know nothing of the family patriarch today, but Barnet's mother — Tzipa Sunenshein Dalitz — was Polish, born in 1854.

Barnet claimed to be Austrian, except in 1897 and 1900, when official documents called him a Russian immigrant. His date of birth was flexible, cited in 1896 as May 8, 1874; in 1960 as October 16, 1875. Between those dates, the census roll for 1910 said he was born in 1872. Brother Nathan was similarly vague, born either in 1882 or 1883.

The Dalitz brothers left no trace of their arrival in America. Barnet claimed that he disembarked at Boston, during 1890, but he could not proffer a specific date. Nine decades later, immigration officers described the absence of a paper trail as "very strange," suggesting that Barnet may have jumped ship or entered the U.S. illegally from Canada. His Austrian birthright was verified, after a fashion, by his service as a charter member of the Austrian Francis Joseph Benefit Association, founded in December 1895.

In Boston, "Bernard" Dalitz made his living as a barber, though city directories called him a "hairdresser" — a term usually reserved in those more chauvinistic times for stylists serving female clients. During 1894–95 he worked alone, then partnered for the next seven years with Morris Messinger. He lived in rented rooms and moved each year from 1894 to 1896.

And then he met a woman. Anna Cohen was another living mystery. A Russian immigrant and "tailoress" by trade, daughter of Joseph and Minnie Cohen, she arrived in the United States, like Dalitz, with no record of her entry. Like her suitor, she played fast and loose with birth dates, variously claiming 1876 and 1881.

They wed, as Barney and Annie, on July 26, 1896. It was a first marriage for both, performed (they claimed) by "Rabbi H. Shenberg" of Congregation Shara Cedek. But the record poses yet another riddle, for the Shara Cedek temple had no Rabbi Shenberg during 1883–1900. The only matching name in contemporary directories (for 1901) is Hyman Shenberg, a dealer in "provisions" with a shop on Rochester Street. Two months after the wedding, on September 28, Barnet swore loyalty to the United States before clerk Frank Mason of Boston's federal court. Two friends, Louis Isenberg and Julius Rosenblum, declared that he had lived in Boston for at least five years. His naturalization also covered Anna and their children yet unborn.

The first of those children, son Louis, arrived on October 22, 1897. Another son, Morris Barney Dalitz, joined the family on Christmas Eve of 1899 — or so he later claimed. When FBI agents went looking for his birth certificate in 1958, they found that none existed. There *was* a birth certificate for Louis *Dolitz,* son of Russian immigrants *Jacob* and Annie. Jacob was a barber whose Lowell Street address matched the residence of "Bernard" Dalitz during 1897–99.

The census roll for 1900 further complicates the search. It found Bernard and Annie *Dalidge* living with sons Louis (two years old) and *Moses* (six months) at 11 Wall Street. Meanwhile, Boston's directory for 1900 placed Bernard Dalitz at 4 Wall Street, moving seven doors down the block a year later. Another tenant in the "Dalidge" home was Aaron Jackson, a Russian born in 1876. The roster marked him with a "c" for cousin, while his citizenship went unrecorded. Subsequent census rolls list Jackson's birth year as 1876, 1877 and 1882.

Changes were in the wind by 1903. The Dalitz-Messinger partnership vanished from Boston's directory that year, while "Bernard" found a new home on Hale Street. It marked his last known residence in Boston, as his family dropped from public view. When they resurfaced three years later, in Detroit, Barnet had a new trade and a new identity.

* * *

Detroit made Boston look like paradise. Its population had ballooned from 116,000 to 286,000 in the 1880s, 466,000 by 1910, and 993,000 in 1920, making Detroit the nation's fourth-largest city. One in every six Detroit families occupied a single room, while beds in all-male boarding houses rented by eight-hour shifts and houses jerry-built on tiny business lots sold off before they were completed.

More than one-fourth of all the new arrivals in Detroit were foreign born, but only one in seven of them earned the $900 yearly wage considered necessary for a family of five. They lived in blighted ghettos: "Corktown" for the Irish, in west Detroit; "Kentucky," for blacks, and "Polacktown" together on the east; "Dutchtown" along Gratiot Avenue; and "Sauerkraut Row," for Germans, on Grand Boulevard. Jews replaced blacks in the blighted area between St. Antoine and Hastings Streets, dubbed "Little Jerusalem" in newsprint. The groups rarely mingled, except to fight for turf, and employers used that ethnic antagonism to frustrate union organizers.

Income was correlated with fluency in English, and second-generation Jews made the best progress among recent immigrants. They learned the language quickly, left their ghettos sooner, and enjoyed pay hikes up to 14 percent. In time, they overtook their Irish predecessors, who clung more tenaciously to jobs held by their fathers.

Detroit's schools did little to prepare immigrant children for success. Russian Jews were accustomed to having their children home-schooled by a private *rebbe* (teacher), or in a *cheder* that focused on only one phase of instruction, but they trusted America's secular schools as a means of integration with society. That trust was not repaid by a system where teachers were often indifferent or actively hostile to immigrant students, prone to lapsing from their lesson plans into racist tirades or insulting lectures on personal hygiene.

The result, predictably, was a system that promoted failure. By fifth grade, 48 percent of all students were branded "retarded" (two or more grades behind their peers), and nearly one-third of all those who enrolled in first grade had quit school. By eighth grade, only 32 percent of the original crop remained, and one-third of those were hopelessly behind the rest. Only one of every thirteen children enrolled in grammar school made it to the final year of high school. German-Jewish children had the best record for advancing to high school. By contrast, a federal study conducted in 1911 found only two Polish children in Detroit's high school system, and no Italians at all. In short, the city's education system was a breeding ground for anger channeled into crime.

* * *

After two years in limbo, "Benjamin" Dalitz appeared in Detroit's city directory for 1906, living and working at 283 Alfred Street. He had given up his comb and scissors for partnership in a laundry, Dalitz & Jackson Towel Suppliers. He and the firm vanished again in 1907, perhaps a printer's oversight, for he resurfaced in the 1908 directory. He was Barnet again by then, teamed with cousin Aaron Jackson and a third partner, Frank Waldham, in the Massachusetts Laundry Company at 305 Alfred. Daughter Helen, last of three Dalitz children, was born that same year.

The three partners labored together through 1911, doing business as the Massachusetts Steam Laundry ("flatwork a specialty"). They handled 90,000 pieces daily in 1909, increased to 100,000 a day two years later. Barnet's brother, Nathan, arrived from Pittsburgh to join the team in 1912, bringing wife Sarah, daughter Ida (four years old) and son Morris (two) to a home on Warren Avenue. In 1913 the Massachusetts Laundry spawned a new enterprise, the Michigan Dry Cleaning Company. Together, in 1916, they boasted the "largest capacity in [the] city" for flatwork.

It was a Motown success story, but Barnet's sons did not fare so well in school. No scholastic records remain for the Dalitz brothers in Detroit. The only trace of their existence in the system is a Central High School yearbook — *The Centralite* — for 1914, listing "B. Louis Dalitz" as a member of House No. 75. The house colors, perhaps auspicious in view of later events, were purple and white. By 1916 Lou was gainfully employed, boarding with his parents and clerking for a dry goods wholesaler, A. Krolik and Company.

Sixty years after the fact, Moe Dalitz told an interviewer that he had attended Bishop Elementary School. In those days, "Old Bishop" was two schools in one, with academic classes for regular students and ungraded job training for "problem" youths. Moe later followed brother Lou to Central High, but did not graduate. Author Hank Messick claims that Moe failed four subjects and quit school in his junior year, circa 1917–18.

Detroit's Bishop Elementary School (Library of Congress).

Moe Dalitz and his fellow Purple Gangsters attended Central High School without graduating (Library of Congress).

In light of Moe's intelligence, amply demonstrated over the next seven decades, the problem may have been his choice of friends. Moe's classmates at Bishop Elementary and Central High included Hyman "The Indian" Altman; Abraham, Isadore, Joseph and Raymond Bernstein; Sam "Fatty" Bernstein (no relation to the other four); Jack Budd; Sam "Gorilla" Davis; Harry and Louis Fleischer; Sam Garfinkle; Harry and Philip Keywell; Morris Raider; Zigmund Selbin; Irving Shapiro; and Abe Zussman.

Together, they later formed the hard core of Detroit's ferocious Purple Gang.

* * *

The gang's colorful name cannot be traced with any certainty today. One version has it that the boys wore purple jerseys at some unidentified gymnasium, another that they took the name from leader Samuel "Sammy Purple" Cohen. Crime historian Paul Kavieff names brothers "Sam and Ben Purple" as Old Bishop students, but no other source confirms their existence. The most common story attributes the nickname to a pair of anonymous Hastings Street merchants, who dubbed the young hooligans "purple" — tainted or "off-color" — for their early crimes. In fact, as Kavieff concedes, the handle may have been invented by some 1920s journalist.

Street gangs had lost their novelty in the United States by 1915. They were part of every

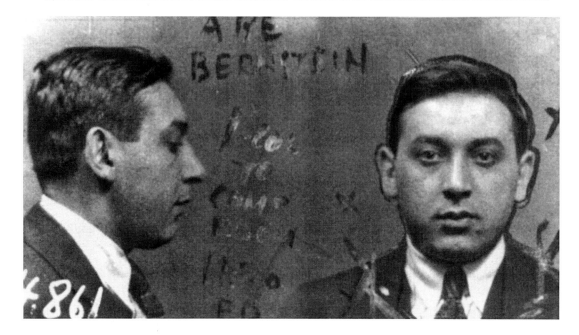

Police mug shot of Abe Bernstein, circa 1920 (National Archives).

urban landscape from New York to San Francisco, robbing, raping, fighting skirmishes with rival hoodlums and police. Some organized initially in self-defense, against attacks by thugs from other ethnic groups. Gangs became surrogate families for youths whose parents worked twelve- and fifteen-hour days. A report issued by Detroit's board of education in 1910 found that many children "come from neglected homes, have cruel stepparents, are feeble minded, suffer from malnutrition, nervous diseases, vicious habits, or physical conditions, many of which can be cured and the child saved from a criminal life. The policeman and the delinquent are not friends, the psychic effect of the policeman is association with crime, hence branding the child as a criminal."

Prior to 1918 most crime in the Jewish ghetto was committed by offenders below age twenty. Older gangsters, dubbed *trombeniks* ("bums"), were a new phenomenon for Russian Jews. Most were gamblers like bookie Sam Solomon, racketeers like "One-Armed Mike" Galfand, or saloon owners like Charles Leiter and Henry Schorr. The senior statesman of *trombeniks* in those days was "Professor" Charles Auerbach, a pimp and strikebreaker from New York City who collected rare books on the side. Greed motivated criminals of every race, but historian Samuel Feldstein observes of the Jewish gangster: "Often he was more merciless and bitter — his criminal passion had no limit."

And mobsters stood out on Hastings Street, ironically nicknamed "Paradise Alley." Their stylish suits and shiny cars contrasted sharply with the humble lives of shopkeepers and pushcart peddlers. Moe and his fellow Purples ran errands for Auerbach and company, collecting pocket money, graduating quickly to illegal chores and management of schoolyard crap games, rolling drunks and offering "protection" (from themselves) to local merchants at a price.

Detroit at large was a sinkhole of crime in the years preceding World War I. In 1910 it boasted 1,600 licensed bars and another 1,000 illegal saloons, dubbed "blind pigs." Prostitution was well organized, with 500 brothels outnumbering the city's churches. As certain streets became notorious, their names were simply changed — Croghan became Monroe, Champlain became Lafayette East, and so forth. Felons could purchase virtual immunity from Police Commissioner John Gillespie, or ensure quick release if convicted. Gillespie's cops were often slow-witted political hacks, with an average I.Q. of 58 (55 for sergeants), earning $2.50 per twelve-hour shift. Most welcomed bribes, while their "investigative" skills were limited to backroom application of the rubber hose. "Curbstone courts" were common, their brutality increasing the contempt that young offenders felt toward those who beat them down.

Shortly before the city election of 1916, Mayor Oscar Marx fired Gillespie and replaced him with James Couzens, a former director of Ford Motor Company whose sole police experience consisted of hiring private detectives to spy on Ford employees and harass union organizers. Despite that suspect origin, Couzens launched a private investigation of crime in Detroit, reporting that he "found conditions far worse than the public dreamed they were. The real inside conditions were never known to the public.... The town was wide open.... Gamblers ran as they pleased; hundreds of houses of prostitution were scattered around, and 1,400 saloons ran all day and all night and on Sundays."

Samuel "Sammy Purple" Cohen (Library of Congress).

Couzens publicly called for a "disciplined city," commanding his men to enforce all laws without fear or favor. He seemed to mean it, and that posed a problem for his wealthy backers, who sought a hands-off policy for Detroit's red-light district in the name of "public welfare." Couzens later complained, "When they asked me to clean up Detroit they didn't mean it. They wanted me to clean it up and not clean it up. They wanted me to make it nice enough for the reformers and let it stay rotten enough to appease the bums."

In October 1917, when Couzens called Detroit "the best policed city in the United States," a local tabloid countered with reports that murders had increased by 53 percent on his watch, while robberies tripled and auto thefts quadrupled. Nearly three hundred policemen were hauled before Couzens on various charges in the last six months of 1917, eighty-nine of them for drinking on duty—but he only fired twenty-nine. Fifty-four holdups were recorded in the first six weeks of 1918, and Couzens conceded defeat in mid–February, enlisting state troopers to patrol the streets at night.

Detroit was bad. But it soon got worse.

* * *

War in Europe struck a blow against Detroit's economy in 1914–15, as reduction of U.S. exports produced widespread unemployment. Congress authorized military conscription on May 18, 1917, with males aged eighteen and over required to register by June 5. The Dalitz brothers stalled for fifteen months, then registered together on September 12, 1918 — two months before the armistice in Europe. Both listed their address as 728 Brush Street, Louis naming his father as Barnet, while Moe called him Barney. Both described themselves as salesmen, Louis for the A. Krolik Company and Morris for a jeweler, S. Lachman. Registrar W.W. Herne judged Louis "medium" in height and build, while Y.E. Fisher found Moe "short" and "slender," tipping the scales at 138 pounds. Neither was drafted, but it hardly mattered. With their cohorts from Old Bishop, they were soon fighting in another war at home, launched by a band of moralists who tried to save America and nearly ruined it instead. Prohibition was coming, and Michigan led the charge.

* * *

Opposition to liquor was nothing new in the Wolverine State or in America at large. The *Michigan Christian Advocate* complained in 1893 of liquor interests dominating politics, and the Anti-Saloon League was organized two years later, in neighboring Ohio. Eight of Michigan's eighty-three counties voted themselves dry in 1908, increased to thirty-six in 1910 and forty in 1911.

America's entry to the Great War helped the drys in three ways: first by centralizing authority in Washington as never before; second, by stressing conservation of food, including various grains used in brewing and distilling; and third, by condemning all things German — which in turn gave temperance crusaders leave to note that many brewers were "enemy aliens." Twenty-three states had some form of prohibition by 1916, and three more went dry in 1917. Michigan was among them, carried on rural ballots while Detroit voted "wet," by a margin of 62,500 to 54,000.

Article XV of Michigan's constitution outlawed sale of alcohol after April 30, 1918, "except for medicinal, mechanical, chemical, scientific or sacramental purposes." New statutes banned any "bringing in" of booze from other states and authorized closure of blind pigs as public nuisances, barred clubs from keeping liquor inventories, restricted the alcohol content of medicines, and assigned enforcement to the state Food and Drug Department under Commissioner Fred Woodworth. An eternal optimist, Woodworth assured the press that he had ample troops on hand to stem the tide of alcohol.

Moe Dalitz and the Purple Gang would prove him wrong.

2

Puller

Michigan officially went dry on May 1, 1918. Over the next twenty months, it furnished a graphic preview of prohibition's "noble experiment," complete with rampant smuggling and bootleg production of liquor, official corruption, and bloody gang wars. But in the early months, it still seemed like a good idea.

In April 1918, Detroit boasted 1,534 licensed saloons and 800 blind pigs. Five years later, police spokesmen acknowledged 3,000 illegal saloons in their city; by 1925 the number jumped to 15,000. Three years later, the *Detroit News* counted 25,000. In some parts of Detroit, the *News* declared, "every house is either a bootleg stand or a blind pig." One reporter found 150 booze emporiums on a single block. By 1928, bootlegging was Detroit's second-largest industry, after automobiles. It employed some 50,000 people, according to Detroit's Board of Commerce. In 1930, official sources pegged yearly retail sales of alcoholic beverages at $239 million. Underworld tattlers placed the total closer to $400 million per year.

Early forms of bootlegging included bogus medical prescriptions and small-scale smuggling or mailing of liquor from neighboring states. Larger consignments traveled by truck or by rail, disguised with false labels as oil, paint, furniture, cement, produce, and so forth. Within two months of prohibition's advent, police in Monroe, Michigan, jailed 300 amateur smugglers caught en route from neighboring Ohio.

That catch was the tip of an alcoholic iceberg. By summer 1918, Detroit's "great booze rush" was on, with thousands of smugglers traversing Dixie Highway—dubbed the "Avenue de Booze"—between Detroit and sopping-wet Toledo, Ohio. Governor Alfred Sleeper sent Colonel Roy Vandercook to Monroe with 24 state troopers, to dam the flood of alcohol. By year's end, Vandercook's squad had arrested 1,102 smugglers, seizing contraband valued at $689,160, but most of the liquor got past them. *Detroit News* reporter Jenny Nolan accurately called the Dixie Highway trade "a dress rehearsal of ingenuity and audacity for the much larger operations to come."

Smuggling methods were diverse and often daring. Liquid cargoes crossed from Canada in speedboats, or on wheels, when lakes and rivers froze. Submarine pipelines and underground tunnels linked Canadian distilleries to Michigan bottling plants. Sunken houseboats housed underwater cable delivery systems. River pirates, known as "go-through guys," posed greater danger to rumrunners than the prospect of arrest. By early 1919, young firebrands of the Purple Gang were renowned as both smugglers *and* hijackers, quick on the trigger when guarding their alcohol shipments or stealing from others.

Despite Michigan's bad example, the rest of the United States pressed on to ratify the

Detroit dry agents raid an illegal distillery (Library of Congress).

Eighteenth Amendment, banning liquor nationwide. America went "dry" from coast to coast at 12:01 A.M. on January 17, 1920. Within the hour, Chicago gangsters set the tone for national prohibition by robbing three liquor warehouses. Before day's end, Detroit officers staged the nation's first booze raids, demolishing two outlaw stills. It was a feeble gesture in the face of a deluge.

* * *

National prohibition lasted for thirteen years, ten months, and eighteen days. By the time it began, Detroit mobsters had eighteen months of hard-earned experience perfecting the manufacture, transportation and sale of liquid contraband, with smuggling routes well established.

For Moe Dalitz and others, the Volstead Act was not a threat.

It was an opportunity.

There was no shortage of booze in "dry" America. Prohibition's advent found 138 million gallons of pre–Volstead whiskey stashed in bonded warehouses, beyond reach of its owners unless they obtained federal permits for export or non-beverage use. During 1920–23, licensed distilleries produced 130 million gallons of medicinal alcohol, 7 million gallons of rum (for use in tobacco products), 8 million gallons of brandy (used in foods and medicine), and 24 million gallons of sacramental wine. Brewers turned out 1 billion gallons of legal "near-

Raiders captured this rumrunner on the Detroit River, while many others escaped (Library of Congress).

beer," with all but .005 percent of the alcohol extracted. Thus resumed, on a national scale, the charade of wholesale medical prescriptions, stolen or counterfeit warehouse withdrawal permits, and manipulation of near-beer, either through misdirection or sale of legitimate stock, which became "needle beer" when bootleggers restored its missing alcohol.

Smuggling, meanwhile, continued apace. Canadian Customs logged 8,335 gallons of liquor exported to the U.S. in 1921, increasing to 1.17 million gallons (worth $19 million) by 1928. The U.S. Commerce Department countered with claims of $90 million shipped in 1921–23, an estimate derided as too low by U.S. Customs. On the Canadian stock exchange, four giant liquor firms showed gains of $73 million in the same period, up 315 percent, while dominion governments made millions from export taxes.

Smuggling methods pioneered by the Purple Gang and others in 1918–19 endured, despite federal disclaimers. Lakes Erie and St. Clair boasted "Rum Rows" rivaling those of the Eastern Seaboard. Ranks of cargo ships anchored outside U.S. territorial waters, off-loading contraband to a mosquito fleet of speedboats that supplied Detroit and Buffalo, New York. Two of those ships, *Geronimo* and *Vedas*, served the Purple Gang exclusively. Detroit received

12,000 gallons of whiskey and 8,000 gallons of beer each day, by boat. More came by truck, rail, and air. After a plane crash at Kalamazoo, in July 1925, police found 100 quarts of whiskey and invoices stamped in Windsor, Ontario.

Canada's premier whiskey smuggler was Samuel Bronfman ("liquorman," in Yiddish), a Russian Jew whose parents fled the pogroms in 1889 and settled in Manitoba. With brothers Harry, Abe and Allan, Samuel grew rich selling whiskey and beer. While Harry managed shipping, Samuel founded the Montreal-based Distillers Corporation, building an empire on brand names including Calvert, Dewar's, and Seven Crown. Later, he merged with Seagram & Sons. Harry kept the home fires burning under massive stills and built the first international whiskey pipeline, while Samuel traveled widely, visiting American customers such as Chicago's Alphonse Capone, Arizona's Kemper Marley, and Detroit's Moe Dalitz. After repeal, Secretary of the Treasury Henry Morgenthau Jr. estimated that Canadian distillers owed the U.S. $60 million in customs and excise duties; Secretary of State Cordell Hull negotiated a $3 million settlement, half of it paid by the Bronfmans from profits of their newly legitimized Seagram's fortune.

Despite their daring and diversity, smugglers could not serve all of Detroit's thirsty scofflaws. Between 1920 and 1933, Detroit police seized 3,000 stills, 500,000 pounds of corn sugar, and 2.5 million gallons of mash. An average-sized commercial distillery, built for $500, might produce 100 gallons of whiskey per day, at a cost of 50 cents per gallon. Sold wholesale for three to four dollars per gallon, the illicit booze turned a profit of 600 to 800 percent.

Some outlaw plants were much larger. In January 1924, federal agents raided a brewery on Michigan Avenue, three-quarters of a mile from City Hall. Its crew produced an average 350 barrels of beer per day. The raiders seized ten 500-gallon beer vats, 142 five-gallon cans of malt, 94 barrels of beer, two loaded trucks, and various brewing paraphernalia. Four years later, authorities found a huge alky complex on Woodward Avenue. The operation filled a city block of basements and most of the buildings above it, boasting three 25,000-gallon beer vats, three 30,000-gallon whiskey tanks, a large refrigerating plant, and a fleet of delivery trucks. Small wonder, then, that one local wag called Motown "a city upon a still."

The net result for Detroit was predictable. In September 1923, the *News* proclaimed: "The law of the jungle rules Detroit." Two years later, the city's deputy prohibition director called Detroit "the wettest city that I have been assigned to." A 1927 Rockefeller Foundation report branded Detroit the most corrupt city in America, "having more blind pigs, houses of ill fame, dope dens and similar places in proportion to population" than any competing metropolis. Bootleggers, if charged, generally escaped punishment: of 1,286 cases filed in Recorder's Court between January 1 and August 15, 1923, half were dismissed for improper evidence; 566 defendants pled guilty and paid small fines; of 35 sent to trial, only 5 were convicted.

* * *

Moe Dalitz and his brother Lou earned fortunes from the liquor trade but left few tracks. Author Hank Messick claims that Lou was twice arrested during 1922, paying a hundred-dollar fine for one offense, but no records remain to prove it. Four decades later, Detroit police told FBI agents that Lou was arrested twice in the 1920s: on February 26, 1920, for "uttering and publishing," and again on April 15, 1929, on a "disorderly person investigation charge." Neither case led to trial. Moe, meanwhile, earned the nickname "Puller" for his skill at bringing liquor out of Canada. The brothers used their father's laundry trucks for after-hours transport, later graduating to barges and speedboats.

Various authors have confused Moe Dalitz's connection to the Purple Gang. Nevada reporter John Smith calls Moe "an associate" of the Purples, while Hank Messick placed him at the gang's "executive level," and Mafia historian Rick Porello calls Moe a "senior member ... a Jewish version of the Sicilian *consigliere*." In fact, while Moe was older than some Purple Gangsters, he was three years *younger* than supposed founder "Sammy Purple" Cohen, and six years younger than Abe Bernstein. William Roemer, an FBI agent-turned-writer, was more confused than most. First, he claimed that Moe "teamed up with members of the Purple Gang," then branded him an "admiral" of the rival Little Jewish Navy. Another Roemer tome declares that Moe was both a Little Jewish Navy admiral *and* allied with the Purples. In his last book, Roemer reverted to the original story, saying that Dalitz "started off as a leader of the 'Little Jewish Navy,'" at war with the Purples. In 1961, Detroit police told G-men (FBI agents) that their "records did not show any information that MORRIS DALITZ was ever active in the 'Purple Gang' or conducted illegal activities in Detroit."

Dalitz himself, in an undated FBI interview, "denied he had ever been affiliated with the Purple Gang," but confessed attending grade school with the Bernsteins and admitted "that he continued this association by trading bootleg whiskey with them and with other members of that notorious gang during the Prohibition era." A separate FBI report alludes to Moe's criminal activity dating from 1921, but the file in question no longer exists. Another link between Moe and the Purples was childhood friend Sam Garfield (né Garfinkle), Russian born in December 1899 or 1900 (reports vary). Garfield became a U.S. citizen in 1907, and met Dalitz at Bishop Elementary School, later teaming with Moe in casinos, oil drilling, and shady stock deals.

While Moe conducted most of the family's booze business, brother Louis maintained a respectable façade. Detroit city directories for 1916 and 1918 found Lou boarding with his parents, still employed by A. Krolik & Company, but Moe vanished from their pages in the wartime years. In 1919–20, Barnet Dalitz appeared as vice president of the Massachusetts Laundry Company, with brother Nathan listed as treasurer. Moe surfaced, joining Lou as boarders with their parents on Brush Street; Lou remained with A. Krolik, while Moe was labeled a salesman for some unnamed firm. Both brothers vanished from the 1920–21 directory, when city planners renamed Brush Street as Hancock, changing Barnet's home address from 726 to 326. Lou reappeared with his parents in 1922–23, as an "agent" of the Massachusetts Laundry.

Love found Moe Dalitz somewhere on the road, in 1922. On March 22, in Indianapolis, he married Edna Louise Keating, a Chicago native born on July 23, 1900. Her parents, John Keating and Clara Steinfeldt, were deceased. The marriage license application lists her residence as the Meridian Apartments, in Indianapolis. Moe, self-described as a salesman for the Massachusetts Laundry Company, claimed residency at the prestigious Claypool Hotel. Marion County Clerk George Coffin performed the civil ceremony — and the couple promptly vanished into limbo.

Back in Detroit, the directory for 1923–24 placed Barnet Dalitz at 2267 Gladstone Avenue, renting rooms to Moe and Lou with no mention of Edna. "Maurice" Dalitz and sister Helen remained as boarders with their parents in 1924–25, while Lou shifted to Blaine Avenue, sharing an apartment with Mrs. Mary Marmer. The same directory named Lou as a partner, with Harry Cohen, in the new Detroit Supply System. Conflicting FBI reports describe Lou as a Detroit Supply partner during 1920–24; Commerce Department files claim that Detroit Supply was founded in 1925 and dissolved in August 1929. Lou retained his job and home address in 1925–26, while Moe vanished again, and Edna surfaced alone, at 99

The Claypool Hotel, where Moe Dalitz registered for his first marriage, in 1922 (Library of Congress).

East Alexander Avenue. In 1926–27, Lou was the sole Dalitz listed for Detroit, living alone at 3039 Gladstone, still working for Detroit Supply.

* * *

As a group, American Jews had little interest in prohibition, but the liquor ban offered hoodlums an unprecedented opportunity. Before prohibition, Detroit's Russian-Polish Jews dominated local trade in grain, sugar, and scrap metal. Their rebel sons thus found the raw materials of liquor and illicit stills already at their fingertips. Huge profits from smuggling and bootlegging kept young *trombeniks* from outgrowing their criminal phase. And, since most Jews rarely drank alcohol, ghetto gangs were forced to invade other neighborhoods, honing their lethal skills against competing, hostile ethnic groups.

No prohibition-era Jewish syndicate was more notorious than Detroit's Purple Gang, merged by 1923 with the Oakland Sugar House Gang of Charles Leiter and Henry Schorr. Purples themselves organized the "Little Jewish Navy" to import Canadian liquor, shipping the surplus nationwide through their Art Novelty Company, and hijacked shipments from competing gangs. They also stole prizefight films and forced theater owners to show them at inflated prices, faked accidents for fraudulent insurance claims, and hired safecracker Morris

Yonnie Licavoli (far right) in custody with Purple Gang members and a Detroit detective (far left) (Library of Congress).

"Red" Rudinsky to pull high-stakes robberies at $5,000 to $15,000 per job. Purples executed contract killings, robbed competitors' blind pigs, and abducted mobsters who could not squeal to police, holding their victims at a fortified "kidnapper's castle" until ransom was paid. Chicago-based jazz musician Milton "Mezz Mezzrow" Mesirow recalled the Purples as "gamblers and big spenders," a group of "flashy good-natured Jews, dressed in loud checked suits and open-necked sports shirts." Crime historian Herbert Asbury saw a darker side, calling them "the most efficiently organized gang of killers in the United States."

Detroit's Italian underworld consisted of various rival families, supervised by gangland diplomat Samuel Catalanotte until his death in 1930. The decade's dominant Italian syndicates were known, respectively, as the Westside Mob and the River Gang, a conglomerate outfit, including both native Detroiters and transplants from St. Louis. Bound by blood, marriage, friendship and business ties, this mob contingent — later Detroit's premier Mafia family — has confused reporters for decades. Primary members included brothers Peter "Horseface Pete" and Thomas "Yonnie" Licavoli, cousin James "Jack White" Licavoli; Joseph "Scarface Joe" Bommarito (Pete Licavoli's father-in-law); Francesco Cammaratta (married to a Licavoli sister); Joseph Zerilli; Guglielmo "Black Bill" Tocco (Zerilli's cousin); Joe Massei; and Joseph Moceri. Pseudonyms confuse the record further, as when Peter Licavoli called himself "Pete Moceri."

The St. Louis prelude of the River Gang is simply told. Mathew Licavoli and his wife emigrated from Sicily around 1900. Son Peter was born in 1902 or 1903, followed by Thomas in 1904, and various siblings thereafter. Most of their neighbors were Jewish, prompting the boys to learn Yiddish as children and to shed the clannish attitudes that prevented other mafiosi from collaborating with non–Italian gangsters. Joe Massei received a similar lesson in tolerance from his Irish mother. The boys ran wild in St. Louis, joining the Hammerhead Gang and terrorizing local merchants. All logged multiple arrests as juveniles: James Licavoli later estimated his St. Louis collars at "maybe a dozen times, maybe two dozen." Over time, police harassment in St. Louis and potential fortunes in Detroit convinced the Hammerheads to relocate.

Legend has it that the Licavolis were imported to Detroit as muscle, but historians cannot agree on who issued the summons. Author Paul Kavieff claims that Joe Moceri first invited Pete Licavoli, while Hank Messick credits the Purple Gang with recruiting Thomas. In either case, once the brothers were settled in Motown, various cousins, in-laws, and crime partners followed their lead. Whether allied with the Purples or simply gun-shy, the River Gangsters avoided Purple territory with their liquor traffic, controlling the upper Detroit River. Pete Licavoli supervised shipments and taxed competitors 25 percent of each whiskey load's value for safe passage through River Gang turf. In Detroit — as later, elsewhere — Horseface Pete and his *amici* also did extensive business with Moe Dalitz.

* * *

Joe Massei (second from left) with his attorney Edward Kennedy Jr. (third from left) and unidentified companions (National Archives).

"Alien" racketeering fueled a brushfire of virulent nativism sweeping America during prohibition. Auto magnate Henry Ford led the charge in May 1920, when his *Dearborn Independent* ran the first of ninety-two articles on "The International Jew: The World's Problem." Ford overstepped his bounds in 1924, with personal slurs against Chicago lawyer Aaron Sapiro. Slapped with a million-dollar libel suit, the Model T's inventor lost his nerve, belatedly attempting to deny his flagrant anti–Semitism. The case ended with a mistrial and a half-hearted apology from Ford, but *The International Jew* soon resurfaced in book form, while Ford kept scores of German-American Bund members on his payroll as strikebreakers. Across the Atlantic, Adolf Hitler admired Ford's style, kept a photograph of Ford in his office, and in 1938 presented Ford with the Third Reich's highest civilian award, the Grand Cross of the German Eagle.

* * *

Moe Dalitz and the Purple Gang did business with the lords of gangland nationwide. Chicago's Al Capone was probably the most notorious, but Purple vendors also sold their whiskey to his mortal enemy, George "Bugs" Moran. Capone cast greedy eyes upon Detroit but would not risk a rumble with the Purples, whom Mezz Mezzrow described as "a hard lot of guys, so tough they made Capone's playmates look like a kindergarten class." In New York City, customers included rival mafiosi Giuseppe "Joe the Boss" Masseria and Salvatore Maranzano, Charles "Lucky" Luciano (who used the Purples for long-distance contract murders), and the Bug-and-Meyer Mob of Meyer Lansky and Benjamin "Bugsy" Siegel. While Siegel took the honors for insanity, insiders dubbed Lansky and Siegel "the Two Bugs" for their impulsive violence in the early 1920s.

Others Purple allies included a *Who's Who* of Jewish mobsters throughout the U.S. New England rumrunning was dominated from Boston by Charles "King" Solomon and Joseph Linsey, with partners Hyman Abrams and Louis Fox. Isadore "Kid Cann" Blumenfeld ran Minneapolis, Minnesota, with his brothers "Harry Bloom" and "Yiddy Bloom" (né Jacob). Next door, in St. Paul, Leon Gluckman called the shots. Solomon "Cutcher-head-off" Weissman struck liquid gold in Kansas City, under Irish boss Tom Pendergast and Mafia watchdog John Lazia. Joseph Reinfeld and Abner "Longy" Zwillman worked Newark, New Jersey. Max "Boo Boo" Hoff and Charles Schwarz ran Philadelphia's Quaker Industrial Alcohol Company, succeeded by Harry "Nig Rosen" Stromberg. Farther west, Dave Berman fought for primacy in Iowa and the Dakotas, waging liquor wars that claimed 375 lives during 1922–26.

One rumrunner who broke the classic mold was Boston's Joseph Kennedy, future U.S. ambassador to England and father of America's thirty-fifth president. Kennedy smuggled booze from Canada, England, and Ireland through his Somerset Importers firm, serving clients who ranged from Harvard alumni to Moe Dalitz, Al Capone, Lucky Luciano, Frank Costello, and Owen "Owney the Killer" Madden. In 1921, Kennedy ran afoul of the Purple Gang by shipping liquor through their turf without permission. Author Nelly Bly reports that Kennedy's "hot temper brought him into a near fatal scrape" with the Purples, before Chicago mobster "Diamond Joe" Esposito intervened to lift the contract on Kennedy's life.

Sometime in 1925–26, East Coast mobsters united as the "Big Seven." Constituent outfits included: (1) Lucky Luciano and John Torrio in Manhattan; (2) Giuseppe "Joe Adonis" Doto in Brooklyn; (3) the Bug-and-Meyer Mob, handling enforcement duties; (4) Waxey Gordon, Harry Stromberg and Irving Bitz in Philadelphia; (5) Longy Zwillman and Mafia ally Willie Moretti, for northern New Jersey and western Long Island; (6) Enoch "Nucky" Johnson, for Atlantic City and the southern Jersey shore; and (7) King Solomon in New England. Informal allies included New York labor racketeers Louis "Lepke" Buchalter and Jacob "Gurrah" Shapiro; Moe Sedgewick (alias Sedway); Bronx beer baron Arthur "Dutch Schultz" Flegenheimer; and Daniel Walsh in Providence, Rhode Island. By 1928, the Seven Group was allied with twenty-two bootlegging gangs from Maine to Florida, ranging westward to the Mississippi River — and Moe Dalitz was a happy member of the team.

* * *

Opposing that rumrunner's army stood a mismatched force of federal, state, and local officers — often corrupt, incompetent, or both — who muddled through enforcement of the Volstead Act by fits and starts. In 1920, 4,550 Customs and Prohibition agents were assigned to watch 18,700 miles of border and coastline, while simultaneously raiding breweries, stills, and blind pigs in forty-eight states. Detroit's police department had 2,023 officers, while local Volstead violators numbered 50,000. Federal booze hunters received no training until 1927, when meager instruction was offered to "key agents" only. Congress appropriated $2.2 million for Volstead enforcement in 1920, from which dry agents drew starting salaries of $1,200 per year.

Small wonder, then, that many lawmen operated with their hands out and their eyes closed. From 1920 to 1933, some 1,600 U.S. dry agents — more than 25 percent of the total force — were sacked for crimes including bribery, extortion, forgery and perjury. Detroit's Customs unit, consisting of 129 agents, suffered a 135-percent turnover within 13 months, as 175 men were fired for joining in a $2 million "graft trust." A.B. Stroup, deputy administrator of federal prohibition enforcement in Motown, resigned in November 1925 with a public complaint that "there is something radically wrong with law enforcement in Detroit."

Volstead enforcement was erratic, typically conducted in large cities as sporadic clean-up drives. Such efforts in Detroit included raiding flurries during August 1921, summer 1922, June 1923, December 1923, and August 1925. Purple Gangsters were not immune to the heat, as demonstrated by ten identified members who logged sixty-five arrests on various charges between 1918 and 1927. Police surveillance was a nuisance, but it seldom won convictions. Author Robert Rockaway claims that two "FBI agents" once infiltrated the B'nai David synagogue, where Harry

Meyer Lansky (right), co-leader of the "Bug and Meyer" gang, escorted by an unidentified federal agent (Library of Congress).

Fleisher's uncle presided, on the Day of Atonement. The spies — most likely members of the Prohibition Bureau — blew their cover when they stepped outside to smoke, unaware that Orthodox Jews light no fires on that day.

Roy Haynes — a close friend of booze-loving President Harding — issued a series of confident statements from Washington. In January 1922, he told reporters, "The Amendment is being enforced to an even greater extent than many of its devoted friends anticipated." April 1923 heard Haynes announce that "bootleg patronage has fallen off 50 percent." Eight months later, he declared, "There is little open and above-board drinking anywhere. The control becomes more complete and thorough with each passing day."

Haynes was half-right on the last account. Control over

Joseph Kennedy — bootlegger, ambassador, and political kingmaker (Library of Congress).

the bootleg trade *was* tightening, but outlaws held the reins.

* * *

Gambling and booze went hand in hand. Many blind pigs offered their patrons games of chance, while major gambling dens served drinks to lubricate high-rollers. Prohibition-era gangsters cut their teeth on dice and poker chips, before the temperance warriors made them rich by banning alcohol. Liquor, gambling, and prostitution were the staples of organized crime nationwide, and Detroit was no exception.

Mert Wertheimer, proprietor of a casino at the corner of Griswold and State Street, became a special friend and mentor to Moe Dalitz during prohibition, later paving the way for Moe's expansion to Nevada. Other thriving members of the Motown "gambling fraternity" included Moe's childhood friend Sam Garfield and Old Bishop classmate Edward Levinson. With brothers Mike and Louis "Sleepout Louie" Levinson — nicknamed for his habit of napping during marathon poker games — Edward prospered in gambling with Dalitz over the next half-century, following Moe's lead from Detroit, through Kentucky, to Miami and Las Vegas.

Purple Gangsters ran their share of Motown gambling spots. Police arrested Abe Bernstein for operating a casino in May 1922, and he received a ninety-day sentence. A casino on Charlevoix Street, raided in January 1924, featured reinforced doors, secret passages for speedy exits, and a steel-lined lookout turret equipped with rifles, shotguns, thirty-odd pistols, and

1,500 rounds of ammunition. (Detroit's *Free Press* named the owners as "Baldy" Jack Ryan and Al Wertheimer, Mert's brother.) Six years later, the *Detroit News* claimed that "big time gambling ceased here at almost the same time the Purple Gang was definitely organized," yet author Court Asher, writing in 1931, found large casinos surrounding City Hall, with riflemen guarding the play from interior catwalks. When Michigan State Police raided the Deutsches Haus, they arrested gamblers including Mayor John Smith, Sheriff Edward Stein, and Michigan congressman Robert Clancy.

* * *

In the mid–1920s, Purple Gangsters tried their hand at labor racketeering. Jews like Barnet and Nathan Dalitz owned most of Detroit's laundries in those days, which made the industry ripe for extortion by ruthless *trombeniks*. Moe and Lou Dalitz, with feet in both worlds, were ideally placed to profit from the Cleaners and Dyers War of 1925–28.

The trouble began when Francis Martel, president of the Detroit Federation of Labor, invited Chicago labor racketeer Ben Abrams to "organize" Detroit's laundries. By early 1925, Abrams had corralled the city's major wholesale cleaners in a price-fixing consortium called the Wholesale Cleaners and Dyers Association. Abrams left town with a $1,500 bonus, while Charles Jacoby Jr.—vice president of Michigan's largest wholesale laundry and a brother-in-law of the Purple Gang Bernsteins—became the WCDA's president. Martel received a $700 check when the WCDA joined his federation, then put on the squeeze for more money. Dues in the WCDA began at twenty-five dollars per week, then jumped to 2 percent of each member's gross income. Martel also required donations for a mythical "construction fund," which went directly to the Purple Gang.

Dissenters quickly saw the darker side of union solidarity. In late summer, after the WCDA doubled wholesale cleaning rates, angry members of the Retail Tailors Union gathered at Detroit's Labor Temple in protest. Martel arrived to chair the meeting, carrying a brick. Whenever tailors stood to air complaints about the rate increase, Martel slammed his brick on the podium, shouting, "Sit down and shut up, if you know what's good for you!" Soon afterward, a group of retail tailors bolted from the union and organized two cooperative cleaning plants, Empire Cleaners and Dyers, and Novelty Cleaners and Dyers.

So the war began.

In the predawn hours of October 26, 1925, bombers struck both "renegade" plants, inflicting damage estimated at $8,000. On November 3, a bomb shattered the retail shop of independent tailor Samuel Davis. Over the next 29 months, the Purples smashed windows in fifty retail shops, stole clothing valued at $65,000 from stores and delivery trucks, and caused another $77,000 damage with stench bombs or acid at 97 shops. Detroit police later pegged that tally as "about half" of the actual mayhem inflicted, since many terrorized victims filed no reports.

The war produced its first fatality on December 9, 1926, when gunmen snatched and executed Sam Sigmund, half-owner of Perfect Cleaners and Dyers. Sigmund's partner, Nathan Shogan, later testified that four Purples—Abe and Ray Bernstein, Ed Fletcher and Irving Millberg—visited their plant in October, demanding $1,000 per week to insure that "there would be no more trouble." Refusal led to Sigmund's death, and other independents got the message. When Abe Bernstein braced Harry Rosman, president of Famous Cleaners and Dyers, demanding a grand per week to keep things "hotsy-totsy," Rosman bargained and paid, shelling out $16,324 in three years. Nathan Shogan also folded in the wake of Sigmund's murder, talking the Purples down to 85 dollars per week—whereupon Francis Martel named

Shogan vice president of the WCDA. The price of his office: another $100 per week to Martel.

No evidence exists that any Dalitz laundry was affected by the Cleaners and Dyers War, but the violence may have encouraged a shift in the family business from Detroit to Ann Arbor, where the Varsity Laundry first appeared in city directories for 1925. Proprietor Nathan Dalitz resided at 2008 Vinewood, while co-owner "Barnett" Dalitz was listed as "res[ident of] Detroit." By 1926, Barnet, Anna, and daughter Helen occupied a home at 1610 Brooklyn Avenue. Son Morris allegedly shared their lodgings and served as the laundry's manager in 1926 — although, as we shall see, he also had a new home in Ohio. After 1926, the only Morris Dalitz listed in Ann Arbor was Moe's cousin, residing with parents Nathan and Sarah, his occupation listed as "student."

Smoke and mirrors confound research into Moe's Ann Arbor sojourn. FBI reports from 1958 claim that Barnet occupied 2008 Vinewood in 1924, remaining until 1942, though various city directories place him in Motown through 1925. G-men declared that Moe "has never had any connection with the Varsity Laundry or any other business in Ann Arbor," adding that he "is not very highly regarded by the family." Moe himself confirmed that story to a friend, Gene Ely, claiming that his parents "shunned" him for dating a gentile classmate at the University of Michigan, who introduced Moe to the seamy world of nightclubs and gambling, thus prompting his move from Ann Arbor to Detroit. Moe's tale founders on two points: the fact that he never attended college, and that he spent twenty years in Detroit *before* settling briefly in Ann Arbor. Yet another variation, offered by Moe to the Nevada Gaming Commission in 1960, charted his moves as follows: Boston, 1899–1903; Detroit, 1903–16; Cleveland, 1916–23, and Ann Arbor "1923–3?"

While most of the Dalitz clan decamped, leaving Louis to cope with business in Detroit, the Cleaners and Dyers War ground on toward its bloody climax. Sam Polakoff, vice president of Union Cleaners and Dyers, was the last casualty, kidnapped and murdered on March 22, 1928. Eight days later, Judge Charles Bowles issued arrest warrants for Charles Jacoby and thirteen Purples. Legal maneuvers left Jacoby and nine Purples facing trial for extortion in June 1928. Bowles directed a verdict of acquittal for defendant Abe Kaminski in August, and jurors acquitted the rest on September 13.

* * *

Two years before the Purple Gang's extortion trial, in 1926, Moe Dalitz undertook another change of residence. While listed by his birth name as a laundry manager and boarder with his parents in Ann Arbor, Moe acquired another home — as "Morris Davis," with wife Edna — on Bittman Street, in Akron, Ohio. In 1928, they moved to an eight-room colonial house on Noble Avenue.

The move placed Moe forty miles south of Cleveland, and introduced his favorite pseudonym. Predictably, the move remains obscured by contradictory accounts. In an undated FBI interview, Moe recalled moving to Akron "about twenty-five years ago," devoting four years to the local liquor trade before his final move to Cleveland. Author Steven Nickel dates Moe's Cleveland arrival from 1928, while other accounts maintain that Dalitz and his best-known Cleveland crime partners were active together by 1925. In fact, that is entirely possible *without* the Akron move, as Dalitz and the Purples had been running liquor into Michigan since May 1918. Today, we only know that Akron failed to publish a directory in 1929, and by the time its next issue appeared in 1930, "Morris Davis" and his wife had vanished.

Why did Dalitz leave Detroit, exactly? Hank Messick claims that Moe "pulled out of the

Purple Gang" because he "was unable to keep them out of trouble." Biographer Alan Balboni says Moe "had a serious dispute" with unnamed Italian mobsters, whereupon Purple Gangster Charles Resnick advised him to flee. Bill Roemer's several books, again, confuse the issue needlessly. In 1989–90, Roemer claimed that Moe fled Detroit after violent clashes with Joe Zerilli's Mafia family — which did not exist, by that name, until 1964. In 1994–95, Roemer wrote that Moe left town because "the Purple Gang in Detroit had proven too much for Dalitz" and his "rival" Little Jewish Navy. Neither of those accounts rings true, since Moe did thriving business with the Purples until their demise in the mid–1930s — and far beyond, with scattered survivors. Testifying in 1951, Moe described himself as a current Detroit resident, and he maintained close ties to Motown mafiosi through the 1980s.

Finally, it may be true that Dalitz, as a gangland diplomat, grew weary of the bloodshed in Detroit — although he never shied away from killing if the need arose, and Cleveland had its own warring gangs. More likely, profit drew him to Ohio. But if certain reckless Purple Gangsters made him nervous, Moe was right to worry, as was demonstrated by the Milaflores Apartments massacre.

* * *

In the wee hours of March 28, 1927, St. Louis mobsters Joseph Bloom, Reuben Cohen and Frank Wright answered a telephone summons to the Milaflores Apartment Building, on Alexandrine Avenue East. Lulled by a friend's voice on the line, vowing a profitable partnership, the three approached Apartment 308 at 4:45 A.M. As one of them prepared to knock, a storm of gunfire blazed from a nearby stairwell. Policemen who surveyed the carnage estimated that 100-plus bullets were fired from a Thompson submachine gun and at least three different pistols. Morgue attendants told reporters that the trio had been shot so many times, it was impossible to count specific wounds.

Inside Apartment 308, police found an abandoned arsenal of three shotguns, twelve pistols, and blackjacks. The Milaflores landlady identified Abe Axler and Ed Fletcher as the tenants of Apartment 308; she also fingered Honey Miller as a frequent visitor. Police nabbed Axler and Fred Burke at 2 A.M. on March 29, lounging in a car with two pistols and a quantity of surplus ammo. Other detectives collared Fletcher, and the three were grilled without result, until attorneys secured their release. No charges were filed, and the case remains officially unsolved.

Moe Dalitz read the garish headlines in Ohio. He visited Motown frequently during the final seven years before repeal of prohibition, and returned to full-time residency in the latter 1940s, but the bulk of his good fortune for the next two decades lay in Cleveland and beyond.

3

Hard Times, Hard Men

Corruption in Ohio rivaled Michigan's, in large part thanks to Mark Hanna. Born in 1837, he befriended future Standard Oil magnate John D. Rockefeller at Cleveland's Central High School. After dropping out of college, Hanna worked at his father's grocery, then served as a Union army quartermaster in the Civil War. Coal and iron merchant Daniel Rhodes opposed his daughter's marriage to Hanna, but Hanna got what he wanted, in matrimony and in business. Soon, he was a millionaire banker, broker, and shipper, dubbed "the Lord of the Great Lakes."

In the 1880s Hanna turned to politics for profit. He managed Ohio Senator John Sherman's unsuccessful bid for the Republican presidential nomination in 1888, then fared better with William McKinley's gubernatorial campaigns in 1891 and 1893. In 1896, as chairman of the Republican National Committee, Hanna raised a record $3.5 million for McKinley's presidential race, fielding 1,400 campaign workers to place his man in the White House. At his death in 1904, Hanna left a thriving political machine — the "Ohio Gang" — that scored another White House victory in 1920, with affable candidate Warren Harding.

* * *

The Ohio Gang took Washington by storm. Its boss in all but name was Harry Daugherty, a Hanna protégé who engineered Harding's presidential campaign. Rewarded with appointment as Attorney General, Daugherty soon transformed the Justice Department into a nest of thieves and thugs nicknamed the "Department of Easy Virtue." Private detective William Burns, handpicked to lead the FBI, wielded that bureau as a bludgeon against labor unions, Democrats, and journalists who criticized the new regime. Author Kathleen Sharp claims that Harding "drank Moe Dalitz's liquor" at White House soirees. While Interior Secretary Albert Fall and Navy Secretary Edwin Denby conspired to loot America's naval oil reserves at Elk Hills, California, and Teapot Dome, Wyoming, Daugherty and longtime friend Jess Smith struck liquid gold without resort to spade or drill.

Their bonanza resided in padlocked warehouses, where oceans of bonded alcohol sat impounded, accessible only through federal withdrawal permits. Millard West, Harding's first internal revenue commissioner, set the tone by releasing 4,000 gallons to Kentucky congressman John Langley, who promptly sold it to mobsters for $100,000. After Langley's indictment, Daugherty named Jess Smith an "unofficial assistant" to William Burns at FBI headquarters. Together, they sold withdrawal permits and pocketed bribes to ignore liquor trafficking. Prominent cogs in the machine included FBI agent Gaston Means and Jacob Stein, a disbarred New York attorney with a record of Volstead Act violations.

Stein met Means in November 1922 at New York's Vanderbilt Hotel. Armed with letters of introduction from Burns and Daugherty, Means demanded seven dollars per case to protect smuggled liquor from federal seizure. At a second meeting, Means offered Stein unlimited access to whiskey from federal warehouses. The price: $200 per barrel, split four ways with $50 each for Means, Daugherty, Burns, and the Republican Campaign Committee. For an extra $50 per barrel, government trucks would deliver the booze. Stein agreed to serve Means as a go-between with various bootleggers, continuing in that capacity until exposure of the Teapot Dome scandal prompted Jess Smith's suicide in March 1923. Four months later, in a tidy bit of scapegoating, Attorney General Daugherty made Stein a federal agent, assigned to investigate Means. In July 1924 Means received a two-year prison term for perjury.

President Harding had died, meanwhile, in August 1923, leaving subordinates to fend for themselves. Successor Calvin Coolidge demanded resignations from Daugherty, Burns, Albert Fall and Edwin Denby. Fall received a one-year prison term and a $100,000 fine, matched by the sentence imposed on oilman Harry Sinclair for his role at Teapot Dome. Daugherty and Burns escaped indictment, while new Attorney General Harlan Stone named young J. Edgar Hoover to command the FBI.

* * *

The storm in Washington had little impact on Ohio, where statewide prohibition took effect on May 27, 1919, one year and twenty-six days after Michigan went "dry." In 1924 jurors convicted Ohio's state treasurer of bribery and conspiracy to protect Cincinnati's breweries. In March 1925 a federal grand jury indicted seventy-one Cincinnatians, including 48 policemen and 10 prohibition agents, on conspiracy charges. Fifty-eight defendants pled guilty, while those who fought the charges were acquitted.

Ohio owed much of its "wet" reputation to George Remus, a German immigrant born in 1869, whose family migrated to Chicago in 1873. At nineteen Remus lied about his age to get a pharmacist's license, working in a drugstore while he studied law at night. In 1920 he moved to Cincinnati, purchasing a series of distilleries, whiskey warehouses, and drug companies authorized to receive medicinal alcohol. The operation was legitimate — or would have been, if any of the booze had reached its rightful destination. Instead, truckers diverted it to Remus's Death Valley Farm, where it sat pending delivery to bootleggers in Ohio, Kentucky, Illinois, Indiana, and Missouri.

By 1924 Remus produced one-seventh of all bonded liquor sold in America. He grossed $2 million dollars in 1920, which increased to $25 million for 1923. To safeguard his illegal business, Remus spent one-quarter of his income on bribes to federal, state, and local officials. Police in Ohio, Indiana, and northern Kentucky's "Little Mexico" district learned to accept graft as a fact of life.

Sadly for Remus, Internal Revenue (IRS) agents had him in their sights before Harding's election. In October 1920 they bugged his office at the Remus Building, in downtown Cincinnati, recording in a single day $1,000 payoffs to forty-four civic officials. The evidence collected brought indictments for Remus and twelve associates, including Kentuckians Buck Brady and Peter Schmidt. At trial, all were convicted, Remus receiving a two-year prison term and a $10,000 fine.

While Remus was in jail, his wife fell in love with one of the feds who arrested him. Together, the lovers squandered $2 million of Remus's money. On the eve of his release, Remus received his wife's divorce petition. In October 1927 Remus shot her on the street, then surrendered to police. Jurors at his murder trial deliberated only nineteen minutes before acquitting Remus on grounds of temporary insanity, while the courtroom erupted with applause.

* * *

Moe Dalitz may have known George Remus, and in light of his protracted dealings with Ohio bootleggers it would have been remarkable if they *were not* acquainted, but no records presently exist to document a link. In any case, Dalitz profited hugely from the Remus-spawned corruption of officials in Ohio and Kentucky.

The date of Moe's first foray to the Buckeye State remains elusive. In 1951, Cleveland Public Safety Director Alvin Sutton claimed that Dalitz had divided his time between Detroit and Cleveland "for the last 30 years." An FBI file from 1958 credits Moe and the Purple Gang with a "considerable amount of criminal activities" in Toledo. For reasons still obscure, Moe chose Akron, forty miles south of Cleveland, as his first Ohio home — and there he met a partner who served him well for half a century.

Samuel "Sambo" Tucker was born in Lithuania on July 11, 1897. The date of his arrival in America is unknown, but he became a naturalized U.S. citizen, with his parents and siblings, in October 1912. In 1926, he lived on Akron's Euclid Avenue, identified in city directories as a clerk for "Sol's Drive-It-Yourself."

George Remus, "king" of Ohio's early bootleggers (National Archives).

Promoted to "salesman" by 1928, Tucker lived on West Market Street, a few blocks from the Noble Avenue home of Moe and Edna "Davis."

Moe Dalitz soon found other partners to the north, in Cleveland. Morris Kleinman may have been the eldest, though his birth date is confused in public records: Hank Messick pegs it as September 19, 1896, while FBI files cite September 18, 1897. With brother Fred, Kleinman worked at his father's Liberty Poultry Company until he chose a sporting life instead. He liked to box and earned the nickname "One Punch" for swift knockouts. In 1919 Kleinman won the featherweight national amateur championship, then lost it to contender Johnny Rini. Kleinman gained ten pounds and tried his luck as a lightweight, but his trainer's verdict said it all: "He's got a lazy streak. Training takes too much time." In his last bout, against Terry McManus on April 18, 1923, Kleinman threw so many low blows that spectators rioted against his victory by judges' decision. One spectator, Mayor Fred Kohler, was so enraged that he banned prize fights in Cleveland.

Retiring from the ring, Kleinman became a fight promoter, then a bookie and bootlegger. Three decades later, Alvin Sutton called Kleinman "an individual here in town that is

Moe Dalitz (left) with partner Sam Tucker (National Archives).

looked up to by a good many people that are up in the upper part of—we will say the social standing in the community. He frowns on any publicity that might come his way. Yet he brought it on himself by his nefarious jobs that he has been in since 1924." Some journalists dubbed Kleinman "Cleveland's Al Capone."

Another Dalitz partner, Louis Rothkopf, was Cleveland born on June 12 or September 3, 1903. Unlike Dalitz, he finished his third year of high school before moving on to the school of hard knocks. Known during prohibition as "the best still man in the business," Rothkopf—alias "Rhody"—traveled widely from his home in suburban Chagrin Falls, supervising construction of mammoth distilleries for customers including New York's Frank Costello.

Together, Moe Dalitz, Tucker, Kleinman, and Rothkopf made criminal history, immortalized as "the Cleveland Four."

But *how* and *when* did they begin? Once more, the record is confused.

The *Cleveland Press*, recounting Kleinman's exploits in December 1933, claimed that he met "Moe 'Puller' Davis" while smuggling whiskey from Canada, where Moe maintained a liquor dock at Leamington, Ontario. Cleveland historian Rick Porello puts the Cleveland Four's debut in 1925, while Hank Messick waffles between 1925 and 1926. Author Steven Nickel offers the latest estimate, placing Moe's Cleveland arrival in autumn 1928. Sam Tucker, under oath in 1951, initially admitted that he had "been with Mr. Dalitz for the past 26 or 27 years," while knowing Kleinman for "about 30 years." As for Rothkopf, "it might have been 15 or 17 or 20 years with him." Moments later, he backpedaled, claiming that his first business venture with Kleinman dated from 1929–30, while "I don't think I knew Mr. Dalitz until later." Cleveland's city directories for 1926–30 do not help: no Dalitzes are listed, but we find six Morris Davises in 1926, four in 1927–28, three in 1929, and six again in 1930.

* * *

Cleveland logged its first acknowledged bootleg murders on January 29, 1920, two weeks after the Volstead Act took effect. Victims Salvatore Russo and Frank Ulizzi came from Buffalo,

Left: Morris "One Punch" Kleinman (National Archives). *Right:* Louis Rothkopf (Cleveland State University Library).

New York, to wind up bullet-riddled in a ditch on Bader Avenue. Police claimed they were "black hand" operators linked to whiskey smuggling in New York. Five days before Christmas 1920, Adam Valaunt was fatally beaten outside his speakeasy on Oregon (now Rockland) Avenue, for withholding payment on his latest booze delivery. By 1925, Cleveland ranked ninth in murders among American cities.

Around the time Moe Dalitz moved to Akron, Cleveland suffered its first "corn sugar war." Primary combatants included the Lonardo brothers — Frank, John, and Joseph — and the seven Porellos: Angelo, James, John, Joseph, Ottavio, Raymond, and Rosario. Joe Porello migrated from Sicily to New York City in 1901, then moved to Cleveland in 1905. Brother John and a host of kinsmen followed, occupying Woodland Avenue as barbers, grocers, and confectioners. Behind those fronts, they organized Cleveland's first Mafia family.

Prohibition changed everything. Overnight, the Lonardos graduated from theft and extortion to booze-baron status. They furnished stills and corn sugar to hundreds of neighbors around Little Italy, paying each family a commission for homemade whiskey. The brothers operated from offices at Woodland and East 9th Street, while Salvatore "Black Sam" Todaro managed their nearby sugar warehouse. Big Joe soon moved from Woodland to a $75,000 home in Shaker Heights.

Gaudy displays of wealth sparked competition. Rival bootlegger Antonio Trioco was the first to die, slain by Lonardo gunmen in February 1925. In April, drive-by shooters killed

William Stamford, a fledgling smuggler from Lorain. August Rini, from Buffalo, had shipments hijacked in March and May 1925 before hitmen killed him in June. Louis Nobile, taken for a one-way ride in June 1926, competed with Lonardo whiskey sales and owed the family money. Angelo Bottaro fueled his stills with 7,000 pounds of sugar stolen from a Lonardo warehouse, until assassins killed him in November 1926. Shotguns blasted police informer Riago de Palma in February 1927. In June 1927, gunmen killed Salvatore Vella for underselling Lonardo whiskey. Rival distiller Luigi Colafato wound up in Shaker Heights, shot in the head and dumped from a speeding car. Booze baron Dominic Farrinacci took five bullets in April 1928.

In April 1927 Joe Lonardo embarked on a five-month tour of Sicily, leaving Sam Todaro to manage the booze trade. The envious Porello brothers saw their chance, hijacking shipments and encouraging a series of police raids on Lonardo stills. Called home from Sicily by brother John, Big Joe dismissed Todaro, who cast his lot with the Porello clan.

Feigning repentance, the Porellos put out peace feelers to the Lonardos. On October 13, 1927, they invited Joe and John to play cards at Ottavio Porello's Woodland Avenue barbershop. Midway through the game, two gunmen shot Joe seven times, killing him instantly. John, despite wounds to stomach and thigh, chased one of the shooters outside. The killer stopped in front of Anthony Caruso's butcher shop and put another slug between John's eyes, leaving him dead on the sidewalk. Butcher Caruso agreed to name John Lonardo's killer in return for a $10,000 reward, but the money was slow in coming. Triggermen killed Caruso at his home on December 5, 1927.

* * *

Moe Dalitz and his three confederates administered their growing bootleg barony from Suite 281 at the Hollenden Hotel. Built in 1885, the Hollenden was a Cleveland landmark, located on "Short Vincent" Avenue (only 485 feet long). A fourteen-story structure with 1,000 rooms, the hotel featured bay win-

"Big Joe" Lonardo (Library of Congress).

The Hollenden Hotel, headquarters of the Cleveland Four (Library of Congress).

dows on all floors, a Crystal Room with mirrored walls and massive chandeliers, plus solid-gold service reserved for heads of state. By the time Moe Dalitz took up residency, ownership had passed to hotelier Julius Epstein and Nathan Weisenberg, the slot-machine "king" of northeastern Ohio.

Bargaining for leniency from a U.S. Tax Court in 1936, Sam Tucker described the new syndicate as follows: "For some years prior to 1936, Messrs. Moe Dalitz, Sam Tucker, Louis Rothkopf, and Morris Kleinman were associated together in various enterprises ... as a sort of entity in various and sundry business transactions involving laundries, real estate, night clubs, and casino operations. They have always been equal partners in these various and sundry transactions." Moe Dalitz acknowledged that he and his partners were "interwoven in various enterprises," but Tucker deplored pejorative labels. "They aren't a syndicate," Sambo insisted. "There are some things that I am in on and some that I am not in on." Profits were equally divided, their scale suggested by Morris Kleinman's admission that he banked $1,674,571 during 1929–30 without filing tax returns. Moe Dalitz kept investigators addled with a host of pseudonyms, including "William Bennett" and "William Martin." FBI files list fifty-nine Dalitz pseudonyms, with several more blacked out on copies released under the Freedom of Information Act.

Aside from its four senior partners, Team Dalitz included thirteen other key members.

Maxie Diamond was a Russian Jew, born in 1902, who emigrated to Cleveland as a child and fell in with the East 105th Street Gang. He practiced bootlegging and labor racketeering in the laundry field, ranked by the *Plain Dealer* as "one of Cleveland's most notorious gang leaders."

Thomas Jefferson McGinty was born in Cleveland on October 17, 1892 or 1894. In 1913, as circulation manager for the *Plain Dealer,* he fielded young thugs against rival vendors of the *Cleveland News.* Next came horseracing at tracks where bettors "contributed" money and split "dividends" if they happened to finance a winner. Prohibition brought new riches, leading U.S. Attorney A.E. Bernstein to call McGinty "King of the Ohio Bootleggers." In 1924 the feds indicted McGinty, his brother Joseph, brother-in-law James Gaul, and eight others for "a gigantic wholesale and retail conspiracy." Convicted at trial, McGinty served six months in Atlanta and returned to active duty in July 1925. Five years later, he was voted Cleveland's best-dressed man.

John and *Martin O'Boyle* were Irish confederates of Tom McGinty who handled his business while McGinty was in prison. John boasted a "terrifically long" police record, while Martin was a disgraced prohibition agent, adept at spotting his former colleagues. With McGinty, the O'Boyles comprised the Irish faction of the Cleveland Syndicate.

Arthur "Mickey" McBride was a Chicago native, born in 1890, who served as circulation manager for William Randolph Hearsts's *Chicago American* in the Windy City's circulation wars. When combat spread to Cleveland in 1913, McBride transferred to Daniel Hanna's *Cleveland News,* opposing Tom McGinty's troops for domination of lucrative street corners. On the side, McBride's Yellow Cab Company monopolized taxi service in Cleveland, while he bought the Cleveland Browns football team and acquired vast real estate holdings.

Samuel Haas was a powerful Cleveland attorney whose father was Mark Hanna's chief lieutenant. In 1916 police charged Haas and Fred McClure, ex-circulation manager of the *Plain Dealer*, with running an auto theft ring. Jurors convicted McClure, while charges against Haas were dropped. Three years later, another jury convicted Haas of arson. Ohio's supreme court overturned that verdict and ordered a new trial in June 1921, but prosecutors dawdled, then dismissed the

Tom McGinty (Cleveland Public Library).

Left: Arthur "Mickey" McBride (National Archives). *Right:* Morris "Mushy" Wexler (National Archives).

case in May 1922. FBI files from the 1930s list Haas among Cleveland's "outstanding racketeers and mobsters." His clients included Mayor Fred Kohler and Tom McGinty, whom Haas also served as general manager of the Bainbridge Breeders and Racing Association, and as owner of record for McGinty's Bainbridge Park racetrack.

Cornelius Jones, a Welshman born in 1897, partnered with Tom McGinty in various gambling enterprises. FBI files list Jones's naturalization as "unverified," yet immigration officers saw no need to investigate.

Maurice Maschke was the boss of Cleveland's Republican Party and a member of the GOP's National Committee, whose name was linked to countless shady deals. Son Maurice Jr. emerged in the 1930s as a Dalitz partner in Cleveland's Pioneer Laundry.

Henry Beckerman was another attorney and one of Maschke's "powers behind the throne" in Cleveland, beginning as inspector of elections in 1915. After the 1929 stock market crash gutted his bank accounts, Beckerman faced indictments for embezzlement and arson. Jurors acquitted him on the first count, while a mistrial was declared on the second amid accusations of jury-tampering. A second jury acquitted him of arson. Beckerman's mob ties included shares in the Thistledown racetrack and the Mayfair Club casino, where his name appeared on both the deed and liquor license. Beckerman's daughter Edie adored Moe Dalitz, whom she called "Uncle Moe."

Morris "Mushy" Wexler, born May 11, 1902, fought for Mickey McBride in the newspaper circulation wars, and was later promoted to drive *Cleveland News* delivery wagons. Prohibition led him into bootlegging and gambling as a member of the Dalitz syndicate. He later ran a wire service for bookies and opened the Theatrical Grill next door to the Hollenden Hotel, in 1937. Reporter Julian Krawcheck said of Wexler, "Mushy was a racketeer in his early years, but he became a gentleman restaurateur and was really a delightful man."

Samuel "Game Boy" Miller was Mushy Wexler's brother-in-law and one of three siblings immersed in Cleveland gambling. FBI files listed Miller as a "chief lieutenant" of Morris Kleinman and Lou Rothkopf, managing their various outlaw casinos.

William "Big Bill" Presser, born in 1907, married the daughter of Cleveland bootlegger Louis Friedman. Maxie Diamond saved Friedman from kidnapping by rival mobsters in the 1920s, thus cementing Presser's loyalty to the Cleveland Four. In years to come, despite three labor racketeering convictions, Presser monopolized Cleveland's jukebox racket and the local Teamsters Union, while his son became the union's national boss and a confidante of U.S. presidents.

Shondor Birns was born in Austria-Hungary. His parents emigrated to Cleveland in 1907, shortening their family name and changing their youngest son's given name to *Alexander.* In trouble with police from age thirteen, Shondor quit school in June 1922 and lied about his age to join the navy. Discharged six months later, Birns returned to Cleveland and served a year for auto theft. Upon release he turned to pimping, and by 1927 controlled every brothel on East 55th Street between Woodland and St. Clair. He later partnered with Mushy Wexler to run the Theatrical Grill.

Detroit had taught Moe Dalitz that business suffered from incessant ethnic warfare. His alliance with Tom McGinty resolved the age-old conflict between Jews and Irishmen, but it was not enough. As in Detroit, where Moe had reached a lucrative détente with the extended Licavoli clan, he knew the Cleveland Four must pacify the local Mafia.

* * *

Cleveland's "Little Italy" centered on Mayfield Road, whose terminus on the Lake Erie shoreline made a handy spot for landing Canadian liquor. While Joe Porello and his brothers ruled the roost, hungry subordinates schemed to unseat them.

Anthony, Frank, and *Peter Milano* were the dominant members of an Italian faction known as the Mayfield Road Gang. Frank was the eldest, born in Sicily in 1891, migrating to the U.S. in 1907 and reaching Cleveland six years later. He also ranked among Moe Dalitz's first Italian allies in Cleveland. Anthony and Frank faced counterfeiting charges in 1912; Frank beat the rap at trial, while Anthony received a six-year sentence and served fifty-four months. In 1951 Frank Milano denied knowing Morris Kleinman, but admitted meeting Lou Rothkopf "occasionally."

Fred, George, and *John Angersola,* alias "King." Fred worked as a lifeguard at Luna Park in 1917 before enlisting with Mickey McBride as a street-fighting newspaper boy. John logged four arrests in Cleveland between August 1920 and January 1921, when he was convicted of armed robbery and sentenced to prison. Paroled in February 1923, he was arrested ten more times between December 1926 and December 1936. Brother George took his first pinch for a Detroit robbery in October 1926. In March 1928 he received a four-month sentence for violating the Volstead Act. All three brothers were later identified as "big-time gamblers" and business partners of the Cleveland Four.

Alfred "Big Al" Polizzi was born in Sicily on March 15, 1900, emigrated to the U.S. at age nine, and quit school five years later to sell newspapers for Mickey McBride. In 1926 Polizzi

Alfred "Big Al" Polizzi (left) with his attorney (unidentified) (Cleveland Public Library).

Chuck Polizzi (left) awaits police questioning with Frank Cammaratta (Cleveland State University Library).

served six months for liquor violations; the following year, police briefly detained him on suspicion of murdering one Hyman Weisenberg. Polizzi partnered with Frank Milano in a Mayfield Road "importing store" and admitted knowing the Angersola brothers "very well." His attorney, when he needed one, was Samuel Haas. As for Polizzi's first meeting with Moe Dalitz, Al testified in 1951 that he sold bootleg liquor both in Cleveland and Detroit, telling the Senate, "I had business in both cities."

Charles "Chuck" Polizzi, born December 13, 1894, is wrongly described in some accounts as Al Polizzi's brother. In 1951 Big Al told Senate investigators, "I have always considered him a cousin." In fact, Chuck Polizzi was born Leo Berkowitz, a son of Russian Jews who died soon after their arrival in Cleveland. His unofficial adoption by Al Polizzi's parents left no records. Chuck himself further confused the matter by sometimes using the name "Albert C. Polizzi." His role as a cultural link between gangland immigrant communities is unrivaled in Syndicate history.

James Licavoli was a Purple Gang ally from Detroit who found Ohio more hospitable in 1929. Licavoli perjured himself before the U.S. Senate in 1951, denying that he ever met Moe Dalitz or Sam Tucker; he admitted meeting Lou Rothkopf "in the fights" and knew Morris Kleinman "not so good."

Further afield, Moe Dalitz also counted Texas mafioso Sam Maceo as a valued ally and business partner. Headquartered in Galveston, Maceo received shipments of Canadian liquor routed through the Caribbean, sending the booze on by train to Cleveland. One shipment seized by prohibition agents included 725 cases of Bronfman whiskey. In the 1930s Maceo dominated vice and narcotics from Galveston to Dallas, and was described in FBI files as "very wealthy and influential in politics."

* * *

With his Jewish-Irish-Italian "combination" firmly in place, Moe Dalitz set about monopolizing illegal liquor traffic from Detroit and Cleveland through western Pennsylvania to Buffalo. Northern Kentucky remained a profitable sideshow to the main event. The Cleveland Four maintained large fleets of trucks, speedboats, and barges, moving booze around the clock. One tactic called for empty semi-trailers to be shipped across Lake Erie on barges, filled with Canadian liquor, and hauled back at night. "If they didn't get a green light," Dalitz later told a friend, "they'd sink the truck and return later for the booze. They'd float a buoy and go after it when the coast was clear." Soon, Lake Erie was dubbed "the Jewish Lake."

One of Moe's fronts was Morris "Ben" Nadel, a ne'er-do-well first arrested in 1920 for "car plundering," later known as a bookie, dope pusher, and vendor of fake jewelry. In 1925, he suddenly had cash to spare for stylish clothes and flashy cars. His secret of success emerged when feds captured the *Ranger*, a 65-foot cabin cruiser with 680 cases of whiskey aboard, at the Huron River's mouth. They found Nadel loitering ashore, with three cars and an empty truck. In 1926, Coast Guardsmen on Lake Erie seized a former U.S. Navy submarine chaser loaded with booze consigned to Nadel, and his reputation soared.

But who owned "Nadel's boats"?

In 1932, facing a tax-evasion charge, Kleinman spoke guardedly concerning his role in the Lake Erie booze trade.

> Q: What was the beginning of it?
> A: I had some partners.
> Q: Who were those partners?
> A: I don't like to mention any names.
> Q: Give the reason why you don't want to mention their names.
> A: I just like to answer all the questions that concern myself.
> Q: Why?
> A: I might get myself into some trouble or something like that by giving these names.
> Q: In what way?
> A: I might get hurt some way by giving their names.
> Q: You mean bodily harm?
> A: That's right...
> Q: At the beginning how many persons were there?
> A: Four or five — four.
> Q: Four?
> A: Yes, four...
> Q: What was the first purchase of equipment that you made?
> A: A boat.

Kleinman later identified one of his partners as "William Martin," neglecting to mention that "Martin's" real name was Moe Dalitz. Kleinman also named Detroit's Joe Massei as one of the "people in Canada" who bankrolled his whiskey shipments.

Before the feds nabbed Kleinman, Ben Nadel was jailed for harboring a thug named Pat McDermott, later convicted of murdering *Canton Daily News* editor Don Mellett. Facing a prison term, Nadel began to mutter threats that he might cut a deal to save himself.

On the night of March 20, 1928, Nadel and Morris Goldman left a Woodland Avenue cardroom with three unnamed "friends." Nadel drove along Lost Nation Road to a Lake County beach where booze landings were common. On arrival, his backseat passengers produced a shotgun and two pistols, blasting fourteen holes in Nadel, twelve in Goldman. A cap found in the car was traced to Solly Hart, roommate of Syndicate rumrunner Morris Komissarow, but police absolved him of the murders. The double homicide remains officially unsolved, but no one doubts who gave the orders.

As Moe Dalitz told an interviewer, decades later, "Hard times make hard people."

* * *

The Cleveland Four's booze fleet survived without Nadel, despite its occasional losses. Late in 1927 their largest, fastest boat — the aptly named *Gray Ghost*—vanished without a trace on the run from Leamington to Cleveland. Months later, two corpses washed ashore at Erie, Pennsylvania, and another at Vermillion, Ohio, thought — but never proved — to be the *Gray Ghost*'s crew.

Lake Erie struck again on December 30, 1928, when the *Hannah* set off through a blizzard with three crewmen and 1,000 cases of liquor. The engines failed three hours out, and *Hannah* drifted for two weeks before her starving crew was rescued off Port Dover, Ontario, consigned to a hotel under guard by "a husky American." No charges were filed, but Canadian authorities seized *Hannah*'s cargo.

Daniel Eberle made numerous Lake Erie runs for the Syndicate before Coast Guardsmen caught him on November 22, 1927, sending Eberle to prison for eighteen months. Eberle's employers offered him a new job on release, as captain of the tugboat *Neptune*. While pretending to accept, Eberle warned dry agents of a scheduled meeting with his bosses in Sandusky. Two strangers named Moe Davis and George Martin met him on the dock, but Eberle declined their job offer and severed his connections to the gang.

Investigators forged ahead without him, learning that Martin and Clarence Andrews had been imported from Florida to man boats for a Syndicate called "the Big Jewish Navy." The *Neptune* had been purchased from United Fisheries in May 1929, by a man who called himself George White. Two other boats, the *Dart* and *Judson*, were also involved in booze traffic. The feds scheduled a raid for May 28, but Marty O'Boyle spotted his former colleagues, and only George Martin remained in the trap when it closed.

Still, the feds were sometimes lucky. On June 7, 1929, Coast Guardsmen caught the *Neptune* running without lights, 100 yards off Cleveland's West 9th Street pier. On board, they arrested Canadian George White, while a second man —"Captain West"— brandished a pistol and leaped overboard. The *Neptune*'s haul included 189 gallons of whiskey and 1,392 bottles of beer. Three years later, Morris Kleinman admitted purchasing the *Neptune* from United Fisheries for "about $4,000."

On June 8, 1929, the Coast Guard scored again. This time it was the *Helen*, spotted off the outer breakwater near 58th Street. After brief pursuit, *Helen* nosed into the seawall and its two crewmen escaped on foot in the fog, leaving behind 360 gallons of whiskey valued at $10,000. One day later, agents seized the *Judson*, a 32-foot speedboat, docked at Cleveland's Clifton Club. Its hold was empty, but Coast Guard spotters identified it as the *Helen*'s convoy boat. Kleinman's confession identified the *Helen* as a Syndicate blockade runner.

On August 2, 1929, Coast Guardsmen chased the *Red Boy* off the Rocky River's mouth, west of Cleveland. While still out of range, they watched crewmen transfer to a speedboat and escape, leaving the *Red Boy* in flames. Despite an exploding fuel tank, the CG cutter towed *Red Boy* to port, where it burned to the waterline. Inside the smoking hulk lay 300 sacks of bottled ale and 200 of beer. Moe Dalitz owned a dock at Clifton Park Lagoon, near the point where *Red Boy*'s crew abandoned her.

More seizures followed. On October 1, 1929, Coast Guardsmen captured the *Fiji* with a liquid cargo valued at $10,000. November 29 brought double success. At 1:30 A.M., rifle fire stopped Captain Harry Wilson and the *Idle Hour* off West 38th Street, with a load of booze valued at $28,000. Eight hours later, a storm pitched *Honey Boy* against the Cleveland break-water, stranding its 100 sacks of bottled whiskey. Two supposed crewmen, found clinging to icy rocks nearby, were freed for lack of evidence. In 1932 Kleinman admitted paying "about $6,000" for the *Idle Hour* and $7,500 for the *Honey Boy*.

* * *

Despite Moe Dalitz's maxim that violence was bad for business, bloodshed dogged the Cleveland Four. In 1933 the press linked thirteen murders to the "Kleinman gang."

Two early casualties were Philadelphia natives Jack Brownstein and Ernest Yorkell. Posing as "tough guys from the East," they toured Cleveland speakeasies and gambling dens, threatening mayhem if they were not paid "protection." Tom McGinty threw them out of his saloon, as did Syndicate casino manager James "Shimmie" Patton. The pair demanded $400 from Phil Selznick at the Club Madrid, then wound up begging in vain for a ten-dollar loan. On October 7, 1927, the hapless hoods told a waitress, "We're going out to get $5,000 or we're not coming back." Hours later, police found their bodies bound with clothesline, blasted with shotguns and pistols in what one reporter called "a bootleg joke."

Soon after the March 1928 Nadel-Goldman murders, gunmen took Harry Sherman for a ride, shot him four times, and dumped him on Woodland Avenue. Sherman survived and named "a member of the [Dalitz-Kleinman] ring" as the shooter, then swiftly recanted his statement before an indictment was filed. The triggerman's identity was never publicized.

On June 10, 1928, hitmen shot booze dealer Abe Warshofsky on St. Clair Avenue, in what the *Cleveland Press* termed "a row over tribute to his silent partners." Two days later, Fred Kleinman and Philip Porris suffered flesh wounds in a shooting at the Bee Smoke Shop, on East 105th. Both crimes remain officially unsolved.

Leo Klein walked the underworld tightrope as a "two-way tipster," earning $150 per month from prohibition agents and doubling his income by briefing corrupt officials on local graft investigations. On April 2, 1929, a tip from Klein sent feds to a Lake Erie beach, where they found "contractor" Morris Komissarow and twenty other men waiting for a midnight booze delivery. Another Klein-inspired raid, at a syndicate plant on Euclid Avenue, cost the Cleveland Four $50,000. On August 1, 1929, police found Klein in his car, stabbed and shot in the head. Towels wrapped around his neck matched those used at the Kinsman Smoke Shop, where officers found two discarded pistols, broken chairs, and other signs of struggle. The *Press* identified the smoke shop as a hangout for "many celebrated rum-runners."

Hard times make hard people.

* * *

On March 6, 1930, Coast Guardsmen aboard CG-106 spied a suspected liquor boat, the *Sambo G*, riding at anchor two miles off the 9th Street pier. As they approached, the rummy fled, ignoring cannon and machine-gun fire before her skipper tried to ram the cutter. Finally, a cannon round and armor-piercing rifle bullets pierced the booze boat's metal hide and forced surrender of the two-man crew. Aboard the *Sambo G* boarders found 540 cases of whiskey alongside 1,000 cases of ale and beer. Wounded skipper Fred Hentrie was hospitalized at Lorain, where CG-106 docked his captured boat.

The Coast Guard's pride in victory was swiftly dashed. Persons unknown raided the *Sambo G* in port and stole back its cargo, while Hentrie made a rope of knotted sheets and escaped from his hospital room. A car stood waiting on the street below, as a pretty nurse lured Hentrie's guard away for a late-night snack. Investigators learned that Morris Komissarow had arranged the getaway, then vanished from his usual haunts. Since his arrest in April 1929, Komissarow had posted bond for Hyman "Pittsburgh Hymie" Martin, jailed as a suspected gangster. Roommate Solly Hart reported Komissarow missing in May 1930, saying that he left home for the last time carrying $5,000 in cash.

Two months later, Moe Dalitz suffered burns in a fire at his dock on Clifton Park Lagoon. According to police reports, a boat exploded at his dock on July 4, resulting in burns that sent him to Lakewood Hospital. Police found evidence of liquor smuggling at the dock, but they could not find Moe.

A garbled account of that incident, published in the *Press* on December 8, 1933, read: "Moe Davis was more frequently seen about Cleveland now, but he kept in the background. His only known police appearance of record here is when he visited Lakewood police. A prominent Cleveland councilman appeared with him as his lawyer. Davis admitted he was owner of a cargoless speedboat, suspected of rum-running. He pleaded for release of William Martin, who had been burned when the craft exploded in the lake. (Sidelight on Davis: He used the name William Martin thereafter as an alias. Under it he is now a fugitive from a rum-running charge in Buffalo.)"

That version of events is all the more confusing since the *Press* itself had run a follow-up on the explosion, dated August 13, 1930. That story described "Moe Davis, reputed Lake Erie rumrunner," surrendering to police for interrogation on murder charges. "Until yesterday," the *Press* reported, "Davis had been missing since July 4 when he was burned in a gasoline explosion which set fire to his cabin cruiser, *Natchez*, in a Rock River lagoon. Davis was taken to Lakewood Hospital that day but never returned for treatment which had been advised." Instead, the *Press* maintained, he had gone off to New York City.

The murder in question was that of Morris Komissarow, who surfaced in Lake Erie near the Rocky River, six weeks after Solly Hart reported him missing. Shot once in the head, Komissarow was bound with wire to a fifty-pound anchor bearing the stamped legend "NAVY." When found, Komissarow had thirty-five cents in his pocket.

* * *

Herbert Hoover's inauguration as president in March 1929 changed the rumrunning scene. Determined to end liquor smuggling from Canada, Hoover chose Detroit as "the laboratory in which to test the noble experiment of prohibition," declaring "war with the full strength of the United States behind it" against smugglers. Under mounting pressure from Washington, Canada's parliament passed new legislation banning export of liquor to America. Signed into law on June 1, 1930, the law closed ten Canadian export facilities, prompted a rash of seizures on Lake Erie, and immediately raised the price of whiskey in Detroit by 50 percent.

Cleveland bootleggers increasingly relied on massive stills to keep the liquor flowing. In June 1929 Captain William McMaster's "axe raiding" team struck an East Side home, destroying several 500-gallon vats and other gear valued at $25,000. The tenant paid a $750 fine, telling police he worked for "a man named Kline or something like that." November 1929 brought discovery of a Merwin Avenue brewery with eighteen 1,000-gallon vats, later acknowledged by Morris Kleinman as a Cleveland Four operation. A year later, police raided an even larger plant on Lexington Avenue, claimed by Kleinman as a tax loss in 1932. A fifth huge plant, on Prospect Avenue, had nineteen 1,500-gallon steel vats. IRS agent Alvin Giesey reported:

> It seems that sometime in 1929, one of the largest stills raided in this city was found within 100 yards of this office. Newspapers at the time made a sensational story of the raid, and it was cited how large that still was and that if it had exploded there would have been little left of the adjoining buildings, which would have included this office, and these examining officers would not now be writing this report. Kleinman admitted that the equipment was part of his operations.

Huge profits fueled expansion into Akron, where local "sugar king" Leo Isaar felt syndicate heat. When his supplies ran low and two of his employees were murdered, Isaar turned to Illinois distributors, two cousins both named Anthony Borsellino. Police found the two Tonys on March 26, 1930, strangled in their car at Brecksville, midway between Akron and Cleveland. After finding a bomb in his car, Isaar quit the business, sold off his Rubber City Sugar Company and fleet of vehicles, then started talking to police. Since 1927, Isaar reported, he had fought a losing war against *two* Cleveland gangs, first Joe Lonardo's, then the syndicate led by "Moe Davis."

* * *

As in Detroit, most Ohio speakeasies included gaming rooms, but 1930 saw a shift in emphasis to lavish "carpet joints" that featured first-rate food and entertainment with their slots, crap tables, and roulette wheels. Tom McGinty's Mounds Club opened that spring in Lake County, managed by M.W. Shaffner, while "a fellow by the name of [Cornelius] Jones had a piece of it too." The Harvard Club, in Maple Heights, welcomed 1,000 players nightly. Other clubs owned by the Cleveland Four were managed by George Gordon, Game Boy Miller, Frank Rosen, and newcomer Ruby Kolod.

Born Reuben Koloditsky on July 27, 1910, in New York City, Kolod was in trouble from age seventeen. New York police jailed him for burglary in March 1929, then for assault and robbery four months later. An August 1929 conviction for illegal entry earned Kolod a three-year prison term, whereupon he fled to Cleveland. Local police held "Ruby Spector" as a suspicious person in August 1930, then as a fugitive from New York justice three months later, but Kolod never served his outstanding sentence. His fifth arrest, for violation of the Volstead Act in August 1932, likewise resulted in no prison time. By then, he was established with the Cleveland Syndicate, as a manager at the Pettibone Club.

Variations on casino gambling in the early 1930s included the steamship *Alabama*, owned by Tom McGinty and George Ralston. Each day the *Alabama* sailed from Cleveland, west to Cedar Point and back, 120 miles in all. McGinty dubbed the craft a "pleasure boat" and vowed that he had "never seen" illegal gambling on board. McGinty also ran racetracks in Cuyahoga and surrounding countries, including Thistledown and Bainbridge Park. When authorities closed Bainbridge Park, outraged farmers protested the plunging price of hay.

Sheriff John Sultzman came under fire in May 1931, when the *Plain Dealer* reported gamblers operating freely in Cuyahoga County. "Big-time resorts they are," the paper said. "No petty bets. The sky's the limit, the house will cover, and sizeable fortunes are won or lost in an afternoon or evening." Mickey McBride's cab drivers steered players to various clubs, while spotters patrolled bus depots, fetching limousines for potential losers. Sultzman described himself as "neutral" on gambling. "I stand as solidly as a phalanx behind my principles and policies," he told reporters. "No one can move me from my stand. I believe in home rule. I'll not interfere until the officials of the villages in which there is said to be gambling ask me to."

Still, heat was heat. Two days after making that statement, Sultzman raided the Airport Tavern, in Brook Park Village, arresting two suspects and seizing dice tables. Another five months passed before Cleveland's public safety director closed the Shawnee Club on Fairmount Road, owned by Detroit's "nationally known gambler and club proprietor" Al Wertheimer. The Harvard Club closed temporarily, on November 18, but the concessions were too little and too late. Judge A.W. Overmyer removed Sheriff Sultzman on December 23, finding him "guilty of refusing and neglecting to enforce the law." It hardly mattered, though, since "home rule" voters swiftly restored him to office.

* * *

Despite brave talk from Washington, Detroit remained as wet and wild as ever. Motown mobsters detonated 170 bombs during 1927–30, and the *News* found 150 whiskey-cutting plants running around the clock in 1928. A year later, on June 13, 1929, the *Free Press* reported that "[f]ormation of a giant combine of Great Lakes rum-runners to challenge the anti-smuggling agencies of the Government, from Buffalo to Mackinac, was completed yesterday at Ecorse at a secret meeting of big operators from all important points of entry on the border."

The Purple Gang maintained its link to Al Capone but lost rival Bugs Moran in an angry dispute over pricing. Moran preferred to hijack booze, a trait that sparked the prohibition era's best-known crime. On February 13, 1929, Moran received a call offering stolen whiskey at bargain rates. He took the bait and ordered delivery to his garage on Chicago's North Clark Street. The next morning, St. Valentine's Day, Purples Eddie Fletcher and the Keywell brothers watched the garage from a nearby apartment, reporting the arrival of a gangster-wannabe optometrist whom they mistook for Moran. Capone's hitmen arrived moments later and machine-gunned seven victims in a bid to finally annihilate the North Side Gang.

While the Valentine's Day Massacre sparked national outrage, the Purples had their own problems at home. In April 1928 authorities charged five gang members with extorting money from Sam Lerner's lumber company; all were convicted and placed on probation. Abe Bernstein beat charges of killing a policeman in broad daylight, but federal prosecutors convicted four Purples of liquor violations in July 1929, resulting in two-year prison terms. Four months later, Phil Keywell received a life sentence for killing a teenaged "spy" at a gang booze cutting plant; Morris Raider got twelve to fifteen years as an accomplice in that case. Gangland bullets dropped Irving Shapiro in July 1929 and Zigmund Selbin three months later. By December 1931, assistant prosecutor Gomer Krise told journalists that "gangs are licked," Motown was "free of crime."

That boast was premature. Surviving members of the Purple Gang still operated in Detroit, along with mafiosi led by Joe Massei and Peter Licavoli. Another local ally of Moe Dalitz, Samuel Stein, was born in 1896 and immigrated from his native Poland in 1913. At age twenty-four he received a two-year sentence for auto theft, followed by arrests for robbery (1923), forgery (1924), armed robbery (1925), liquor violations (1925), and grand larceny (1928). Prosecutors dismissed all those charges, but a jury convicted Stein and Joe Massei of carrying concealed weapons in 1933. Stein fought that case all the way to the U.S. Supreme Court, which ruled the police search illegal and freed Stein to relocate in Cleveland, as manager of Freddie's Club on Vincent Street.

Lou Dalitz kept his nose clean in Motown, listed as an employee of the Detroit Supply System in city directories for 1926–27, acquiring wife Lillian and graduating to vice presi-

Al Capone (right), shown here with one of his attorneys, planned the St. Valentine's Day massacre with members of Detroit's Purple Gang (Library of Congress).

dent of Rogers Cleaners and Dyers in 1928. Directories for 1928–29 list Moe Dalitz as the company's secretary/treasurer, residing in Ann Arbor. In 1929–30 Louis emerged as president of Michigan Modern Overall Cleaners. Fellow bootleggers smiled at his fondness for laundries, dubbing Louis "Lou the Chinaman."

* * *

By early 1929 America had spawned a breed of "new gangsters," molded by wealth and mock-respectability into patterns of dress, speech, and behavior far removed from those of their ghetto forebears. Mimicking the robber barons of "legitimate" industry, liquor and gambling tycoons wormed their way into the upperworld that made their *under*world both profitable and essential. Mob historian Nicholas Gage notes that Moe Dalitz and his Cleveland partners "were more subtle, and often more effective, than crime leaders in the east." Leading modest personal lives, preferring bribes to bullets in the main, the Cleveland Four would "lead organized crime in the United States into a new era."

Thus, Moe Dalitz filled the classic role of *rebbe* (teacher) from the Old World *shtetl*, schooling his associates in subjects ranging from the art of money laundering to social graces. Former G-man William Roemer notes Moe's "close alliance" in those years with eastern mobsters Lepke Buchalter, Gurrah Shapiro, and Longy Zwillman. Moe was "especially close," says

Members of Chicago's North Side Gang, slaughtered on St. Valentine's Day, 1929 (Library of Congress).

Roemer, to Meyer Lansky and future Mafia "prime minister" Frank Costello. To succeed in the long term, he counseled, outlaws must adapt and organize.

On May 13, 1929, gangsters from eight states converged on Atlantic City, New Jersey, for the Mob's first national convention. Dalitz had offered Cleveland for the gathering, but others preferred the safety of Jersey kingpin Enoch "Nucky" Johnson's bailiwick. Delegates to the Atlantic City convention included Moe Dalitz, Lou Rothkopf, and Chuck Polizzi from Cleveland; Capone, Jacob "Greasy Thumb" Guzik, Moses Annenberg, and Frank McErlane from Chicago; Joe Bernstein and Charles Resnick for the Purple Gang; King Solomon from Boston (though his days were numbered, indicted in October 1929, murdered in January 1930); Max Hoff and Nig Rosen from Philadelphia; John Lazia and Solly Weissman from Kansas City; Longy Zwillman, Waxey Gordon, and Willie Moretti from New Jersey. New York's delegation was the largest, including Lansky, Lucky Luciano, Frank Costello, John Torrio, Dutch Schultz, Owney Madden, Lepke Buchalter, Albert Anastasia, Vincent Mangano, Frank Scalise, Joe Adonis, and top bookie Frank Erickson. While Jews and Italians mingled freely, Madden and McErlane were the only Irishmen invited.

The first order of business in Atlantic City was a national delineation of bootleg territories, coupled with a moratorium on gang warfare. Al Capone later claimed that an actual contract was signed to minimize bloodshed, and he agreed with the convention's vote that he

Shown here in 1902, Atlantic City's Boardwalk was little changed when it hosted the first Mob convention in 1929 (Library of Congress).

should "cool off" with a one-year prison term on Pennsylvania weapons charges. Gambling was another major topic, with Frank Erickson anointed heir to Arnold Rothstein's "layoff" betting empire (used by local bookies to defer expensive losses). Moses Annenberg, a veteran of Chicago's newspaper circulation wars and owner of the *Daily Racing Form*, took charge of a new transnational wire service — "The Trust," in Mob parlance — that supplied split-second race results to bookies throughout the United States, Canada, Mexico, and Cuba. By the time he died in 1942, Annenberg was the fifth richest man on Earth.

Moe Dalitz left Atlantic City satisfied — and unaware that federal spies were following his every move.

* * *

Dry agents established their first wiretap on "Moe Davis" in May 1929, as part of a Detroit liquor investigation. On July 20, the eavesdroppers heard Davis discuss booze shipments with

Edward Downing, owner of a Buffalo trucking company, and a Canadian beer broker at Port Colborne, Ontario. Two days later, "M.M. Davis and wife, Akron, Ohio," checked into Buffalo's Hotel Statler. On July 23 Moe telephoned Sam Tucker in Cleveland, telling him "the deal went through" and ordering an $8,000 payment to Port Colborne for 700 cases of whiskey and ale. Moe also told Tucker to send John O'Boyle to Buffalo, to oversee the shipment. On July 24, Moe called Tucker again, announcing his return to Cleveland and reporting that bad weather had prevented loading of the full shipment.

While Moe packed his bags in Buffalo, the tug *Ballinas* left Port Colborne with four barges in tow. John O'Boyle met the *Ballinas* on Lake Erie, transferring 400 cases of whiskey and ale from the *Idle Hour* (captured by feds four months later) to one of the barges. That shipment reached Cleveland's 9th Street pier at 9:00 P.M. on July 24, but some were not so fortunate.

On Christmas Day 1929, CG-2245 waylaid the barge *Loretta*, allegedly loaded with 1,159 cases of Canadian liquor. Eugene Downey Jr., son of a Cleveland police lieutenant, raced the Coast Guard to Woodlawn Beach and died when federal bullets ripped through his groin. Coast Guardsmen arrested brother George Downey and searched the *Loretta*, finding three quarts of whiskey and some empty sacks. While local

Super-bookie Moses Annenberg, founder of America's racing wire service (National Archives).

prosecutors threatened manslaughter charges, U.S. Attorney Richard Templeton issued a federal gag order and Seymour Lowman, Assistant Secretary of the Treasury, told reporters, "The fact that no liquor was found in the boat had no significance, because there was plenty of time to throw the liquor overboard into the lake." In fact, he said, Coast Guardsmen had chased the *Loretta* on six prior occasions, and Eugene Downey was free on $20,000 bond from a prior rumrunning charge when he died.

On January 20, 1930, a federal grand jury in Buffalo indicted ten defendants for violation of the 1922 Tariff Act and conspiracy to defraud the U.S. government. Those charged included: "Moe Davis," Morris Kleinman, "Sammy" Tucker, both O'Boyle brothers, Edward Downing, former navy lieutenant Glenn Farr (an officer of Hedger Transportation Company, which owned the *Loretta*), and three barge captains: Arthur Barth, Engval Monson, and Alphonso Peeters. A press release announced that four other defendants — barge captains Edward Hawkins, Frank Loomis, Joseph Loomis, and William Lahr — had agreed to plead guilty. Barth pled guilty on April 4 and was sentenced to time already served, granting immediate release. On November 21, 1930, prosecutors filed an entry of *nolle prosequi,* dismissing all counts against the nine remaining defendants.

FBI files from June 1958 claim that federal court records reveal another indictment of Moe Dalitz, as "William T. Martin," for Tariff Act violations on October 14, 1930. The file further claims that "Martin" pled guilty to one count on October 13, receiving a thirty-day suspended sentence with six months probation. Tellingly, the Bureau notes, "The U.S. Attorney, the U.S. marshal and the U.S. Probation Officer, Buffalo, have no records available on above case." Neither did the federal court in Buffalo, when I obtained its files in 1983. The charge and guilty plea, in short, did not exist.

Buffalo G-men apparently garbled the facts of a second indictment filed against four defendants on October 4, 1933. That case involved delivery of 1,955 gallons of whiskey to the Kit-Kat Club at Neptune Beach, in New York's Chemung County. Those charged included "William Martin, alias Moe Davis"; club owner Anthony Mistretta; Pennsylvania trucker Joseph Genovese; and Harry Milford. On October 18 the Fruehauf Trailer Company sued "Martin" to recover two semi-trailers purchased for $699 on April 7, 1933, with $2,876.50 outstanding on the bill. No record exists of the indictment's disposition.

Two decades later, when questioned by Senate investigators, Dalitz professed ignorance of the Buffalo indictments.

> Q: Now, you were indicted on some barge deal in 1934 [*sic*], were you not?
> A: That is news to me.
> Q: Were you or were you not?
> A: Nobody ever said a word about it to me. They must have kept it a secret.
> Q: You never heard a word about it?
> A: I was never in Buffalo in my life.
> Q: Who said anything about Buffalo?
> A: I read it; it was in the papers.

* * *

Rumrunning and indictments still left time for romance. Moe Dalitz was a ladies' man who married four times and enjoyed many extramarital flings. His first marriage, to Edna, ended mysteriously sometime between their July 1929 trip to Buffalo and August 7, 1930, when Moe married Dorothy Brazzel of Akron, before Justice of the Peace W.E. Van Camp in St. Louis, Missouri. Dorothy was seven years Moe's junior, four days short of her twenty-third birthday when they married.

A second marriage did nothing to curb Moe's wandering eye. Within days of the ceremony, he hosted a meeting at the Hollenden Hotel, between Longy Zwillman and Hollywood siren Jean Harlow. The bicoastal lovers met in Cleveland for an emotional farewell, prior to Zwillman's incarceration on an attempted murder charge. Hank Messick writes that Dalitz hung around Zwillman's suite, ogling Harlow, until Zwillman pointedly asked him to leave. Author Gus Russo further names Dalitz as the "first lover" of Mob floozy Virginia Hill, famous for trysts with Joe Adonis and Bugsy Siegel.

* * *

Shock waves of violence rocked the Mafia in 1930, emanating from New York. Moe Dalitz marked the tremors and chose sides.

Early in prohibition, Salvatore "Toto" D'Aquila deposed "boss of bosses" Piddu Morello, then lost his throne (and his life) to Joe Masseria in October 1928. Meanwhile, in 1925, Salvatore Maranzano arrived from Castellammare del Golfo, Sicily, fleeing Benito Mussolini's war against the Mafia. Surrounding himself with homeboys like Giuseppe "Joe Bananas" Bonnano, Maranzano cast himself as a modern Julius Caesar, lecturing his troops on ancient Roman history and sneering at "greasers" like Masseria. Huge stills in Pennsylvania and upstate New York, coupled with demands for tribute from subordinates, kept Maranzano solvent. After three years of sporadic skirmishing, Masseria's gunmen executed Maranzano underboss Gaetano Reina in February 1930. By the time snipers killed Steve Ferigno and Al Mineo in November, battle lines in the Castellammarese War were drawn nationwide.

Masseria's New York allies included Lucky Luciano and Vito Genovese. Al Capone pledged support from Chicago. Maranzano risked parallel war with the Big Seven by hijacking their booze trucks and shipments of clothing protected by Lepke Buchalter. In Cleveland, Joe Porello created an Italian-American Republican Club to rival Frank Milano's political machine, with Maurice Maschke and other luminaries attending the group's kickoff banquet on June 30. Five days later, Al Polizzi invited Joe Porello and Sam Tilocco to a meeting at Milano's Venetian Café, where both were murdered in the presence of John Angersola, Charles Colletti, and Chuck Polizzi. Shotgunners dropped Vincenzo Porello outside a Woodland grocery store on July 26, and bombers demolished Raymond Porello's home. On August 2 unknown killers dumped Christine Colletti, Charles's sister-in-law, near Cleveland's airport. Police jailed husband Tony as a suspect, and he "hanged himself" on October 13, in the cell he shared with mafiosi Frank Brancato and Dominic De Marco.

New York's balance of power shifted in spring 1931, when Joe Masseria, suspecting Luciano of treason, asked Joe Adonis to execute Lucky. Adonis tipped Luciano instead, and thus signed Masseria's death warrant. On April 15, 1931, Luciano dined with Masseria at Scarpato's Nuova Villa Tammaro on Coney Island, then stayed to play cards. After several hands, Luciano excused himself to use the restroom. In his absence, gunmen entered the café and executed Joe the Boss.

Maranzano convened a national Mafia confab on April 21 and proclaimed himself Boss of Bosses. Luciano, now the head of Masseria's family, feigned agreement but quickly traveled with Meyer Lansky to Cleveland, for a meeting with Moe Dalitz and Frank Milano. Santo Trafficante Sr. came by train from Tampa, while Al Capone sent an emissary from Chicago. In Luciano's words, "I told 'em that [Maranzano] was nothin' better than a big tub of horseshit who was still livin' with the *capo* crap he brought over from Sicily, and now he married it to Julius Caesar.... It took most of the day to explain what I had in mind and to answer their questions and lay everythin' right on the line. They hadda know we just couldn't dump

Charles "Lucky" Luciano (center), shown here socializing with friends, Americanized the Mafia in 1931 (Library of Congress).

Maranzano's plans, that we hadda eliminate him entirely. All the guys ... agreed with every-thin' I said."

After the meeting Dalitz took his guests to a prize fight, but police arrived during the preliminary bout and arrested the out-of-town hoodlums. Lansky and Luciano were released next morning, but Maranzano heard of the arrests and doubted Luciano's story that he simply went to Cleveland for the fights. Quietly, Maranzano drafted a new list of murder contracts.

At the same time, violence wracked New York's Amalgamated Clothing Workers of America. Leaders of the 50,000-member union asked Luciano to counter incursions by Lepke's racketeers, but Lucky declined for friendship's sake. The contract went to Maranzano, just as Luciano learned of Maranzano's plan to kill him at a meeting scheduled for September 10. Lepke's killers reached Maranzano's office first, posing as IRS agents before they shot and stabbed him at his desk. After Maranzano's death, Luciano declined coronation as Boss of Bosses, establishing instead a national Mafia commission including the heads of New York City's five families, plus the dons of Buffalo and Chicago.

More meetings were required to formalize Luciano's plan and clarify the Mafia's role within the larger national Syndicate. Al Capone hosted the first at Chicago's Congress Hotel in early autumn 1931. In February 1932, the *New York Times* reported a two-day meeting of booze barons from Detroit, New York, and New England in Halifax, Nova Scotia. A second meeting in Chicago, in April 1932, mourned Al Capone's tax-evasion conviction and conferred his authority on Frank Nitti. Over the next two years, Moe Dalitz and his partners attended other gangland summits in Kansas City and New York. Cleveland police also tracked Morris Kleinman on repeated trips to Hot Springs, Arkansas, where Kleinman met repeatedly with Frank Costello and Joe Adonis, New Jersey mafioso Gerardo Catena, Phillip "Dandy Phil" Kastel and Sheriff John Grosh from New Orleans, and political fixer Art Samish from California. Authorities reported that "these get-togethers are something in the nature of policy meetings."

Those meetings clarified the boundary lines of territories ruled by different gangs, established Miami as the Mob's first "open city," and established procedures for settling disputes short of open warfare. Moe Dalitz counseled against killing journalists or other public figures on the rare occasions when they proved immune to bribery. For those occasions when only a bullet would serve, the Mob created a special Brooklyn-based enforcement unit, led by Lepke and Albert Anastasia. Fielding killers nationwide, that group claimed at least 400 lives before its exposure as "Murder, Incorporated" in 1940. Dalitz emerged from the Syndicate meetings a figure of national prominence. Mob lawyer Dixie Davis wrote in 1939: "Moey Davis became the power in Cleveland, and anyone who questioned it would have to deal with Lucky and Meyer and the Bug [Siegel]."

* * *

By early 1932, Moe and his cohorts knew that prohibition was a doomed experiment. They would continue bootlegging for years beyond repeal, but the emphasis now shifted toward illegal gambling. Dalitz and company already owned Ohio's best casinos, but independent operators still controlled some quarters of the sporting scene. The Great Depression found their territories ripe for plunder by the Mob.

Lawyer Dixie Davis (right, with client Dutch Schultz) leaked details of the Mob's national power structure (Library of Congress).

First up, the numbers racket, a poor man's lottery in which gamblers bet on three- or four-digit numbers selected at random by drawings or from published figures (daily race results, the stock exchange, etc.). Bets were typically small, with most of the action confined to black urban ghettos. Racist mobsters shunned policy until Dutch Schultz took an interest, demonstrating that the "penny-ante" games yielded millions of dollars per year. In 1931, police estimated Cleveland's *daily* take at $6,000 to $10,000, split among four operators: Frank Hoge, John Johnson, Rufus Jones, and Willie Richardson. Of the four, only Hoge was Caucasian.

The Mob went for Richardson first, sending three carloads of gunmen to snatch him from Central Avenue on January 26, 1931. Richardson fought back, then feigned death when the mobsters started shooting. While *Plain Dealer* editorials bemoaned the "injection of the spirit of vendetta into the formerly pacifist policy game trust," Richardson named mafioso Charles Colletti as one of his assailants. On January

28 Richardson and six other independents signed waivers confessing their crimes and announcing retirement from the numbers game. A four-year term for tax evasion rescued Rufus Jones from the Mob, but Richardson remained a target. On October 3, 1931, drive-by shotgunners missed Richardson again but blew off a bodyguard's arm. Richardson recanted his statement at Charles Colletti's trial, later receiving a ten-year sentence for perjury. He emerged from prison to work as a Syndicate flunky for $55 per week.

Other casualties of conquest included Godfrey McDonald, dumped in Moreland Heights Village with "quite a lot of lead in his body"; Willie Wiggins, shot and thrown from a car in Pepper Pike Village; Prudence Thompson, killed while riding on Scovill Avenue; and Frank Handy, slain outside a candy store on Central Avenue. John Johnson, wounded at his home, told reporters, "I'm quitting because of this here depression." Frank Hoge knuckled under and kept 60 percent of his business, while Shondor Birns consolidated the Mob's new policy empire from his base at the Alhambra Inn.

From policy, the Syndicate moved on to slot machines. Nate Weisenberg first felt the heat in 1928, when Mob spokesmen demanded a piece of the action he shared with partner Frank Joiner. Refusal prompted a bombing of Weisenberg's home. Detectives questioned Al and Chuck Polizzi, then freed them for lack of evidence. Weisenberg stood firm until December 16, 1932, when he joined the Polizzis and John Angersola as a partner in Buckeye Enterprises, renamed Buckeye Catering on January 1, 1935. Frank Joiner left the firm in January 1934, his corpse recovered on August 21 from a lime pit in Solon. Weisenberg's capitulation bought him another decade, until he outlived his usefulness to the Mob. Asked about Buckeye and Weisenberg in 1951, Moe Dalitz testified, "I don't remember that company. I was never interested in that and don't know that man." Subsequent investigation demonstrated that the Cleveland Four owned 50 percent of Buckeye Catering.

* * *

William Potter left a Chicago orphanage at age eight, in 1892, to support himself as a newspaper boy and bricklayer. Moving to Cleveland as a young adult, he entered local politics and won election to the city council in 1919. On October 15, 1929, a grand jury indicted Potter, Harmon Atwater, and Fred Thomas for swindling the city out of $33,000 on real estate transactions. Potter and Robert Bunowitz faced additional charges for harboring Atwater as a fugitive from justice. Atwater pled guilty to fraud, while jurors convicted Bunowitz and acquitted Potter on both counts. Unsatisfied with that result, a new grand jury charged Potter with perjury in 1930.

Out of office and short on cash, Potter grew desperate. He sold his house, moved his family into a small bungalow, and tried in vain to support himself by selling insurance. The depression crushed him. Rumors spread that he would "squeal" on Cleveland's Powers That Be to save himself from prison.

Potter left home for the last time at 9:00 A.M. on February 3, 1931, "to transact some business." Seven hours later, he telephoned to warn his wife that he "would be a little late." On February 6 Mrs. Potter received an anonymous phone call, informing her that William's car was parked outside an apartment house on Parkwood Drive. She had the car towed home, then called police. According to their files, "Mrs. Potter informed us that she did not want an official report of the absence of Mr. Potter made until further word from her."

Two days later, an unknown caller told police, "There's a dead man in suite four at 880 Parkwood Drive. Looks like a suicide." Detectives found Potter sprawled on the sofa, drilled through the head with a .38 caliber bullet, his skull crushed by heavy blows. A second shot, from a .32-caliber pistol, pierced Potter's overcoat but missed his flesh, striking a nearby wall. Police found two shell casings, but no weapons. Prosecutor Ray Miller declared, "This crime was committed by someone who feared that Potter might reveal what he knew about the graft in city land deals. He was killed to close his mouth."

An upstairs neighbor, prostitute Mildred Scribano, told police that she had seen bootlegger Hyman Martin — previously bailed out of jail by Morris Komissarow in May 1929 — enter the murder flat on February 1. Another witness, Esther Morgan, reported seeing Martin enter the apartment twice. GOP spokesman Alex Bernstein claimed that "two men from Detroit" left Potter a note at City Hall on February 3. Coroner A.J. Pearse opined that Potter died sometime that night. Patrolman Harry Mizer belatedly recalled finding a bloodstained .38 revolver on Bryant Avenue, on February 4. He took the gun home and was fired for dereliction of duty.

Hymie Martin, a rumrunner with contacts in Akron, Cleveland, and Detroit, surrendered to Pittsburgh police on February 12, 1931. Cleveland detectives snatched him in the midst of a *habeas corpus* hearing and charged him with murder. Akron witness Mary Outland surfaced on March 15, stating that Martin was with her on February 3 and "would not hurt a fly" in any case.

Hymie Martin (third from right) with attorneys and detectives at the Potter murder scene (Cleveland Public Library).

Jurors convicted Martin of first-degree murder on April 3, sparing his life with a recommendation of mercy. Martin served ten months of his life sentence before an appellate court reversed his conviction, citing "an amazing dearth of evidence." Meanwhile, Mildred Scribano recanted her previous statement and blamed police for coercion. Another key witness admitted taking money from police on "twelve or thirteen occasions." Esther Morgan claimed that strangers had offered her $5,000 to change her original statement. Confused jurors acquitted Martin on June 16, 1932.

So, who killed William Potter?

In August 1936 William Edwards, director of Cleveland's Association of Criminal Justice, told G-men that Lou Rothkopf "figured in the murder of City Councilman Potter along with Hymie Martin and Akron Mary [Outland]." FBI files from May 1939 report that "FRED FLAUB [*sic*], the principal witness in the trial of HYMIE MARTIN..., indicates that MORRIS KLEINMAN engineered the murder and that LOUIS ROTHKOPF also was involved, the latter having been located and apprehended in a hideout furnished by MORRIS KLEINMAN." Another FBI report, from 1958, says that "MOE DAVIS and LOU ROTHKOPF were key figures in the official attempt to locate POTTER'S murderer." According to that file, "Both DAVIS and ROTHKOPF disappeared after POTTER'S murder. Both were readily found, questioned and released. A great deal of information ... is in the possession of the police, politicians and reporters and has never been made public since they are libelous unless they are proved and proof is not available."

Supporting those accounts, a police memo dated August 17, 1931, reads: "Woman called Freed says that Hoot Gibson and Morris Kleinman are at Sam Miller's on Harvard Avenue. This woman heard them talking, and they said they were with H. Martin at murder of Potter." On October 28, 1931, the *Plain Dealer* named Rothkopf as a "missing witness" and "pal of Hyman Martin," reporting that the search for Uncle Lou had "narrowed to Cleveland" after forays into Canada and Cuba.

Two years later, the *Cleveland Press* reported that Hymie Martin placed calls to Pittsburgh from the Prospect Advertising Company, a bookie joint run by Dalitz and Kleinman. Police also traced checks written by an unnamed city official through Prospect Advertising to Dalitz, Kleinman, and gambler Dave Langman. Langman denied knowing Martin, but his brother, bootlegger Jack Langman, was seen with Potter at a "cottage colony" in Euclid. Unknown gunmen killed Jack Langman in June 1931, leaving police to speculate that he "talked too much about Potter." According to the *Press*, Kleinman answered questions about Potter's death, while Moe Dalitz went on the lam. Ex-mayor Ray Miller later called Kleinman "the fountainhead" of Potter's slaying, claiming that Potter offered one prosecution witness "a nice soft job" in return for clearing Hymie Martin.

In 1951, Chicago Crime Commission chairman Virgil Peterson told the Kefauver Committee, "Moe Davis and Lou Rothkopf were with 'Pittsburgh' Hymie until a few hours before the [Potter] slaying. Davis was also with Hymie until an hour prior to the arrest of Hymie." Asked to respond, Dalitz told the committee, "I have never been questioned on that. I have never been talked to about it and I never had any connection with it of any kind. I have never even been questioned about it even as a witness or by influence, or anything else." Senator Kefauver replied, "Let's go ahead with more specific details in connection with that"— then abruptly veered off into questions concerning Ohio casinos.

Author Howard Beaufait, profiling the Potter case in 1947, wrote that after his acquittal "Hymie Martin left Cleveland immediately.... He went back to Pittsburgh, and bought a night club there, and that is all the news there has been of him since."

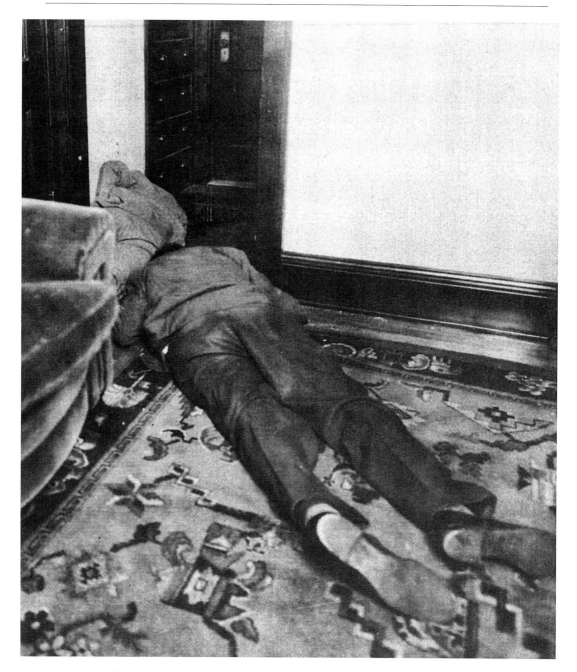

Victims of the Collingwood Apartments massacre (National Archives).

Well, not quite.

In 1960, Martin surfaced on Florida's Gold Coast. His new job: overseeing local gambling for Moe Dalitz and the Cleveland Syndicate.

* * *

More murders followed Potter's. On June 28, 1931, bootlegger-florist Rosolino Visconti was shot while driving along Kinsman Road with a pistol tucked under his belt. Detectives questioned the same "Captain West" who escaped from the *Neptune* in June 1929, then freed him for lack of evidence.

On July 21, 1931, police found East Side bootleggers Harry Gertzlin and Al Jaffe murdered in their car, parked beside a rural highway often used by rumrunners between Detroit and Cleveland. Jaffe ran a Buffalo distilling ring. In 1932 Morris Kleinman cited Jaffe for a $5,000 "bad debt."

A tantalizing note from FBI files claims that in early 1932 G-men and prohibition agents "were interested in locating Moe Davis for questioning in connection with the disappearance of [DELETED]. In March 1930 [DELETED] had been employed by 'Moe Davis and gang' of Cleveland as a liquor runner."

In a footnote to the Potter killing, two hitmen beat and shot Joseph Redlick, brother of state witness Julius Redlick, on February 2, 1935. He died on Woodhill Road, clutching an unfired pistol. Police discounted robbery as a motive, blaming his death on a "Mayfield feud."

* * *

The Purple Gang was up to its old tricks in 1931, defending local turf against Chicago infiltrators Joseph Lebovitz, Herman Paul, and Isadore Sutker. The trio had worn out their welcome in Chicago by extorting "protection" from Capone speakeasies, then moved to Detroit and forged an alliance with the Little Jewish Navy. In 1930 they resumed their shakedown rackets, targeting Purple-protected casinos. Their final mistake was hijacking a shipment of liquor earmarked by the Purples for Detroit's 1931 American Legion convention.

On August 20, 1931, a man calling himself James Regis rented a flat at the Collingwood Manor Apartments, two blocks from the home of Moe Dalitz's paternal grandmother. Ray Bernstein then approached Solly Levine, a Little Jewish Navy member friendly with Lebovitz, Paul, and Sutker. The Purples, Bernstein said, wanted Levine and his three friends to serve the gang as liquor agents. They would finalize the bargain on September 16, at Collingwood Manor.

What followed was a replay of the 1927 Milaflores Apartments massacre. Levine and the others entered Apartment 211 to find Ray Bernstein, Harry Fleischer, Harry Keywell, and Irving Millberg waiting. Bernstein left, ostensibly to fetch the gang's bookkeeper, whereupon his cronies drew pistols and fired at point-blank range, killing Lebovitz, Paul, and Sutker. Levine "sat there in a daze," then fled with the slayers, but later told all to police. On September 21 authorities charged Bernstein, Fleischer, Keywell, and Millberg with first-degree murder. Fleischer escaped, while police took his three cohorts into custody and held Levine as a material witness. Jurors convicted Bernstein, Keywell, and Millberg on November 11. All three received life sentences.

* * *

The 1932 presidential campaign offered mobsters a unique chance to influence national policy. Prohibition was dying, and President Hoover clearly had slim hope of re-election. That left two "wet" New Yorkers, Franklin Roosevelt and Alfred Smith, as prime contenders for the Democratic nomination. Smith, New York's governor and a friend of Lucky Luciano, had lost the party's nod in 1928 because he was a Catholic. That obstacle remained in 1932, while Roosevelt made overtures to New York mobsters, vowing through proxies to curtail investigations of Big Apple graft.

The Mob turned out in force for the Democratic National Convention, held in Chicago

The Collingwood massacre trail. Right to left: Defense attorney Edward Kennedy, Harry Keywell, Ray Bernstein, Irving Millberg, prosecutor Miles Culihan (National Archives).

between June 27 and July 2, 1932. Moe Dalitz, Luciano, Meyer Lansky, Frank Costello, and Longy Zwillman occupied lavish quarters at the Drake Hotel, spending quality time with Louisiana's Huey Long and Kansas City boss Tom Pendergast. Delegates who resented paying for whiskey or beer at Frank Nitti's undisguised liquor stands found free alcohol available around the clock in the Mob's hospitality suite. Side meetings advanced the spread of illegal casinos from coast to coast, but choosing America's next president remained the first order of business.

To that end, rumrunner Joseph Kennedy donated $100,000 to the Roosevelt campaign, backed by a matching check from William Randolph Hearst, and twisted arms on the convention floor. Al Smith led a movement to stop Roosevelt, while Dalitz and Luciano waited until the last moment, then used their influence for FDR on the fourth ballot. Lucky broke the news to Smith, ignoring Smith's prophetic warning that Roosevelt would break his campaign promises. On November 8, 1932, Roosevelt buried Hoover with 89 percent of the electoral vote, effectively dooming prohibition.

* * *

Repeal came too late for Morris Kleinman, already ensnared by tax-evasion charges that mirrored Al Capone's federal prosecution. IRS agent Alvin Giesey launched the probe in 1931, after press reports on the Potter case named Kleinman as Cleveland's top bootlegger. Investigation proved that Kleinman had banked $931,667 in 1929 and $742,904 in 1930, while reporting no income. Kleinman's secretary, Sylvia Regar, admitted depositing bundles of cash in eight different accounts, under various names. At Merchants Bank, depositor "Frank Clark's" signature card bore a typed name instead of a signature, with the phone number for Kleinman's Liberty Poultry Company. Moe Dalitz, as "William Martin," used money from Clark's account to buy his dock at Clifton Park Lagoon. Another five grand from the same account had bailed out Harry Wilson, captured with the *Idle Hour* in November 1929.

Chuck Polizzi (right) with unidentified companion (Cleveland State University Library).

Kleinman hired Maurice Maschke to settle the case, admitting his lapse while claiming deductions for lost liquor boats, captured stills, bail bonds, and "bad debts" from murdered associates. While refusing to name his partners, Kleinman admitted ownership of a dozen blockade-runners. The feds pegged Kleinman's traceable profits for 1929–30 at $303,000, a *very* conservative estimate. Maschke later claimed that IRS agents promised to waive prosecution if Kleinman paid his debt, then double-crossed Kleinman by filing a criminal indictment on February 3, 1933. Some authors view that move as Franklin Roosevelt's first visible betrayal of the mobsters who supported his campaign.

Kleinman promptly vanished, remaining at large until feds found him in Washington, D.C., on October 12, 1933. With wife Gizella at his side, Kleinman pled guilty to tax evasion in Cleveland on November 27, receiving a four-year prison term and a $15,000 fine. The next day, before Kleinman departed for prison, his partners staged a lavish going-away party in Sheriff Sultzmann's office. Pending Kleinman's parole on September 1, 1936, Moe Dalitz chose Chuck Polizzi to fill Kleinman's seat on the Syndicate board of directors.

4

New Deals

Prohibition died by stages. Congress passed a Twenty-first Amendment to the Constitution, repealing the Eighteenth, and sent it to the states for ratification on February 20, 1933. Michigan was first to ratify the new amendment, on April 10, while Utah provided the crucial 36th stamp of approval on December 5, 1933.

The nation's liquor syndicates were ready for repeal. Sam Bronfman went legit with Seagram's. Lewis Rosenstiel, indicted for bootlegging in 1929, offered stiff competition with Schenley Distillers. Joe Reinfeld partnered with Longy Zwillman and Joseph "Doc" Stacher in Browne Vintners. "Retired" mafioso John Torrio helmed Prendergast & Davies liquor wholesalers. Frank Costello, Max Hoff, and Irving Haim created Alliance Distributors. Al Capone's heirs ran Gold Seal Liquors, Chicago's top wholesaler. Boston's Joe Linsey handled Schenley booze as president of Whitehall Distributors. Joseph Kennedy and James Roosevelt, son of the president-elect, founded Somerset Importers in September 1933, securing the franchises for Gordon's gin, Ron Rico rum, Dewar's Scotch, and Haig & Haig.

Moe Dalitz chose a different route. Repeal was fine, but why should he pay Uncle Sam a liquor tax, when he had fifteen years' experience in selling homemade hooch?

* * *

Eleven days before Repeal, on November 25, 1933, Molaska Corporation registered with Ohio's secretary of state. Ostensibly, the firm existed to manufacture dehydrated molasses for use in liquor, ice cream, candy, and other products. Two secretaries and a clerk from Samuel Haas's law office signed the incorporation papers. Molaska's officers of record included:

President: John Drew, né Jacob Stein, was the same disbarred New York attorney who had peddled liquor warehouse withdrawal permits with Gaston Means in 1921–23. Already dabbling in powdered molasses by 1932, Stein hit the big time a year later, when he gained financial backing from "some people out in Cleveland." That same year, 1933, Stein legally changed his name.

Vice President: Theodore Black was a New York co-conspirator with Stein and others in various bootlegging rings. Stein/Drew credited Black with procuring Molaska's wealthy Cleveland investors.

Secretary: Sidney Kyman was a Cleveland produce dealer and longtime friend of Sam Tucker. He later told authorities, "Sam Tucker came to me and asked my permission to use my name in connection with the Molaska Corporation.... I have never taken any interest, active or otherwise, in the affairs of Molaska Corporation, nor have I attended any of their meetings or put one red cent into that corporation."

Treasurer: Ray Tobein was a partner with Chuck Polizzi in the Cleveland-based Ray Coal Company. His sole duty as treasurer was "to sign a quantity of blank checks ... in advance for John Drew."

Assistant Treasurer: Moses Citron was Meyer Lansky's father-in-law and partner in a New York produce business. Citron invested $121,000 in Molaska, afterward explaining that "all the business he did with Molaska was transacted through Meyer Lansky."

Director: David Kyman, Sidney's brother, fronted for Moe Dalitz. Kyman's statement read: "Moe Davis called on me and stated that as he did not wish to use his name, would I permit him to use my name in connection with a corporation that he, Davis, was interested in. I had known Davis for several years, and I told him that as a favor to him I would permit the use of my name in the Molaska Corporation." He closed by saying, "I really don't know what my connection is with Molaska, if any."

Legal Counsel: Aaron Sapiro was the same attorney who sued Henry Ford for libel in 1925. Three months before Molaska organized, Chicago prosecutors indicted Sapiro, Al Capone, and 22 other defendants for labor racketeering. All were acquitted, but the bad publicity prompted Sapiro to quit Molaska in January 1934, ceding his post to Samuel Haas.

While John Drew and a cast of hapless stooges ran Molaska on paper, its *real* owners included the Cleveland Four and the Polizzi "cousins," Lansky, Peter Licavoli, Lucky Luciano, Frank Costello, Joe Adonis, Lepke Buchalter, and Longy Zwillman. Lansky secured Molaska's sugar supply through Fulgencio Batista, a Cuban army officer who seized power in September 1933 and ruled the island until 1944. Molaska established its first factory in a six-story building that covered a square block of Cleveland's Stanton Avenue, the scene of a bungled insurance-fraud arson attempt on November 30, 1932. FBI files described landlord Edward Strong, a legal associate of once-convicted arsonist Sam Haas, as "well known in gambling circles."

Post-repeal bootlegging was a variation on the old, familiar theme. Molaska's outlaw stills produced untaxed whiskey at a cost of fifty cents per gallon, shipped to wholesale buyers for two dollars per gallon (half the price of liquor taxed by Treasury officials). A single Molaska distillery, located in Zanesville, Ohio, produced 5,000 gallons of alcohol each day, for an estimated profit of $2.74 million.

Molaska operated without interference until August 1934, when Treasury agent Eliot Ness assumed command of IRS Alcohol Tax Unit in northern Ohio. On arrival, Ness found Cleveland agent Robert Bridges seething over official disinterest in a huge bootleg distillery on Sweeney Avenue, disguised as the Sweeney Metal Company. Sidetracked by corrupt superiors since July 1933, Bridges joined Ness in raiding the still on September 7, 1934. The agents found no booze, but Bridges surreptitiously scratched his initials on three large steam boilers, for future reference.

Within days of the Cleveland raid, Chief of Detectives Milton Stotts began tracking "three foreigners" in Zanesville, 150 miles south of Cleveland. Stotts identified two of the men as Clevelanders Harry Bader and William Goldenberg. Goldenberg was a partner of Al Polizzi's in Toledo's Lubeck Brewery, founded by Polizzi in January 1933. Moore had negotiated with Zanesville councilman Solomon Berman and safety director Charles Barron to transfer Lubeck's equipment from Toledo to Zanesville's abandoned J.B. Owens Pottery and Tile plant, on North Dearborn Street. Barron resigned as safety director on August 16, 1934, one day before Bader took over the plant and renamed it the Baltic Feed Company. Barron's furniture store subsequently sold various items to Baltic Feed, and furnished a house Bader leased across the street from his new factory.

Stotts mounted surveillance on Baltic Feed, tracing visitors back to the Hollenden Hotel, where a house detective identified them as members of "an alky ring." Neighbors of Baltic Feed complained about the smell of cooking mash, but Barron led Stotts on an inspection tour that revealed no improprieties. Still, Stotts kept digging. On December 3, 1934, Bader met Stotts at the county courthouse, handing him $100 and two pints of whiskey. In return, Bader asked that "if one of my boys gets picked up, you can stop them from being fingerprinted." At a second meeting, one month later, Bader told Stotts that "he was not worried about being knocked off, as he had the state and federal fixed and his outfit had connections right in Washington. If any knocks went in they would be notified to leave."

On January 16, 1935, ATU agents raided Baltic Feed and captured the largest illegal distillery in U.S. history, valued in excess of $250,000. Harry Bader and several employees escaped through a tunnel leading to their house across the street. Feds traced Bader to a house in Kansas City, vacated for his convenience while its owner went to stay at Lou Rothkopf's farm in Ohio. That favor was explained when ATU investigators learned that Bader's wife was related to Blanche Rothkopf. Any doubts concerning ownership of Baltic Feed vanished

"Untouchable" Eliot Ness failed to crack the Dalitz syndicate in Cleveland (Library of Congress).

when Robert Bridges found his initials on three of the boilers seized in Zanesville. According to the ATU's final report: "This still was owned and operated by the Moe Davis Syndicate here in Cleveland. This plant almost in its entirety was formerly located at 5301 Sweeney Avenue, Cleveland."

The Zanesville raid produced 23 indictments. Harry Bader spent two years in federal prison. William Goldenberg was sentenced to one year, while Tom McGinty aide John O'Boyle received a six-month sentence.

Ten days after the Zanesville sweep, on January 26, federal agents struck another Molaska alky plant in Elizabeth, New Jersey. Leased from Texas Oil on September 13, 1934, the distillery was camouflaged by surrounding oil tanks and refineries, with waterfront access for shipping. Authorities valued their haul at $200,000, reporting that the still was "large enough to flood New York and New Jersey with illicit alcohol." One of those detained later told agents that Ben Siegel and Lucky Luciano "had a piece of the Elizabeth plant."

But they were not alone. Three blocks away, at 150 South Front, stood Molaska's eastern headquarters, leased

The control room of Molaska's huge distillery at Zanesville, Ohio (National Archives).

The Zanesville plant's distilling columns (National Archives).

from Bethlehem Steel by Sam Tucker, John Drew, and Theodore Black in October 1934. Tucker drew a paycheck as the factory's supervisor. His telephone records showed calls to Morris Kleinman's brother-in-law at Liberty Poultry; to a Cleveland bookie joint; to congressman Martin Sweeney, whose legal partner, Martin McCormick, pled for leniency at Kleinman's tax-evasion trial; and to "Fred Bennett," residing at the home address of Moe Dalitz.

Molaska Corporation filed for bankruptcy on March 2, 1935. One day later, the Elizabeth plant closed its doors and shipped its fixtures back to Cleveland. The firm officially dissolved on November 15, 1935. Buckeye Enterprises partners Moe Dalitz, Lou Rothkopf, Sam Tucker, Al Polizzi, Chuck Polizzi, Martin O'Boyle, and John Angersola each claimed a loss of $16,661.80 from Molaska on their 1935 tax returns. The IRS accepted those deductions after Buckeye's owners agreed to pay taxes on pro rated shares of $50,000 additional income for 1933–35. Dalitz explained the compromise by saying that "any newsboy thirty inches high knew we had to pay something for ice [graft]."

Meanwhile, business continued as usual. A new Molaska Company, Inc., organized on October 9, 1935, with John Drew as president and "M.B. Davis" as vice president. New stills went up in Buffalo and Chicago, reported to ATU agents only after they had closed. Cleveland was Molaska's distribution center, with a "canning plant" on East 105th Street and a fleet of trucks housed at the Diamond-T Garage on Rockwell Avenue. Business offices moved frequently, with federal eavesdroppers complaining that they had to shift their wiretaps five times between October 1935 and March 1936. Eliot Ness was on Molaska's case by March 1935, raiding Fred Morello's bootleg distribution office on East 90th Street. ATU agents manned Morello's phones after the raid, taking orders from dozens of local saloons, then fanned out to jail Morello's customers. Ness's report claimed that Morello had obtained 4,925 gallons of booze from Maxie Diamond, and 2,035 gallons from Anthony Milano. Payments by check simplified the process of indictment.

Lou Rothkopf's luck ran out in December 1935, when feds trailed him to Kansas City for meetings with local bootleggers. On December 16, wiretappers heard Blanche Rothkopf urge her husband to call Cleveland, where his partners wanted to discuss "the agreement." Soon after the Rothkopfs returned to Cleveland, K.C. received its first shipment of Molaska alcohol. The feds indicted Rothkopf, Diamond, and ten others, all of whom were convicted on May 18, 1937. Four days later, Rothkopf received a four-year sentence and a $5,000 fine. On June 9, he entered the federal lockup at Lewisburg, Pennsylvania.

Still, all was not lost. On May 21, the day before Rothkopf's sentencing, the Molaska Company filed for bankruptcy. Its assets sold at public auction for $3,817.10, while private parties bought "three air fans and one lot of miscellaneous steam pumps located at Mitchen, New Jersey." Sam Haas claimed a loss of $2,500. Lou Rothkopf was the big winner, in April 1938, when an appellate court reversed his conviction on grounds that wiretap evidence was inadmissible.

* * *

While Molaska rose and fell, the FBI declared a "war on crime." J. Edgar Hoover claimed that with repeal, the nation's "big-time" criminals had switched from bootlegging to ransom kidnapping. Hoover's "war" languished until June 17, 1933, when gunmen ambushed a party of FBI agents and local policemen escorting fugitive bandit Frank Nash from Arkansas to Leavenworth Penitentiary. When the gunsmoke cleared at Kansas City's Union Station, Nash and four lawmen lay dead. FBI agents commandeered the case, despite a total lack of jurisdiction, eventually naming the killers as ex-sheriff Vernon Miller, Oklahoma bank robber Charles

J. Edgar Hoover (left), ironically posed with an unloaded Tommy gun, denied the existence of organized crime for decades. He is accompanied here by an unidentified federal agent (Library of Congress).

FBI files linked Moe Dalitz to the Kansas City massacre but provided no evidence (National Archive).

"Pretty Boy" Floyd, and Floyd sidekick Adam Richetti. An FBI file from 1933 contains "information concerning reported contacts by Moe Davis of the Cleveland underworld with both Floyd and Miller about the time of the Kansas City massacre. It was also indicated that Davis was in contact with [DELETED] and [DELETED] who were associates of Floyd and Miller." Despite that claim, no evidence exists that Moe was ever questioned in the case.

Floyd and his trigger-happy ilk preoccupied Hoover's G-men through the mid–1930s, while the Mob spread its tentacles from coast to coast. Empowered by new federal laws passed in 1934, FBI agents earned their "gang-busting" reputation by shooting bandits and jailing their "gun moll" girlfriends. Bureau reports for the era list America's major crimes as homicide, rape, robbery, burglary, auto theft, and aggravated assault — with no mention of illegal gambling, bootlegging, racketeering, or narcotics. Today, the FBI's Internet website claims that "[t]he legal tools given to the FBI by Congress ... resulted in the arrest or demise of all the major gangsters by 1936."

In fact, only one of the era's "public enemies" was linked to organized crime. Alvin Karpis robbed banks and kidnapped wealthy Minnesota businessmen with "Ma" Barker's sons in 1933–34. While on the lam in 1935, he worked as a hired gun in Cleveland, guarding the Harvard Club and terrorizing independent gamblers. Karpis escaped when raiders hit the Harvard Club in January 1936, thanks to a timely tip-off. G-men traced the call to the Cleveland Police Department, where "conditions [were] such that practically no police work can be accomplished." Finally captured in New Orleans, on May 1, 1936, Karpis told agents that he had rejected job offers from the Chicago syndicate, but failed to mention Moe Dalitz, insisting, "I'm no hood! I'm a thief!"

Historians still debate J. Edgar Hoover's stubborn refusal to tackle organized crime. Biographer Anthony Summers notes that the Mob's national expansion "coincided precisely" with

Bandit Alvin Karpis (in handcuffs) worked for Moe Dalitz in Cleveland, while a fugitive from kidnapping charges (Library of Congress).

Hoover's reign at FBI headquarters, from 1924 onward — but why? When IRS agents jailed prominent bootleggers and Thomas Dewey gained fame by prosecuting New York's leading racketeers, how could Hoover dismiss reports of syndicated crime as "baloney"?

Hoover and second-in-command Clyde Tolson were close friends with columnist Walter Winchell, frequently dining with Winchell at New York's Mob-infested Stork Club. When visiting Miami, Hoover often dined at Joe's Stone Crabs, a seafood restaurant frequented by Al Capone, Frank Costello, and Meyer Lansky. Owner Jesse Weiss considered Hoover a "very, very, very close friend." In La Jolla, California, Hoover stayed free of charge at oilman Clint Murchison's Del Charro hotel, also patronized by Ed Levinson, Molaska's John Drew, and Chicago mafioso John Rosselli. Estimates of Hoover's "comped" vacations at Del Charro total $19,000 during 1953–59.

Nor can such incidents be chalked up to coincidence. An inveterate gambler, Hoover timed his annual "inspection tours" of FBI field offices to coincide with racing seasons at horse tracks in New York, Florida, California, Maryland, and West Virginia. For appearance's sake, Hoover placed two-dollar bets, while anonymous G-men lined up at the hundred-dollar windows. Still, it hardly qualified as gambling, since Frank Costello furnished Hoover with tips on fixed races from layoff bookie Frank Erickson. In 1961, Costello told Justice Department attorney William Hundley "that he knew Hoover, that they met for lunch." Another New

York mafioso, Carmine Lombardozzi, confirmed that Hoover and Costello "had contact on many occasions and over a long period. Hoover was very friendly towards the [Mafia] families. They took good care of him, especially at the races." As a result, Lombardozzi said, "Hoover was in our pocket. He was no one we needed to fear."

* * *

With Molaska's demise, Moe Dalitz made illegal gambling his primary focus. He had run casinos from the early days of prohibition in Detroit, but gambling had always been an adjunct to illicit liquor sales. Repeal and Lou Rothkopf's near-miss with prison changed all that, expanding Syndicate horizons and increasing profits exponentially.

While Cleveland G-men showed no interest in tackling organized crime, their secret reports from the mid–1930s name members of "the MORRIS BARNEY DALITZ criminal syndicate" as Morris Kleinman, Lou Rothkopf, Sam Tucker, Game Boy Miller, Sam Haas, Mushy Wexler, Martin O'Boyle, and Nate Weisenberg. Their casinos included Cleveland's Mayfair Club, the Ohio Villa in Richmond Heights, and the Thomas Club in Maple Heights. Operations erroneously labeled "independent" included the Harvard and Arrow Clubs, 139 bookie joints, and 100 brothels. Agents reported that Sam Miller "usually goes around the country making gambling contacts," and handled bookmaking at New York racetracks during the spring-summer months.

Investigators singled out Nate Weisenberg for special attention. Wiretaps on his phone revealed frequent calls to police officers, and FBI agents found him "closely aligned with [Arthur] Hebebrand," a partner of record with Shimmy Patton and Dan Gallagher at the Harvard Club, in Newburgh Heights. William Edwards, director of Cleveland's Association for Criminal Justice, told agents that Weisenberg was "only a front for the Mayfield Road gang and only owns a 20% interest in the [slot] machines he places for this mob." At the Mayfair Club, Weisenberg "own[ed] part interest but there are other parties that own the majority of the stock in the enterprise that are not known to the public."

Edwards also gave G-men a financial audit of the Thomas Club, performed by someone named "Geiser or Geisey," listing the casino's owners as "Morris Dolitz," Sam Tucker, Lou Rothkopf, "Mar[t]y J. O'Boyle," Albert and Charles Polizzi, John Angersola, and Harry Potter. The audit pegged total profits for 1935 at $101,745, with $12,717.88 paid to each owner. Edwards opined that the audit "was made purposely in order to defeat any subsequent income tax suits," and that "the earnings of the club were well in excess of the above figure." FBI agents identified the Mob's accountant as ex-IRS agent Alvin Giesey, whose investigation sent Morris Kleinman to prison in 1933. Retired from government service since 1934, Giesey later claimed that Kleinman hired him as a bookkeeper 1936, but his name appeared on a list of Molaska Corporation's creditors in March 1935. In 1951, Kefauver Committee counsel Rudolph Halley asked Giesey, "What is the inducement to you? Why do you do these things?" Giesey's reply: "For the almighty dollar."

Another money-hungry Syndicate employee was Louis "Lew" Wasserman, whose Russian-Jewish parents ran a restaurant on Woodland Avenue. From selling candy in a burlesque theater, he graduated to service as an advertising agent for Harry Propper's Mayfair Club, downtown. Ex-owner Herman Pinchner, who sold the club in 1933, called Propper "a front man for the Syndicate — four Jewish gentlemen." Mob lawyer Henry Beckerman's name appeared on the Mayfair's deed and liquor license. Around the time of Beckerman's arson acquittal, Wasserman married Beckerman's daughter Edie (who fawned over "Uncle Moe" Dalitz) and moved into the lawyer's home. In 1936, Wasserman accepted a job offer from

Chicago ophthalmologist Julius "Jules" Stein, becoming an agent of Stein's Music Corporation of America. Dalitz subsequently sold the Mayfair to Louis Blumenthal and Jacob Shapiro, Lepke Buchalter's longtime partner in New York's labor rackets.

Aside from Cleveland and surrounding Cuyahoga County, FBI files reveal that Dalitz also dominated gambling in Cincinnati. Other thriving outposts included the Jungle Inn (Trumbull County), the Mounds Club (Lake County), the Pettibone Club (Geauga County), and the Colony Club, on the Ohio River. The Pettibone's managers included Ruby Kolod, Alfred Goltsman, and George Gordon; Mafia "grand councilman" John Scalish worked at the club for $100 per week, when Kolod remembered to pay him. In each locale, police and politicians turned a blind eye to gambling, while Moe claimed to believe the clubs were legal. "There were so many judges and politicians in them," he told a reporter, "I figured they had to be all right."

* * *

Moe's casinos operated so brazenly that they served as lighting rods for civil litigation. Between August 1937 and April 1942, three dozen lawsuits were filed against Moe and various partners in Cuyahoga County, seeking reimbursement of gambling losses or other alleged damages. The plaintiffs generally sued "Moe Davis," with sundry variations and aliases, including "Frank Bennett" and "M.B. Dalitz." Other defendants included Moe's various partners in the Arrow and Thomas Clubs.

Willing participants in illegal gambling may not recover their losses in court, but that did not stop some of Moe's unhappy players from trying. The angry wives of losing gamblers comprised another class of litigants against Moe's Cleveland clubs. Plaintiffs claiming physical injuries fared somewhat better in lawsuits arising from limousine crashes en route to the clubs. Most cases were dismissed or settled quietly, but some losing gamblers dropped their lawsuits out of fear. Ex-judge Frank Lausche cited the case of a Cleveland butcher who lost his life savings and two butcher shops while gambling at the Harvard Club. The butcher sued for $2,500, whereupon a carload of gunmen called at his home, warning the plaintiff, "If you love your wife and your child, you had better not appear in that courtroom and testify in support of the petition which you filed." The butcher delayed his lawsuit, then withdrew it entirely when the thugs paid a visit to his wife.

Another class of Cleveland cases involved criminal charges filed against gamblers who stole money to replenish their losses. After sentencing a gambling-addicted school superintendent to prison for embezzlement in 1933, Judge Lausche called for a grand jury investigation of local casinos, but authorities proved reluctant to act. On July 22, Cleveland safety director E.E. Adams told police "in words they couldn't help but understand" that slot machines must be eradicated from the city. Police chief George Matowitz echoed that call to action eight days later, but his efforts to stamp out gambling were largely ineffectual.

On October 11, 1933, raiders struck five gambling clubs identified by grand jury foreman William Feather, but found no evidence of any violations. Three weeks later, Captain Emmett Potts handed Chief Matowitz a list of forty clubs, but the two resultant raids turned up no evidence. On November 23, new mayor Harry Davis shifted the city's priorities. The *Plain Dealer* announced that "a liberal policy of regulation, rather than suppression, of vice and gambling will be adopted, although no written orders to that effect are likely to find a place in the police archives."

In June 1934, after a few half-hearted bookie raids, police spokesmen blamed the Mayfield Road Gang for Cleveland's gambling problems. Mafiosi were "intent on gaining control of all gambling activities," the *Plain Dealer* reported. Already, they controlled 40 percent of Cleveland's policy rackets, while collecting $50 weekly from most bookmakers. The Harvard and Thomas Clubs closed briefly, during Sheriff John Sultzman's race against reformer William McMaster, then reopened to celebrate "Honest John's" victory. Sultzman, for his part, denied any knowledge of outlaw casinos, while prosecutor Frank Cullitan pledged action despite local pleas for wide-open "home rule." After a string of bungled raids in February 1935, Chief Matowitz proclaimed his department's record "brilliant, considering the handicaps." In fact, he claimed, the force had "made unrelenting war on organized crime; it has made Cleveland a very poor refuge for the criminal element."

As Matowitz postured in Cleveland, Moe Dalitz moved to annex the Arrowhead Club, in Clermont County. Prosecutor Frank Roberts "tolerated" the casino, explaining that he "never felt obliged to enforce laws to the letter." Owner Joseph Bauer, described by Roberts as "a real gentleman," died under mysterious circumstances in 1934, while Roberts was "on vacation out west." Successor Sam Nason was known as a bootlegger and bookie during prohibition. He welcomed the Cleveland Four as partners in his new operation and settled a local minister's complaints against the club by donating $75 per month to the preacher's salary.

While Moe's casinos reaped huge profits through the Great Depression, racing supplied another steady stream of income. Cleveland's top bookie was Frank Rosen, who doubled as Mob office manager at the Hollenden Hotel. By the mid–1930s, with pari-mutuel betting legalized in Ohio, the Syndicate reported taxable profits from Tom McGinty's Bainbridge Park, the Thistledown track in North Randall, and a greyhound track at Caledonia. In Cincinnati, Moe and his partners cast covetous eyes on the Coney Island racetrack, owned by volatile Dutch Schultz.

* * *

Cleveland's Mafia was often troublesome, but also useful for the larger Syndicate. FBI agents, groping their way through the underworld labyrinth without support from headquarters, dubbed Moe Dalitz the "Czar" of the all-Italian Mayfield Road Gang, but came closer to the truth in other classified reports. One memo sketched Cleveland's gangland history, noting "considerable difficulty in the ... area, between the Italians and the Jews, each group attempting to gain control of the rackets. Finally Moe Dalitz ... was credited with making peace with the 'Dogos' [*sic*]." Another file explains Moe's revolutionary move more simply: "MOE DAVIS brought about a combination of the Italian and Jewish mobs of gangsters." Forty years after the fact, *Cleveland Magazine* correctly identified Mayfield Road's mafiosi as "the strong-arm branch of the Cleveland Syndicate.... While the Mayfield Road Gang gained all the publicity with their bloody tactics, the Big Four amassed a huge fortune ... behind the scenes in a more sophisticated manner."

Future Mafia turncoat Aladena "Jimmy the Weasel" Fratianno immigrated from Naples to Cleveland at age four, in 1917. By 1933 he was a Mayfield Road Gang wanna-be, booking bets at local racetracks. A year later, Fratianno bought a used limousine and began ferrying gamblers to Syndicate casinos — for which Lou Rothkopf paid him seven dollars per carload. Citing the difference between Mafiosi and Jewish mobsters, Fratianno told author Ovid Demaris:

> The Jews in Cleveland — Dalitz, Kleinman, Rhody — they were running all them gambling joints and they tell the Italians they've got to put so much money aside for taxes. After seven, eight years, they've made millions of dollars and declared 20, 30 percent to the government. At that time taxes ain't that high, which means they're building operating capital....

Now look at the Italians. They stash their money. They can't invest it without going through fucking fronts. Them Italians in Cleveland made millions and what good is it? They live like peasants. Everything's under the table. Even when they die, their heirs got to hide the money. Why don't they declare some of it? Uncle Sam don't give a shit how you earn your money as long as you give him your cut.

* * *

Back in Detroit, the Purple Gang continued to disintegrate. In November 1933, police found Abe Axler and Eddie Fletcher dead in the backseat of Axler's car, holding hands, each shot repeatedly in the face. Detectives surmised that they were slain for cheating fellow Purples on some unspecified business deal. In December 1934, Henry Schorr left home for a business meeting with Charles Leiter, then vanished forever. Police blamed his presumed death on Sam Davis and Harry Fleischer, but they filed no charges. In April 1936 federal agents charged four Purples—John Gettleson, Jack Selbin, Harry and Sam Fleischer—with running a 6,000-gallon still valued at $100,000. Jurors convicted all four, resulting in eight-year prison terms and $20,000 fines.

Harry Millman was the next to go. A renegade by any standards, he robbed Mafia brothels and blind pigs for pocket money. In 1936 he fought an hour-long brawl with Joe Bommarito, later accosting Bommarito in a barbershop and spitting in his face. Retaliation was inevitable, but the Italians missed on their first try, in August 1937, when a bomb in Millman's car killed a parking valet. Three months later, Millman entered Boeskey's Bar with Harry Gross and Hymie Cooper. Two gunmen soon arrived, and a shootout erupted. Millman died on the spot, shot ten times, while Gross was mortally injured and five bystanders suffered flesh wounds. Police found the killers' bloodstained getaway car on December 11, with two fingerprints on the driver's door, but the door was removed and subsequently "lost."

Louis Fleischer—paroled from Leavenworth in November 1934, after serving two-thirds

Weapons confiscated by Detroit police from Louis Fleischer (National Archives).

of a ten-year hijacking sentence — moved to Albion, Michigan, where he ran a safecracking ring. Police suspected Fleischer of fifty-plus break-ins by June 1936, but their best evidence only supported a charge of possessing burglar's tools. Fleischer jumped bail in May 1937, then resurfaced in April 1938, when a tipster gave Highland Park police the license number of his car. When officers stopped the vehicle, Fleischer's wife fled to a nearby tailor's shop, where patrolmen caught her hiding a homemade submachine gun. Outside, they handcuffed Fleischer and passenger Sidney Markman, wanted for murder in New York. A search of Fleischer's apartment revealed two more pistols converted to full-auto fire, three normal handguns, six silencers, 500 rounds of ammunition, and brass knuckles. In April 1939, jurors convicted all three prisoners of federal firearms violations. Lou Fleischer and Markman received thirty-year prison terms, while Nellie Fleischer got off with ten years.

The Purple Gang was now officially extinct, but its name proved too colorful to die. Reporters simply transferred the label to Detroit's Mafia family, and the legend endured.

* * *

Legitimate enterprise sheltered some Purple Gang survivors. Joe Bernstein quit the gang after the Collingwood Apartments massacre, changing his name to "Burnstein" when he opened a men's clothing shop, but the Depression scuttled that attempt to go straight. Late in 1933, Bernstein emerged as treasurer of Garfield Oil and Gas, a corporation owned by former grade-school classmate Sam Garfield.

Garfield Oil and Gas had a strange history. It sprang from Isaiah Leebove's Mammoth Petroleum and Refining, ranked in 1932 as the largest independent oil company east of the Mississippi. Leebove was a lawyer who left his New York practice and struck black gold in Michigan's oilfields. In 1933, for no apparent reason, Leebove gave Sam Garfield 25 percent of his business, chartered on November 1 with $5,000 capital. Garfield served as president, hired Joe Bernstein as treasurer, and welcomed brother Isadore Bernstein as a stockholder. Garfield Oil's first well came through in November 1933, producing 2,000 barrels per month. A second well scored in February 1934, producing 3,000 barrels daily. Soon, Garfield and Joe Bernstein occupied two of the finest homes in Mount Pleasant, Michigan, Bernstein sporting a $12,000 ruby ring and threatening his critics with litigation. "I'll sue anybody for $5 million who calls me a racketeer," he told reporters. "I never have been a racketeer!"

Moe Dalitz kept a lower profile than his old schoolmates, while pursuing legitimate interests. On September 15, 1938, he received Social Security number 277–16–8986. Moe's application listed his employer as Pioneer Linen Supply, in Cleveland, with a starting date of September 14, 1938. FBI files list other "apparently legitimate" firms owned by Dalitz as Liberty Ice Cream, Lubeck Distributing, and Ray Coal. Dalitz Brothers & Company, incorporated in Detroit on June 28, 1940, listed Lou Dalitz as its resident agent. The firm changed its name to Colonial Laundry on August 1, 1940, and dissolved on August 31, 1958. Moe also owned the Dalitz Realty Company, Michigan Industrial Laundry, and Pioneer Laundry. Further investments included Berdeen Realty (with Henry Beckerman), the Chicago & Rock Island Railroad, D.J. Krause Realty, the Liberty Company, Michigan Modern Land Company, Milco Sales, and Union Enterprise.

Involvement with legitimate industry forced Moe to interact with labor unions, chief among them the International Brotherhood of Teamsters (IBT), organized in 1903. By the mid–1930s, Detroit's most visible Teamster was James Riddle Hoffa.

Jimmy Hoffa was the son of a coal miner, born in Brazil, Indiana, on February 14, 1913. Hoffa's father died in 1920, and his mother moved the family to Detroit in 1924. Hoffa quit school at fourteen to work full-time and led his first strike at a grocery warehouse in 1932. After forming his own mini-union, Hoffa merged with IBT Local 299 in 1936 and began his relentless drive for control of the union. Somewhere along the way, he met Moe Dalitz and the Mob.

No consensus exists as to how or when their first meeting occurred, but logic dictates that young Hoffa must have mixed with mobsters in his early strikes. Hoffa told author Oscar Fraley, "I knew guys in the Purple Gang in Detroit. We fought them with bombs and billy clubs in 1935 and both sides got hurt bad. We made up our mind to meet them, get to know them, and work out an agreement under which they'd stay out of our business and we'd stay out of theirs."

Journalist Lester Velie paints a different picture, reporting that Hoffa recruited Purple Gang members to counter Mafia strikebreakers. As a result, Hoffa and a friend, "barely out of their teens," faced a Mafia tribunal, charged with spilling

Sam Garfield inspects one of his oil wells (Library of Congress).

Italian blood. Hoffa escaped execution, Velie says, by convincing mafiosi he would be worth more to them alive. Meanwhile, author Paul Kavieff asserts that Joe Bommarito ran ITB Local 299 in the mid–1930s, while former Justice Department attorney G. Robert Blakey claims Hoffa bribed Detroit mafiosi Angelo Meli and Santo Perrone to keep their family neutral during citywide strikes, in 1937.

All of which ignores Hoffa's longstanding relationship with Moe Dalitz. Reporter Nick Tosches writes that Dalitz was "a friend of Hoffa's from the days when Hoffa was nothing, and who was instrumental in Hoffa's rise to power." Crime historians Frank Browning and John Gerassi claim that Hoffa met Dalitz in the 1920s, when Hoffa's mother worked in "commercial washhouses." In the late 1970s, Doc Stacher recalled, "We knew Jimmy Hoffa right from the early days, because of Moe Dalitz. It's a complicated story, but Jimmy once had a girlfriend who married a Detroit man named John Paris [*sic*]. And it was at her house in Detroit that Jimmy Hoffa met Moe when he [Dalitz] was just a young man in a group of Jewish boys who worked for Norman Purple in the Purple Gang." The lady in question, described in most accounts as Hoffa's "former mistress," was Sylvia Pagano O'Brien, a union clerk whose second husband — John Parris — owned a Detroit laundry. The Dalitz introduction may have occurred while Hoffa served as muscle to Joe Wilder's International Laundry Workers Union, fighting to organize Detroit's laundries.

Hoffa biographer Arthur Sloane put a different spin on the O'Brien connection, claiming that Dalitz met Hoffa in the 1920s, then "lost touch" with him until 1940, when Mrs. O'Brien — Hoffa's mistress from the early 1930s — moved into Hoffa's home with her six-year-old son. While Sloane denied any impropriety, rumors branded Chuckie O'Brien as Jimmy's illegitimate son. Moe Dalitz, meanwhile, knew Sylvia's various ex-husbands and allegedly "had a thing for her, too," renewing his acquaintance with the IBT's rising star when he came to visit Mrs. O'Brien at Hoffa's home.

Hoffa himself recalled it somewhat differently. "Hell, yes, I knew Dalitz," he told Oscar Fraley. "I've known him since way back when he owned a string of laundries in Detroit and we threatened him with a strike. Those were the laundries Ike Litvak was organizing and where they kept beating the hell out of him. We finally got our contract.... [S]omebody put a mob price on Ike's head. Did Dalitz have it done? Hell's bells, I don't know. People don't put ads in the papers about that kind of stuff. But I know we got a contract, a good contract, and the Dalitz laundries lived up to it."

The strangest version of the Dalitz-Hoffa meeting came from Moe himself, decades after the fact. In 1963 an FBI bug caught Moe claiming that "he was raised with Hoffa in the same town." Fifteen years later, in a newspaper interview, Moe reminisced about attending high school with Hoffa in Detroit. At Central High, Dalitz recalled, Hoffa was "well known and well liked by his classmates." The paper published that account without researching it, but the problems are obvious: Moe was thirteen years older than Hoffa; he quit Central High in eleventh grade, while Hoffa was an Indiana preschooler.

* * *

While Moe forged ties with Teamsters in Detroit, Dutch Schultz had problems in New York which greatly pleased the Cleveland syndicate.

The fuss began with Thomas Dewey, who, as U.S. District Attorney for southern New York, sent Waxey Gordon to prison for tax evasion in 1933. Next, Dewey filed an

Jimmy Hoffa shared a mistress with Moe Dalitz and welcomed mobsters into the Teamsters Union (Library of Congress).

identical charge against Schultz, but Dutch beat the rap after winning a change of venue to a small town where jurors were easily bribed. Undaunted, Dewey left federal service and continued his pursuit of Schultz as New York City's special prosecutor, prompting Dutch to pull up stakes and move his headquarters to Newark, New Jersey. Still, Dewey hounded him, until Dutch asked the Mob's board of directors for permission to kill Dewey. The vote went against him, cooler heads fearing that Dewey's murder would provoke an inquisition leading to destruction of the Syndicate. Enraged, some say insane, Schultz vowed to deal with Dewey by himself.

Another gangland board meeting convened, this time without the Dutchman, and his fate was sealed. On October 23, 1935, Schultz met gang members Otto Berman, Abe Landau, and Bernard Rosenkrantz at Newark's Palace Chop House. At 10:30 P.M., three shooters from Lepke's Murder Inc. entered the restaurant. Rosenkrantz took seven bullets and two shotgun blasts, Berman absorbed four slugs and one buckshot charge, while Landau collapsed with three wounds. A single bullet struck Schultz, but it was enough. He died 24 hours later, raving deliriously.

Much speculation surrounds the Dutchman's final words, including disjointed references to "the boss," "Hitler's commander," and "the Chinaman's friends." Hank Messick surmised that "the Chinaman" was Louis Dalitz, but Schultz biographer Paul Sann fingers Charles "Chink" Sherman, a longtime rival of Schultz whose corpse was found in a Catskills lime pit twelve days after the Newark massacre.

Whatever Schultz meant to say in his last fevered hours, no question exists concerning the fate of his empire. Longy Zwillman annexed the New Jersey rackets, New York mafioso Michael Coppola seized Schultz's Harlem numbers banks — and the Cleveland Four took over Dutch's Coney Island racetrack in Cincinnati, renaming it River Downs.

As Sam Tucker later explained it, in his tax court deposition, "Moe Davis" somehow learned that the track could be purchased for $1,000 and moved to obtain it. Moe "knew he could not be a party to the actual operation of the racetrack, but he was interested in acquiring it with his other associates, for the purpose of the real estate venture and with the idea in mind of leasing it to a race-track operation. Mr. Davis was acquainted with one Samuel T. Haas, of Cleveland ... whom he knew was acquainted with Mr. E.P. Strong, who was engaged in the business of operating racetracks."

The Cleveland Four paid one-third of the purchase price, while Haas and Strong paid two-thirds, leaving the track in Strong's name. Strong's role, as described by Tucker, "was to form a corporation known as the River Downs Racing Association, with the understanding that the company would enter into a lease with River Downs, Inc., for the purpose of conducting horse-racing operations." One of the corporation's officers was Harry Rose, subsequently named in 1937 bankruptcy proceedings as an officer of Molaska Company.

River Downs turned a handsome profit in its first racing season before the Ohio River overflowed its banks in January 1937, drowning a tri-state area and inflicting some $20 million damage. To rebuild the track, Moe Dalitz borrowed money from Louis Jacobs, a former Buffalo rumrunner who, with his brothers Charles and Marvin, owned the Emprise sports concessions firm, founded in 1915. Jacobs shared ownership with various mobsters in Detroit's Hazel Park racetrack, and his loan allowed River Downs to reopen in 1938. Two decades later, Moe repaid the favor with a $250,000 loan to Emprise.

Moe's role at River Downs became public knowledge in 1948, when Ed Strong died and River Downs, Inc., sold its stock to another syndicate front, Daleview, Inc. The "sale" produced net long-term capital gains of $373,838.13, divided as follows: Samuel Haas and Strong's estate each received $124,612, while the Cleveland Four got $31,153.18 each — a 374-percent profit on their 1936 investments of $83.33 each. Moe and his partners reaped a further wind-fall in March 1950, when Daleview sold out to River Downs of Ohio, Inc., for $470,000. The principal buyer, New Jersey native Henry Green, once worked for Tom McGinty at Cleveland's Thistledown track, then opened Randall Park racetrack in 1940. In 1955, Green sold River Downs and moved to Las Vegas — where his dealings with Moe's Desert Inn casino produced charges of income-tax evasion.

The more things change, the more they stay the same.

* * *

Cleveland voters were ready for change in 1935, unseating Mayor Davis, replacing him with Harold Burton. Burton, in turn, named 32-year-old Eliot Ness to replace Martin Lavelle as director of public safety.

Ness seemed ideal for the job, described in one newspaper profile as "[s]ix feet and 172 pounds of fight and vigor, an expert criminologist who looks like a collegian but can battle crime with the best of them." Hired on December 11, 1935, Ness staged his first gambling raid three days later, but it flopped. His officers stormed a barbershop and caught five men listening to race results, but found no gambling paraphernalia. Mobsters and civilians alike laughed at Cleveland's new "Boy Scout," while Ness drew up fresh battle plans. "I hope to take necessary action first," he told reporters, "and talk about it later." Mayor Burton's son conducted stakeouts for Ness during college vacations, and Ness hired a squad of anonymous agents (the "Unknowns") to mimic his Chicago "Untouchables," fielding them to tap phones, trace bank accounts, and recruit gangland informants.

"Racket-busting" special prosecutor Thomas Dewey of New York (Library of Congress).

Ness was a self-styled liberal on "amusements," but he understood illegal gambling's pernicious impact on society. On January 10, 1936, he told the Cleveland Advertising Club that local gamblers earned at least $200,000 weekly, half of that from numbers alone. "Gambling," he said, "brings into financial power citizens recognized as law violators." Furthermore, "In

Dutch Schultz, mortally wounded in Newark's Palace Chop House (Library of Congress).

any city where corruption continues, it follows that some officials are playing ball with the underworld.... The dishonest public official hiding behind a badge or political office is more detestable than any street criminal or mob boss."

While Ness addressed his audience, prosecutor Frank Cullitan mounted raids against two suburban casinos. Game Boy Miller offered no resistance at the Thomas Club, but it was a different story at the Harvard Club, where Shimmy Patton cursed the raiders from behind steel doors and threatened bloodshed if they entered. Cullitan phoned Sheriff Sultzman, only to learn that he was out of town and deputies refused to budge unless the mayor of Newburgh Heights requested them. Cullitan retreated, watching shamefaced while gamblers fled the club and a caravan of trucks began evacuating its illegal gear.

At last, Cullitan called Ness for help. Ness had no jurisdiction outside city limits, but he enlisted Lieutenant Ernest Molnar and 43 off-duty policemen to join the raid as private citizens. When Ness demanded entry to the club at 10:30 P.M., one of Patton's men opened the door. Art Hebebrand warned the raiders to "act like gentlemen while you're in here or you'll wish the hell you had," then fled to his office and out through its window. Cullitan's men seized one blackjack table and four empty safes. Next morning, Ness ordered the Harvard Club's owners of record arrested on sight, but police never managed to find them.

Ness rarely moved against Mob casinos in Cleveland. In fact, his only raid of note occurred six months after the Harvard Club fiasco, on July 22, 1936. His target was the Hermitage Hotel on West 25th, described in newspaper reports as a gambling den complete with secret passageways, armed guards, and a full-dress casino. Plainclothes rookies infiltrated the hotel before Ness hit the doors, only to find the casino vacated. As consolation prizes, they seized ledgers and stationery belonging to Tom McGinty. Ness subsequently learned that McGinty employed three sons of police inspector Timothy Costello, who was also friendly with Art Hebebrand.

Ness knew that his raids failed because corrupt police had tipped the gamblers in advance. To remedy that problem, he transferred 28 lieutenants, 63 sergeants, and 400 patrolmen to new posts, while a handful of cops resigned to avoid prosecution. Ness assigned gambling raids to "Molnar's Raiders," but ignored reports that Molnar himself—later imprisoned for bribery, in 1948—ran one of Cleveland's largest numbers banks. Meanwhile, the Unknowns discovered that Captain Louis Cadek had banked $150,000 on a yearly salary of $3,500. He drove two Cadillacs, both gifts from local mobsters. At trial, in June 1936, jurors convicted Cadek of four counts of bribery.

After ten months in office, Ness presented Francis Cullitan with a 100-page report on Cleveland's underworld, including statements from 26 witnesses who agreed to testify before a grand jury. That panel indicted one deputy police inspector, two captains, two lieutenants, one sergeant, and three patrolmen for bribery—all of whom were later convicted and imprisoned. The shakeup made headlines, but no fundamental changes in how the Mob did business.

One obvious problem was Ness's inability to see beyond the Mayfield Road Gang and a handful of flamboyant Jewish racketeers. Ness raided Maxie Diamond's betting parlor in 1937, calling it "downtown Cleveland's busiest and biggest bookie and gambling joint," but it remained for the Molaska trial to briefly take Diamond out of circulation. In October 1938, Ness led a raid against the Mafia's largest numbers bank, operating from a private home on East 36th Street. The evidence seized there secured indictments against George and John Angersola, Angelo Lonardo, Chuck Polizzi, Angelo Scirrca, Shondor Birns, Maishe Rockman, and sixteen others in April 1939. Most escaped conviction, while FBI files confirmed that those indicted "are considered muscle and front men for the powerful new Mayfield Road gang [*sic*] under Moe Davis and his associates."

Ness fared worse in other areas, including labor racketeering. Bill Presser survived a drive-by shooting in January 1939, expanding from his dominance of jukeboxes and vending machines to control Ohio's Teamsters Union. Ness lost his mayoral race in 1941, and disaster struck in March 1942, when Ness left a late-night cocktail party at the Hollenden Hotel, collided with another car, then fled the scene. He resigned in April and spent World War II touring the country on a crusade against venereal disease. Moe Dalitz survived Ness's clean-up, acknowledged by Mafia historian Rick Porello as "the supreme power" in Cleveland through the 1940s.

5

Beachheads

Having achieved dominion over gambling and associated rackets in Ohio, with continuing influence in Detroit, Moe Dalitz and his partners looked for other worlds to conquer in the 1930s. One such land of golden opportunity lay just across the border from their Cincinnati stronghold, in northern Kentucky. George Remus had prepared the way, during the early years of prohibition, but the residents of "Little Mexico" were far from innocent when he arrived.

George Remus protégé Peter Schmidt, described by one acquaintance as "a man of vision with the soul of a miser," returned from prison to the Newport alky trade in 1924. He bought a hotel on Monmouth Street, renamed it the Glenn Rendezvous, and ran it as a full-service vice den until Treasury agents staged a raid. Schmidt wounded one of them and drew another five-year sentence, but the club was waiting for him when he hit the street. He expanded the casino and built another, the Playtorium, on Fifth Street, but neither fulfilled his ambition. In 1932, Schmidt bought the Old Kaintuck Inn, in Southgate, and remodeled it into the lavish Beverly Hills Club. That same year, Remus-Schmidt compatriot Buck Brady bought the Bluegrass Inn, in Wilder, and renamed it the Primrose Club.

Moe Dalitz gazed across the river from Ohio, and he saw that it was good.

* * *

Conventional histories maintain that Cleveland racketeers "discovered" northern Kentucky in 1940 and rose to dominance overnight, by making local operators the proverbial offer they could not refuse. FBI reports from 1944 claim that "the Moe Davis Mob" obtained control "by contacting the established gamblers in that area, and furnishing financial backing." In fact, however, Moe's conquest of Kentucky capped a five-year struggle for supremacy.

And as in every war, there would be casualties.

Moe's first Kentucky venture was a greyhound track at Dayton, in Campbell County. The track operated for thirteen days before Governor Albert "Happy" Chandler ordered its closure. Local authorities indicted "Maurice Davis" for illicit gambling, then dismissed the charge in October 1935. A quarter-century later, Moe explained the episode by saying, "If I remember correctly, there was a question about an option, some kind of a legal technicality that just didn't work out. It just wasn't there and they closed it."

Next, Moe offered to buy the Beverly Hills Club, but Pete Schmidt refused to sell. Undeterred, Dalitz hired away three of Schmidt's toughest employees, Albert "Red" Masterson, Samuel Schraeder, and David Whitfield. On February 3, 1936, a friend saw Masterson filling gasoline cans at a local service station. Asked about the purchase, Red advised his chum to read the next day's newspapers. That night, fire leveled the Beverly Hills Club. Live-in caretaker Carl Filbert and wife Viola escaped from their upstairs apartment, but five-year-old niece Mary Rardin suffered fatal burns. Arsonist Edwin Garrison, with burns on hands and legs, sought refuge with Dave Whitfield.

Police initially blamed the fire on an exploding still, then charged Whitfield as an accessory. Convicted in a hasty trial, he served a short prison term and returned to serve the Mob as a casino manager in Newport.

Pete Schmidt refused to see the writing on the wall. Renamed and rebuilt on a grander scale, the Beverly Hills Country Club resumed operations in April 1937.

Kentucky governor Albert "Happy" Chandler (Library of Congress).

Happy Chandler led the parade of officials at Schmidt's grand opening, while a local reporter declared: "Peter was toasted opening night by the official life of four states. His rise has been meteoric. There's none, 300 miles around, that stands shoulder high to him now. His Beverly Hills dominates its world."

And Cleveland's imps were nowhere to be seen — at first. A 1936 narcotics rap sidelined Red Masterson, but others soon filled the void. A long war of attrition began when six bandits robbed the Beverly Hills in June 1937. Thereafter, fights broke out among Schmidt's patrons, while skilled card "mechanics" with bottomless pockets challenged his dealers. Casino employees deserted Schmidt, with his guards close behind. In desperation, Schmidt invited a Toledo gang to run the club, but they bailed out after three months. Schmidt's last resort, arming local blacks to guard the club, was sheer humiliation for a southern "sporting gentleman."

Finally, in May 1940, Schmidt bit the bullet and welcomed his new Cleveland partners into the Beverly Hills Country Club. Sam Tucker moved from Cleveland to Southgate as the casino's manager, bringing brother Garson along for the ride. Newport attorney Charles Lester handled the paperwork when the club officially changed hands on November 18, 1940. Schmidt received a payout of $125,000 from the club's profits, while Lester built a web of corporations to divide the spoils. Boulevard Enterprises held the club's real estate; Beverly Hills, Inc., managed the restaurant and bar; and Country Club Enterprises supervised the gambling. Alvin Giesey served as secretary of the first two groups, while carefully avoiding any public contact with the third. Top-flight entertainment soon distinguished the Beverly Hills Country Club as "the Showplace of the Nation."

* * *

From his Newport bastion, Moe cast eyes across the Licking River into Kenton County, where another Remus protégé, James Brink, had rivaled Pete Schmidt. Brink's Lookout House casino stood atop a hill in Fort Wright, with a view of the Ohio River and Cincinnati's skyline. In June 1936, authorities indicted Brink, Lou Levinson, and layoff bookie Ed Curd for gambling, but jurors acquitted all three. A permanent injunction banned gambling at the Lookout House after 1936, but Brink and the police ignored it. A new grand jury charged Brink with 45 counts in April 1938, but friendly businessmen raised his $50,000 bond and he won acquittal once more. Meanwhile, thugs blackjacked one grand juror and blinded another with ammonia.

The 1938 grand jury's complaint of "laxity in law enforcement" was a classic understatement. Kentucky law required sheriffs to conduct monthly inspections of roadhouses and any other facility offering music, reporting violations to a county prosecutor, but the statute was ignored in Little Mexico. Kenton County Sheriff Henry Berndt raided two large casinos, the Kenton Club and the 627 Club, but told feds that "I cannot get the little ones." Ten years after Moe and company arrived, Berndt said he "never heard of" them. In fact, he testified, "I do not believe there is a person in Kenton County that ever heard of any one of those fellows.... I do not believe any of them come to the county." Judge Joseph Goodenough admitted gambling at the Lookout House, yet claimed his first-hand observation "would not charge me as a judge with any responsibility to awaken the [anti-gambling] injunction." Leonard Connor, owner of the Turf Club in Latonia, served double duty as a county election commissioner and sergeant at arms for Kentucky's state senate.

James Brink had learned from Pete Schmidt's mistakes. When Cleveland came calling, he haggled briefly over price with Sam Tucker — whom Brink dubbed "the gentleman of the boys" — then struck a deal. In return for his cooperation, Brink received $125,000, kept 10 percent of his club, plus 10 percent of the Beverly Hills Country Club and 4 percent of Newport's Yorkshire Club. Sam Miller took charge of the casino and claimed 15 percent of the club. On paper, Brink's partners in the Lookout House divided their holdings as follows: "M.B. Davis," Lou Rothkopf, Morris Kleinman, and Louise Tucker, 10 percent each; Sam Schraeder, 9 percent; Chuck Polizzi, 8 percent; Charles Carr and Mitchell Meyer, 5 percent each; B.W. Brink, 4 percent; and John Carr, 2 percent. As in Newport, Alvin Giesey kept the books, trusting his clients to report their full income on tax returns. In 1951, Moe Dalitz denied owning any part of the Lookout House, then admitted receiving $20,000 from the club on one occasion. His explanation: "It might have been a dividend."

Back in Newport, Moe and his partners owned at least two-thirds of the city's twenty-odd gambling dens. Newport's largest downtown clubs were the Flamingo and the Yorkshire, followed closely by the Merchants Club. Moe Dalitz granted the Levinson brothers a piece of Art Dennert's Flamingo, for Meyer Lansky and Mike Coppola, as a trade-off to New York for Cleveland's grazing rights in Florida. Ace Research, near the Flamingo on York Street, supplied local bookies with race results, courtesy of Mushy Wexler in Cleveland.

The Yorkshire was another classic Dalitz operation, though his name did not appear on any paperwork related to the club. Officially, the ownership broke down as follows: Fred Hallam of Bellevue, Kentucky, 12 percent; Morris Nemmo, Maurice Ryan, and Abe Schneider, 8 percent each; John Croft, 7 percent; Robert Bergin, 6 percent; Sam Tucker, John Angersola, Chuck Polizzi, Alfred Goltsman, and George Gordon, 5 percent each; James Brink, Ruby Kolod, Red Masterson, Edward Rogers "Butts Lowe" Lowenstein, Claude Hines, and George Bregal, 4 percent each; and Richard Fox, with 1 percent.

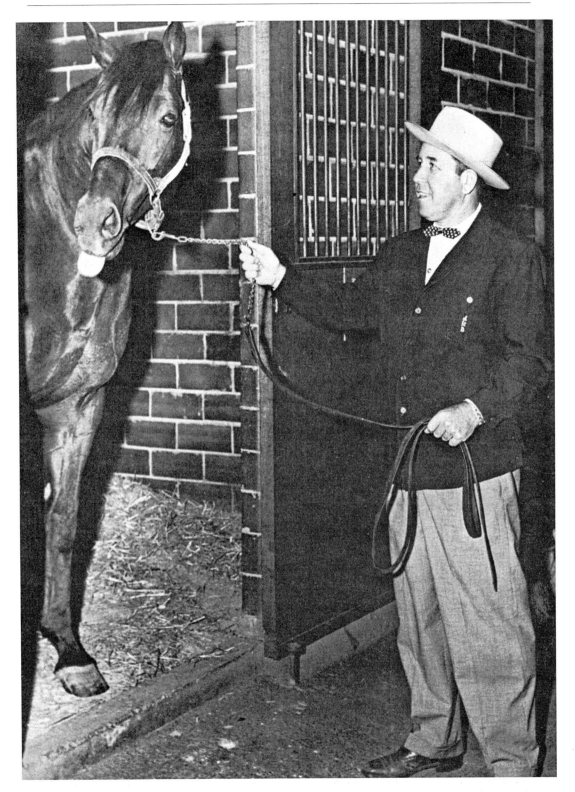

Gambler James Brink, with one of his prize thoroughbreds (Library of Congress).

Brink's Lookout House, in Covington, Kentucky (Library of Congress).

Gambling in Kentucky was no secret; it did not need to be. Governor Chandler publicly supported "the right of the people to have it dirty," and Moe's connections reached beyond the Bluegrass State, to Washington, D.C. Louisville native Flo Umberhocker served as secretary for Kentucky congressman Alben Barkley, remaining at his side when he went to the U.S. Senate in 1927, and when he was elected as Harry Truman's vice president in 1948. Along the way, she met her future husband, realtor Frank Bratten, at Kentucky's Laurel Race Track. As lifelong racing enthusiasts, the Brattens befriended Red Masterson and often stayed at his home during visits to Newport.

Soon, familiar faces graced Moe's clubs in Little Mexico. Hymie Martin owned a share of several clubs in Newport, prior to settling for the remainder of his life on Florida's Gold Coast. Another veteran, Samuel Nason, ran Ohio's Arrowhead Club until crusading prosecutors closed it in 1938, then briefly opened another casino in Cincinnati, disguised as the Valley Catering Company. When that joint closed, he crossed the river to Newport, managing the Yorkshire Club's race book.

* * *

Mobsters are only human. They complain about cold weather and enjoy a sunny beach, like any normal working stiff. They also profit from their knowledge of the latest trends in tourism, which made Florida an irresistible target.

A haven for pirates and smugglers since colonial times, Florida maintained that reputation through the rumrunning years of prohibition. Sammy "Purple" Cohen fled Detroit and settled in Miami Beach, where he joined four partners to create the S&G Syndicate, bribed local police, and took the local bookmaking racket by storm. Attorney Ben Cohen, Sam's brother, defended the syndicate's bookies in court. Frank Erickson invested $250,000 in the Tropical Park racetrack, at Coral Gables, and also owned a piece of the Colonial Inn, a casino located near Hallandale's Gulfstream racetrack. His partners in that club, guarded by uniformed sheriff's deputies, included Joe Adonis, Meyer and Jake Lansky, Vincent "Jimmy Blue Eyes" Alo, and Detroit's Mert Wertheimer.

Detroit mafioso Joe Massei registered with Miami Beach police as a convicted felon in March 1936. Local authorities jailed him twice for vagrancy, in January 1937 and February 1940, but the charges were quickly dismissed in each case. Massei accepted the harassment as a price of doing business, both in gambling dens and in legitimate firms like the Miami Provision Company, which provided meat and groceries to Gold Coast hotels. Moe Dalitz acknowledged friendship with Massei, but denied any business partnership. Massei, for his part, was amused when newspapers described him as a member of Detroit's Purple Gang. Hank Messick reports that Massei liked to tease Dalitz, offering Moe membership in the Mafia, if Dalitz would make him an honorary Purple. Moe always declined, explaining that the Purple Gang was "an even bigger joke" than the Mafia.

Tom McGinty was next, invading Carter's, a South Miami Beach casino described in local newspapers as "the biggest gambling establishment from a standpoint of money handled that had ever been operated in the United States since the days of the Gold Rush." Owner George Carter initially resisted McGinty's overtures, then surrendered to threats from hired goon "Honest Frenchy" Gips. When the dust settled, partners of record in Carter's included McGinty (holding 65 percent for Cleveland), William Schwartz from the Colonial Club (25 percent for New York), and Carter (10 percent). From Carter's, McGinty moved on to acquire the Dixie Inn, in West Palm Beach.

An FBI file from 1938 reports that "Moe Davis [*sic*] arrived in Miami for the season, and during that month was seen in the Continental Club sitting at a table with Augie Pisano, owner of the Club." *Time* magazine described Pisano (né Anthony Carfano) as "Al Capone's East Coast viceroy," but in fact he was a graduate of Joe Masseria's New York Mafia family. In 1931, after Lucky Luciano deposed Masseria, Augie went south and fronted New York's gambling interests. His meeting with Dalitz probably concerned the Frolics Club, a joint venture launched in 1937. Sam Miller ran the club, and while FBI files named Moe as its sole owner in 1939, silent partners included Carfano, Meyer Lansky, Longy Zwillman, and Morris Wolinksy. Miller also lent a hand at Lansky's Island Club, while Dalitz and company ran the nearby Isle d'Capri (spelled that way in FBI files). An FBI report spanning the years from 1938 to 1941 noted that Dalitz "was engaged in gambling activities with numerous individuals during this period."

Despite those observations, the Florida Mob had nothing to fear from G-men. J. Edgar Hoover patronized their restaurants, hotels, and horse tracks, accepting any favors thrown his way. In March 1940, society columnist Inez Robb criticized Hoover in print for vacationing at Mob resorts, and Hoover never forgave her. A quarter-century later, he scrawled a memo branding Robb "a bitch" who "vilified the FBI and me personally when I was in Miami."

Eliot Ness encouraged the Mob exodus to Florida, when he indicted Cleveland's leading numbers racketeers in 1939. According to subsequent media reports, several of those indicted, including brothers George and John Angersola, fled Cleveland aboard the *Wood Duck*, a forty-foot boat owned by Mickey McBride. McBride disputed that tale, claiming that the *Wood Duck* was already docked in Miami Beach when the Angersolas left Cleveland. The *Wood Duck*'s flight to freedom, in McBride's view, was a simple case of "poor reporting." Al Polizzi agreed, telling the Kefauver Committee, "You couldn't get [George Angersola] on a boat if you stood on your ear."

Be that as it may, the Angersola brothers *did* migrate to Florida in 1939, and thus avoided trial in Cleveland. Two years later, they joined Frank Erickson, Abe Allenberg, and Augie Pisano in taking over the Wofford Hotel. Max Marmonstein, a Cleveland hotelier friend of John Angersola, represented Angersola when he signed a ten-year lease on the Wofford. Erickson ran his bookmaking operation from the hotel, with branch offices in the Roney Plaza, Boca Raton, and Hollywood Beach Hotels. Over the next four decades, reporters claimed that half of Miami Beach's hotels were run by the Mob through willing fronts like Abe Allenberg and Lansky associate Morris Lansburgh.

Al Polizzi started buying Gold Coast real estate in 1937, seven years before he finally left Cleveland to become a full-time Florida resident. Upon arrival in the Sunshine State, Big Al joined John Angersola to form the Polkin Company (*Polizzi-King*), a construction firm that built most of Coral Gables, along with several Catholic schools and lavish homes for mobsters Joe Massei, Mike Coppola, and Tom McGinty. On the side, Polizzi and Angersola leased a hotel from the wife of Chuck Hall, a failed gubernatorial candidate and future chairman of the Dade County Commission.

Around the same time, Sam Tucker and Boston's Joe Linsey pooled their resources for a series of Florida land deals. Tom McGinty followed their example, expanding from his Palm Beach home to acquire "a sixth of four or five lots" plus "25 percent of another piece of property." As explained in 1951, Edward Strong of Strong Estates owned one-sixth of the land, while partner Sam Kay held 50 percent. Strong's fellow Cleveland lawyer, Samuel Haas, also owned "a piece" of Strong Estates.

The cash for those investments came primarily from gambling, now well-organized in Florida. Aside from bookmaking, casinos, and racetracks, the Mob reaped millions from local versions of the numbers racket, known as *bolita*. In Broward County, from 1931 to 1950, Sher-

Sunday morning in Coral Gables, Florida. Al Polizzi (#1) and Mickey McBride (#3) with friends, after church (Cleveland Public Library).

iff Walter Clark ran the bolita racket from his Fort Lauderdale office. Clark also held a one-third interest in a firm licensed to manufacture pinball games and slot machines.

Transplanted mobsters brooked no interference with their new empire. When Miami Beach councilman Melvin Richard opposed gambling, Sam Cohen's S&G Syndicate financed a recall campaign, spearheaded by Mickey McBride's radio station WMIE. Later, when ex-FBI agent Richard Danner became Miami's city manager, he found himself embroiled in a feud over gambling that had divided the city's police department. Officers in the pro-gambling faction sent two men to Newport, Kentucky, where they were jailed in a well-timed brothel raid. At their booking, the poseurs identified themselves as Danner and Miami Mayor Leonard Thomson, whereupon Miami's crooked cops sought to blackmail their official opposition. It was not Newport's first frame-up, and it would not be the last, but this one failed. After a tense investigation climaxed by a midnight meeting in a gravel pit, Newport police admitted their complicity and sank the scandal.

* * *

Cuba lay just ninety miles off Florida's Gold Coast, ruled by Fulgencio Batista from September 1933 to October 1944, and Mob negotiations for Cuban gambling rights began soon after Batista seized power. According to Doc Stacher, Meyer Lansky and Lucky Luciano raised the

Dictator Fulgencio Batista (at microphone) opened Cuba to the Mob (National Archives).

subject at a syndicate meeting in New York. The buy-in price for anyone desiring a share of the Cuban action was $500,000 apiece. As Stacher told Lansky biographer Dennis Eisenberg:

> At the end of the speech Charlie [Luciano] said he was in on the deal and ten of the others, including Bugsy Siegel, Moe Dalitz, Phil Kastel, and Chuck Polizzi, also chipped in half a million bucks. Lansky and I flew to Havana with the money in suitcases and spoke to Batista, who hadn't quite believed we could raise that kind of money.
>
> Lansky took Batista straight back to our hotel, opened the suitcases, and pointed at the cash. Batista just stared at the money without saying a word. Then he and Meyer shook hands and Batista left. We had several meetings with him over the next week and I saw that Meyer and Batista understood each other very well. We gave Batista a guarantee of between three and five

Left: Richard Nixon allied himself with mobsters from his first congressional campaign, in 1946 (Library of Congress). *Right:* Jack Dragna led L.A.'s "Mickey Mouse Mafia" (Library of Congress).

million dollars a year, as long as we had the monopoly on casinos at the Hotel Nacional and everywhere else on the island where we thought tourists would come. On top of that he was promised a cut of the profits.

Lansky's next investment in Havana, during 1937, was a racetrack previously coveted by Tom McGinty, who had failed to raise the necessary cash. His guests at the Nacional, in June 1940, included newlyweds Richard and Pat Nixon. Six years out of law school, serving as a small-town California prosecutor, Nixon was "exploring the possibilities of establishing law or business connections in Havana." That plan fell through, but Nixon's honeymoon excursion laid the groundwork for his thirty-year collaboration with the Mob.

* * *

California was another haven for Midwestern mobsters in the Depression. Prohibition had destroyed most of the state's wineries, but as elsewhere, it failed to stem the tide of bootleg alcohol. The Stralla brothers — Anthony, Frank, and Louis — smuggled booze into Los Angeles on shrimp boats, trucking their product as far east as tiny Las Vegas, Nevada, before the Coast Guard caught Anthony with 1,000 cases of liquor and sent him to prison for two years. With repeal, the Strallas switched to gambling on boats anchored beyond the twelve-mile limit.

While the Strallas plied the seas, the Mafia planted its flag in Los Angeles. Pioneer Jack Dragna was born in Sicily, in 1891, and emigrated to Chicago at age 23. He moved to L.A. during prohibition and established himself as a "rancher," with a farm near Cucamonga. Dragna's underboss was John Rosselli, sent west by Al Capone in 1925 to cure his asthma and to escape narcotics charges. Some authors consider Rosselli the brains behind Dragna's crime family, derided in Syndicate circles as "the Mickey Mouse Mafia."

John Rosselli (right, with his lawyer) represented the Mafia in Las Vegas (Library of Congress).

Moe Dalitz found his way to Hollywood in 1931, when he occupied a bungalow at the Garden of Allah on Sunset Boulevard. Erected in 1928, the stylish complex housed visiting mobsters Meyer Lansky, Ben Siegel, Frank Costello, and Longy Zwillman (with girlfriend Jean Harlow), alongside celebrities F. Scott Fitzgerald, Ernest Hemingway, the Marx brothers, Errol Flynn, Greta Garbo, and Humphrey Bogart. On one such vacation, Costello met Howard Hughes — then struggling to escape a quagmire of debt — and declined to invest $250,000 in a film, *The Outlaw*, starring Hollywood newcomer Jane Russell.

Mob-watcher Dan Moldea credits Dalitz with a key role in helping the Mob take over the International Alliance of Theatrical Stage Employees in 1933–34, although traditional histories of that affair rarely mention Moe. The trouble began in July 1933, when the IATSE struck against Hollywood's major film studios. John Rosselli fielded strikebreakers to keep the cameras rolling. Meanwhile, in Chicago, George Browne of the local stagehands' union schemed with pimp Willie Bioff to seize control of the IATSE. It was a goal beyond their

The Garden of Allah, where Moe Dalitz socialized with Howard Hughes and other celebrities (Library of Congress).

reach, until Frank Nitti and Lepke Buchalter joined forces to grab the brass ring. In March 1934 Rosselli met Nitti at Al Capone's Florida mansion, to refine their strategy for capturing the union. At that meeting, Nitti predicted "a permanent yield of a million dollars a year" from the IATSE.

It went like clockwork when IATSE members convened in Louisville, Kentucky, in June 1934. Reporters were excluded, thus preserving anonymity for "delegates" Lepke and Nitti, Al Polizzi, Longy Zwillman, Meyer Lansky, and Ben Siegel. Browne ran unopposed for president and won easily. Soon afterward, the IATSE called its first strike in New York, against the RKO theater chain, which paid $87,000 for "strike insurance." By June 1935 the Mob had earned $1.5 million from Hollywood in protection payments and union "surcharges." Rosselli banked $25,000 on the side, from MGM, for suppressing a porn reel that featured headliner Joan Crawford.

Bioff overstepped his bounds in 1937, when he tried to muscle in on the Screen Actors Guild. After a spate of violent incidents failed to arouse corrupt authorities, SAG president Robert Montgomery launched a private investigation of Bioff, Browne, and the IATSE. In 1939 the IRS indicted Bioff for income-tax evasion, while New York authorities belatedly moved to enforce a 1922 pandering conviction. Browne retaliated by inviting the House Un-American Activities Committee to investigate Hollywood "communists," but the subsequent blacklist of innocent actors and writers would not spare the Mob from its fate. Bioff entered prison in April 1940. A year later, he and Browne faced federal racketeering charges stemming from the IATSE takeover. Both pled guilty in October 1941, with sentencing deferred pending identification of their syndicate masters. When the axe finally fell, it struck at Chicago, leaving Dalitz and Cleveland unscathed.

* * *

The Hollywood extortion racket was a sideshow for the Mob's main interest in Los Angeles, its million-dollar yearly take a pittance next to the rewards from gambling and vice. The Syndicate at large did not trust Dragna or Rosselli with such grave responsibilities, nor were the overlords of crime content to let Chicago rule the roost.

Ben Siegel made his first trip to Los Angeles in 1934, seeking to install a casino in Thelma Todd's Sidewalk Café, but that effort collapsed after Todd's mysterious death in December 1935. Siegel then returned to New York, but came west again for good soon after Lucky Luciano's June 1936 prostitution conviction. From prison, Luciano ordered Jack Dragna to cooperate with Siegel, dividing the L.A. basin between them: Siegel's territory encompassed western Los Angeles, including Hollywood and Beverly Hills; Dragna's spanned central L.A. and the valley suburbs.

Siegel's mission, in a nutshell, was to gain control of gambling for the New York Mob. Frank Costello smoothed Jack Dragna's ruffled feathers after Siegel muscled in on Tony Stralla's gambling ships, but rumors of war persisted, while Angelenos pondered the corruption of their city. Voters recalled Mayor Frank Shaw in 1938, replacing him Fletcher Bowron, but graft payments continued in the city and in L.A. County, where Sheriff Eugene Biscailuz and District Attorney Buron Fitts shared the proceeds of organized crime.

As Siegel forged a California empire, Moe Dalitz shopped around for someone to represent Cleveland's interests in the Golden State. His choice was curious, to say the least. L.A.'s police chief dubbed Cleveland's man "essentially stupid." The Kefauver Committee called him "a simian figure," while New York prosecutor Burton Turkus branded him "the small shot who goes for the sandwiches when the big boys have their hotel-room sessions." TV commentator George Putnam labeled Cleveland's West Coast ambassador "a horsefly on the rump of public decency."

And yet...

Meyer Harris "Mickey" Cohen was born to Russian-Jewish parents in Brooklyn's Brownsville district, in July 1914. His father died soon afterward, and Mother Cohen moved her brood to Los Angeles in 1920. The family ran a pharmacy with a backroom still, and Mickey handled the deliveries until his first arrest at age nine. Authorities dropped that charge due to Cohen's youth and an older brother's connections, but Mickey was destined for trouble. After more arrests in L.A. during 1933, Cohen hopped a freight to Cleveland and joined the Mob there, earning $100 per week for muscle work, while pulling freelance holdups on the side. It was, in Cohen's terms, "a meeting of the minds."

With blessings from the "Big Combine," Cohen organized the Hill Gang, robbing cafés, brothels, and gambling joints that operated without Mob protection. Cohen later boasted of 300 heists and burglaries before the game went sour, in 1934. A messy holdup landed one of Cohen's sidekicks in prison, while Mickey wound up on probation. Lou Rothkopf— described by Cleveland safety director Alvin Sutton as "a very close friend" and "a very strong supporter" of Cohen— sent Mickey to chill in Chicago with gambler Joe Barron. Next, Cohen moved to Detroit and considered putting down roots, but a phone call from Rothkopf changed his mind. As Cohen recalled, Rothkopf said, "Look, Benny Siegel's out on the coast and we want you to go right out there as soon as you can." Mickey understood "we" to mean the Cleveland Four, inferring that Rothkopf, Dalitz, and company wanted him to "stand in for their end of the action" in California.

The Mob sent Bugsy Siegel (center) to control rackets in Los Angeles. He is accompanied here by two of his attorneys (unidentified) (Library of Congress).

Cohen was happy to oblige, although the details of his final westward move remain obscure. Siegel biographer Dean Jennings puts Cohen in L.A. from 1939 onward, while journalist Ed Reid offers three different dates — 1937, 1938, and 1939. The circumstances of Cohen's first meeting with Siegel are equally nebulous. Mickey credited their introduction to Lou Rothkopf, while Reid claims that Cohen telephoned Siegel to "plead for a job."

In any case, upon arrival in L.A., Cohen assumed his post as Siegel's second-in-command. He was Bugsy's pit bull, subduing independent bookies and gamblers while Siegel enjoyed the Hollywood high life. On the side, he established a narcotics pipeline from Mexico into southern California. Mickey's reach also extended into San Diego, where he worked closely with bookie Morris "Moe" Morton.

* * *

California's political boss in those years was Arthur Samish. Born in East Los Angeles and raised in San Francisco, Samish entered politics as a clerk for the state legislature, then lobbied against prohibition on behalf of California's liquor interests. He lost that fight, but honed his skills and seldom lost another. Twenty years later, Governor Earl Warren told reporters that "[o]n matters that affect his clients, Artie unquestionably has more power than the governor."

Author Gus Russo describes Samish as a "childhood friend" of Mickey Cohen, but Samish was a 23-year-old San Francisco resident when Cohen moved to L.A., at age six. Still, there *was* a connection. Cohen described his relationship with Samish as follows: "If I had any problems with legislators in Sacramento on things like slot machines on premises, he nipped it in the bud. I was his right hand, and he was my godfather, my senior statesman."

The Cohen-Samish introduction may have been arranged by Murray Chotiner, a Pittsburgh native who quit school at fifteen, yet still obtained a law degree four years later. A lifelong Republican, Chotiner campaigned for Herbert Hoover in 1932 and managed Earl Warren's gubernatorial race ten years later. An ally of Chicago syndicate attorney Sidney Korshak, Chotiner represented underworld clients including New Jersey's Angelo "Gyp" DeCarlo and Philadelphia's Marco Reginelli. Mickey Cohen was another famous client, who followed Chotiner's post-war lead to bankroll Richard Nixon.

Mickey Cohen represented Cleveland's interests in California (Library of Congress).

* * *

Arizona and New Mexico had been states for less than two decades when Moe Dalitz arrived to survey their terrain. Author Alan Balboni cites two southwestern sojourns in the late 1920s, with Moe accompanied on each by "business associates from Ohio and Michigan." No further details are available, but the visitors could not have failed to meet Kemper Marley, Arizona's premier bootlegger and client of Sam Bronfman. Marley bankrolled Harry Rosenzweig, who shared the largess with

Republican candidates statewide. Phoenix gambler Clarence Newman, a childhood friend of the affluent Goldwater brothers, operated from a building owned by Rosenzweig. Another Phoenix resident, Gus Greenbaum, had been sent by Meyer Lansky from New York in 1928, to organize gambling and manage the Mob's race-wire service.

The next time Dalitz went to Arizona, in the latter part of 1936, he blamed his sinuses. He lingered through the spring of 1937, adding the Tucson Steam Laundry to his chain of washhouses, while entertaining visitors that included Al Polizzi, Pete Licavoli, Lepke Buchalter, Mike Coppola, and Frank Costello aide Joe Zucker. Lepke was a fugitive from New York justice when he joined Moe on hunting trips around Tucson. Coppola occupied a house on Tucson's East 5th Street from February 5 to April 30, 1937, during which time G-men claimed he "was frequently observed in the company of Davis [*sic*] and other individuals, who were affiliated with

California governor Earl Warren welcomed Mob support in his political campaigns (Library of Congress).

criminal activities in Cleveland." Telephone records document Moe's calls from Tucson to Frank Costello, vacationing in Hot Springs, Arkansas, during March 1937. Al Polizzi acknowledged crossing the Mexican border to hunt deer with Dalitz, and FBI files place a ranch owned by the Cleveland Mob "in Arizona near the Mexican border," years before Pete Licavoli bought a spread outside Tucson.

Licavoli's Grace Ranch — named for his wife — became a focal point for Mob activity in Arizona. Frenchy Gips, fresh from his work in Florida for Tom McGinty, came west to help Licavoli corral Tucson's independent gamblers. That gave Licavoli more time to dabble in real estate, manage Tucson's race-wire service with Kemper Marley, and invest in local restaurants with Robert Goldwater. *Tucson Weekly* reporter Tim Vanderpool described Goldwater — brother of a future U.S. Senator — as a "longtime buddy" of Moe Dalitz. By then, Arizona had proved so attractive that New York mafioso Joseph Bonnano bought a Tucson ranch near Licavoli's spread. Meanwhile, an FBI summary of Moe Dalitz's activities for 1931–39 maintains that "during this period he arranged for an individual (not identified) to work the numbers racket in Houston, Texas."

* * *

Lepke's Arizona hunting trip was occasioned by charges arising from Mob infiltration of the

Louis "Lepke" Buchalter (in plaid tie) hid out with Moe Dalitz before his 1939 surrender (Library of Congress).

fur-dressing industry. In 1932, Lepke and partner Jacob Shapiro organized the Protective Fur Dressers Corporation and the Fur Dressers Factor Corporation. In exchange for a $50,000 yearly payoff, Lepke's "special service" to dues-paying members included the standard campaign of terrorism against independent fur dressers. As tabulated by the FBI, one year of Lepke's assistance included "more than fifty anonymous telephone threats, twelve assaults, four stench bombings, ten explosive bombings, one kidnapping, three acid throwings, and two cases of arson."

In November 1933, federal jurors convicted Lepke and Shapiro of violating the Sherman Antitrust Act. They received two-year prison terms and matching $10,000 fines. Released pending appeal, both men jumped bail and went on the lam, hunted by FBI agents from coast to coast. The Bureau's "Furdress" file mentions Cleveland mobsters John Angersola, Morris Kleinman, and Lou Rothkopf, but its most telling entry concerns Moe Dalitz. When interviewed by G-men, "Moe Davis" confessed "that just prior to the disappearance of the fugitives they visited him in Cleveland. He also admitted that he saw them at Madison Square Garden, New York City, in 1937, but denied that he had seen them since that time. He admitted that he was well acquainted with them during the prohibition era." As a sidebar, the file claims that "racketeer lawyer" Sam Haas was "associated with Davis in the fur dressing case."

* * *

Another goldmine for the Mob, from the 1930s through the early 1950s, was the wire service that furnished bookies with results of horse races. Its founder and proprietor was Moses Annenberg, a Prussian Jew who emigrated to America in 1885. He quit school at eleven to sell newspapers during Chicago's circulation wars. By 1927 Annenberg was a multimillionaire controlling forty different businesses, including the *Daily Racing Form.*

That same year, Annenberg bought the General News Bureau, later called the Nationwide News Service. Between 1933 and 1936, Annenberg received $20 million from Nationwide, investing his bounty in fifty-odd corporations handling real estate, theaters, insurance, laundries, and newspapers. In 1938 Annenberg estimated his personal worth at $20 million; a year later, he pled ignorance when asked how much money he had.

The IRS had a fair idea. In 1939 it charged Annenberg, his son Walter, and other associates with evading payment of $9 million in taxes, plus penalties and interest. Moses cut a deal, agreeing to pay $9.5 million and accept a three-year prison term, in return for dismissal of charges against his son. Before he entered prison, however, Annenberg needed a strong man to run Nationwide.

He chose Mickey McBride.

As McBride later explained the transaction, it was all his mother's doing. Mrs. McBride complained to Mickey that Annenberg's downfall would leave countless wire-service employees jobless, including Mickey's own brother-in-law. Always a dutiful son, McBride conferred with Annenberg and struck a bargain. Nationwide News Service disbanded on November 15, 1939, and McBride's new Continental Press Service sprang to life five days later, capitalized with a $20,000 investment. For counsel, he retained the law firm of Kahn, Dillon & Arthur, whose partners allegedly told him "the logical thing to do would be to sell [race results] to nobody but scratch-sheet operators."

Thus encouraged by fine legal minds, McBride set about dividing his newfound empire among loyal subordinates. Mushy Wexler would control the service in Ohio, while James Ragen Sr. covered Illinois from Chicago. William Molasky, a friend of McBride's for twenty-odd years, served St. Louis with his Pioneer News. Russell Brophy, in Los Angeles, controlled "practically everything west," except for the Arizona enclave managed by Gus Greenbaum and Kemper Marley.

McBride always claimed that the wire service "didn't make money," but Senate investigators traced $148,000 from Continental to his pocket over three years. In August 1942, McBride sold Continental to James Ragen Jr. Fourteen months later, Ragen Jr. welcomed his father and Eddie McBride (Mickey's son) as partners. Eddie, lately drafted into military service, received $16,000 cash and a one-third share in Continental's future earnings, in return for which, said Ragen Sr., he "will never have to do a thing."

* * *

While Moe's empire expanded nationwide, he hit a snag on the domestic front. Sometime in 1939, Dorothy left the family home on East 107th Street and took a room at the Allerton Hotel. Moe sued for divorce on January 13, 1940, charging Dorothy with "gross neglect of duty and extreme cruelty." Maurice Maschke Jr. represented Moe, while Dorothy retained attorney A.N. Jappe. The property settlement granted Dorothy her jewelry and Cadillac, 300 shares of common stock in the Mullens Manufacturing Company, and $50 per week until the divorce was final. That decree ended the marriage and Moe's financial responsibilities to Dorothy on April 3, 1940.

Moe's divorce was still pending when he allegedly met future hitman Harold Konigsberg, in February 1940. Writing from prison six decades later, Konigsberg described his encounter with Moe at the "Holland Hotel," where he drove two unnamed men to visit Dalitz and Morris Kleinman. The next day, Konigsberg claims, he drove Kleinman and the anonymous VIPs to Cicero, Illinois, on business that "involved President Roosevelt and the leader of the combination, and a fellow involved in the labor movement named Sidney Hillman." Konigsberg's extravagant demands for cash precluded further correspondence, but Hillman *was* a major labor leader of that era, leading the Amalgamated Clothing Workers of America and the International Ladies' Garment Workers' Union, which placed him in contact with Lepke Buchalter. In 1935 Hillman helped found the Committee for Industrial Organizing, renamed the Congress of Industrial Organizations in 1937.

Hillman was certainly a friend of FDR, who named him to serve on the Labor Advisory Board of the National Recovery Administration in 1933, and on the National Industrial Recovery Board in 1934. In 1935 Hillman helped draft the National Labor Relations Act, and three years later he lobbied successfully for passage of the Fair Labor Standards Act. In May 1940 FDR appointed Hillman to the National Defense Advisory Committee, followed by service with the Office of Product Management in 1941, and as head of the War Production Board's labor division in 1942. All this is fact, but still we must ask why Dalitz and Kleinman would choose Harold Konigsberg, just eleven years old in 1940, as their interstate chauffeur. Whatever the relationship, Konigsberg recalled Moe and Kleinman in 2007 as "two of the finest caring, honorablest [*sic*] and respected people on the face of the Earth."

* * *

Old habits die hard. In August 1939 Detroit rumrunner Abe Moss called Moe Dalitz to reminisce about the good old days, when their boats had challenged the Coast Guard's blockade. He mentioned, too, that untaxed alcohol could presently be purchased in Chicago for $1.10 and sold in Canada for $9, an 820-percent markup. Would Moe be interested?

Moe was.

The Cleveland Four bankrolled Moss, but left him to handle the details. First, Moss arranged to purchase bootleg alky in Chicago. Next, with brother Louis, he set up shipping headquarters at Ecorse, Michigan. Shipments were dispatched to Ontario, where drivers met the boats and carried off the liquid gold. To double his profit, Moss decreed that the booze boats should not return empty, instead bearing loads of Canadian furs for resale in the States. It was a profitable enterprise, until the feds nabbed Abe and indicted him for smuggling. In July 1941 he received a ten-year prison term and a $10,000 fine, all suffered without naming Dalitz or his Cleveland partners.

In 1940 Al Polizzi bought Cleveland's Sunrise Brewing Company and changed its name to Tip Top Brewing. With him came veterans of the defunct Lubeck Brewery, including Fred Garmone (another friend of Mickey McBride). Polizzi opened a Cleveland bank account in Garmone's name, to guarantee repayment of loans to Tip Top's retail customers — a "tied-house system" banned by federal law. Ohio's state government monopolized liquor sales, while FDR's Office of Price Administration fixed a ceiling price on booze. Ignoring the law as in days of yore, Polizzi and Garmone bought 1,501 gallons of whiskey from Ulrich Vogt's Peerless Liquors in Chicago — a prohibition-era link in Morris Kleinman's smuggling chain — and sold the booze in Ohio for $9 per gallon above the OPA ceiling. Vogt received $5 on each gallon, while Polizzi and Garmone split $4. Polizzi and Garmone dispensed their product through Mushy Wexler's Theatrical Grill and other Mob-owned saloons, where ardent drinkers cared less for quality than quantity.

Enter Samuel Stein, a Russian-Polish Jew who emigrated to America in 1913, at age seventeen. He landed in Detroit, where police arrested him for auto theft in 1920, resulting in a two-to-five-year sentence. Stein learned nothing from incarceration, rolling on to log arrests for armed robbery (1923, 1925), forgery (1924), liquor violations (1925), and grand larceny (1928). In 1933, police caught Stein with Joe Massei and a carload of guns. Convicted of carrying concealed weapons, Stein and Massei fought their verdict all the way to the U.S. Supreme Court, which ruled the police search illegal and ordered return of the weapons. Stein then moved to Cleveland, joining Freddie Myers as a partner in Freddie's Club, near the Hollenden Hotel and Theatrical Grill.

April 1943 found Stein involved in the Polizzi-Peerless liquor racket. Polizzi had registered Peerless with Ohio's state government as agent for out-of-state whiskey transactions, but he still needed warehouse receipts to legitimize the traffic. Stein traveled to Kentucky and purchased warehouse receipts from bona fide liquor wholesalers, bankrolled with a $17,000 loan from Pete Licavoli. Bardstown's Fairfield Distillery furnished the whiskey required.

In May 1943 Stein forged a new alliance with Cincinnati wholesaler Robert Gould, who controlled three distilleries with an inventory of 23,935 barrels, valued at $1,451,530. Acting on Garmone's instructions, Stein purchased 500 barrels at $5 per gallon, $3.85 above the OPA ceiling. Around the same time, Stein, Pete Licavoli, and Chuck Polizzi purchased a Milwaukee distillery and its stockpile of whiskey for $420,000. As revealed in subsequent court hearings, Polizzi's $75,000 investment included "unnamed associates."

The feds indicted Stein for his part in the liquor ring in December 1943, but the charge was later dismissed on a technicality. Al Polizzi was next, indicted for alcohol tax violations. He liquidated Tip Top and pled guilty in October 1944. Upon release from prison in 1945, Polizzi followed his Mayfield Road cohorts to Florida, ostensibly intending to "go straight." In 1951 he told Senate investigators, "I made no money on that transaction." Furthermore, he said, "I want to tell you that, so far as taxes or any of that stuff was concerned, everybody got their taxes, and the only one that lost any money was me."

* * *

The Tip Top scheme was not Sam Stein's first business venture with Moe Dalitz and the Cleveland Syndicate. In 1938 a relative of Sam's, Jack Stein, was shot and killed by mobsters in Toledo. Jack's widow fell for Morris Wasserman, whose brother Irving was related by marriage to one Nat Levitt. In 1939, Toronto police caught Levitt with 118 cases of Abe Moss's untaxed whiskey. He served a brief jail term but did not go straight. Smuggling was in his blood, and while the alky trade had soured for him, he was primed to smuggle something else.

Like gold.

In 1940, Canada ranked third among the gold-producing nations of the Earth (after South Africa and the Soviet Union). Canadian officials estimated that stolen gold worth $75,000 found its way to the U.S. each week. Stein and Levitt moved most of that swag, until police nabbed accomplice Irving Wasserman in Milwaukee, in April 1942. Wasserman gave up Levitt and two other cohorts, one of whom — Marlin Landau — agreed to lay a trap for Stein.

Landau claimed plans were afoot for a Chicago buyer to receive 125 pounds of gold from Stein on September 13, 1942, at Detroit's Book-Cadillac Hotel. FBI agents were watching at

1:35 P.M., when Stein met Bennie Kray and Charles Lipshitz in the hotel's café. At 4 P.M., Lipshitz drove Stein to the airport, where Stein had booked a flight to Buffalo. A surreptitious search of Stein's luggage revealed no contraband.

More G-men waited for Stein at Buffalo's airport. They tracked him to a phone booth, eavesdropped on his conversation, then followed him to the Statler Hotel. There, instead of checking in, Stein left his bag with the concierge and met one Michael Menneci in the hotel's dining room. Two hours later, Stein and Menneci walked several blocks to a waiting car, then drove *back* to the Statler, retrieved Stein's suitcase and put it in the car's trunk, then drove to Buffalo's railroad terminal. There, agents watched Menneci park the car, open the trunk, and slip something into Stein's bag. A second search of the suitcase, inside the terminal, revealed four large gold buttons valued at $8,900.

Agents arrested Stein and Menneci, then released them on bond. Surveillance of Stein's movements revealed frequent trips to Cincinnati, where he met with members of the Cleveland Syndicate. In April 1943 Stein's phone records showed calls to Game Boy Miller, the Lookout House casino, various jewelry dealers, and a company that supplied slot machines in Newport, Kentucky. The next month, G-men logged more calls to Miller and Stein's first conversation with wholesale liquor dealer Robert Gould.

Stein and Menneci received two-year prison terms in September 1943. Both were immediately freed again, pending appeal, and Stein kept busy with the Mob, pursuing the booze deal that saw him indicted three months later. In November 1943 he canceled a flight to Detroit after chatting by phone with Morris Kleinman, then flew to Cincinnati instead. The next morning, Stein left his hotel in a car registered to Louise Tucker and drove to Sam Tucker's home in Kentucky. At 4 P.M., Tucker's wife drove Stein back to his Cincinnati hotel, where he phoned a "Mr. Simons" in Detroit with news that he was planning to sell 17,000 cases of "gin" to "the Man in Cleveland." Stein then caught a flight to Cleveland. Convinced that Stein was only dealing booze, G-men suspended further investigation "unless information is again received that he is dealing in the smuggling of gold."

* * *

Gambling in Cuyahoga County took a double hit in January 1941, when Frank Lausche became Cleveland's mayor and Joseph Sweeney took office as county sheriff. Local casinos closed, but other counties still welcomed Mob "sportsmen." It would take Lausche's election as governor, in 1944, to finally shut down the state's most infamous gambling dens.

Meanwhile, in 1943, state lawmakers stripped Common Pleas judges of the power to issue search warrants, handing that authority to local magistrates who were more easily bribed. At the same time, legislators changed the statute concerning removal of negligent sheriffs, requiring petitions signed by 15 percent of a county's total population. Raiding instantly decreased, and Mayor Lausche deemed the new obstructions to reform "virtually impossible" to overcome. In Trumbull County, gambling proponents established the "artificially created city" of Halls Corners, with its mayor and other civic leaders linked to owners of the thriving Jungle Inn. Statewide, Buckeye Catering still distributed slot machines, though accountant Alvin Giesey later claimed that he thought the slots "went out in 1938." Al Polizzi, questioned in 1951, first was "positive" that he quit Buckeye before 1940, then said, "I don't like to answer those questions. It just takes me back and tears me all apart."

In Detroit, Moe Dalitz turned his mind to refinement of the laundry game, hiring technicians to create an invisible marking ink that became legible after garments were washed. Its purpose: to reduce theft of uniforms by laundry employees. Moe filed a patent application for the ink, which trademark attorney Albert Ely called "an extremely promising development for the linen supply business." Unfortunately, government restrictions on industrial materials stalled production. On December 7, 1941, one of Moe's aides met with Ely to discuss how the invention could be "put on ice" for the duration. Their lunch was interrupted by news of the Japanese raid on Pearl Harbor.

* * *

At forty-two, Moe was exempt from the draft, but this time he chose to enlist, joining the army as a private at Fort Hayes, Ohio, on June 29, 1942. While older men saw combat in World War II, Moe was not fated for a foxhole. Rather, his extensive knowledge of the laundry trade made him a godsend for the quartermaster corps, a catchall army branch that handled everything from general supplies and groceries to graves registration. On December 23, 1942, Moe was transferred to Fort Lee, Virginia, where he was commissioned as a second lieutenant.

Decades later, Gus Russo claimed that Moe owned his commission to Mob attorney Sidney Korshak, who served as a Fort Lee desk sergeant, vetting prospects for Officers Candidate School. Russo quotes an unnamed source who allegedly heard Dalitz say: "During the war, it was Sidney, who I had not met at that point, who recommended me for OCS. I'll never forget it." As a result, the source claimed, "Dalitz didn't go to the bathroom without checking with Sidney." Unfortunately, Russo's tale contains a fatal flaw. By his own admission, Korshak was not drafted until April 9, 1943, fifteen weeks *after* Moe received his commission.

Lieutenant Dalitz was next assigned to the 2nd Service Command on Governor's Island, New York, supervising laundry operations. Rather than endure barracks life, he stayed at Manhattan's Savoy-Plaza Hotel, where Meyer Lansky and other old friends kept him in touch with Mob activities. He also had plenty of free time, as evidenced by a wartime photograph of Oscar-winning songwriter Jimmy Van Heusen, posed with a salmon. The photograph's inscription reads: "Fishing trip to Alaska, salmon catch with Moe Dalitz and Bing Crosby—1943."

Others followed Moe's patriotic example. Mob accountant Alvin Giesey donned a uniform, emerging from the war as a major in the field artillery reserve. George Gordon registered for the draft in October 1940, but army psychiatrists rejected him as "a psychopathic personality." FBI files note "that in approximately April of 1945, GEORGE GORDON was ... a member of the Bayonet Club which was operated by the Moe Davis and Morris Kleinman Syndicate."

Moe was happy at the Savoy-Plaza, where his wealthy neighbors in uniform included Lieutenant Colonel Sam Becker and naval officer Robert Goldstein, late of Universal Pictures. In civilian life, Becker was Goldstein's lawyer. Together, in the post-war years, they invited Moe to participate in the phenomenon of television.

* * *

Contradictory FBI reports from 1944 name Moe Dalitz as a "key syndicate figure" and "head of the Cleveland gambling syndicate," while claiming that the Mayfield Road Gang was "the only known organized gang operating in the Cleveland area." Of course, the muddled feds still branded Moe "the Czar" of Mayfield Road. Unable to imagine any larger Syndicate, they missed another chance to halt its growth during the war.

G-men acknowledged that the "MRG" engaged in casino gambling, numbers rackets,

Lieutenant Moe Dalitz in uniform (Las Vegas Historical Society).

horse racing and bookmaking, sale of black-market alcohol and other rationed products, plus "illegal use of gasoline ration stamps ... fraudulently obtained from Ration Board 6 in Cleveland with the aid of corrupt rationing officials and others." On March 29, 1944, the *Cleveland Press* reported that 1,194 cases of booze, valued in excess of $71,000, had been stolen from state-owned liquor stores over the past twelve months. That traffic produced at least one murder, when George Gladish was shot near Cuyahoga Falls in May 1943. FBI files called Gladish "a well-known hoodlum and member of the Mayfield Road Gang," speculating that his bosses killed him for stealing Mob funds. Specifically, Gladish told a girlfriend that he had to do a job in Akron, retrieving $20,000 in cash for Lou Rothkopf and George Gordon. Other men had died for less.

Frank Rosen sent his son to North Carolina's Duke University: Allard "Roen" graduated in 1943, with a B.A. in business administration, then served as a naval ensign until 1945. Police jailed Mushy Wexler for gambling in May 1942, but later dropped the charges. Wexler borrowed $10,000 from Mickey McBride to pay his 1944 income taxes, and secured McBride's signature on a bank loan to remodel the Theatrical Grill. Sam Haas invited Major Alvin Giesey to invest $1,500 in the Melody Music Company, an Arizona operation co-owned by Nate Weisenberg's son. Giesey took the plunge, also investing in Denver's Century Music Company and Modern Music, based in Colorado Springs. Other partners included Morris Haas (Sam's son) and Tom McGinty. Giesey, while placing the stock in his wife's name, later claimed that he thought Melody Music was a simple "music-box business," created to sell jukeboxes. In fact, all three firms distributed slot machines.

* * *

California simmered during the war years, with tension escalating between Ben Siegel and Jack Dragna. Their latest feud involved the race-wire service and a scheme by Chicago mobsters to grab the racket for themselves. As later reconstructed by investigators, members of the old Capone gang serviced local bookies through R&H Publishing, a subsidiary of Continental Press. R&H withheld payments from Continental, and the ripples spread westward to Los Angeles, where Russell Brophy managed Continental's action for his father-in-law, James Ragen Sr.

The sequence of events remains obscure. Author Andy Edmonds says Dragna tried to muscle in on Siegel's bookies, while Brophy employee George Redston described Siegel and Dragna collaborating to squeeze Brophy out of the business. In either case, Mickey Cohen and Joe Sica invaded Brophy's office on July 21, 1942, ripping out his phone lines and beating Brophy severely enough to put him in the hospital. Brophy declined to press charges, but authorities still fined Sica $200, while Cohen paid $100.

Dragna subsequently placed a $100,000 contract on Siegel, while Siegel responded with a five-cent bounty on Dragna, suggesting that Dragna's life was not worth a "plugged nickel." Mickey Cohen sent gunmen to ambush Dragna outside Sherry's Restaurant, on the Sunset Strip, but Dragna learned of the plot and canceled his reservation. On July 10, 1944, Joe Adonis, Frank Costello, and Chicago mobster Charles Fischetti arrived in Long Beach to negotiate peace. In Bugsy's absence, they met with Dragna, John Rosselli, and Siegel cohort Allen Smiley. The conference produced a fragile, short-lived peace treaty — and, Andy Edmonds says, enlisted Smiley as the Mob's "mole" to spy on Siegel and volatile mistress Virginia Hill.

* * *

Events in Kentucky had more immediate concern for Moe Dalitz. Friendly governor Keen Johnson was scheduled to leave office on December 7, 1943, along with state attorney general Hubert Meredith and assistant Jesse Lewis. Before departing, Johnson named attorney William Wise as Campbell County's prosecutor and appointed Judge Ray Murphy to the circuit court. Both men would serve for two decades without disrupting Mob activities, but Cleveland's latest headache emanated from another quarter.

Pete Schmidt, stripped of his interest in the Beverly Hills Club, still dreamed of a comeback. His unlikely ally was lawyer Charles Lester, still on the Mob's payroll after handling the casino transfer in November 1940. Dissatisfied with his syndicate stipend, Lester joined in Schmidt's plan for a coup d'état and enlisted lame ducks Meredith and Lewis. On September 20, 1943, Lester and Lewis filed a lawsuit seeking an injunction against Newport's gamblers and officials who supported them, 92 defendants in all. Armed with an order from Judge C.D. Newell that authorized seizure of gambling equipment, Lester and Lewis forced Newport police chief George Gugel to raid five prominent clubs: the Beverly Hills, Glenn Rendezvous, the Merchants, the York Tavern, and the Yorkshire. Officers seized gambling equipment valued at $100,000, burning some of it and placing forty-one slot machines in storage.

So the battle was joined. Judge Murphy vacated Judge Newell's order, only to find himself named as a defendant in the Lester-Lewis lawsuit. Hubert Meredith got Judge Murphy's ruling overturned on appeal. Meanwhile, Sam Tucker's lawyers exposed Lester's role in Mob acquisition of the Beverly Hills Club, revealing his conflict of interest. Forced to choose between dumping Lester or dropping the Beverly Hills from their lawsuit, Meredith and Lewis chose the latter course. Embarrassed by the furor, Campbell County's grand jury indicted eight gamblers on December 22, 1943. The defendants included "Maurice Davis," Sam Tucker, Samuel Schraeder, John Croft, Red Masterson, Sam Nason, Elmer Gerrein and Agnes Schmidt. Masterson pled guilty on two counts and paid a $400 fine, while Croft pled to one count and paid $200. The other charges were dismissed. Nason moved on to run the Fox and Crow Club, a plush casino in Montgomery, Ohio. The rest resumed business as usual.

As for the confiscated slots, they vanished within hours of the raids. Chief Gugel set Patrolman Wallace Sweeney to guard them, but Campbell County police chief Julius Plummer called Sweeney from his post at 8:15 A.M. on September 21 and kept him in conference until 9:35. By the time Sweeney returned to guard duty, "persons unknown" had decamped with the slots. Judge John Vest cited Tucker, Schraeder, Plummer, and three patrolmen for contempt of court. Tucker and Schraeder appealed their citations on grounds that the slots were "not in legal custody." The appellate court disagreed, but Vest later dismissed Schraeder's charge, while fining the patrolmen $25 each. On January 31, 1944, Vest convicted Tucker and Plummer, ordering both men jailed until the missing slots were returned. Appeals dragged on until July 4, 1945, when Newport gambler William Motz confessed ownership of the missing machines. Motz paid $1,530 in fines and received a thirty-day jail term. Tucker and Plummer thus saw their charges dismissed, without spending a day in custody.

By that time, Tucker had survived a second, unrelated prosecution. In October 1944, U.S. marshals arrested Sam and associate Mike Wenzel for violating OPA price regulations on whiskey served at the Beverly Hills Country Club. They also charged Richard Hopkins, a former state revenue agent, as an accomplice. Jurors failed to reach a verdict at trial, and prosecutors continued the case before Judge Mac Swinford until the court's next term, in April 1945. No second trial was held, and FBI files listed the case as still "pending" in March 1958.

* * *

Kentucky authorities never served their December 1943 arrest warrant on "Maurice Davis," and dismissal of those gambling charges fazed Moe Dalitz no more than the original indictment. Aside from gambling and other rackets in half a dozen states, he was also cleaning up on various legitimate investments. By May 1944, when he rejected a $1 million offer for Cleveland's Pioneer Laundry, Moe was immersed in his biggest industrial caper to date.

The story began in July 1943, when Max Zivian became president of the Detroit Steel Company. His promotion coincided with merger negotiations between Detroit Steel and Cleveland's Reliance Steel, owned by Sol Friedman. The first attempt failed when Friedman demanded control of the new corporation, but Zivian planned to skirt that obstacle by purchasing Friedman's stock in Reliance. Friedman placed his stock in escrow, while Zivian and other Detroit Steel executives collected $480,000 of the proposed buyout price. They were still $100,000 short when Zivian went to Cleveland and "bumped into Moe Dalitz," home on leave from the army.

In fact, Moe and Max were longtime friends. They golfed together, Zivian once spent six days on Moe's yacht, and Moe had borrowed cash from Zivian several times, including one loan of $60,000. Now, as Zivian later explained, "I met Mr. Dalitz on the street outside the Statler Hotel. I told him we were short $100,000, and he said, 'Let me arrange to get it.' A couple of hours later we went over to his lawyer's office." The lawyer was Samuel Haas. According to FBI files, "HAAS made phone calls, the result being that Morris Plan Bank of Cleveland did the financing and HAAS bought 3333 shares while DALITZ, MORRIS KLEINMAN, LOU RHODY [sic] and their partner in dice joints, SAMUEL TUCKER, bought 3337 shares." The Bureau's tabulation was faulty, however: Dalitz and his three partners actually divided two-thirds of 10,000 shares — a total of 6,667 at $10 per share. Alvin Giesey arrived in time to finalize the deal.

And what a deal it was. The merger went through on schedule, with Zivian installed as president of the new Detroit Steel Corporation. Giesey subsequently bought 100 shares of stock on four separate occasions, rewarded with his masters as the stock split twice, increasing Cleveland's share from 10,000 to 40,000 shares, worth $1,360,000 in 1951. Asked by investigators if he personally made $230,000 on the deal, Moe replied, "It might have been a little more." Small wonder, then, that Moe should say of Zivian, "I regard him as a very, very good and loyal friend."

* * *

On January 14, 1945, unknown burglars stole jewelry valued at $300,000 from the premises of Schneider & Son, in Atlanta, Georgia. FBI agents entered the case on a presumption that the loot was sold across state lines, and the trail led them to Cleveland's swank Ohio Villa, "operated by the Mayfield Road gang under the leadership of MOE DAVIS." The file mentions the Angersola brothers as potential suspects. It also notes that, while Morris Kleinman and Lou Rothkopf were not jewel thieves, "they have connections all over the United States which could be used to good advantage in disposing of stolen property."

The case remains officially unsolved.

Six weeks later, "Slots King" Nate Weisenberg suffered through the worst day of his life. He had no way of knowing it would be his last.

February 23 began with a clamoring alarm on Cleveland's Chester Avenue, where prowlers had hacked through the wall of a warehouse and tried to steal some of Weisenberg's slot machines. Weisenberg declined to file a police report, but he visited Chief Matowitz at headquarters, then stopped by the prosecutor's office, finally huddling with his masters at the Hollenden Hotel. Nate treated himself to a steam bath that afternoon, then returned to the Hollenden for dinner, followed by a meeting with Judge Frank Merrick in the hotel's Artists and Writers Club. At 10 P.M. Weisenberg joined two good-time girls for drinks at the Hollenden's bar. The trio left at 11:45, stopped briefly at another bar, then Weisenberg dropped the ladies at Euclid and East 107th Street.

At 1 A.M. on February 24, a boy walking home from a dance in Cleveland Heights saw Weisenberg's Lincoln coupe parked on Silsby Road, with its headlights on. A closer look through the shattered driver's window revealed a body slumped behind the steering wheel. Two close-range shotgun blasts had nearly beheaded Weisenberg.

A search of Weisenberg's files revealed a letter from former associate Thomas Gerak, in Seattle. Gerak wrote:

> You never saw so many people, soldiers and sailors, as well as civilians, in a town of this size in your life. And they're out on the streets at all hours of the day and night. It's a seaport town. Its lumber, canning, and trading industries are not affected by the depression. It's the Gateway to Alaska, and it's a young and growing town.... The important thing is that there is plenty of action and money in circulation here so let me know if you're interested. You have nothing to live for in Cleveland now — since your old pal Frank Noonan died. Let me hear from you.

Detectives returned to the warehouse on Chester Avenue and seized sixty-nine slot machines, then went on to question the owner of record, elderly Herbert Gove. Under repeated questioning, Gove reluctantly acknowledged that other slots had been stolen during the February 23 break-in. Cleveland safety director Frank Celebreeze reported that Weisenberg's contacts on the last day of his life included George Gordon, Morris Kleinman, Chuck Polizzi, Lou Rothkopf, and Frank Rosen. Lieutenant Martin Cooney's report to the coroner's inquest explained that:

> These men can be found in the afternoon and night around Vincent Avenue in the lobby of the Hollenden Hotel, and in Room 281 of the Hollenden Hotel, a gambling place operated by Frank Rosen. I have had several telephone calls that Nathan Weisenberg was in this room the night he was killed. Nearly all the aforementioned men live outside Cleveland and have no legitimate business in Cleveland.

Which is not to say they had *no* business interests. Following Weisenberg's death, various silent partners divided his Skill Amusement Company among themselves. The lucky group included Edward Kleinman (Morris's nephew), Joe Polizzi and son Alphonso Polizzi (brother and nephew of Alfred), Jerry Milano (kin to Frank and Tony), John and William McGinty (sons of Tom), Regis Duddy (Tom McGinty's son-in-law), Richard Moriarty (McGinty's lawyer), Gladys Giesey (Alvin's wife), and lawyer Samuel Haas. Francis Weisenberg and his widowed mother retained a small share of the business until 1946, when Francis died in an "unexplained" single-car crash. Authorities blamed a heart attack, and the Mob paid his estate a final stipend of $22,139.

* * *

Around the time of Nate Weisenberg's death, Moe Dalitz received two letters from Detroit. One came from his attorney, the other from the Colonial Laundry, where Moe's services were urgently required. The War Manpower Commission promptly declared Colonial "essential" for national security. On March 1, 1945, Moe wrote to his commanding officer and asked to be relieved of duty. Two months later, on May 29, he was honorably discharged at Fort Sheridan, Illinois, as a first lieutenant, his commission extended for six months after the wartime emergency "unless sooner terminated."

FBI agents interviewed Moe at their Cleveland field office on June 25, 1945, and apparently received forthright cooperation. The censored reports say Moe "furnished information concerning his associates and activities while he was serving in the U.S. Army, 1942-June 1945 [sic]. He stated that during that period he maintained a financial interest in certain gambling establishments in Ohio and Kentucky. He also mentioned his gambling activities during 1941 in Ohio and Kentucky, and individuals with whom he had associated." More specifically, "DALITZ advised that while he was serving in the Army, MORRIS KLEINMAN was in charge and probably made arrangements to finance other gambling establishments located in Cleveland and elsewhere. DALITZ stated the names of these establishments were unknown to him, although he did recall that there was a gambling operation near Cleveland managed by GEORGE GORDON."

Additionally, Moe "advised the Bureau that THOMAS McGINTY, member of the Cleveland Gambling Syndicate, controlled all gambling and rackets in Lake County, Ohio, as a result of his political connections there." He also acknowledged a financial interest in Suite 281 at the Hollenden Hotel, but claimed the operation was terminated after Nate Weisenberg's murder.

Such revelations were safe, from Moe's viewpoint, since the feds had no interest in local Mob activities, and J. Edgar Hoover refused to look farther afield. The FBI was preoccupied with communism, launching a crusade against the Red Menace that would consume Hoover's energy and most of the Bureau's man-hours over the next fifteen years.

Or maybe Moe was simply in a chatty mood.

But why?

By summer 1945 Moe Dalitz was in love — again.

6

Chutzpah

Leonne Gladys Clark, known to her friends as "Toni," was a vivacious twenty-four-year-old fashion model when she met Moe in Detroit, in 1943. Hank Messick claims that they were introduced by Sam Stein, whose new bride was a friend of Toni's, but Toni recalls meeting Moe for the first time at Sammy Sofferin's Wonder Bar, after a fashion show. They subsequently met again in Buffalo — "the first time that we really got together," Toni said — and she moved to New York City to improve her prospects, while Moe was in the army. They married in Miami, with Morris and Gizella Kleinman as witnesses, on December 8, 1945. The newlyweds built a home in Detroit, but Moe left no tracks. As late as 1948, city directories showed Toni Clark Dalitz living alone at 400 Parkview Drive.

In fact, Moe shared the same address through 1951, and he was not alone with Toni. Nine months after their wedding, on September 21, 1946, they adopted a four-day-old boy in New York City and named him Andrew Barnet Dalitz. FBI agents reported that Moe and Toni registered at the Hotel New Yorker, where "a spot surveillance was being conducted on DALITZ." While there, Moe telephoned Kleinman's unlisted number in Cleveland and received a call from boxing promoter Harry "Champ" Segal. Moe and Toni flew home to Detroit with baby Andrew on September 26.

The marriage was a happy one in those days. Moe bought a yacht and christened it the *Toni Kid,* subsequently replaced by the larger *South Wind.* Toni, unmarred by baby fat, continued her successful modeling career, while Moe pursued his varied interests. The Dalitzes vacationed in Mexico, and generally behaved like a loving couple. If Toni recognized her husband's roving eye, she kept it to herself. Moe's travels in pursuit of cash concealed a multitude of sins.

* * *

In November 1945, Moe's Modern Overall Cleaners became the Michigan Industrial Laundry. Brother Louis drew a $17,500 yearly salary from Michigan Industrial, while Moe and partner Maurice Maschke Jr. banked $9,600 each. Lou formed his own U.S. Industrial Glove Company in 1945, but delayed obtaining a state charter until September 1948, when he changed the firm's name to Inglasco. Capitalized with $50,000, Inglasco was reborn as Industrial Glove Corporation in November 1948, and again as U.S. Industrial Glove in May 1949.

The Dalitz brothers had no shortage of "straight" firms in those post-war years. Together, they owned Detroit-based Milco Sales, described by Moe as a company "that disposes of the salvage and materials, resulting from the laundry business." Dalitz Realty, "quite a large com-

Moe Dalitz (left), bride Toni, and father Barnet Dalitz in Miami Beach, 1946 (Toni Clark Drago).

pany" by Moe's assessment, owned "land and buildings" in Wyandotte, Michigan. So did Berdeen Realty. As Moe explained to federal investigators, "Out in Wyandotte there is this development, land development, going on. We built a big supermarket and leased it to a tenant. These companies are rent-collecting realty companies."

Detroit Steel was still a lucrative concern for Dalitz and his partners. Sam Tucker invested $75,000 in Pioneer Linen, and also owned a share of Michigan Industrial Laundry "for a very short time." Moe Dalitz launched Pioneer Linen in 1938, with 75 percent of its stock shared equally by himself, Kleinman, Tucker, Lou Rothkopf, Chuck Polizzi, and Maurice Maschke Jr. Polizzi sold his share to Dalitz and Tucker in 1943. Kleinman and Rothkopf sold out to Dalitz and Tucker in 1945. Four years later, Tucker sold his share to Dalitz for $120,000.

Moe kept various other irons in the fire. An FBI report described his entry into "the credit collection industry," and he also doubled as a talent agent. Struggling singer Sonny King shared a New York apartment with Youngstown native Dean Martin — and introduced Martin to pal Jerry Lewis — before a chance encounter changed his life in 1946. A friend of King's informed him that Moe Dalitz, "a key booker around the country," was passing through town. "She called him up," King later said, "and I sang to him right over the phone. He offered me a job in D.C. right then." King's two-week gig at Washington's Tradewinds Club grew into a two-year engagement, while Martin and Lewis were left to fend for themselves.

Other syndicate forays into semi-legitimate business included a Pennsylvania Lincoln-Mercury dealership, established in 1946 to furnish syndicate leaders, their relatives and friends with new cars. Sam Tucker bought cars there for two of his children in 1949, shortly before Alvin Giesey took over the firm. Crown Investment Company — later renamed Cleveland Arena, Inc.— existed solely to purchase stock in the Cleveland Hockey Company, using $200,000 on loan from the Fidelity Trust Company of Indianapolis.

And the wheels kept turning. Liberty Ice Cream, established by Kleinman during prohibition, survived into the Cold War era. Dean Rothkopf, Lou's brother, ran the business

Sam Stein aboard Moe's yacht, the *Toni Kid* (Toni Clark Drago).

Moe and Toni in Mexico, 1946 (Toni Clark Drago).

until 1945, when Edward Kleinman replaced him. Edward's wife owned Roxy's, a Cleveland burlesque theater. Allen Kleinman managed the Warfield Drug Company, expanding from one shop to four. Mob lieutenants also ran Pierre's Restaurant on Euclid Avenue, and another restaurant, Hatton's Corners, at Lexington and 55th. Both featured gambling as well as fine cuisine.

One venture with vast potential, which nonetheless flopped, was Consolidated Television, organized in 1947. Partners of record included Joe Adonis, Frank Costello, and Meyer Lansky. Consolidated's president was Louis Pokrass, a Russian Jew who immigrated to the United States in 1915. Jailed four times for Volstead violations between 1925 and 1931, Pokrass emerged from prohibition as general manager of New York's Capitol Wine & Spirits. After World War II, he led Gotham Liquor, which rented office space in the same Fifth Avenue high-rise that once housed Molaska Corporation's headquarters.

Pokrass believed that the golden future of TV lay in saloons, rather than private homes. He approached friends in the New York syndicate because, as Lansky later said, "We had knowledge of distribution of juke boxes. We knew every place that had a juke box and that would be a good place to have television." Beyond simply placing sets, however, Consolidated Television aimed at producing "soundies"— short features with music and dancers — to keep tavern patrons amused.

Moe Dalitz joined Consolidated's cast of characters, although he shared Hollywood's view that TV would be a short-lived fad. None of the "experts" thought Americans would stay at home and watch the tube, when they could be out on the town. Still, if the TV bar scene

Moe and Toni with unidentified friends in Montreal, 1946 (Toni Clark Drago).

prospered, mobsters on the ground floor had an opportunity to corner yet another facet of the entertainment industry.

Consolidated Television's vice president was Terrill Murrell, an ex-lieutenant colonel in the army who found his way into the TV business with help from New York mafioso Joe Bonanno. Soon after joining the firm, Murrell launched a tour of Midwestern saloons, including Cleveland's Theatrical Grill, where he met Moe Dalitz. Moe recommended Sam Stein as a pitchman for Consolidated in Detroit. Stein accepted the job, but Murrell quit the business around the time Pokrass changed Consolidated's name to Tele-King. A new addition to the team, Robert Goldstein of Universal Pictures, knew Dalitz from their wartime service at Manhattan's Savoy-Plaza.

Despite such talent and connections in show business, Tele-King ultimately failed. Meyer Lansky later said, "I think we went in at the wrong end of it. We thought that the commercial end was the best part. We should have gone into the home-set end, and maybe I would have been a very rich man today." Moe Dalitz, already rich, was not finished with TV, however. His next foray into the field, two decades later, would add more millions to his fortune.

* * *

While still unknown to the public at large, Moe was increasingly notorious in law enforcement circles. The sluggish FBI took notice of his post-war movements, but predictably misunderstood them. When J. Edgar Hoover launched the Bureau's first, short-lived investigation of organized crime in 1946, he focused on Chicago as the center of the Mob universe. Cleveland G-men opened a file on Moe because he was "friendly with remnants of the Capone gang," then proclaimed long-absent Frank Milano "the big one in Cleveland ... who controls all the rackets." In March 1947 a new report declared George Angersola the "number one man

Peter "Horseface" Licavoli (National Archives).

in control of the operations of the Mayfield Road Gang." Or was he? Four months later, confused G-men claimed that Thomas Scalish's death had cleared the way for brother John to command the gang.

Hoover could not imagine a syndicate run by non–Italians. Thus, in Bureau eyes, Moe remained a fringe player, acknowledged as Cleveland's "principal contact with the PETE LICAVOLI mob in Detroit," but otherwise reduced to the role of a Jew on a Mafia leash. In October 1949, FBI files noted a "definite indication that the so-called Mayfield Road Gang has a specific interest in the enterprises owned by the gambling syndicate of MORRIS B. DALITZ, MORRIS KLEINMAN, and LOUIS ROTHKOPF. The representative of the Mayfield group in this connection is JOHN SCALISH." Another file came closer to the truth, noting that Scalish "had been a chauffeur for Dalitz in Cleveland."

While Hoover's FBI suffered from Mob myopia, Ohio governor Frank Lausche had a better grasp of reality. Lausche challenged Moe's gambling empire in 1945–47, but local lawmen refused to cooperate. Lausche lost his bid for a second term, but rebounded to run the state from 1949 to 1957. Upon his re-election, Lausche wasted no time in attacking the Mob. His weapon was the state's Department of Liquor Control, led by Director Anthony Rutkowski.

Rutkowski started small, in tiny Elmwood Place, closing the Maple Club and its adjacent bookie parlor. Next, he hit the Jungle Inn, in Trumbull County, which had never closed despite state revocation of its liquor license. Rutkowski's raiders struck in August 1949, bagging 36 employees and 700 patrons, 83 slot machines, three dice tables, plus chuck-a-luck, roulette, and a racing board. Putative boss John Farah threatened Rutkowski's life, then surrendered, pleading guilty with nineteen others and paying $4,500 in fines. Fire marshals demolished the casino, but it soon reopened as the Jennings Inn, prompting another raid.

Rutkowski's next target was Chesapeake's Colony Club. Clarence Lenz managed the club, while his wife worked for the Lawrence County sheriff's office. Sheriff Peter Burke declined to raid the club, and later found it awkward to explain why the casino paid his private utility bills during 1944–48. The casino's lawyer also managed Burke's political campaigns, perhaps explaining why Burke ignored not only the Colony Club, but other casinos including the Hickory Club, the Swan Club, and the Valley Club.

Rutkowski stormed the Colony Club in December 1949, catching 250 gamblers at the tables. The club's safe yielded a letter from Alvin Giesey, addressed to Kentucky gambler Sam Schrader at the Beverly Hills Country Club — a circumstance Giesey professed himself unable to explain. Lenz stalled for nine months, challenging Rutkowski's search warrant, then pled guilty and paid a $500 fine.

In Youngstown, meanwhile, Chief of Police Edward Allen found himself "engaged in more or less of a continuous battle" with the Licavoli gang, but he saw no link between mafiosi and the Cleveland Four. Of Dalitz and company, he said, "Those men I don't believe would resort to murder, organized murder, in order to protect their financial interests." They were merely "professional gamblers," Allen insisted, while Licavoli's Sicilians were "organized criminals."

Sheriff George Timiney of Lucas County suffered from a similar naiveté, influenced by his 25-year friendship with local gamblers. Questioned in 1951, Timiney admitted knowledge of several casinos within his jurisdiction. They included the Victory Club ("not a very big place") and the T&T Club ("a wire place"), while the Pines Club and Webster Inn were full-service "gambling joints and bootlegging places." None of that inspired Timiney to raid the clubs, but he *was* willing to accept campaign advice and contributions from "retired tavern keeper" James McGrath, as well as Mob defense attorney Edwin Lynch.

* * *

At 12:15 A.M. on September 3, 1947, ten bandits invaded the Mounds Club during its second dinner show. Actor Peter Lind Hayes was on stage with wife Mary Healy, when four men armed with submachine guns entered the dining room. Six more rushed the casino and corralled startled gamblers. Manager Buck Schaffner opened the club's safe at gunpoint. Estimates of the gang's total haul, including pocket money and jewelry seized from club patrons, range from $250,000 to $500,000.

The police reaction was peculiar. As later described by Governor Lausche, "The sheriff of Lake County did not want to hear about it; the prosecutor laid back." The Mounds Club's owners filed no official complaint, and no police manhunt ensued. Local newspapers *did* report the event, proclaiming it "the first robbery at the Mounds Club in its seventeen years of existence."

But it was not the last heist at a syndicate joint. Within days, a six-man gang raided the Continental Club in Chesapeake, escaping with an estimated $60,000. Once again, law enforcement officers were stricken by a strange bout of lethargy.

Which does not mean the bandits went unpunished.

Long after the fact, G-men heard "through the grapevine" how rough justice was administered. Moe Dalitz used his influence within the underworld to learn the bandits' names. A trial of sorts was held, sentence was passed, and manhunters hit the ground running. By March 1948, it is said, every one of the robbers was tracked down and killed. To this day, they remain anonymous, their graves unmarked.

* * *

The Lausche offensive in Ohio hastened relocation of the Mob's casinos into other states. One outpost was the Huntington Athletic Club, in West Virginia. Brothers Howard and William

Swarts, formerly employed by Shimmy Patton at the Continental Club, paid $100,000 for an old hotel in Huntington and spent another $300,000 transforming it into a plush casino. Its profits fell short of projections, however, so Dalitz looked for greener pastures in the Mountain State.

He settled on White Sulphur Springs, where natural hot springs and the historic Greenbrier resort had lured visitors since 1758. The Cleveland Four sent Abe Goodman — one of Sam Tucker's in-laws — to scout the terrain in April 1948. Goodman found property for sale, its $40,000 asking price divided equally among Dalitz, Tucker, Morris Kleinman, Lou Rothkopf, and Tom McGinty. Architects drew plans for a hotel to rival the 650-room Greenbrier, with a lavish casino attached.

But then, the planners hit a snag. The Greenbrier's owners, they discovered, also owned the Chesapeake & Ohio Railroad, which had carried Moe's bootleg whiskey during prohibition. Despite that history, C&O executives were livid at the thought of competition for the tourist trade. Any attempt to build a gambling den, they threatened, would produce indictments. Rather than pursue the matter, Moe retreated to Kentucky, where officials had no quaint ideas about enforcement of the laws.

Campbell County was a perfect case in point. Sheriff Ray Diebold, prior to his election, spent fifteen years as a traveling "good will man" for Cincinnati's Hudepol Brewery, stocking casinos along with legitimate taverns. As sheriff, Diebold pled ignorance of state laws requiring monthly inspection reports on saloons within his jurisdiction. Police Chief George Gugel was equally oblivious to gambling in "liberal" Newport. A 25-year friend of Red Masterson, Gugel left gambling investigations to a myopic chief of detectives who handled "outside work," while Gugel devoted himself to jail maintenance.

Despite official collusion, Mob operations in Kentucky were not trouble-free. Brothers Rip and Taylor Farley retired from pimping to work for Sleepout Louie Levinson, but Rip had a wild streak. In February 1946 he stole $2,500 from the Yorkshire Club at gunpoint, neglecting to wear a mask. Four days later, a drive-by shooting dropped both Farleys outside the Flamingo; Rip died on the spot, while Taylor survived a shot to the chest. Chief Gugel called the shooting a bungled holdup, but Taylor craved vengeance. War was averted when one of the hitmen, Aaron "Danny Meyers" Meyervitz, was killed by persons unknown in Pittsburgh. Public outcry led to revocation of the Flamingo's liquor license, but the move backfired. Reopening days later, the Flamingo saved money on bribes, since state liquor inspectors were barred from entering an unlicensed joint.

Meanwhile, Buck Brady's Primrose Club had grown sufficiently to steal its share of gamblers from the larger Beverly Hills Country Club. Red Masterson, speaking for Cleveland, warned Brady against further poaching, "or else." With the Farley murder in mind, Brady decided that the best defense was a preemptive strike.

On August 5, 1946, Masterson left the Merchants Club in his new Cadillac. A block from the casino, when he stopped for a red light, a second car pulled alongside and its passenger called out, "Hi, Red." Masterson turned to find a shotgun pointed at his face, but the close range betrayed his would-be killer. Instead of spreading to shatter Red's skull, most of the buckshot hit the Caddy's window frame. Red bailed out, while his Caddy struck cars at the curb. Several gunmen fled the other car, which also crashed.

While an ambulance rushed Masterson to Dayton's hospital, Newport police scoured the scene for suspects. They found Buck Brady in an outhouse, with a rifle and a pistol lying nearby. Brady said he was strolling through the neighborhood when he heard shots, explaining, "I always run when I hear shooting." Charged with disturbing the peace, Brady faced a hometown jury. George Remus emerged from retirement to testify as a character witness, calling his former employee "the salt of the earth." When Masterson claimed inability to recognize the gunmen, charges were dismissed. Brady subsequently sold the Primrose to his Cleveland adversaries and retired to a Florida citrus plantation. Moe Dalitz renamed Brady's Primrose the Latin Quarter, and installed paroled arsonist Dave Whitfield as manager.

Enter Frank "Screw" Andrews, a Cincinnati native who logged the first of forty-plus arrests at age thirteen, when he killed a bystander while playing with a loaded gun. After World War II, he reopened the old Remus booze routes through northern Kentucky, shipping untaxed liquor from Tennessee and the Carolinas. In 1947, bankrolled by Mike Coppolla, Andrews expanded to invade the Newport numbers racket.

As in Depression-era Cleveland and Detroit, black gamblers dominated Kentucky's numbers. Major players included Melvin Clark, Steve Payne, and A.L. Schmidt. Andrews moved first against Payne, bribing Newport police to raid his Sportsman's Club in May 1947. Payne hung on until early 1948, when he was taken for a one-way ride and dumped in a ditch outside town. Within a month, ownership of the Sportsman's Club passed to Coppolla associate Irving "Nig" Devine, then to Andrews. In August 1948, City Solicitor (and Screw's attorney) Morris Weintraub raided Schmidt's operation. Schmidt won acquittal at trial, but saw the light and went to work for Andrews.

Melvin Clark proved more resistant. Andrews sent a black employee, Oliver Payne, to pick a fight with Clark, on grounds that Clark had brought a white woman to Newport's all-black Alibi Club, but Payne was slow on the draw. Clark killed him and blamed Andrews for setting up the duel. Indicted for murder, Clark beat the rap but was "probated out of Kentucky" by white authorities.

Next door, reformers organized the Kenton County Protestant Association to oppose gambling. The group went public in January 1947, and four months later presented grand jurors with proof of local corruption. No indictments followed, prompting the KCPA to seek disbarment of county prosecutor Ulie Howard, who died in October 1947, with charges of misfeasance pending against him. KCPA leaders invited local lawmen to a public meeting in March 1950, but those who attended remained noncommittal.

The sluggish reaction was no surprise. Alfred Schild, a Covington's police chief since 1939, doubled as president of the local Peace Officers Association, accepting advertisements for casinos in the POA's newsletter. Exposure of a local "profit sharing" plan in 1951 revealed that Covington commissioners received $100 weekly from gamblers, while the mayor got $150, and city detectives pocketed $150 per month.

Another reform group, the Newport Civic Association, organized in 1949 with the goal of finally enforcing anti-gambling injunctions which police had ignored for the past six years. In 1951, Newport prosecutor Fred Warren told the Senate that "gambling has been eradicated ... except for, oh, minor cheating that may go on, which has been reduced," but investigators easily disproved the claim.

* * *

Florida remained another land of opportunity for Dalitz and his partners in the post-war years. Sam Tucker left Kentucky "for my health" in 1948, settling in Surfside, near Miami Beach. It must have felt like Old Home Week to Sambo, with so many refugees from Cleveland and Detroit already there ahead of him.

One thriving firm was the S&G Syndicate, organized in 1944 by Purple Gang survivor Sam Cohen and four other Florida bookmakers. By 1948 the group held betting concessions at 200 hotels in South Florida. Formerly independent bookies paid half of their weekly take to S&G headquarters. According to its own ledgers, the syndicate booked more than $26.5 million in bets during 1948, reporting a net income of $466,504. Outside observers called those figures conservative, estimating a yearly gross of $30-$40 million, with profits of $4-$8 million per year. Sam Cohen's brother Benjamin, a lawyer, represented S&G bookies in court and spearheaded the recall movement against Miami Beach's anti-gambling councilman Melvin Richard, aided by Mickey McBride's radio station WMIE.

As for McBride, he reaped huge profits from Florida real estate with partner Al Polizzi. Asked about the ethics of collaborating with Polizzi, McBride replied, "In my way of thinking, he is all right. He is a good citizen." Polizzi assessed himself by saying, "What somebody else considers wrong, I might think it is right. Maybe there is something wrong with me." Their joint projects in 1948 included the H&I Holding Company, the University Estates in Coral Gables, and a Shriners golf course.

Polizzi, independent of McBride, shared ownership in Miami's Sands Hotel with John Angersola and three convicted Philadelphia bookies. Daniel Sullivan, director of Dade County's crime commission, branded the Sands a hangout for members of Nig Rosen's Philadelphia syndicate, while the nearby Wofford Hotel "became the meeting place for notorious racketeers and gangsters from all over the country, and headquarters for [Frank] Erickson's very extensive bookmaking operations in Florida." Dade County Sheriff James Sullivan responded by naming Wofford manager Abe Allenberg an honorary sheriff's deputy.

Another of Polizzi's enterprises, Thompson & Polizzi Construction, built much of Coral Gables in the post-war decade. Forrest Thompson and Polizzi formed the company in 1947, assisted by attorney Nick Mangine, brother of mafioso Vincent "Doc" Mangine. Together, Thompson and Polizzi built Joe Massei's $90,000 mansion, two theaters, an A&P Food Fair supermarket, and various other Coral Gables landmarks.

Gambling remained a primary Syndicate interest in Florida. Joe Massei ran a dice game with William "Lefty Clark" Bischoff in Palm Beach County. Mert Wertheimer, as one-third owner of the Colonial Club, reported net profits of $222,800 during 1948's three-month winter season. Moe Dalitz, questioned in 1951, initially denied any Florida gambling investments, then hedged and granted that he "might have had" an interest in the Frolics Club. "I don't remember," Moe maintained, adding, "I knew who the operators were." Moe went on to perjure himself, claiming, "I have only vacationed in Florida once in my life." In fact, official records document at least two visits: once in January 1938, when G-men saw him with Little Augie Paisano at the Frolics Club, and again in December 1945, for his marriage to Toni.

* * *

The post-war years witnessed a new "crime wave" in the United States. FBI reports claimed a 20-percent increase in various offenses (none of them Mob-related) during 1944–46. J. Edgar Hoover and Attorney General Tom Clark blamed juvenile delinquents, citing a 198-percent rise in arrests of teenage girls since 1939. Even so, ex-G-man Virgil Peterson encouraged creation of citizens' crime commissions patterned on Chicago's, to look more closely at organized rackets.

One governor who listened, despite his own suspect associations, was California's Earl Warren. Warren's California Crime Commission reported that New York's Frank Costello had placed slot machines throughout the state, while Attorney General Frederick Howser turned a blind eye. Howser went hunting for slots in Kern County, but claimed to find none. The crime commission followed and found scores of one-armed bandits, owned by the Kern

County Music Operators Association. Kern's sheriff pleaded ignorance of any gambling, and requested proof from the commission's files. Meanwhile, the KCMOA levied "special assessments" on its subscribers to support police fund-raising efforts and sponsor the California Highway Patrol's pistol team.

Liquor and gambling went together in California. Alfred Hart paid his dues as a Chicago beer runner, then partnered with Outfit leaders Joe Fusco and Charles Gioe in Gold Seal Liquors before moving to California as proprietor of Glencoe Distilleries & Pacific Brewing Company. Hart logged eight gambling arrests in Los Angeles during 1928–31, then built San Diego County's Del Mar Race Track in 1937, with co-investors Bing Crosby, Pat O'Brien, and Paramount Studios. One of Hart's best customers and closest friends at Del Mar was J. Edgar Hoover, despite the fact that FBI files said "Hart has a reputation of associating with known hoodlums." Ben Siegel had a box at the Del Mar Turf Club and persuaded Hart to invest $75,000 in his Las Vegas dream resort, the Flamingo. Hart also loaned $7,000 to Mickey Cohen for his bookie operation, launched with hustler Jack Morton. Morton, a friend of Cary Grant, Al Jolson, and other Hollywood celebrities, had Del Mar Turf Club privileges that boosted Cohen's status in the horseracing fraternity.

Early in 1947, Cohen moved the operation to a haberdashery on Sunset Boulevard. The shift placed him outside LAPD's jurisdiction, thereby narrowing his bribes to the sheriff's department. Cohen bought a fleet of fast, expensive cars complete with secret compartments for money and weapons, moved wife Lavonne into a $150,000 Brentwood home, and spent another $50,000 furnishing the place. His closet ran the length of the master bedroom, housing more than 200 suits.

Part of California's problem in the post-war era was the quality of its elected officials. Fred Howser was perennially blind to Mob incursions, both as L.A.'s district attorney and as state attorney general. Future governor Edmund Brown, a gambler's son, did no better as San Francisco's D.A. Richard Milhous Nixon was the poster child for corrupt California politics. Nixon attended North Carolina's Duke University Law School, where he burglarized the dean's office during his last semester. In 1937, while working for his first law firm, Nixon bungled a civil case so egregiously that Judge Alfred Paonessa threatened him with disbarment for unethical behavior.

Nixon rubbed shoulders with mobsters in Florida and Cuba on his 1940 honeymoon. Two years later, he joined the navy and served in the Pacific. On Green Island, in the Solomons, he ran a high-stakes poker game and won enough money to partially bankroll his first bid for Congress. Even so, he needed help to beat incumbent Jerry Voorhis in 1946, and Nixon got it from the Mob.

Early that year, Nixon's supporters offered attorney Murray Chotiner $580 per week to manage their candidate. Chotiner and his brother Jack were well Mob-connected, defending a reported 221 gambling cases during 1949–52. One of the first connections Chotiner forged for Nixon was a link to Mickey Cohen, who donated $5,000 to Nixon's 1946 campaign. Chotiner also set Nixon on the Red-baiting path that would define his career, branding Voorhis "a friend of the communists." It worked, as frightened voters sent Nixon off to Washington and a seat on the witch-hunting House Un-American Activities Committee. By 1955, when *Behind the Scenes* magazine dubbed Chotiner "Nixon's secret link to the underworld," Nixon was Vice President of the United States.

A quarter-century later, Professor Trowbridge Ford of Boston's Holy Cross College discovered another of Nixon's Mob links. A 1947 FBI memo included a G-man's affidavit reading: "It is my sworn statement that one Jack Rubenstein of Chicago, noted as a potential witness for hearings of the House Committee on Un-American Activities, is performing information functions for the staff of Congressman Richard Nixon.... It is requested Rubenstein not be called for open testimony in the aforementioned hearings." Before year's end, Rubenstein moved from Chicago to Dallas, Texas, and changed his name to Jack Ruby.

In 1950 Nixon challenged Democratic congresswoman Helen Douglas for a U.S. Senate seat. Nixon went back to the Mob for support, including $75,000 raised by Mickey Cohen from a banquet in L.A.'s Knickerbocker Hotel. According to Cohen, "It was all gamblers from Vegas.... There wasn't a legitimate person in the room." When the donors fell twenty grand short of their quota, Cohen's gunmen barred the exits until they raised the remainder. Cohen's lawyer, Sam Rummel, leased Nixon's L.A. campaign headquarters, with Mickey paying the bills. Cohen later claimed that his support for Nixon was inspired by orders from Meyer Lansky.

Nevada senator Pat McCarran, the gamblers' friend (Library of Congress).

* * *

Much of California's daily action fell to Mickey Cohen in the post-war years, as Bugsy Siegel was distracted by Nevada — home of legal gambling since 1931. Reno was then Nevada's largest city, controlled by bootleggers in prohibition, and by gamblers afterward. Las Vegas, far to the south, was little more than a whistle stop on the railroad line between Chicago and Los Angeles until work began on nearby Hoover Dam. A sudden influx of construction workers spiked demand for liquor, prostitutes, and games of chance. Casino licensing was localized and hit-or-miss until 1945, when the state Tax Commission assumed control of "gaming."

Nevada politics represented a classic old boy's club, and the biggest old boy on the block was Senator Patrick McCarran, a Reno native born in 1876. Elected to the U.S. Senate in 1932, McCarran earned a reputation as a bitter enemy of communism and unfettered immigration. He also opposed any federal moves against gambling and organized crime, a side effect of his friendship with sundry notorious mobsters.

Among those were the hoodlums who colonized Reno during and after prohibition. William Graham and partner James McKay, ex-convicts who served time for mail fraud in New York, built Reno's Bank Club in 1926 and managed the town's largest brothel. They welcomed Al Capone and Doc Stacher as investors, while Capone cousin Charles Fischetti helped finance their Cal-Neva Lodge at Lake Tahoe. Purple Gang survivors owned a stake in Reno's Riverside Hotel, while brothers Mert and Lou Wertheimer built their Nevada Club with $975,000 from FDR's Reconstruction Finance Corporation, ceding management to convicted Michigan gamblers Lincoln Fitzgerald and Daniel Sullivan. Fitzgerald barely survived a shotgun ambush outside his home, in November 1949, but he pacified investigators by forgiving his would-be killers, and Judge Harry Watson declined to extradite Fitzgerald for trial on pending charges in Michigan.

Two Vegas landmarks opened for business in 1941. First, attorney Clifford Jones teamed with Marion Hicks and J.K. Houssels to build the El Cortez downtown. Hicks befriended Kirk Kerkorian, a Los Angeles entrepreneur whose fledgling charter airline service got a boost from desert hops to Las Vegas. Bugsy Siegel bought half-ownership for $600,000, then sold it to brothers Dave and Charles Berman for $1.3 million. Meyer Lansky received a $160,000 "finder's fee."

The first casino on Highway 91—later the Las Vegas Strip—was El Rancho Vegas, opened in April 1941 by Thomas Hull. In 1945, gambler Wilbur Clark purchased 25 percent of the El Rancho for 10 percent of its future net earnings. By 1947, Purple Gang alumnus Charles Resnick owned part of the resort. Cleveland's first man on the scene, in 1943, was Carl Cohen, who later said, "I came to Vegas with all I had to my name, a thorough background in gambling." In fact, Cohen was far from destitute, in either cash or friends with influence.

In 1945, "big-idea man" Billy Wilkerson, founder of the *Hollywood Reporter,* bought 33 acres on Highway 91 to build another carpet joint. His dream was going nowhere until Bugsy Siegel surfaced in November, purchasing the land for $63,000. Wilkerson remained a one-third partner, promised "operational control" of the Flamingo Hotel and Casino. Siegel estimated the resort would cost $1 million to complete. Eastern mobsters signed on to bankroll construction, but Siegel was soon distracted by a national struggle for control of the racing wire service.

* * *

By the time James Ragen Sr. brought Mickey McBride into Continental Press, he was at odds with the Chicago Outfit. Mob leaders offered Ragen $100,000 for control of his goldmine, with permission to remain as manager, but Ragen declined. Worse yet, he furnished G-men and local prosecutors with a ninety-page rundown of his feud with the Outfit.

On November 4, 1945, Jack Dragna phoned New York, demanding a meeting with Frank Costello, Joe Adonis, Meyer Lansky, Charles Fischetti, and Ben Siegel to settle ownership of California's wire service. Siegel refused to attend, telling Costello, "Things stay the way it is. No deal with any of the Chicago dagos. If they want the wires, let them try and get them. They'll have to go through me." Chicago responded in March 1946, creating Trans-American Publishing to compete with Continental Press. From that point on, confusion reigns in various accounts of the wire-service war.

The war's first shots were fired in California. On May 2, 1946, Mickey Cohen triggerman Harold Rothman killed holdout Paulie Gibbons in Beverly Hills. Five months later, Rothman slew Gibbons partners Benny Gamson and George Levinson. Cohen personally killed rival Max Shaman, persuading D.A. Fred Howser that his action constituted self-defense.

Meanwhile, James Ragen Sr. ran out of luck in Chicago. Badly wounded in a drive-by shotgun ambush on June 24, 1946, Ragen lingered until August 14, when he was killed by soft drinks spiked with mercury. Ex-G-man Bill Roemer told author Anthony Summers,

"The Ragen affair is a very, very significant moment for any study of J. Edgar Hoover and organized crime. When Ragen started talking, the FBI opened a real operation against organized crime in the city for the first time ever. But as soon as Ragen was killed, Hoover dropped the investigation. For eleven years afterwards, that was the end of it."

The wire service war dragged on for seven months beyond Ragen's death. Early negotiations faltered, and while an FBI report from August 1946 claimed "Cleveland key figures" including "Moe Davie" were bound for Chicago, subsequent airport surveillance "failed to reflect" their arrival. At last, in March 1947, James Ragen Jr. visited the McBrides in Florida, asking Eddie to buy him out of Continental. Eddie agreed "to take a shot at it," since, as his father said, he "didn't have to have any money" for the transaction. As finally agreed in May, Ragen Sr.'s estate received $215,000 in nine annual payments, plus 6 percent interest; Ragen Jr. accepted $130,000 in ten yearly payments, also at 6 percent, plus $25,000 spread over five years to ensure non-competition. Aside from $16,000 personally paid by Mickey McBride, all payments came from Continental's net income. While Eddie McBride was the owner of record, his father testified that Eddie played no real part in the business, leaving Continental's management to Mickey and brother-in-law Tom Kelly.

With its business concluded, Trans-American disbanded in June 1947. The war's last casualty was renegade California gambler George Bruneman, who refused to join the Siegel-Cohen network. Three ambushes failed to drop Bruneman, before he was finally killed in a local restaurant. Siegel allegedly demanded a $2 million bonus for his part in the wire-service war, but the ultimatum came at a bad time for Bugsy, beleaguered by problems on every side.

* * *

The Flamingo was supposed to be a gold mine, but it turned into a quagmire. Siegel's partners were tight-fisted, when their investments produced no immediate returns. Gus Greenbaum helped Siegel borrow money from Kemper Marley's Valley National Bank, in Phoenix, where Robert Goldwater served as a director from 1947 onward.

But it was never enough.

Del Webb Construction built the Flamingo, acceding to Siegel's most extravagant demands. Proprietor Delbert Webb earned his fortune during World War II, building relocation camps for Japanese-Americans, rubbing shoulders with Howard Hughes, the Goldwater brothers, and Moe Dalitz's friend Bing Crosby. At the Flamingo, some critics claimed Webb's employees were looting the site, but nothing was proved. When

Virginia Hill, mistress of the Mob (National Archives).

Las Vegas, 1948: Right to left: Sam Tucker, Moe Dalitz, Toni Dalitz, unidentified companions (Toni Clark Drago).

Webb voiced concerns for his safety to Siegel, Bugsy replied, "Don't worry. We only kill each other."

And then, there was Virginia Hill.

She moved from Lipscomb, Alabama, to Chicago at seventeen, working as a prostitute at the 1933 World's Fair, then attached herself to Jake Guzik lieutenant Joseph Epstein, moving on in turn to Mob luminaries including Frank Nitti, Tony Accardo, Joe Adonis, Frank Costello — and, some say, Moe Dalitz. Gus Russo describes Moe as Hill's "first lover," while declaring that their affair is "still known only to a handful of insiders." Hill explained her appeal by calling herself "the best damn cocksucker in the United States," but she also served as a "mule," carrying bags of cash to Switzerland on Mob-financed vacations. Sometime in 1945–46, Hill fell into a semblance of love with Ben Siegel. Siegel's investors fretted over Hill's trips to Europe, suspecting that some of their money had vanished across the Atlantic.

Ex-agent Bill Roemer claims that Moe Dalitz visited Vegas in 1946, dispatched "on the sly" by Lansky and Costello to assess Siegel's progress. Ex-wife Toni supports that story, placing her move with Moe from Detroit "shortly after" they adopted Andrew. According to historians Sally Denton and Roger Morris, Moe reported that Bugsy was stealing from the Mob. Swiss contacts confirmed Hill's deposits of $500,000 in Zurich. In September 1946, Siegel received another $1 million-plus from Lansky, pushing the Flamingo's tab $5 million over budget. Lansky warned Siegel that Dalitz and Longy Zwillman were growing impatient, with Cleveland casting covetous eyes on Las Vegas. Hank Messick claims Siegel replied, "Shit on them. The Flamingo is my baby.... They'll get their cut, but I don't want them butting in on my territory. Let them go to Reno if they want to."

Lansky telephoned Lou Rothkopf. "It's that bitch," Rothkopf opined. "She's driven him out of his mind." Rothkopf called Mickey Cohen with orders to keep close watch on Hill and Siegel, while accountants studied the Flamingo's books. In Vegas, Carl Cohen stood by, slated to serve as one of the Flamingo's pit bosses. Lansky watched from Florida, while storm clouds gathered over Cuba.

* * *

In May 1945, New York's parole board recommended freedom for Lucky Luciano. Governor Dewey agreed in January 1946, contingent upon Lucky's deportation to Italy. On February 9, aboard the S.S. *Laura Keene,* Luciano enjoyed a *bon voyage* party attended by mobsters Moe Dalitz, Meyer Lansky, Joe Adonis, Frank Costello, Albert Anastasia, Willie Moretti, Joe Bonanno, Carlo Gambino, Phil Kastel, Owney Madden, Longy Zwillman and Ben Siegel. Immigration agents had promised the press a shipboard interview with Lucky, but Anastasia's longshoremen held reporters at bay until the ship sailed.

Luciano soon resurfaced in Havana, where recent changes in leadership failed to discomfit the Mob. Fulgencio Batista, barred by law from succeeding himself as president in 1944, retired to Florida, ceding control to President Ramón Grau San Martin and his protégé, Carlos Prío Socarrás. In Havana, from his suite at Meyer Lansky's Hotel Nacional, Luciano tackled problems that included turmoil in the New York Mafia, wartime disruption of heroin traffic from Europe, and the unrest caused by Siegel's Flamingo.

On December 22, 1946, Lansky closed his Hotel Nacional for a Mob summit conference. Mobsters from every part of the U.S. flew down to discuss their concerns with Luciano. Dalitz came from Cleveland, mingling with Lansky, Costello, Anastasia, Adonis, Bonanno, Willie Moretti, Zwillman, Joe Profaci, Vito Genovese, Doc Stacher, Carlos Marcello, Tony Accardo, and Florida's Santo Trafficante Sr. Siegel was notable for his absence. Luciano received "Christmas presents" exceeding $200,000 in cash.

When they got down to business, Lucky discussed establishment of a new heroin route from Italy, through France to Cuba and America. Next, he proposed a peaceful settlement to the increasing rivalry between New York mafiosi Anastasia and Genovese. The peace that Lucky dictated endured for a decade, before it was drowned in blood.

At last, the delegates addressed the "Siegel situation." Lansky acknowledged that Bugsy was $5 million over budget, but he dismissed the overrun as "peanuts" compared to potential profits. Dalitz countered with a warning that Siegel might flee to Europe if his brainchild collapsed. Stories differ on what happened next. Some authors contend that a vote sentenced Siegel to death, with a stay of execution until the Flamingo's opening night. Lansky biographer Dennis Eisenberg says that Meyer and Longy Zwillman left Havana with appeals for Siegel to reform "before it was too late."

* * *

Siegel's Flamingo, barely half finished, opened on December 26, 1946. Lew Wasserman sent band leader Xavier Cugat to headline the party, but freak rainstorms grounded Kirk Kerkorian's planes in L.A., preventing most of Hollywood's glitterati from attending. Siegel tried again on December 28, with Lucille Ball, William Holden, and others on hand, but the casino lost $300,000 in its first week and closed in the second.

In early February, during a typical quarrel, Siegel beat and raped Virginia Hill at her home in Beverly Hills. Soon afterward, crooner Frank Sinatra flew to Havana with mobster Rocco Fischetti, bearing another suitcase of cash for Luciano. American reporters learned of the visit, producing calls for Lucky's deportation back to Italy. Cuban police took Luciano into custody on February 23, and he left Havana aboard a Turkish freighter on March 29.

Meanwhile, L.A. G-man (later county sheriff) Peter Pitchess claimed that Siegel turned stool-pigeon for the feds. Pitchess told Anthony Summers, "When Siegel took it upon himself that he would like to talk to me, I was afraid even to tell the Bureau…. Siegel gave me information on his enemies, but we just put it in some intelligence file — we didn't dare call it 'Mafia.' That, we'd been told, didn't exist." If true, this breach of gangland etiquette was grounds for execution, in and of itself.

Del Webb finished the Flamingo on March 1, 1947, and the resort reopened on March 27. Within three weeks, the red ink turned to black. In May, Siegel's casino earned $300,000 profit. Siegel may have been elated, but his time was running out.

In June 1947, Virginia Hill flew to Chicago, then on to Paris. Siegel returned to L.A. on June 19, to find Hill's mansion occupied by brother Charles Hill and his girlfriend. Siegel spent most of his last 24 hours with Allen Smiley, described in some accounts as a spy for Jack Dragna. Smiley was seated on the living room couch with Siegel at 10:45 P.M. on June 20, when a sniper fired nine rapid shots through a nearby window. Four bullets struck Siegel, killing him instantly. Moments later, in Vegas, mobster Moe Sedway took charge of the Flamingo. With Gus Greenbaum, Dave Berman, Charles Resnick of the Purple Gang, and Minnesota's Israel "Icepick Willie" Alderman, Sedway ran the Flamingo until 1954.

Various authors have named Siegel's killer in print — Frankie Carbo, Dragna gunman Eddie Cannizzaro, even Mickey Cohen — but who gave the order, and why? Was Bugsy killed for stealing, for informing on the Mob, or was there another reason?

Bill Roemer claimed Moe Dalitz's report on Siegel's embezzlement "was the major reason" behind Bugsy's death. Others also fingered Moe, but claim he acted from a different motive. Author Nick Tosches, writing for *Vanity Fair* in 1997, quoted an alleged remark by Sidney Korshak to Hollywood screenwriter Edward Anhalt. Korshak said, "You know that bullshit about Ben being killed because he spent too much money? Absolute fiction." According to Korshak, Siegel's death was ordered by "the guy from Detroit … the guy from the Purple Gang." The mobster in question — presumed by Tosches and Gus Russo to be Dalitz, Hill's "first lover" — was "very offended" by Bugsy's beating of Hill. "He warned Siegel, and Siegel paid no attention to the warning, and they whacked him," Korshak claimed. Lew Wasserman biographer Kathleen Sharp says that "Wasserman knew" of the contract on Siegel, issued to defend "one of Dalitz's old flames."

True or false?

Hill never spoke a public word concerning Dalitz in her life, which ended with an overdose of sleeping pills in March 1966. Moe, likewise, never mentioned Hill in any context during his rare interviews. Korshak, although a Mob insider, had a tendency to lie, as demonstrated by his false tale of promoting Moe to officer status in World War II. The truth, like so much else about Moe's life, may never be revealed.

* * *

The years immediately after Siegel's murder were a period of change and challenge for the Mob. California was a crucible of violence, exacerbated by Bugsy's death. Mickey Cohen, believing Siegel's killers were holed up at L.A.'s Roosevelt Hotel, invaded the lobby with twin .45 automatics, firing shots into the ceiling and demanding that the gunmen meet him

Bugsy Siegel in death (Library of Congress).

outside for a duel. When no one appeared, Cohen fled the scene with sirens wailing in his ears.

Unknown to Cohen, LAPD had thoroughly bugged his Brentwood mansion before Mickey and his wife moved in. Cohen eventually found the hidden microphones, but not before officers eavesdropped on conversations with Tony Milano, Lou Rothkopf, and Louis

Gus Greenbaum (right) and Moe Sedway (center), shown here with an unidentified companion, controlled the Flamingo after Siegel's murder (Library of Congress).

"Babe" Triscaro (later an Ohio Teamsters leader under Jimmy Hoffa). In October 1947, Cohen told Rothkopf, "Lou, I'm afraid to show my face.... You have been so goddamned good to me." In another chat with Rothkopf, in February 1948, Cohen told Rothkopf that "the deal was well in hand [and] that everything was O.K. on the west coast."

In fact, it was not.

Cohen's abiding problem was Jack Dragna, who made repeated attempts on Mickey's life. Once an assailant armed with a lead pipe cornered Cohen in a cardroom, forcing Mickey to flee through a window. After a machine-gun ambush two blocks from his home, Cohen insisted that Lavonne travel in a separate car when they went out together, telling her, "You gotta understand, honey, there's a war on." In August 1948, gunmen raided Cohen's haberdashery, killing Hooky Rothman and wounding two other victims, while Mickey slipped out the backdoor. Another ambush, at a hospital benefit, was scrubbed when Cohen showed up with Harry Cooper, an aide to state attorney general Fred Howser. In June 1949, Jimmy Fratianno and Louie Dragna planted a bomb under Cohen's bedroom, but a defective fuse spared Mickey's life. On July 20, 1949, Cohen and his entourage left Sherry's, on Sunset Boulevard, and walked into a blaze of gunfire. Harry Cooper was wounded, while gunman Neddie Herbert died, and Cohen took a bullet in the shoulder.

Frank Costello intervened, trying to negotiate a truce, but he was unsuccessful. Cohen won public sympathy in 1949, when he sent seven goons to beat up radio repairman Alfred

Mob banquet in Los Angeles, 1948. Clockwise from lower left; Mrs. Joe Bommarito, Pete Licavoli, Grace Licavoli, Lou Rothkopf, Mickey Cohen, Petey Mack, Hooky Rothman, comedian Joe E. Lewis, Neddie Herbert, Blanche Rothkopf, Lavonne Cohen, Sally Herbert (National Archives).

Pearson. Pearson's crime consisted of suing an elderly customer over an inflated bill, forcing foreclosure on her home at auction, which Pearson bought for $26.50. Cohen's sluggers, dubbed "the Seven Dwarves" by local newspapers, were caught in the act of hammering Pearson, and Mickey — hailed as "Snow White" in Hearst headlines — mortgaged his home to post their $300,000 bond.

Dragna next decided to bankrupt Cohen by killing the Seven Dwarves, thus forcing Mickey to forfeit their bonds. Two of the seven, Frank Niccoli and David Ogul, were murdered and secretly buried by October 1949. Cohen lost $75,000, but jurors acquitted his surviving soldiers. Enraged, Dragna bombed Cohen's home in February 1950, but wounded only a teenage neighbor. Ten months later, shotgunners blasted Cohen attorney Sam Rummel outside his home.

Despite his long war with the Mafia, Cohen stayed busy. An FBI report from October 1949 declares that "information received on the telephone taps and microphone installations in the residence of MICKEY COHEN ... reflected frequent communications and associations between COHEN and the prominent members of the gambling syndicate and the Mayfield Road Mob." G-men specifically named Lou Rothkopf and John Scalish. Cohen later admit-

Members of the Dragna gang await questioning in the bombing of Mickey Cohen's home. Left to right: **Louis Dragna, Tom Dragna, Frank Dragna, Guillermo Adamo, Paul Dragna** (National Archives).

ted running six or seven illegal casinos in L.A. County, plus three more inside city limits. One was located in the Ambassador Hotel, owned by Myer Schine and his son David (later a colleague of Red-hunters Joseph McCarthy and Roy Cohn). Cohen also ran a casino at Lake Arrowhead, in San Bernardino County.

Despite its mayhem, L.A. still appealed to Moe Dalitz. While Cohen fought his battles in the streets, Moe and Morris Kleinman leased the Moulin Rouge, on Sunset Boulevard, from Doc Stacher. The club later passed to Frank Sennes, a friend and employee who served Moe well in Cleveland, Newport, and Las Vegas.

* * *

Cuba's underworld survived Luciano's 1947 deportation, despite the brief retirement of Fulgencio Batista. Carlos Prío succeeded Ramón Grau in 1948 and continued his tradition of corruption. Batista campaigned for a Cuban senate seat that year, and won the election without leaving Florida. President Prío barred Batista's return until Meyer Lansky placed $250,000 in Prío's Swiss bank account. Thus pacified, Prío allowed Lansky to build a new Riviera casino, while ownership of the Nacional passed to the Cleveland Four.

In far-off Phoenix, citizens rebelled against a city council that had fired thirty city managers within 35 years. Establishment of a city charter in 1948 insulated city managers from the panel's malicious whims, but it smelled like business as usual in 1949, when critics accused manager James Deppe of selling favors. Reformers nominated their own slate of candidates, oddly including Harry Rosenzweig and Barry Goldwater, whose brother's bank helped finance the Flamingo. Barry admitted that he "didn't particularly object" to gambling or prostitution, as long as Phoenix had a stable government. In that, he succeeded. Phoenix took honors as an "All American City" in 1951, and Goldwater won a Senate seat the following year.

Meanwhile, corruption flourished. Willie Bioff, Chicago's point man in the IATSE extortion scandal, left prison to seek a healthier climate and wound up in Phoenix, befriending Barry Goldwater and Gus Greenbaum. James Hensley went to work for Kemper Marley after World War II, as general manager of Marley's United Liquor. In 1948, despite the best efforts of attorney William Rehnquist, Hensley and 51 others were convicted of falsifying records to conceal illegal whiskey sales. Hensley received a six-month sentence and was banned from the booze trade, but Marley later put him in charge of a beer dealership, valued at $200 million in the 21st century. Hensley's daughter married future U.S. Senator and presidential candidate John McCain.

Transplanted mobster Willie Bioff befriended Arizona's elite after serving time in prison for extortion (Library of Congress).

On those rare occasions when Arizona journalists tackled the Mob, they focused almost exclusively on Pete Licavoli and Joe Bonanno, in Tucson. Few noticed Game Boy Miller, handling Cleveland's action from Tucson's Santa Rita Hotel, with help from Butts Lowe of Newport. Lowe owned 80 percent of the layoff book, but split his take with Licavoli. In 1949, Lowe and Licavoli established Silver City News, in Albuquerque, handling bets from New Mexico bookies. When questioned about his ties to Licavoli in 1951, Moe Dalitz admitted, "I know who he is," but denied any business connection. "Never in my life," Moe testified.

Moe devoted as much attention to legitimate business in Arizona as to illegal gambling. In 1947, front man Robert Brickman paid $450,000 for the Tucson Steam Laundry, then bought land nearby for a 356-room hotel. Brickman, a former fight promoter linked to Lou Rothkopf and Tom McGinty, left Cleveland after he matched young Jimmy Doyle against Sugar Ray Robinson with fatal results. Coroner Samuel Gerber complained that "a great deal of unholy pressure has been put on me to divert this investigation," but Brickman beat the heat by leaving town. In Tucson, he joined George Darnell to form Tucson Motels, Inc.—whose owners of record included George Gordon, Al and Chuck Polizzi.

* * *

Jewish Americans followed the troubled course of post-war history in Palestine, where Zionist guerrillas of the Irgun waged terrorist campaigns against British authorities, battling for establishment of a Jewish homeland. Jewish mobsters shared that fascination, and author Jim Hougan reports that Meyer Lansky furnished weapons to the Irgun during 1946–48. Oth-

Arizona senator Barry Goldwater was Bioff's most prominent friend in public life (Library of Congress).

ers also aided Israel, or pretended to, with mixed results.

Menachem Begin, a future Israeli prime minister and head of the Irgun in 1943–48, fled Palestine following his organization's bombing of a Jerusalem hotel, which killed fifteen persons in January 1948. While hiding in Los Angeles, Begin met Mickey Cohen and other undesirables, including Jimmy Fratianno. Fratianno claimed that he promised to raise $1 million for the Irgun by taxing his bookies and holding a benefit concert with Art Samish and top hoodlums present. Cohen himself pegged the total at $375,000, but it hardly mattered. His alleged boatload of weapons sank somewhere in transit, leaving critics on both sides of the Atlantic convinced that Mickey had kept the cash for himself.

In Las Vegas, attorney and ex-Flamingo publicist Hank Greenspun had a better idea. When Israel was created in May 1948 and faced invasion by its Arab neighbors, Greenspun plundered an inactive Navy depot in Hawaii for 6,000 tons of surplus weapons, shipped them across the Pacific, then hijacked a yacht in California to complete the delivery, all while posing as an agent of the Chinese government. Israel got the weapons, and Greenspun got off easy, paying a $10,000 fine in July 1950.

Moe Dalitz tried a different method, with help from Sam Stein, in a near-disastrous spin-off from their Consolidated TV venture. Terrill Murrell had left Consolidated to create Masthead Export Corporation, with outposts in London and Morocco. Robert Goldstein of

Consolidated TV and Universal Pictures served as Masthead's president, while Stein and Dalitz became vice presidents. During a visit to England, Murrell met Cochrane Hervey, director of Empire Films, whose police record included convictions for housebreaking and larceny. Hervey's movie career took a backseat to international arms smuggling, with Arab nations ranked among his biggest customers.

In September 1948 Murrell returned from London, for meetings with Egyptian entrepreneur Sami Salim, alias "Sam Hannah," a partner in the Middle East Commercial and Transport Company. Salim agreed to purchase twenty-one aircraft from Masthead, including twenty AT-6 single-engine planes and one B-25-J bomber, built for high-altitude precision bombing. The AT-6s, while designed as training craft for fighter pilots, were convertible into armed fighters.

In October 1948, Murrell ordered the war-surplus planes on behalf of Hervey's Empire Films. In Detroit, he met with Masthead's leaders to discuss the impending transaction. On November 1, Dalitz and Stein resigned from Masthead; Goldstein followed suit on November 19, while new players joined the team. Arthur Leebove, a friend of Stein's who owned the El Dorado Club in Las Vegas, introduced Murrell to a St. Louis flight instructor who had a spare B-25 on his hands. Others new to Masthead included Detroit machine-shop owner George Wilson, Leonard LaBella, and Leonard de Pippo.

FBI files reveal what happened next. On November 10, 1948, Murrell, Leebove, Wilson, Stein, and Dalitz "purchased approximately twenty airplanes known as AT-6s and caused them to be flown and delivered to Newark Airport." Two days later, Murrell told Wilson to hire a four-man crew, to fly the B-25 from St. Louis to Newark. Customs agents plagued Murrell with red tape in Newark, while the Civil Aeronautics Board challenged his claim that the B-25 would be used as a cargo plane. Murrell changed his story, calling the bomber his personal "executive-type" aircraft. The CAB demanded an Affidavit of Temporary Sojourn, which Murrell vowed to provide. On December 7, Murrell received $28,108 from his Egyptian buyers.

Six days before the cash arrived, Murrell and Wilson hired a British crew for the B-25 and arranged their passage to St. Louis. On December 6, Dalitz, Stein, Leebove, and Salim met in New York and cabled Wilson to return from London, signing the telegram "Art, Moe, and Sam." On December 10, Dalitz, Murrell, Leebove, Stein, and Wilson arranged for the AT-6s to be disassembled and crated for shipment aboard the Egyptian steamer *Mohammed Ali El Kabir*. That same day, G-men reported that Stein, Murrell and Wilson had procured a crew to fly the B-25 from St. Louis to Newark. On December 23, Murrell met Stein, Leebove, de Pippo, and Salim in New York, to discuss their problems with Customs. Four days later, Murrell paid Leonard LaBella to sign a fictitious Affidavit of Temporary Sojourn, using the pseudonym "Lawrence Labeulla," then met De Pippo in Newark and filed the fraudulent document with Customs. Agents remained suspicious, however, and LaBella was forced to repeat the signing in person, on December 28.

Bad weather ultimately foiled the plot. Murrell's crew flew the B-25 to Albany, New York, where storms grounded it. Customs agents there refused to honor Newark's clearance for continued flight to Montreal and Iceland. The bomber returned to Newark, where Murrell produced *another* affidavit, but permission was rescinded when Customs could not find "Lawrence Labuella." Murrell explained that the false signature was used "purely for business reasons, to cut insurance costs." Unimpressed, Customs seized all twenty-one planes on January 6, 1949. Eleven months later, a federal grand jury charged Murrell, de Pippo, and LaBella with making false statements to Customs. Masthead associates "Hannah," Leebove,

Stein, and Wilson were faced conspiracy charges. Their trial was postponed, pending further investigation.

Moe Dalitz dodged indictment, for the moment, and ex-wife Toni recalls that he was "furious" on learning that the planes were bound for Egypt, for use against Israel. Be that as it may, Moe's continued involvement with Masthead following his resignation produced a new indictment in December 1951.

* * *

President Harry Truman, meanwhile, was locked in the political fight of his life. Truman's public approval rating had slumped to a disastrous 36 percent in 1948, while southern racists bolted from July's Democratic National Convention to form their own Dixiecrat Party, and Henry Wallace led liberals into a breakaway Progressive Party. Pundits predicted Truman's landslide defeat by Republican Thomas Dewey. To recoup his losses, Truman launched a marathon cross-country tour — and behind the scenes, he reached out to the Mob.

When Truman hit Cleveland, he rode with Mayor Thomas Burke and Ohio Governor Thomas Herbert in a Cadillac supplied by Shondor Birns. Doc Stacher later claimed that Meyer Lansky and Lucky Luciano supported Dewey, convinced that he "would accept financial support from them and in return they would be allowed to operate their gambling without much interference." J. Edgar Hoover also lent his influence and secret files to Dewey, expecting a Supreme Court seat as his reward, but Chicago mobsters swung the balance in Truman's favor on election day. After Truman's stunning upset victory, Chicago's Sam Giancana told friends, "We own him. We own the White House. We had to beg, borrow, and steal to swing the son of a bitch. No way the man doesn't know who got him elected."

Truman's second administration was plagued by scandals, including bribery of senior officials and tax-fixing at IRS headquarters, prompting dismissal and indictment of 166 employees. The taint touched Vice President Barkley's office by way of Newport, Kentucky, where secretary Flo Bratten partied with Red Masterson and pressured Kentucky highway engineers to grace her newly purchased mansion with a private road at taxpayers' expense. In 1951, critics accused her of "peddling the influence of the Vice President's office" to help her friends get loans from the Reconstruction Finance Corporation.

Named as suspects with Bratten were Henry Jenisch, regional manager of the RFC, and Charles Shaver, general counsel for the Small Business Administration. Senate investigators, led by Richard Nixon, found that Flo and Shaver "operated as a team" in processing RFC loans that included payouts to Miami hotels and to Chuck Polizzi in Cleveland. Still, despite what Nixon termed "irreconcilable conflicts" in Bratten's testimony, Flo was "absolved" of any criminal wrongdoing. Shaver was less fortunate: indicted for influence peddling, he pled guilty, paid a $1,000 fine, and received a two-year suspended prison term.

* * *

In 1949, pressures in Cleveland and Detroit distracted Moe Dalitz from projects in the West. June brought news of a bombing that nearly killed Joe Allen, a Cleveland numbers operator who refused to employ Shondor Birns as his "insurance agent." Police named a Birns crony, Chuck Amata, as the bomber. Authorities indicted Birns, but his first jury split eight-to-four in favor of conviction. Birns won acquittal at his second trial, in March 1950, then received a six-month sentence and $1,000 fine for jury-tampering.

Moe's troubles in Detroit were less explosive, and more easily concealed. Isaak Litvak, head of Teamsters Local 285, sought a five-day week and higher pay for truck drivers employed

by members of the Detroit Institute of Laundering, which included Moe's Michigan Industrial Laundry. When owners balked at the demands, Litwak threatened a strike. DIL leaders
called on Dalitz to intercede with the union. Soon, Jimmy Hoffa sent IBT representatives
Jack Bushkin and Joseph Holtzman to meet DIL spokesmen Howard Balkwill and John Meiss-
ner. Bushkin and Holtzman promised the DIL a sweetheart contract for $25,000 cash, then
bargained down to $17,500. Hoffa signed off on the contract without a five-day-week provi-
sion and without informing Litvak, who was furious on learning of the sellout. Holtzman
later explained the $17,500 payment in terms of "expenses," while Balkwill told investigators,
"There was never any doubt in [my] mind at all except that this was a payoff."

* * *

Moe's 1946 Nevada scouting mission piqued his interest in legalized gambling. For all his flaws,
Ben Siegel's vision for Las Vegas was prophetic. Moe and his partners wanted to cash in on
the bonanza, but they needed the perfect front man.

They found him in Wilbur Ivern Clark.

An Illinois native, Clark left home at nineteen and hitchhiked to California, working
various menial jobs before he found his calling as a craps dealer. He worked Tony Cornero's
gambling boats, drifted to Reno's Bank Club in 1931, and from there to illegal casinos in Palm
Springs and Saratoga, New York. In 1939, Clark bought part ownership of Cornero's SS *Rex*,
along with a hotel, a stable of racehorses, and several restaurants that featured backroom gambling. In post-war Las Vegas, Clark owned a share of the El Rancho, then built his own Monte
Carlo Club downtown. In 1947, Clark prepared to take the gamble of his life.

With his brother and two other investors, Clark gathered $250,000, bought land on the
Strip, and began construction of his Desert Inn in May 1947. Hank Greenspun bought 15
percent of the DI's stock and proclaimed Wilbur Clark "a man I soon came to love as a
brother." Construction proceeded by fits and starts, still far from complete when Greenspun
returned from his globe-trotting Israeli arms deal in 1949. He noticed that everything had
changed.

Sometime in 1948, Clark met Moe Dalitz. The circumstances of that meeting are
unknown, but it creates a curious discrepancy in subsequent reports of how the Desert Inn
was finally completed, with the Cleveland Syndicate in charge. Moe waffled on the subject,
telling Senate investigators that he first met Clark in 1949, later admitting that they actually
met a year earlier. As Moe explained to the *Las Vegas Sun*, in 1983:

> A dear friend of mine in Detroit named Mert Wertheimer went to Reno to buy the Riverside
> Hotel-Casino. Mert couldn't handle the deal. It was too big for one individual, so he asked me
> to fly there and talk to him about a possible partnership. When I got to Reno, I wasn't really
> convinced that it would be a sound investment. Oddly enough, while I was there, I got a call
> from Wilbur Clark. Wilbur asked me if I would please come and talk to him. It sounded urgent,
> so I said my goodbyes to Wertheimer and flew to Las Vegas.

In Vegas, Moe reviewed the DI's ledgers and blueprints. "I liked Wilbur's plans the
instant they were laid," he told the *Sun*. Moe caught the next flight to Cleveland, to brief his
partners on the project. "It wasn't long," he said, "before we agreed to assume all responsibility for finishing the development and construction of the resort."

Sam Tucker told a different story in 1951, reporting that Moe summoned him to Las
Vegas in October or November 1948, "to see the place or look over the deal." Dalitz and Morris Kleinman were already there, Tucker said, when he met Clark for the first time and agreed
to come in on the deal.

FBI files from 1949 confuse the issue further, reporting that Moe moved to Nevada in 1945, when "[DELETED] reportedly accompanied Moe Dalitz, and others, as the representative of the 'Italian Group.'" The date may be a typo, since other FBI reports describe a three-day series of negotiations with Clark in May 1949. According to G-men, Moe and his partners returned to Vegas on August 28, 1949, and booked rooms at the Last Frontier, across the street from their new acquisition, through September 5.

"All in all," Moe said, four decades after the fact, "the opportunity in Las Vegas was too good for me and my associates to pass up. I was fifty years old then and I could breathe easier in this climate."

Clark needed $90,000 to complete the hotel; an operational casino ran the tab up to $3.6 million. Cleveland supplied the cash, obtaining effective control of Clark's brainchild. Dalitz became vice

Wilbur Clark with a photo montage of his celebrity friends (Las Vegas Historical Society).

president of the DI, while Ruby Kolod moved in as the casino manager, and Allard Roen became the "expediter of construction." In 1951, Moe testified that he, Sam Tucker, and Morris Kleinman each owned 13 percent of the DI, while Tom McGinty and Cornelius Jones held "approximately 20 percent." Moe neglected to mention shares owned by Roen, Lou Rothkopf, and Ruby Kolod, which inflated Cleveland's piece of the action to 74 percent.

The DI was expensive, but it hardly mattered, since much of Cleveland's investment came from others.

Some, like mafiosi Joe Massei and Frank Milano, were silent partners in the project; others moved in the realm of legitimate business. Tom McGinty paid $175,000 for his "very small interest" in the DI, borrowed from hotelier Max Marmonstein, Miami Beach attorney Herman Cohen, and one M.J. Burnette in the "railroad supply business."

Who else owned shares in the DI? Unsubstantiated rumors named Benny Binion, a transplanted Texas gambler and convicted murderer who later built the Horseshoe Club downtown, as a DI investor. Chicago's Outfit may have had an interest, explaining Sam Tucker's rented Windy City office space at 134 North LaSalle — the same building occupied by Mob lawyer Sidney Korshak. FBI files suggest New York's interest, revealed in the role of Doc Stacher. According to the files: "On one occasion in 1949, Starcher [*sic*] sat in on a meeting in Las Vegas which was also attended by Dalitz, in financing the Desert Inn Hotel." Even accountant Al Giesey was on board, borrowing $7,500 from Samuel Haas, which Giesey then loaned to the DI at 4.5 percent interest.

The Desert Inn hotel-casino (Las Vegas Historical Society).

Through it all, Wilbur Clark remained the smiling front man, memorialized in head-lines as the "Ambassador of Las Vegas." Moe Dalitz earned a nickname, too. He became the "Godfather of Las Vegas," whose influence often made the crucial difference between success and failure for new projects.

* * *

Despite that influence, casino licensing was problematical. Lieutenant Governor Clifford

Jones acknowledged that prior to 1949 "little or no effort was made to screen applicants," but that was changing when Cleveland bought the DI. Virgil Peterson, of Chicago's Crime Commission, made things worse with a scathing report to the Nevada Tax Commission, which passed judgment on prospective licensees. Robbins Cahill, chief of the Tax Commission's Gaming Division, called Peterson's report "a masterpiece of literature [that] painted in the darkest terms the shadowy world that [Dalitz] operated in.... It was enough to scare the life out of you."

To counter that portrait, Moe retained ex-governor Edward Carville as the DI's attorney. In Cahill's view, "They chose a person for their political influence, or background, far more than their ability as attorney." Carville introduced the Cleveland team to Cahill, and all submitted fingerprints, which revealed "nothing unusual" beyond illegal gambling, Kleinman's tax-evasion rap, and Lou Rothkopf's Molaska's conviction. Tom McGinty was "a very hard man to get a rundown on." Ultimately, Cahill discovered McGinty's 1925 Volstead conviction, but deemed that rejection of a license on those grounds "just wouldn't hold water," since most Reno gamblers had similar records. Cahill likewise ignored Kleinman's tax rap, since "income evasion was charges [*sic*] that happened to the best people."

Still, Cahill stalled approval, traveling to Cleveland for Nevada's first-ever out-of-state background investigation. Twenty years later, he said, "I went there with the opinion that we were dealing with a mob of hoodlums, and that we were going to be the savior of Las Vegas by keeping them out." Local sources acknowledged that the Cleveland Four were criminals, but said, "They run a good, tight business. An ethical business." One union boss described Moe's gang as "probably the most ethical people that he'd dealt with." Reporter Forrest Allen, with the *Cleveland Press*, told Cahill, "These people make a special effort to keep their hands clean," thus distinguishing them from the Italian "dirty hands boys." Police files were no help, since Moe had paid crooked cops to purge them before he left town.

Cahill returned from Ohio convinced that Moe and his partners "were not gangsters in the true sense, but merely men who wanted to come to Nevada and do legally what they had been doing illegally in other states. They were silk glove men." In later years, Cahill's opinion depended on who asked the questions, and when. In 1972 he called Morris Kleinman "a man who I've known for many years, and still think a lot of." By contrast, "I had my problems in the earlier times with Moe Dalitz because he was the kingpin." Twenty years later, Cahill told authors Carole Case and Ronald Farrell that he "greatly admired" Dalitz. In Cahill's final view, Moe had "done more good for the city of Las Vegas and done more to build Las Vegas than any single man connected with the industry."

Some others disagreed. Norman Biltz, a millionaire developer known as "the Duke of Nevada," branded Dalitz one of "the southern Nevada racketeers." An alternative tale of the DI licensing wrangle, advanced by authors Ed Reid and Ovid Demaris, contends that Texas mafioso Sam Maceo greased the wheels for Moe and company by bribing Senator McCarran. On February 27, 1950, in what the *Las Vegas Review-Journal* called "a surprise move," Cahill's Gaming Board granted casino licenses to Dalitz, Kleinman, Tucker, and McGinty, but rejected Lou Rothkopf because his 1937 bootlegging conviction came four years after Repeal, and thus qualified as "criminal." Taking the slight in stride, Rothkopf "loaned" the DI $112,500 in March 1950, and another $30,000 in April, but he received no stock. Nephew Bernard Rothkopf stood in for Uncle Lou on the DI's staff, joining Allard Roen as a member of what Hank Messick dubbed the "second-generation syndicate." Robert Kaye, a partner in Cleveland's Empire News with Game Boy Miller and Mushy Wexler, came aboard in the guise of a lowly cashier.

* * *

One figure overlooked in the DI investigation was Allen Smiley, who shared a sofa with Ben Siegel on the night a sniper killed the Bug. An IRS report from 1949 claims that Smiley steered a rich female rancher to the Beverly Club in New Orleans, where she lost "a small fortune," then introduced her to "Moe Davis in Chicago," who promptly "took" her for $160,000.

Around the same time, an LAPD microphone in Jack Dragna's home recorded Dragna's side of a phone conversation with Smiley. The transcript read:

> I don't know what in hell they've got to do with it. After all, you got in here.... It's for you to say, and them to.... All you've got to say is that whatever you've got there is no special name and that is enough.... Them dirty bastards.... Yeah.... There is plenty that goes out with the dish water in there.... No, I was told they were supposed to give you five and now they're going to give you money instead.... That's what I was told.... Well, he didn't specify what he was going to give you.... I mean Lou himself.... That is a lot of crap.... He didn't go in there because.... People work like that.... He didn't go because of business.... Because he's too good natured for that, you understand.... So he sent the other guys out to do it.... I know how them people work.... I know how they work.... I could tell you a mouthful.... You know how to deal with the lousy....

Hank Messick contends that Dragna's tirade referred to the DI's owners and a promise to give Smiley a piece of the action. And, indeed, a second tape-recorded conversation found Dragna advising Smiley to hold out for 2.5 percent of the resort.

> If you can get in there, why take the money?...You and I could live it up here instead of there.... I don't know when in the hell they start putting out of their own pockets.... I'd show them people whether you could face it, or if I could face it.... We're as clean as them, anytime.... What?... Well, don't settle with them.... All you have to do is tell them you're splitting up with me, and that would end it....

But tough talk from the Mickey Mouse Mafia carried no weight in Las Vegas. Dragna and Smiley missed the DI's grand opening on April 24, 1950, when Governor Vail Pittman led a delegation of officials including Lieutenant Governor Jones, Mayor Ernie Cragin, and ex-Senator Carville. Lew Wasserman flew in from Hollywood for the festivities, bringing a troupe of clients that included ventriloquist Edgar Bergen, Bud Abbott and Lou Costello, Van Heflin, Gail Storm, the Ray Noble Orchestra, and the Donna Arden Dancers. Also present in the crowd, unnoticed by reporters, were old partners Joe Massei, Pete Licavoli, Sam Maceo, Frank Milano, and Black Bill Tocco.

FBI agents reported that the DI's grand opening cost more than $150,000. Moe granted $10,000 credit to each of 150 selected high-rollers. On opening night, players bet $750,000 on the casino's gaming tables, with no tabulation revealed for the slots. That night, the casino reported a 4-percent profit of $30,000. Five days later, on its first Saturday, the DI lost $87,000 in eight hours — including $36,000 to a single lucky crap-shooter — but by Friday, May 5, the casino had rebounded with weekly profits of $750,000.

At least, that's what Moe and his partners told the IRS.

* * *

Wilbur Clark's Desert Inn set new standards for Nevada "gaming." At 2,400 square feet, the DI's sprawling casino was one of Nevada's largest, and its first year's take was second only to that of Harold's Club, in Reno. The resort's 170 acres included the Strip's only eighteen-hole golf course, a health club and solarium, spacious outdoor terraces, and a gourmet restaurant under Chef Maurice Thominet, formerly of the Parisian Ritz Hotel. Tenants of the DI's 300 guest rooms were treated to round-the-clock room service, with an array of specialty shops including the pricey Goldwater's of Phoenix. The Painted Desert dinner theater seated 450 guests, while the Sky Room Lounge treated daredevil guests to a rooftop view of A-bomb detonations only 65 miles distant.

In addition to his longtime partners and their relatives, Moe Dalitz brought a coterie of trusted friends to the DI. Pete Bommarito came from Motown, employed for two years as a pit boss overseeing Moe's dice tables. In his spare time, Bommarito served as president of the Italian American Club of Southern Nevada, fraternizing with Dean Martin and Frank Sinatra. Cleveland gambler Pete Brady also followed Moe to the DI, working the blackjack and roulette tables. Frank Sennes Sr., late of Cleveland via Newport, served as the DI's entertainment director, staging lavish productions before he moved on to the Mob-owned Moulin Rouge in Hollywood. Dalitz spared no expense for the amusement of his guests, spending $2.7 million on entertainment in the DI's first three years of operation.

Periodic FBI surveillance determined that the DI did "a consistently larger business than any of the casinos in the larger hotels on The Strip," but those files failed to mention Director J. Edgar Hoover's visits to the casino.

Hank Greenspun handled publicity for the DI's grand opening, later claiming that he viewed Clark's Cleveland partners with "a vague instinct of ever-growing mistrust," but had no knowledge of their criminal backgrounds prior to April 24, 1950. "Days later," Greenspun wrote in 1966, he clashed with Dalitz over an advertisement in the *Las Vegas Free Press*, a tri-weekly published by blacklisted members of the International Typographical Union. Greenspun bought the ad as a gesture of union solidarity, and to defy the *Review-Journal's* alliance with Senator McCarran. Moe soon appeared in Greenspun's office, informing him that "all of us hotel owners" were joining ranks to boycott the *Free Press*. Greenspun stood firm, but only long enough to sell his DI stock and use the proceeds to buy the *Free Press*, renamed the *Las Vegas Sun* in July 1950. Over the next four decades, Greenspun veered from one extreme to the other on Dalitz, sometimes reviling Moe, then meeting him for pinochle and praising him as the architect of Vegas; denouncing Moe's mob ties, then vilifying G-men who investigated them; campaigning for clean government, while praising Jimmy Hoffa as a working-class hero.

One thing was clear: a change of address for Moe Dalitz and his partners signaled no change in the way they did business. FBI agents logged a telephone call from Mickey Cohen to Moe's DI office on November 4, 1950, and other mobsters also had his ear. The DI's "skim"—cash siphoned from the daily take before it was reported to the IRS—filled underworld pockets in Vegas, Cleveland, Detroit, and beyond. The Mob's greatest gold rush since prohibition had begun—and it was legal.

More or less.

7

Heat

America woke slowly to the grim reality of organized crime. In September 1949 the American Municipal Association convened in Cleveland for a racketeering conference. Mayor DeLesseps Morrison of New Orleans requested a federal investigation of Mob influence on city governments, echoed by pleas for special assistance from the mayors of Los Angeles and Portland, Oregon. When no response was forthcoming, the AMA formally appealed to the Justice Department in December 1949, declaring that the "matter is too big to be handled by local officials alone."

J. Edgar Hoover disagreed, opposing any federal moves against the Mob, dismissing syndicate leaders as "a bunch of hoodlums" who were best handled by local police. FBI headquarters listed America's major crimes as homicide, rape, robbery, burglary, auto theft, and aggravated assault, with no mention of racketeering. President Truman supported Hoover's stand, but he could not ignore the groundswell of contrary public opinion.

In February 1950 Attorney General J. Howard McGrath invited mayors, prosecutors, and police chiefs from various cities to Washington, for another conference on the Mob. Truman opened the proceedings with a lecture on the post-war "crime wave," blaming most of it on aftershocks from World War II. Local enforcement was the answer, he declared, but most delegates agreed with Dallas district attorney Will Wilson, who described the Texas gambling syndicate as a spin-off from Chicago's Outfit, maintained by "killing of the most reckless kind." Mayor Morrison of New Orleans told reporters, "We do not have the whole picture, but each of us present ... [have] seen small segments of this national scene of organized ... crime. These pieces fit together in a pattern of mounting evidence concerning several highly organized ... syndicates whose wealth, power, scope of operations, and influence have recently grown ... to alarming proportions."

A lone dissent came from Chicago's federal prosecutor, Otto Kerner. Incredibly, Kerner opined that "[t]here is no organized gambling in the city of Chicago." Furthermore, he "[did] not know that the Capone syndicate exists. I have read about it in the newspapers. I have never seen any evidence of it."

That seemed absurd to Estes Kefauver, the freshman senator from Tennessee, elected in 1948. While on the campaign trail, he decided that a public drive against the Mob could serve America, while furthering his own ambitions. If he played the game correctly, it might even send him to the White House. In January 1950, Kefauver introduced Resolution 202, calling on the Senate Judiciary Committee to investigate Mob ties to "interstate gambling and racketeering activities."

Kefauver's gambit faced immediate opposition, led by Senate Majority Leader Scott Lucas of Chicago and Nevada's Pat McCarran. As co-chairman of the Judiciary Committee, McCarran hoped to sidetrack Kefauver's resolution, or to control hearings if the Senate approved an investigation. Meanwhile, Wisconsin's Joe McCarthy sought to claim the Mob probe for his Special Investigations Committee, then lost interest after *Newsweek* documented his ties to Frank Costello. President Truman, through Lucas, supported Arizona Senator Ernest McFarland's proposal for a Rules Committee investigation, which would focus solely on gambling. Sworn to defend Nevada, McCarran grudgingly passed Kefauver's resolution in late March, slashing appropriations from $100,000 to $50,000 and imposing a July 1950 deadline. Virtually crippled at the outset, Resolution 202 made its way to the Senate floor, where partisan debate threatened to drag on past the deadline.

The story might have ended there, but Kansas City mobsters gave Kefauver's campaign a push, in April 1950, executing two mafiosi in the very First Ward Democratic Party headquarters that launched Harry Truman into politics. Before the echoes of those gunshots faded, Republican leaders demanded full disclosure of Democratic ties to the Mob; Democrats feared that the Judiciary Committee's Republican majority would highlight Democratic sins, while whitewashing their own. Their compromise produced a Special Committee to Investigate Crime in Interstate Commerce, with its budget expanded to $150,000 and its deadline extended through February 1951.

The committee held its first meeting on May 11 and chose Kefauver as chairman. The panel's other members included Senators Lester Hunt (Wyoming), Herbert O'Conor (Maryland), Charles Tobey (New Hampshire), and Alexander Wiley (Wisconsin). Chief counsel Rudolph Halley did most of the work, drawing information from Harry Anslinger's Federal Bureau of Narcotics and the IRS; from prosecutors, sheriffs, and police chiefs; from civilian crime commission chairmen like Chicago's Virgil Peterson and Daniel Sullivan in Miami; and from investigative journalists.

One source that stonewalled from the start was Hoover's FBI. Newsman Jack Anderson described an interview with Kefauver, wherein Kefauver "told me the FBI tried to block it.... Hoover knew that if the public got alarmed about organized crime, the job would go to the FBI. And he didn't want the job." Associate committee counsel Joseph Nellis recalled, "We had a long series of meetings with [Hoover] ... at which he told us, 'We don't know anything about the Mafia or the families in New York. We haven't followed this.' He told us what we were learning about the Mafia wasn't true, but we didn't believe him. It was dreadful. We tried to enlist the FBI's help in every major city, but got none." Decades later, declassified FBI files revealed Hoover's collection of derogatory information on Kefauver, held in reserve should Kefauver publicly criticize the FBI.

* * *

Despite that roadblock, Kefauver forged ahead. He planned to launch his hearings in New York, but District Attorney Frank Hogan beat him to the punch in May 1950, with a raid on bookie Frank Erickson's headquarters. Kefauver shifted his sights to Miami, where gamblers suddenly made themselves scarce. After two days of closed hearings, Kefauver left Florida to seek larger game, leaving the local search to investigator Downey Rice. Gambling records secured by Rice included checks totaling $75,000, written to Mickey Cohen by John O'Rourke, Frank Erickson's partner in the Boca Raton Club. O'Rourke professed amazement, though the Miami *Daily News* had aired his business links to Cohen in 1949. Overall, Kefauver determined, the S&G Syndicate's bookies had grossed $26.5 million between 1944 and 1948, while 52 "more or less elaborate gambling casinos operated in Broward County alone."

Between July and October 1950, Kefauver held closed hearings in St. Louis, Kansas City, Chicago, New York City, and Philadelphia. Scott Lucas asked Kefauver to avoid Chicago until the new year, while Lucas campaigned for a third Senate term, but Kefauver refused. Strategic leaks from hearing testimony, coupled with Joe McCarthy's speeches branding Lucas "soft on communism," tipped the balance in favor of Republican contender Everett Dirksen, thus ending Lucas's political career.

* * *

Kefauver brought his committee to Las Vegas on November 15, 1950, prompting an exodus of mobsters. Only six witnesses finally testified. Lieutenant Governor Jones and Tax Commissioner William Moore admitted their involvement in gambling and defended the state's practice of licensing felons to run casinos. Louis Wiener, attorney for the Ben Siegel's estate, briefed Kefauver on the Flamingo's finances and judged Siegel's share of the Golden Nugget horse book as being worth "zero, nothing." Henry Phillips, operator of the Last Frontier's commission room, complained that "I try to operate, but I haven't been doing anything since I have been here." Robert Kaltenborn, lately released from federal prison on a tax-evasion rap, described his interests in copper mining and the El Rancho Hotel. Reno police chief Lawrence Greeson briefed Kefauver on mobsters in northern Nevada, including the Wertheimer brothers, Doc Stacher, and Bill Graham.

Missing from the witness chair were Moe Dalitz and his DI partners, along with every other major player in the city. Kefauver saw "no question as to the character of" witnesses Jones and Moore, but he left Vegas convinced that "the caliber of the men who dominate ... gambling in ... Nevada is on a par with that of professional gamblers operating illegal ... establishments throughout the country." Officials were complicit in Mob control of casinos, since "[n]o attempt had been made ... to eliminate the undesirable persons who had been operating in the State before [1949]."

* * *

Hearings in Cleveland were scheduled for January 17–19, 1951. A month before that date, federal marshals fanned out in search of witnesses, but many vanished as they had in Vegas. An FBI memo noted Kefauver's request for Bureau assistance in serving subpoenas on Dalitz, Kleinman, Rothkopf, Tucker, Sam Haas, Mushy Wexler, Game Boy Miller, and the Angersola brothers. Gloating in his office, Hoover scrawled a note across the memo, reading: "We can check our files & that is all. This is getting to be a farce. If they would stop alerting proposed witnesses in advance this problem would never arise."

Despite missing the biggest fish, Kefauver still found witnesses aplenty in Ohio. They included Governor Lausche; Mayor Thomas Burke of Cleveland; Mickey McBride; Alvin Giesey; Cleveland safety director Alvin Sutton; Al Polizzi; lawyer Richard Moriarty and his client, Tom McGinty; Anthony Rutkowsky; Lawrence County Sheriff Peter Burke; Youngstown police chief Edward Allen; Lucas County Sheriff George Timiney; former sheriff Charles Hennessy; James Licavoli; hotelier Max Marmonstein; Newport police chief George Gugel; and Cleveland mafioso Anthony Milano.

Most of the lawmen summoned from Ohio and Kentucky offered vague excuses for their failure to suppress gambling. Some lacked money and manpower, while others were preoccupied with tax collection and other chores. Chief Gugel brought gambler's attorney Charles

Lester to advise him, seemingly oblivious to any hint of impropriety. Alvin Giesey frankly explained his transformation from IRS agent to Mob accountant in pursuit of "the almighty dollar."

The path of least resistance had been paved with gold.

* * *

From Cleveland, the committee moved on to New Orleans and its first televised hearings. By the time Kefauver reached Detroit, mobsters were all the TV rage. A Motown station canceled *Howdy Doody* to air the spectacle of senators interrogating Pete Licavoli, Black Bill Tocco, and others. While focusing chiefly on Mafia links to the Ford Motor Company, the panel also found time to question Max Zivian's sale of Detroit Steel stock to Moe Dalitz. On February 19, *Time* magazine noted that "[t]he committee is still looking for Stockholder Dalitz, to question him."

Kefauver got his chance nine days later, in Los Angeles. Moe scored his first coup by arriving with attorney Charles Carr, a friend and classmate of Kefauver's from Yale Law School. After that awkward moment, Dalitz sparred with Kefauver concerning his evasion of subpoenas.

> KEFAUVER: Efforts were made to serve a subpoena on you at various and different places but without any success. You were aware of that; were you not?
> DALITZ: I assumed that there was a subpoena for me from what I read in the papers...
> KEFAUVER: The marshals at Cleveland, Detroit, and other places had a subpoena for you but could not locate you.
> DALITZ: Nobody came to my home with a subpoena...
> KEFAUVER: You were not there; you had left.
> DALITZ:. I have been back and forth a few times, yes...
> KEFAUVER: Why didn't you let us know where you were so we could have you come in and testify at Cleveland or Detroit?
> DALITZ: Well, Senator, I, frankly, was just alarmed at the whole thing and all the publicity. I have never had any publicity in the past.

That was not strictly true, as Kefauver revealed by quoting Dixie Davis's 1938 confessions to *Colliers* and Virgil Peterson's summation of the William Potter slaying. "To start off with this thing about Dixie Davis," Moe replied, "I never saw him in my life, and wouldn't know him if he was in this room. I know that he couldn't have known me." As for the Potter case, he said, "I have never been questioned on that. I have never been talked to about it and I never had any connection with it of any kind. I have never even been questioned about it even as a witness or by influence, or anything else."

Moe held his own throughout the hearing, refusing to answer questions that might incriminate him, responding honestly on certain subjects where the statute of limitations had expired, clearly lying on others. He admitted knowing Longy Zwillman, but denied ever meeting Lucky Luciano and claimed that he had only seen Al Polizzi "three or four times in the last ten years." He denied the 1930 bootlegging indictment and falsely claimed that "I never was in Buffalo in my life." Otherwise, Dalitz made no apologies for his adventures in the liquor trade.

FBI memos mention a perjury investigation related to Moe's testimony, concerning Luciano. According to that file, "numerous persons could place Dalitz and Luciano together on many occasions." Another memo stated, "Dalitz also lied when he stated that he did not have an apartment at the Hollenden Hotel in Cleveland." The Bureau was right, but the effort went nowhere. No perjury charges were filed.

Sam Tucker followed Dalitz to the witness chair. Once again, Kefauver led off his interrogation with questions concerning Tucker's evasion of federal subpoenas.

> KEFAUVER: Why didn't you let us know about your whereabouts?
> TUCKER: I was home every day; I never went anywhere. Nobody served me with a subpoena.
> KEFAUVER: You do not feel that there is some obligation to make yourself available in the event it is known that you are wanted?
> TUCKER: The only time I knew I should be available is when they mentioned something about a warrant.

Tucker followed Moe's lead, evading questions where he might face prosecution, admitting partnership in older outlaw operations, lying freely when he felt the need. A case in point was the Buffalo liquor indictment from 1930. "I remember hearing about it," Tucker said, "but I don't know why they would have indicted me. If they had me indicted they should have picked me up and charged me, or something like that."

The panel also questioned Wilbur Clark in Los Angeles, but the result was disappointing. The following exchange suggests Clark's take on life, and the committee's inability to pin him down.

> Q: What is your function at the hotel? What do you do there?
> A: Well, I am supposed to be the general manager.
> Q: Are you?
> A: I think so...
> Q: You have the most nebulous idea of your business I ever saw. You have a smile on your face but I don't know how the devil you do it.
> A: I have done it all my life.

* * *

After televised hearings in New York City, the panel returned to Washington, where Kefauver predicted that some "important witnesses from the government and odds and ends from the underworld [were] due to appear." The New York hearings prompted Senator Wiley's complaint that the hearings had devolved into "a three-ring circus, a fourth-rate style production with hamming and phony theatrics, an unjust inquisition of people under klieg lights, particularly people who might not be able to testify under such conditions." That observation paved the way for startling events on March 26, 1951.

Longy Zwillman was the first witness to testify that day, hedging his answers with a semblance of cooperation and emerging from the hearing chamber as what one newspaper termed a "telegenic hit." Any pretense of cordiality evaporated, though, when Morris Kleinman took the witness stand. Lou Rothkopf waited in the wings, both men detained on special warrants. In Cleveland alone, an estimated three million viewers tuned in to hear their hometown mobsters testify.

Kleinman arrived with lawyers William Corrigan and Timothy McMahon, who had also represented Alvin Giesey. McMahon opened with protests against TV lights and cameras directed toward his client. "Under these circumstances," he said, "I would like the indulgence of the committee for the witness to read a statement on a question which we want to develop at this time."

Kleinman then launched into a recitation of professed concern that "[m]y manner of sitting, of talking, using my hands, the clothes I wear, may all be the subject of movies and unfavorable comment, and may be used against me. My voice, which is not trained, may make an unfavorable impression, and my entire appearance, as given, or compared to others, may be distorted." He was equally concerned that strangers might profit from his testimony. He declared:

Left: **Moe Dalitz confronts the Kefauver Commission (Cleveland State University Library).** *Right:* **Lou Rothkopf defies the U.S. Senate (Cleveland State University Library).**

> If the television industry wants me to aid in boosting the sale of TV sets, and the sponsors, saloons, and restaurants want my aid in boosting their business, I am entitled to be compensated just the same as any other American amusement enterprise.... I do not know to what extent this question has been raised before the committee, but I am stating now that I believe that such procedure is a violation of my constitutional rights, and before I have anything further to say, I wish to respectfully inform the Senate committee that I will not, in danger of my rights, perform to aid the TV industry, the radio industry and the newsreels, and I will proceed no further until this apparatus is shut off and removed.

Kefauver replied, "Well, Mr. Kleinman, if we had been able to find you in Cleveland, where we tried very hard to get you in, you wouldn't have had this difficulty, because that hearing, I don't think, was televised." Kefauver then ordered the TV cameras be turned off, but balked at banning other media from the hearing.

"I want everything off," Kleinman said.

"Not everything," Senator Tobey replied.

Kleinman turned stubborn, letting "the statement speak for itself" when Joe Nellis asked his whereabouts over the past fifteen weeks. Senator Tobey weighed in once more, asking, "You knew this committee was looking for you for a long time, did you not?"

"The apparatus is still on, Senator," Kleinman replied.

"The television is not on, sir."

"The other newsreels are on, the radio is on, the lights are on."

Tobey fumed, "You sat back there ten feet behind for an hour and three-quarters. You took the lights then in good part, but the minute you come on the stand for questioning, then you quail under the lights.... Good Lord, let me say something to you, sir. You evaded this committee for two or three months. No honest man would do that. He would come a running and say, 'Here I am, nothing hidden.' You skulked away somewhere, and you won't tell us where you were, but I am telling you something. The people of this country are outraged at the likes of you, and when we all get through you will come up to the bar of justice. I promise you that."

Kleinman absorbed the lecture and sat mute through fifteen questions until Tobey barked, "I've had enough of this opéra bouffe." Tobey requested that Kleinman be held under $25,000 bond for contempt of Congress. Kefauver reduced the bail to $10,000 and ordered the Senate's sergeant at arms to place Kleinman under arrest.

Lou Rothkopf was next on the hot seat, flanked by the same attorneys. Before the senators could ask him anything, Rothkopf secured permission to read a statement that echoed Kleinman's verbatim. He then sat mute through fifteen questions of his own — including two about phone calls to Mickey Cohen in L.A.— and was removed under $10,000 bond.

Cleveland's *Plain Dealer* rated Kleinman and Rothkopf as a pair of "entertainment duds." Three days later, a unanimous Senate voted to cite the pair and ten other mobsters — including Frank Costello, Joe Adonis, Frank Erickson, Meyer Lansky, and Jake Guzik — for contempt. The maximum penalty, one year in prison and a $1,000 fine on each count, applied to each specific instance of contempt — that is, each question which a witness refused to answer under specific directions from Kefauver. If convicted on all counts, Kleinman and Rothkopf thus faced up to fifteen years in prison.

* * *

In June and July 1951, more witnesses from Kentucky and Ohio testified in Washington. Campbell County witnesses included Yorkshire Club secretary-treasurer Virginia Moore, county police chief James Winters, Sheriff Ray Diebold, Newport city manager Malcolm Rhoads, city solicitor Fred Warren, commissioner Charles Eha, county prosecutor William Wise, Judge Ray Murphy, and Newport police chief George Gugel. From Kenton County came James Brink, Judge Joseph Goodenough, prosecutor James Quill, Sheriff Henry Berndt, Covington commissioner John Moloney, police chief Alfred Schild, Sharon Florer from the Kenton County Protestant Association, and Turf Club owner Leonard Connor. Other witnesses included Mob accountant Jack Kuresman of Cincinnati, agent Theo Hagen from Kentucky's State Alcohol Board, and committee investigator Lawrence Goddard, who had penetrated various Kentucky gambling joints.

As in the previous Ohio hearings, politicians and policemen provided the comic relief. John Moloney explained the gamblers' "profit sharing" scheme in Covington, while Sheriff Berndt proclaimed, "We do not really try to make any attempt at the law enforcing." Campbell County's Sheriff Diebold denied ever setting foot in a casino, much less raiding them. Chief Gugel of Newport acknowledged his recent suspension from duty on insubordination charges.

Thus ended the road show, after ten months of hearings in fifteen cities, involving more than 600 witnesses. The committee had traveled 52,000 miles and compiled 11,500 pages of testimony. New York TV executives announced that 30 million viewers had watched the hearings.

But what did the investigation accomplish?

In November 1950 initiatives to legalize gambling appeared on state ballots in Arizona, California, Massachusetts, and Montana. All were defeated, with anti-gambling forces crediting Kefauver for their victories. By contrast, a federal bill that would have imposed a 10-

percent tax on gambling profits nationwide died after Pat McCarran warned that its "cumulative effect would spell tragedy for the state of Nevada." Mickey McBride's Continental Press survived until March 1952, then disbanded. Nevada authorities ignored Kefauver's findings, while some mobsters pretended that the hearings had led them to wholly legitimate lives. A quarter-century after the fact, Dalitz associate John Licini told a reporter, "The best thing that ever happened to us was the Kefauver investigation which forced us to move to Nevada.... And you can see what a man like Dalitz, with his ability, was able to do once given the opportunity." Licini and the newspaper conveniently forgot that Moe assumed control of the Desert Inn two years *before* Kefauver's hearings began — and continued his illegal enterprises far beyond them.

Kefauver made it briefly stylish to harass famous mobsters. Twenty-four illegal aliens identified by the committee were deported, including Joe Adonis. The Justice Department briefly expanded its racket squad, then disbanded it in 1952. The IRS proved more resolute, conducting 28,742 racketeering investigations over the next six years and sending 874 mobsters to prison. Several states empanelled "little Kefauver committees," while Kefauver investigator John McCormick became Cleveland's public safety director. Senator Tobey's Commerce Committee rolled on to investigate Mob domination of waterfront labor, but that probe collapsed with his death in July 1953.

None of Kefauver's nineteen proposed anti–Mob bills survived the gauntlet of partisan politics on Capitol Hill.

Congress cited 46 Kefauver witnesses for contempt, but only three served any time. Twenty-two were acquitted at trial, ten cases were dismissed, and five convictions were reversed on appeal. Part of the problem was Kefauver's approach, as described by appellate judge David Bazelon in reversing Maryland gambler Charles Nelson's conviction: "The committee threatened prosecution for contempt if he refused to answer, for perjury if he lied, and for gambling if he told the truth." Kleinman and Rothkopf found an early ally in Washington Senator Harry Cain, who condemned Kefauver's "television extravaganza tactics" in August 1951. During that speech, Cain called Kleinman and Rothkopf "victims of a wave of emotion over which they had no control. I was disturbed and shocked by the manner in which they were treated.... I saw no effort to get at the truth." TV executives, fearing lawsuits if the televised hearings produced convictions, soon joined the chorus pleading for withdrawal of contempt charges.

Both sides in the Kleinman-Rothkopf case waived their rights to trial by jury, submitting the matter to Judge H.A. Schweinhaut. Observing that the only purpose for interrogating any witness is to get "a thoughtful, calm, considered and ... truthful disclosure of facts," Schweinhaut declared that batteries of lights and cameras "necessarily ... disturb and distract any witness to the point that he might say today something that next week he will realize was erroneous. And the mistake could get him in trouble all over again." Accordingly, he wrote:

> It is said that these defendants are hardened criminals who were not and could not have been affected by the paraphernalia and atmosphere to which they were exposed. That may be so, but the court cannot take judicial notice that it is so. Moreover, it cannot be said that for John, who is a good man, one rule applies, while for Jack, who is not a good man, another rule applies. Such reasoning is incompatible with our theory of justice. Under the circumstances clearly delineated here, the court holds that the refusal of the defendants to testify was justified and it is hereby judged that they are not guilty.

Meanwhile, questions arose about Kefauver's personal integrity. When committee hearings began, his bank account was overdrawn by $1,700. In January 1951 Kefauver deposited an untraceable $25,000, immediately writing a $10,500 check to pay off his mortgage. By autumn 1951 he was back in the red, with a $1,600 overdraft. One of Kefauver's closest friends at home was Flora Brody, whose husband ran the Knoxville numbers rackets. Rumors spread that Kefauver had received a $5,000 campaign donation from Brody in 1948, while reporting only $100 to federal authorities.

Kefauver's bid for the vice presidency failed in 1952, although he made a comeback four years later. Historian Hal Rothman writes that "the defeat of Kefauver emboldened the Vegas mobsters. It made them feel that they had much greater control over this place, had much greater control over the industry than they probably previously realized, and it made them certainly more willing to venture throughout the 1950s." By 1956, when Kefauver tried again, his time was past and the Mob had a friend a heartbeat away from the White House.

* * *

Personal business distracted Moe Dalitz from much of the Kefauver drama, starting with the breakup of his third marriage. Matrimony weighed heavily on a man with Moe's roving eye, and Nevada granted instant divorces to any resident of six weeks' standing. One sweltering afternoon in June 1950, attorney E.R. Miller drove Toni Dalitz 245 miles north through the desert to Ely, seat of White Pine County, where a judge annulled the 42-month marriage. The file is sealed by court order and county clerk Donna Bath refused to provide a specific date for the annulment, when contacted in July 2006. Toni was surprised, that year, to learn of the annulment, having thought for over half a century that she and Moe had simply been divorced.

Despite that sudden move, Moe did not banish Toni altogether from his life. Soon after the annulment, he visited Toni and son Andrew in Detroit, where the couple became "re-engaged" in a bid to reconcile. As Toni recalled it in 2006, "He asked me if we could try it again, and so I shook hands, but then it didn't work out that we tried it again." Moe drove Toni and Andrew to Florida, where he kept a yacht moored at Bahia Mar, but the reconciliation came to naught. Even then, Toni notes that Moe "said that I could come back any time, he'd give me three years after the divorce," but it was not to be. Moe kept in touch, "not very often," and while Toni would visit the Desert Inn with Andrew on occasion, by 1953 Moe had another Mrs. Dalitz on the line.

Meanwhile, G-men kept track of Moe. In April 1951 they marked his presence at the Toll Gate Inn and Fishing Lodge, "a combination gambling joint and fishing camp" in the Florida Keys. FBI files contain the statement of an unnamed informer, describing another Dalitz yacht — the *Howdy Partner*— which he kept during the summer months at Michigan's Riviera Yacht Club or at Wisconsin's Port Washington marina, heading south to Florida each autumn. On one such trip, Moe spent time with Longy Zwillman off Miami Beach, aboard a yacht owned by Sam Tucker.

Legitimate business demanded much of Moe's attention, liquidating the Thistledown racetrack and merging Colonial Laundry with Michigan Industrial Laundry in 1951, maintaining his interest in various laundries around Detroit and Cleveland. In August 1951 partners Kleinman and Rothkopf sold a Shaker Heights apartment house to Mutual Mortgage and Investment Company, turning a $94,000 profit on their 1947 investment. An FBI memo from February 1952 claimed that "[a]s of the above date [Dalitz] restricted himself to legitimate investments but was still recognized on a national basis as a leading racketeer." Twelve months later, G-men claimed that Moe "apparently had no financial holdings in Cleveland … [but] had been mentioned in connection with the investigation of fraudulent activities on the part of Willy's Overland employees at Toledo." Real estate investment briefly soured for the Mob in 1953, when Ohio state auditor James Rhodes withheld rent payments on a state office building in Cleveland, owned by Kleinman and company. Another tenant was the IRS, which paid the Mob $505 monthly in rent.

* * *

Another thorn in Moe's side was Masthead Exports. On December 18, 1951, a federal grand jury indicted Moe, Sam Stein, Arthur Leebove, Leonard La Bella, Leonard de Pippo, Sami Salim and George Wilson for conspiracy to defraud the government and to register various aircraft under fictitious names. Prosecutor Grove Richman called Moe "the main financier" of the plot, but it took agents three weeks to find him. Arrested on January 8, 1952, Moe posted $10,000 bond and pled not guilty at his arraignment, on January 11.

Once Moe was indicted, G-men had more plausible reason to follow his movements. They noted his departure from Miami on February 1, 1952, and his return on February 12. Two weeks later, agents interviewed Moe in Miami Beach, concerning the Senate's attempt to secure his testimony on a case captioned "Consolidated Laundries vs. U.S. Court of Claims." Moe said "he was not desirous of testifying ... but that if he did testify he would be a willing rather than a hostile witness." He also "furnished information concerning general gambling activities in Las Vegas." No subpoena was forthcoming in the laundry case, nor do the FBI's files provide any details.

The Masthead case dragged on until April 7, 1953, when H.M. Goldschein, a special assistant to Attorney General Herbert Brownell Jr., asked Judge Alfred Modarelli to dismiss Moe's indictment. Goldschein explained that "the government has been unable to corroborate the charges," consisting chiefly of statements made by Terrill Murrell.

Salim's charges were also dismissed. On April 10, Murrell was fined $1,000 for filing false Customs documents, while LaBella and de Pippo paid $100 each for the same offense. On May 23 defendants Stein, Leebove, and Wilson paid $1,000 fines.

Moe explained the case, after a fashion, to Nevada's Gaming Control Board in August 1960. As summarized by the FBI, Moe testified "that he had loaned a sum of money to Sam Stein, who was an old friend. Stein went into the exporting business and Dalitz helped him make contacts for purchasing cotton. Stein, unknown to [Dalitz], started exporting contraband in the nature of airplane parts. Stein, Dalitz, and others associated with the venture were indicted for violation of the Neutrality Act. [Dalitz] was indicted because of his financial interest. He later explained his position and the case against him was dismissed. The others pleaded nolle contenders [*sic*]."

In fact, that statement was misleading on several points. Moe was an ex-vice president of Masthead, not a mere investor, and the plan involved export of fully functional warplanes, not "parts." Likewise, his case was not dismissed based on his "explanation" to authorities, but rather on the fact that prosecutors lost faith in their star witness. Still, it was good enough for the GCB, whose members saw and heard no evil where Moe Dalitz was concerned.

* * *

Kefauver heat upset the Mob in California, where Mickey Cohen was indicted in 1951. Fifty-five years later, Gus Russo claimed that Sidney Korshak "ratted out ... Cohen ... to the FBI in 1951" because "Mickey was becoming an all-around pain in the ass, setting up crap games just to rob the players." In fact, Cohen was arrested by IRS agents who charged him with ducking $156,000 in taxes. Convicted in June 1951, Cohen received a five-year sentence and served four, emerging from prison to resume his criminal career in 1955.

The sentence may have seemed like a vacation to Cohen, whose home was bombed by mafiosi in February 1950. Shortly before he went away, Cohen fielded an offer from televangelist Billy Graham press agents. According to Cohen, Graham's team promised $10,000 in return for Mickey's appearance at Madison Square Garden, where he would publicly convert to Christianity. Cohen went to New York, bankrolled by W.C. Jones, who served on Graham's board of directors. Jones recalled praying with Mickey, after which Cohen tapped him for a $1,000 loan. Mickey ran up a $500 tab in Manhattan, then embarrassed Graham by spilling his story to the L.A. *Herald-Express.* Reporter Ed Reid says that Mickey's abortive salvation cost the Graham crusade $18,000, while evidence produced at his trial suggested a $50,000 offer for Mickey's participation in a nationwide speaking tour. Cohen called the payments "brotherly love gifts" from minister James Vaus, who gave Cohen at least $6,000 and introduced him to other suckers.

A May 1953 report from California's Crime Commission named Mal Clark of Palm Springs as a character "associated with hoodlums in the gambling casinos in Las Vegas, among whom is Moe Dalitz." Two months later, FBI memos cited a "confidential informant of known reliability"—the standard designation for a bug or wiretap—who "advised that Mo Dalitz and Morris Kleinman ... were working through the Governor of Ohio to exert pressure in delaying the impending deportation of Jack Dragno [*sic*]." In December 1951, San Diego County liquor control officer Jack Graves was "surprised" to learn from the commission that his car was registered to Pete Licavoli's home address. Graves acknowledged visits to Licavoli's Tucson ranch, but he denied any taint of impropriety.

Publicists for the Rev. Billy Graham paid Mickey Cohen for his promise to become a Christian (Library of Congress).

*   *   *

Despite the FBI's claim that Dalitz "restricted himself to legitimate investments" after 1951, Moe kept his fingers planted in various illicit pies. Gambling was his primary interest, with a list of Ohio joints including the Hickory Club, Swan Club, and Valley Club in Lawrence County. Lucas County was busier still, with the Benor Club, Chesterfield Club, Devon Club, Pines Club, T&T Club, Victory Club, Webster Inn, and the Woodville Club. An FBI memo from August 1951 acknowledged that Moe "has been a king-pin of Cleveland's gambling syndicate for years."

By 1951, Ohio gambling had spilled across the Indiana border, with slot machines infesting counties along the Ohio River. Hank Messick blamed Frank Costello for planting the first slots in Lawrenceburg, but Cleveland soon absorbed the river-counties action. That winter, Sheriff Frank McDonald raided the Gar-Dan Oil Company office in Evansville, owned in part by Moe's old classmate Sam Garfield. McDonald found basketball handicapping sheets printed on Gar-Dan stationery, plus other gambling paraphernalia. The "Dan" in Gar-Dan, Milton Danenberg, was a Chicago bookmaker. Garfield blamed an unnamed "friend" for turning one of his spare rooms into a bookie joint, yet he pled guilty to gambling and paid a $500 fine.

While Hoover's G-men filed and forgot their memos on Dalitz, IRS agents put pressure on the Mob. In Cleveland, Shondor Birns saw his Alhambra Inn go bankrupt while he battled deportation. In 1952 the IRS charged him with evading $111,972 in taxes on income from the Alhambra, the Theatrical Grill, and the Ten-Eleven Club. Convicted in July 1953, Birns received a three-year sentence.

Meanwhile, in March 1951, California congressman Cecil King released a "secret list of underworld characters" facing IRS investigation for tax evasion. Among the 126 names were those of Moe Dalitz, Pete Licavoli, and Cleveland's Angersola brothers. IRS agents requested an FBI "name check" on Dalitz through the Cleveland field office, in October 1951, but nothing came of it. Likewise, no charges resulted from Morris Kleinman's default on his 1950 income tax, revealed by Alvin Giesey to the Kefauver Committee. Chuck Polizzi found himself in tax court during 1952, as did Sam Tucker the following year, but neither served any time. In 1953 the IRS indicted Wilbur Clark, but he beat the rap at trial in August 1954, with a verdict that Ed Reid and Ovid Demaris dubbed "miraculous."

* * *

While his interests were far-flung, Las Vegas was the center of Moe's universe from 1950 onward. In May of that year, local police department suffered a humiliating scandal. Chief Archie Wells dismissed four officers on charges including illegal moonlighting, obstructing justice, corrupt fraternization with casino owners, leaking classified material to "perfect strangers," and conspiring "to undermine and set up the department as they saw fit." Attorney Harry Claiborne fought the charges and won reinstatement for all four officers, despite what Chief Wells called "a cancerous condition of internal dissension, unrest, insecurity, and a dangerous lack of authoritative leadership within the police department."

That kind of law enforcement suited Dalitz perfectly. The state of local politics may be inferred from Gus Greenbaum's 1950 election as mayor of Paradise, a mini-municipality consisting of fifty-four square miles surrounding the Las Vegas Strip. In 1950's gubernatorial race, Dalitz opposed incumbent Vail Pittman's re-election bid, fearing that Pittman might use his second term as a launching pad to challenge Senator Pat McCarran in 1952. Accordingly, the DI crowd threw its weight and cash behind ex-state senator Charles Russell, who won the race and served two terms as governor.

Moe's support for McCarran also placed him at odds with former DI publicist Hank Greenspun. Despite close ties to gamblers, Greenspun's *Sun* covered the Kefauver hearings and blasted McCarran for his alliance with witch-hunting Senator Joseph McCarthy. In 1951, pro-McCarran mayor Ernest Cragin lost his seat to *Sun*–backed independent C.D. Baker, while McCarran fumed and plotted vengeance. He tried the carrot before the stick, throwing Greenspun a lucrative advertising account for Bill Graham's Bank Club in Reno, but while Greenspun ran the ads and kept the money, his attacks on McCarran continued.

The storm broke in 1952, when Greenspun backed ex-newsman Tom Mechling in

Nevada's Democratic senatorial primary, against McCarran candidate Alan Bible. Mechling scored a narrow victory, whereupon McCarran covertly gave his support to incumbent George Malone. In March 1952, eight months before Malone defeated Mechling, Gus Greenbaum and Benny Binion visited Greenspun, begging him "on bended knee" to stop attacking McCarran. Greenspun refused, and four days later saw 30 percent of his casino advertising cancelled within a span of two hours. When the Desert Inn account was pulled, Greenspun called Dalitz and found him "unavailable." Rushing over to the DI, Greenspun cornered Moe for a showdown later recorded in the memoir *Where I Stand.*

"What's behind all these ad cancellations?" Greenspun demanded.

"You should know," Moe replied. "Why did you have to attack the Old Man?"

"What business is it of the Desert Inn, or any other hotel, what I print in my paper?" Greenspun challenged.

"You've put us all in a terrible position," Moe said. "You know as well as I that we have to do what he tells us. You *know* he got us our licenses. If we don't go along, you know what will happen to us."

Greenspun left Dalitz with an ultimatum: restore the ads within twenty-four hours, or else. On March 25 the *Sun* ran its first exposé on the boycott, followed by allegations that a McCarran phone call launched the boycott. El Cortez owners Fred Soly and J.K. Houssels admitted as much, in a meeting with Mayor Baker, Greenspun, and Lieutenant Governor Jones. Baker raged, "I'll be damned if any hoodlums from the Strip are going to put a newspaper out of business in this city! I'll cancel every downtown gambling license if this boycott continues!"

But continue it did. Greenspun sued McCarran and forty casino executives, charging conspiracy to ruin the *Sun* and seeking $1 million in damages. At a preliminary hearing in May 1952, before Judge Roger Foley, Dalitz and other casino proprietors denied any pressure from McCarran. Moe further charged that Greenspun had threatened to "expose every stockholder in the Strip hotels with information from his files" if the casino ads were not restored. Mayor Baker's testimony, summing up the meeting at his office, tipped the balance in Greenspun's favor. Judge Foley ruled that the matter should proceed to trial, but limited Greenspun's recovery to treble damages — a maximum of $225,000.

McCarran tried to block that order in October, moving for dismissal on grounds that Greenspun had "failed to prove any complicity" in the boycott. Foley reserved judgment until McCarran was deposed in December 1952. In an eight-hour grilling, McCarran acknowledged "comped" visits to various Strip hotels, but denied any link to the Mob or involvement in the boycott. Two days before trial was scheduled to start, in February 1953, attorneys for the Strip executives requested "the minimum acceptable basis for a settlement." Greenspun demanded $86,000, plus written guarantees of three years' steady advertising. The bosses balked at that, and trial proceeded on schedule.

The final event was anticlimactic. Before ex-Thunderbird secretary Charlotte Furer could describe phone calls received between October 1951 and June 1952, defense lawyers renewed their pleas for a settlement. Greenspun accepted $80,500 in cash and an unwritten "gentleman's understanding" that ads in the *Sun* would resume without attempts to influence editorial policy. McCarran branded the deal "an admission by Greenspun that his charges had been unsubstantiated," but he fooled no one. A heart attack killed him on September 28, 1954.

* * *

When not in court or legislative hearing rooms, Moe Dalitz enjoyed his role as the DI's "entertainment director." Those whom he entertained included MCA's Lew Wasserman, wife Edie, and their daughter Lynn — who shared her mother's habit of calling Dalitz "Uncle Moe." Another favorite was Antoinette Giancana, daughter of Chicago mafioso Sam Giancana. In her autobiography, Antoinette recalled meeting Dalitz and wife Toni three decades earlier. On that occasion, Giancana admired a diamond necklace of Toni's that spelled out her name. Six weeks later, Giancana claims, she received an identical necklace from Moe.

Problems arise when Toni Giancana dates the encounter within the year after her mother's death, which occurred in 1954. By then, Moe had already wed his fourth wife, but his third ex explained the discrepancy in a 2006 interview. Toni Dalitz recalled meeting Toni Giancana during one of her post-annulment visits to Las Vegas. The bauble in question was, she said, "a pinky ring that said 'Toni' in diamonds, but they were very small, nothing much. She [Giancana] had liked it, and so, when she was telling Moe about it, I guess in the office upstairs, he had one made for her."

Moe's other special friends included Bob Hope, Bing Crosby, and comic-musician Phil Harris. Singer Sonny King owed his career to Dalitz, who launched him on Las Vegas with a four-week stint at the Bingo Club. From there, King played the Sahara and teamed with Jimmy Durante at the DI, forging a partnership that endured until Durante's death in 1980.

Frank Sinatra also owed much to Dalitz. Following a rage of "bobby-soxer" popularity, Sinatra's career hit the skids in 1950. Encouraged by Paul "Skinny" D'Amato, a New Jersey club owner who met Moe at the 1929 Atlantic City conference, Dalitz booked Sinatra into the DI's Painted Desert Room, where players got a floor show and steak dinner for six dollars per head. Those Vegas gigs kept Sinatra solvent until 1954, when he revitalized his image with an Oscar as Best Supporting Actor in *From Here to Eternity*. Still besotted with gangsters, Sinatra craved their company and once told singer Eddie Fisher, "I'd rather be a don of the Mafia than President of the United States."

* * *

From Bugsy Siegel's murder through the 1990s, it was *de riguer* for local newspapers to tease subscribers with reports on the "supposed" extent of Mafia influence in Vegas. Most accounts were vague, some openly dismissive, but Sin City seemed to relish a flavor of gunsmoke and garlic. To this day, the subject of Mafia involvement in Nevada still inspires heated debate.

There is no question that the Mob built Vegas and controlled it more or less completely through the mid–1960s, while retaining major influence for years. As for the Mafia — meaning the oath-bound clique whose membership is restricted to Italians — the matter remains obscure. Two inside spokesmen for the Vegas-Mafia cabal were Jimmy Fratianno and John Rosselli. Speaking through biographers and courtroom testimony, both men cast themselves as lords of Vegas, living like a pair of sultans on The Strip.

The facts paint a different picture.

It is true that mafiosi from Detroit and Cleveland shared Moe's bounty at the Desert Inn. Joe Adonis and Frank Costello owned "points" in the Sands casino, with Meyer Lansky, Doc Stacher, Kid Cann, and Ed Levinson. Tom Dragna bought a desert ranch outside Vegas in 1951, but brother Jack's attempt to colonize Nevada ended with his arrest by immigration agents. According to FBI files, it required intervention from Dalitz and Morris Kleinman to save Dragna from deportation. Jimmy Fratianno recalled dining with Tom Dragna and Lou Rothkopf and claimed that Rothkopf boasted of skimming $36 million from the DI.

Moe Dalitz employed singer Frank Sinatra (left, with Ava Gardner) when Sinatra's career was on the skids (Library of Congress).

That story may be true. Conversely, Fratianno also claimed that he personally introduced the Cleveland Four to Wilbur Clark. Another Fratianno fable described the murder of gambler Mert Wertheimer — who actually died from leukemia in July 1958.

Fratianno's wildest claims involved the Mafia's supposed domination of Jewish mobsters in Las Vegas and nationwide. A former chauffeur for the Cleveland Four, Fratianno regaled Ovid Demaris with tales of physically assaulting Doc Stacher, Moe Sedway, and Morris Kleinman. The latter incident supposedly occurred in 1954, when Kleinman used profanity in front of Fratianno's wife. Such stories only surfaced decades later, when Fratianno suddenly recalled telling colleagues, "The Jews don't fuck with the Italians. I'd whack Meyer [Lansky] tomorrow if Jack [Dragna] gave me the word. And he'd stand there and take it like the rest of them." Even John Rosselli shunned such flights of fancy, telling Fratianno in 1960, "There's been a power switch in Nevada, from Reno to Las Vegas. Today it's the Dalitz crowd that has the clout."

Toni Giancana did her part for the Mafia myth in 1984, describing how Dalitz "practically did cartwheels" to serve her father. A measure of respect for Sam Giancana was only natural, since he served as Tony Accardo's underboss, then led Chicago's Outfit until 1974. Meanwhile, Giancana was banned from setting foot in any Nevada casino after June 1960, when he joined ten fellow mobsters as original entrants in Nevada's "Black Book." Moe certainly knew Giancana, and showed him the respect due to a rattlesnake, but no evidence exists that Giancana "owned" Moe or his partners at the Desert Inn.

Others of note in Vegas, who carried no Sicilian taint, were familiar faces. Ed Levinson came west in 1952 and took his place as an executive at

Many reports exaggerate Chicago mobster Sam Giancana's influence over Moe Dalitz (Library of Congress).

the Sands. Nevada authorities approved his gambling license in 1953. Soon, Levinson also owned 20 percent of the Fremont and 27.5 percent of the Horseshoe. Joseph Kennedy was another Nevada investor, splitting ownership of Lake Tahoe's Cal-Neva Lodge with Sam Giancana. FBI memos also suggest a Kennedy connection to the Desert Inn. Specifically, they cite two letters written to Dalitz by DI employee Annie Patterson, noting Kennedy's claim of friendship with Meyer Lansky. Kennedy told Patterson that Lansky had complained to him, asking Kennedy to find out why Lansky "was not receiving his full share of the take" from Moe's skim at the Desert Inn.

* * *

Convinced that Vegas needed more attractions for quality players, Dalitz convened a meeting of hotel owners to discuss construction of a golf course. Moe's rationale was simple: "We need to give our customers something to do besides gamble, swim, and sleep." Gus Greenbaum opposed the idea, so Moe pressed on alone, building the Desert Inn Country Club with southern Nevada's first eighteen-hole course. The project involved importation of 10,000 trees and diversion of water from other precincts, but Dalitz finished the job late in 1952. One problem remained: what would lure big-name players to Nevada?

Moe's answer was the Tournament of Champions, conceived to reap publicity and cash.

For years, as tour director of the Professional Golfers' Association, Howard Capps — the DI's new golf pro — had promoted a "showdown" match for PGA champions only. Now, he had his venue, with an added twist. While pros faced off for an initial prize of $10,000, Moe guaranteed a minimum donation of $35,000 to the Damon Runyon Cancer Fund. Celebrities flocked to the event and bet on the match, while others — including Dalitz chums Bob Hope, Bing Crosby, and Phil Harris — joined in a spin-off putting contest.

Moe Dalitz smiled all the way to the bank.

He also profited from real estate, a venue long familiar to the Cleveland Four. Hotels, apartment houses, tract homes, shopping malls — no project was too large, if Moe could find the right associates.

He found them in Mervyn Adelson and Irwin Molasky. As with Dalitz, confusion shrouds their early movements in Vegas. Alan Balboni claims that both arrived in the 1940s, while Molasky dated his arrival from 1951–52. Adelson's father was a prosperous grocer in Los Angeles. His son, born in 1929, borrowed $10,000 to open Market Town on Las Vegas Boulevard. Irwin Molasky, born in 1927, was a nephew of St. Louis bookie William Molasky. Indicted with Mickey McBride in 1939 for running an interstate lottery, William pled guilty to that charge, and to tax evasion in 1940. Ten years later, when he drew attention from the Kefauver Committee, William was a major stockholder in Pioneer News Service, which transmitted race results via Western Union until police cut the link in 1950. Balboni says Irwin entered Vegas through the motel business; Molasky describes himself as a construction pioneer, starting with home remodeling and working up from there.

Molasky and Adelson met in the early 1950s, becoming partners at the Colonial Inn, which authors Reid and Demaris call "a bistro noted as a haven for prostitutes." Reid and Demaris say that after meeting Dalitz, Adelson and Molasky sold the Colonial and embarked on the road to riches. Vegas locals called them "guys who fell into it" when they met Moe. Meanwhile, FBI files state that Dalitz "and others" bought the Colonial *House* from Wilbur Clark and assumed its gambling license with state approval in January 1954. Soon afterward, Moe borrowed $200,000 from one of his shell companies to expand the joint. An FBI memo from June 1955 listed Moe as sole owner of the Colonial House. Another from May 1963 says Moe owned 75 percent of the business, with 25 percent held by Robert Brooks of Los Angeles. Concerning his ties to the DI crowd, Molasky told author Wallace Turner, "We were socially connected."

Dalitz knew talent when he saw it. With Allard Roen from the Desert Inn, he joined Molasky and Adelson to form a new construction firm, Paradise Developments. Together, the partnership of Dalitz, Roen, Adelson, and Molasky — "DRAM," for short — remodeled Las Vegas and expanded beyond Nevada, striking gold in California.

* * *

Mob operations in California and Nevada intertwined with projects in Florida and the Caribbean. In October 1951 Moe Dalitz sailed his *Howdy Partner* south from the Great Lakes to Miami, where police noted an influx of mobsters. Those identified in print included Morris Kleinman, Lou Rothkopf, Al Polizzi, Longy Zwillman, Joe Massei, Max Weisberg and "Big Shooey" Segal from Nig Rosen's Philadelphia syndicate. FBI files say Dalitz was "in and out of Miami Beach several times" during the winter of 1951–52, with another appearance noted in June 1952.

By that time, America was caught up in another presidential race. Democrats snubbed Estes Kefauver to nominate former Illinois governor Adlai Stevenson. Republican war hero

Dwight Eisenhower tapped Richard Nixon as his running mate, due in equal parts to Nixon's Red-hunting and the persuasive powers of Mob attorney Murray Chotiner. Between July's Republican convention and September 1952, Chotiner steered $18,000 in illegal contributions into Nixon's pocket. Exposure of that slush fund threatened Nixon's place on the GOP ticket, but Chotiner saved him by drafting the now-famous "Checkers" speech, televised on September 23, which portrayed Nixon as a virtual pauper.

Irwin Molasky became a millionaire through his association with Moe Dalitz (Las Vegas Historical Society).

In fact, he was anything but poor. During 1952 Nixon bought land in Florida, financed by friend Bebe Rebozo's bank. Rebozo also used Polizzi Construction to build Miami's first Cuban shopping center. In Chicago, Sam Giancana told friends, "I like Ike, but I like his running mate, Nixon, even better." J. Edgar Hoover helped the GOP by spreading rumors that Adlai Stevenson was bisexual. On election day, Ike and Nixon trounced the Democrats by a margin of 6.5 million votes.

Ninety miles from Miami, Fulgencio Batista staged a nearly bloodless coup in March 1952, removing President Carlos Prío Socarrás. The U.S. State Department cheerfully bestowed its recognition on the new regime. For the sake of appearances, Batista subsequently staged an election and ran unopposed, achieving victory despite reports that 75 percent of Havana's voters abstained in protest.

Nixon's ties to Cuba were well known. Aside from honeymooning there, he enjoyed spending time and money at Havana's Mob-owned casinos. In August 1952, Nixon penned a letter to the State Department, asking U.S. diplomats to help an old friend, Dana Smith, avoid prosecution for writing bad checks to cover his Cuban gambling debts. In October 1952, the *St. Louis Post-Dispatch* reported that Nixon was with Smith in Cuba when the incident occurred. Nixon predictably denied it.

American mobsters welcomed the news of Batista's return to power, seeing Cuba as an antidote to the Kefauver-inspired gambling crackdown in Florida. Batista announced that his government would match any foreign construction investments exceeding $1 million. Working under cover, Meyer Lansky built a new Riviera hotel-casino, siphoning half of the $14 million price from Cuban banks. Batista also waived import duties on casino building materials and extended work visas to two years for casino "technicians." Licenses cost $25,000, while yearly taxes came in well below the Cuban norm. The exception was Batista's brother, who as Cuba's Sports Director claimed 50 percent of all slot-machine income.

Batista and the Mob brought new prosperity to Cuba, for the lucky few. By the mid–1950s Havana had more telephones and Cadillacs per capita than any American city. Still, poverty, corruption, and police brutality left peasants simmering in discontent. Cuba's Communist Party supported Batista until mid–1958, but young revolutionaries schemed to unseat him. One such was Fidel Castro, who led 160 guerrillas against the army's Moncada Barracks in

July 1953. Sixty-one of the rebels were killed and fifty-odd captured, half of them tortured to death by Batista's police. At trial, where he received a fifteen-year sentence, Castro told the court, "History will absolve me."

* * *

The Mob's Kentucky operations suffered briefly from Kefauver scrutiny, but any changes were cosmetic. Newport's Chief George Gugel weathered his suspension in December 1950, while members of the Newport Civic Association, secretly funded by Red Masterson, campaigned on a vow to "clean up, not close up." Local police files told the story: of 1,733 arrests made in 1950, only 41 involved gambling offenses, while 518 miscreants were jailed for traffic violations.

Moe Dalitz denied any ongoing link to Kentucky's casinos, but FBI files told a different story. A memo from July 1950 noted that Moe maintained "financial interests in Northern Kentucky, including gambling establishments in Newport." Lou Rothkopf, Chuck Polizzi, and John Croft allegedly sold their interests in the Lookout House to local gamblers in 1951, yet Croft remained spokesman for Bluegrass Amusements, founded the previous year to manage Kentucky casinos. Accountant Jack Kuresman served Bluegrass as bookkeeper for the Yorkshire, Merchants, and 633 Clubs, the Latin Quarter, and the Oak Grove Restaurant. In Senate testimony, Kuresman identified Croft as his Bluegrass contact but conveniently forgot who owned the company. The Beverly Hills Club also "changed hands," with Dalitz, Kleinman, Tucker, and Tom McGinty allegedly selling their interests to Rothkopf, Chuck Polizzi, John Croft, and Harry Potter.

Covington's hot spots included the Kentucky Club, 514 Club, and 627 Club (two blocks from the courthouse). The Kentucky Club suffered a raid in February 1951, after reformers published its address, but the action was hardly crippling. Four months later, myopic grand jurors declared that "the gambling situation in Kenton County is solved." Nonetheless, in March 1952 state police raided the Lookout House, seizing gambling equipment valued at $20,000. In August, James Brink and gambler Charles Drahman died when Brink's plane crashed near Atlanta. Rescuers found $16,200 spilling from the plane, with records for a Miami dog track.

In 1953 Newport's alleged reformers elected Judge Fred Warren as mayor. Warren immediately fired the town's police chief and retained an "incorruptible" replacement — who immediately struck a deal with Wilder's Marshal "Big Jim" Harris, owner of the Hi-De-Ho Club brothel and several casinos. Harris had irritated Dalitz by organizing Cincinnati's cabbies to supply his clubs with suckers, drawing business from Mob casinos, and blackmailing prominent whorehouse clients with covert audio recordings. Now, he sent Newport's police chief around to extort further bribes. Mob leaders met at the Yorkshire Club and agreed to pay Harris $5,000 per month, while they schemed to depose him. Soon, county prosecutors "remembered" a March 1952 raid on one of the marshal's casinos and charged Harris with illegal gambling. Harris retained Charles Lester, then complained that "he never even showed up in court." Convicted at his second trial, Harris received a three-year prison term. Departing for the lockup, he described Newport as "a wonderful town for framing somebody."

In November 1950, armed robbers stole $75,000 from the Kentucky Club's counting room. Chief Gugel identified "two or three suspects," but made no arrests in what he called Newport's all-time greatest holdup. The culprits were never publicly identified. Their shallow graves remain unmarked.

Fidel Castro's revolution ultimately drove the Mob out of Cuba (Library of Congress).

* * *

Moe Dalitz's exposure by the Kefauver Committee brought more heat down upon him in 1952–53. The source was New York's State Crime Commission, belatedly turning a spotlight on labor racketeers. Governor Dewey launched the hearings in March 1951, and extended their life with a second order in November 1952.

Dalitz made his first appearance before the commission on October 16, 1952. He admitted knowing Mafia boss Thomas Lucchese, but refused to say when they first met. As for Albert Anastasia, Moe said, "I ran into him once or twice, I guess. I don't know. I met him when I was in the army."

Recalled to testify on January 26, 1953, Moe suffered a memory lapse. This time, he denied knowing either Anastasia or Lucchese, until commission special counsel Theodore Kiendl read excerpts from the previous interrogation. Thus cornered, Moe admitted knowing Lucchese "by sight," and said of Anastasia, "Well, I didn't know that name.... I don't think he'd know me, and if I met him on the street I wouldn't know him well enough to stop and say hello to him."

Others whom Moe acknowledged knowing "by sight" included Irish mobsters Connie Noonan and Tommy Whalen, Art Samish, Allen Smiley, Jake Guzik, and millionaire ex-convict oilman Larry Knohl. Moe acknowledged his acquaintance with Phil Kastel, Joe Adonis, Frank Erickson, Meyer Lansky, Ben Siegel, and California gambler Elmer Reemer, but denied ever meeting Lucky Luciano, Mickey Cohen, Lepke Buchalter, or Jack Dragna. Abner Zwill-

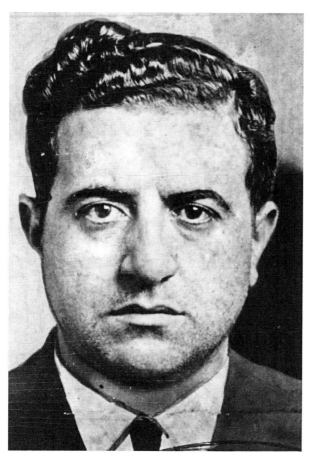

Moe Dalitz, under oath, offered contradictory statements concerning his ties to mafioso Albert Anastasia (Library of Congress).

man was a longtime friend and frequent guest aboard the *South Wind*, Moe admitted, as was Edward McGrath, boss of New York's violent "Westies" gang during 1934–49. In February 1952, McGrath spent several days aboard the *South Wind* and played golf with Moe in Nassau.

Another topic of interest was Moe's September 1952 dinner meeting with McGrath, Reemer, a woman named Marion Taft, and "a man by the name of Samish." While uncertain of the date, Moe recalled meeting "during the fight"—perhaps Rocky Marciano's September 23 defeat of Jersey Joe Walcott. In any case, the hearing ended with a feeble anticlimax. Moe had left to watch the fight on television, with a friend identified only as "Benjamin," while Samish, McGrath, and Reemer "went to another one."

The commission ultimately accepted Moe's denials that he knew Luciano, Lepke, Mickey Cohen, or Jack Dragna. The evidence that could have jailed him for perjury was hidden in FBI memos spanning two decades. Another memo, penned in February 1953, cited an informer's reference to a "bookmaker in partnership with Moe Dalitz," accepting illegal wagers in Cleveland and New York.

Moe had no reason for concern. Only the IRS seemed bent on trapping him, and his accountants, led by Alvin Giesey, held that threat at bay. Far to the west of Cleveland and New York, Moe had a new love in Las Vegas and an ever-growing list of golden opportunities. No one in California or Nevada was inclined to question him or shun his money.

Life was good.

8

Happy Days

Moe's new love was Averill Marie Knigge, born in 1925. She left Texas with gambler Jake Friedman, serving as his executive secretary when Friedman opened his Sands Hotel-Casino on the Vegas Strip in December 1952. Rumor named Friedman's silent partners as Meyer Lansky, Doc Stacher, Kid Cann, Ed Levinson, and Frank Costello.

When Moe met Averill, it was lust at first sight. Alan Balboni describes Averill as "stunningly attractive," and her Texas background helped. Raised with guns from childhood, she joined Moe on hunting trips to Utah's Shivwit Indian Reservation and posed for newspaper photographs with deer she killed. Their "torrid romance" rated mention in the *Sun*, with Hank Greenspun proclaiming that their marriage on May 1, 1953 "took no one by surprise."

Overnight, Averill graduated from secretary at the Sands to queen bee at the DI, joining Toni Clark and Evelyn Roen to coordinate social events. She also gave Moe a daughter, Suzanne, though circumstances surrounding the birth are confused. As noted by reporters Don Bauder and Matt Potter in 2006, voter registration documents for Suzanne Dalitz place her birth in 1957, while court documents claim she was born in 1951. The latter date, two years before her parents wed, is clearly incorrect.

* * *

Moe's main focus, in post–Kefauver Vegas, was expansion of his western empire, anchored at the Desert Inn. While new casinos opened nearby, the DI reigned as the Strip's centerpiece and classiest joint. Honored guests included Robert Goldwater and Bing Crosby — who, according to the FBI, cavorted with prostitutes and paid $10,000 hush money to a blackmailing pimp. G-men noted Bing's association with Moe, tagged by the Bureau as a former member of "the old Detroit Purple Gang."

Other DI visitors included Sidney Korshak and Chicago mafioso Louis Rosanova, whose golf foursome included Dalitz, Allard Roen, and Jimmy Hoffa lieutenant Frank Fitzsimmons. Also present was Bill Presser, tapped by Hoffa and Tony Milano to rule Ohio's Teamsters as head of IBT Joint Council 41. That post gave Presser a monopoly on Buckeye jukeboxes, and a 1954 report from the Chicago Crime Commission noted that he also "figured prominently in the manipulation of Detroit juke box operators." Son Jackie Presser, who accompanied his dad on visits to Nevada, told friends that billionaire Howard Hughes had smuggled Lucky Luciano into Vegas as a favor. According to Jackie, "Luciano along with Moe Dalitz and a half-dozen other Mafia members [*sic*] were in Vegas to greet us."

Meanwhile, a group of investors applied to buy the Flamingo in November 1953. Chief among them were Ed Levinson and Albert Parvin, who sold Ben Siegel the Flamingo's first carpets. State tax authorities approved Levinson's license in December 1954, placing him in charge at a cost of $8.35 million. Levinson hired Parvin to preside at the Flamingo, then decamped in July 1955 to serve as president and general manager of the new Fremont.

Moe Dalitz also had a stake downtown. In early 1954, Moe and his partners bankrolled construction of the Showboat, situated at the eastern end of Fremont. Proprietors J. Kell Houssels and William Moore theoretically owned the Showboat, but Dalitz applied for a license to run its casino in June 1954. Vegas historian Deanna DeMatteo claims that authorities denied Moe's application in July, but FBI files say the license was granted in August. The Showboat opened on September 3, 1954, with a speech by Las Vegas mayor C.D. Baker and an "aquatic exhibition" by seven-year-old Annette Kolod. Annette's father, Ruby Kolod, was frequently seen at the Showboat in company with DI casino manager Cornelius Jones, Cleveland gambler Pete Brady, and manager Joe Kelley (a veteran of Tony Cornero's gambling boats).

Despite such talent, the Showboat endured "several rough years" before breaking even. Dalitz booked actor George Jessel to lure players, but the Showboat struggled, hampered by its poor location. Reports differ on the date of Moe's withdrawal from the enterprise, but a July 1962 listing of officers includes Ruby Kolod as president, Morris Kleinman as vice-president, and Bernie Rothkopf as secretary-treasurer. At some point thereafter, Joe Kelley bought the Showboat, added bowling lanes, and struck gold with the Professional Bowlers Association Tour.

* * *

Casino expansion was buoyed by loans from the Bank of Las Vegas, established in 1954 as a branch of Walter Cosgriff's Continental Bank and Trust of Salt Lake City. Cosgriff's man in Vegas was Parry Thomas, who brought colleagues Nate Mack and son Jerry along for the ride. While older banks shunned contact with casinos, Thomas welcomed loan applications "outside of conventional channels." As one old-timer told Sally Denton and Roger Morris, "Parry came to town with his own juice, and everyone on the Strip knew it." Another said, "The casinos knew what was coming the minute the [BLV] charter was granted."

Specifically, the BLV granted "character loans" to casino owners and front men, approved by Thomas without stifling demands for collateral. The first such loan, for $750,000, went to the Sahara in 1955. More quickly followed to the DI, Sands, Fremont, Riviera, Stardust, and Thunderbird — all known for Mob affiliations. Thomas frequently explained, "I'm in the banking business and these people were good loans." He also said, "I never met a hoodlum."

Money and politics go hand in hand. Incumbent Governor Charles Russell surprised gamblers when he first agreed to license a crony of Reno's Bill Graham, then changed his mind. Addressing a Republican Women's Club in August, Russell noted that state legislators had defeated his attempt to invest Nevada's attorney general with power to revoke casino licenses. If the bill fared no better in 1955, Russell warned, Nevada gaming might fall "into the hands of syndicates and undesirable persons." Despite such statements, Robbins Cahill recalled that Morris Kleinman "loved" Russell and was "emotional in his support of Charlie."

Pat McCarran supported Democrat Vail Pittman, but McCarran's voice was stilled forever in September 1954, when he collapsed during a campaign speech. The Lansky brothers and Lieutenant Governor Jones persuaded moguls on the Strip to back the sitting governor with votes and cash. Throughout the latter days of the campaign, reporter Edward Olsen says, "You'd find guys like Moe Dalitz ... showing up to push or pull something" in the state capital. On election day, Russell defeated Pittman with 53 percent of the vote.

The result was stricter regulation, of a sort. In 1955 state legislators created a new Gaming Control Board with an ex-G-man in charge, ostensibly to "clean up" legal gambling. Governor Russell told reporters, "I am determined that Nevada's licensed gambling shall not be invaded by hoodlums or organized crime." Authorities suspended the Thunderbird's license, pending resignations from Marion Hicks and Cliff Jones, and imposed a ninety-day moratorium on new license applications. Those already in the works were not affected. The effort proved haphazard at best, as when the GCB licensed Ed Levinson while banning other applicants from the Flamingo.

The problem was one of perception. Robbins Cahill freely granted that men like Moe Dalitz "were not ... bishops of the church, or pillars of the community. They were ... gamblers. That's the reason they came out, and built, and spent millions in a gambling place, and knew how to run the gambling business." In Cahill's view, "most accusations of racketeering ... were probably exaggerated" by outsiders.

* * *

As proof that Governor Russell's "cleanup" had failed, skeptics pointed to the Riviera, opened next door to the Thunderbird in April 1955. It was Nevada's first high-rise, costing $10 million. Liberace was the Riviera's headliner, earning $50,000 per week, while actress Joan Crawford served as hostess. Dean Martin held court in his own lounge, Dino's Den.

The real story lay with the men behind the "Riv." Its mastermind was Detroit mobster William Bischoff, whose acquaintance Moe Dalitz acknowledged before the Kefauver Committee. Bischoff launched his project as the Casa Blanca, with a gaming license granted in January 1952, then withdrew a year later. Next in line was a clutch of Miami investors led by Samuel Cohen, formerly known in Detroit as Sammy Purple. The state approved Cohen's license in September 1953, and the Riv opened on schedule. Then, in June 1955, Tax Commission spokesman Paul McDermott called for an investigation of the club's owners and employees. In July the Riviera closed, claiming bankruptcy from casino losses in its first three months.

What went wrong? Today, the Riviera's website says that Cohen and company "were unaccustomed to gaming and they ran into trouble." Gus Russo adds a twist, saying that Cohen's team was "unaccustomed to gaming while being simultaneously skimmed." Clearly, neither version is true, since Cohen had grown rich among illegal gamblers in Detroit and Miami, later moving on to skim prodigiously from the Flamingo with Meyer Lansky. Whether the early Riviera bankruptcy was real or staged, its net result was pure gold for the Mob.

Next up at the Riv was Gus Greenbaum, who applied for a license as managing director in July 1955. Most sources claim Greenbaum was lured from retirement by the Chicago Outfit, his reluctance conquered when assassins smothered his sister-in-law at her Arizona home. Curiously, that murder occurred in April 1955—one week after the Riviera's grand opening, and two months before its bankruptcy. Further confusion arises from the Riviera's website, which credits Greenbaum's employment to the Gensbro Hotel Company, owner of the desert soil beneath the Riviera.

Whatever the point of those machinations, Sam Cohen retained control of the Riviera's hotel, while Greenbaum took over the casino with a crew including Dave Berman, Willie Alderman, and other ex-Flamingo officers. A new face on the staff was that of entertainment director William Nelson, from Phoenix—previously known as Willie Bioff. That choice by Greenbaum may seem odd, since most reporters claim Gus was a tool of the Chicago syndicate, while Bioff was the Outfit's most hated informer. Still, Bioff survived three months of service at the Riv.

His passing, when it came, was swift, loud, and safely removed from Vegas. On November 4, 1955, a car bomb killed Bioff in Phoenix, blowing his cover as "Nelson" and embarrassing his friends, including Senator Barry Goldwater. *Why* was Bioff killed so publicly, a dozen years after he testified against Chicago's top gangsters? Conventional wisdom contends that Chicago lost track of Bioff, then "rediscovered" him in 1955 and ordered Greenbaum to kill him. In fact, though, Willie was not hiding. He traveled with the Goldwaters, loaned cash to Harry Rosenzweig, and dropped $28,000 in Vegas while gambling. Author John Tuohy suggests that Pete Licavoli and Chicago mobster Paul Ricca were squeezing Bioff for money, jointly deciding to kill him when he stopped paying.

Even without Bioff, Greenbaum put the Riviera in the black. He weathered a still-unsolved $5,000 casino holdup in February 1958, but his luck ran out ten months later. On December 3, his maid found Gus and wife Bess at their Phoenix home, both bludgeoned, their throats slashed so deeply that both were nearly beheaded. Again, most authors blame Chicago, claiming that Greenbaum was hooked on heroin, gambled excessively, and stole more cash from the casino than his Outfit masters would allow. The Riviera's website claims that Tony Accardo and chief enforcer Marshal Caifano spent Thanksgiving at the Scottsdale home of Pete Licavoli, thirty minutes by auto from Greenbaum's house — but Licavoli lived in *Tucson.* Jimmy Fratianno blamed the hit on Meyer Lansky, while Hank Messick claims Greenbaum was killed on orders from Moe Dalitz, after rejecting Moe's overtures to buy the Riviera. Robbins Cahill deemed the hits "too messy" for the Mob, "more like a crime of passion." The GCB found nothing to connect the deaths with legal gambling in Nevada.

Whether he made the fatal call or not, Moe had an interest in the property. Riviera vice-president Ben Goffstein succeeded Greenbaum and reported a pending sale to Ed Levinson, then changed his mind in August 1959, announcing plans for a $2 million expansion. Eleven months later, Goffstein told the GCB that he would have to close the Riviera soon, without fresh infusions of capital. His proposed solution involved selling 38.4 percent of the casino to Dalitz and the DI crowd for $760,000. Moe applied for a license to run the Riv on August 5, offering to pay $152,000 for 7.6 percent of the casino. On his application, Moe reported assets worth $2,239,320.20, with an adjusted gross income of $114,985.39 for 1958. The state rejected Moe's application, citing fears of "monopolistic growth," arranging instead a bank loan "guaranteed by the Desert Inn organization." Various reports peg the loan at $250,000 or $285,000.

In either case, Moe had his foot in the door. FBI reports from November 1960 placed Dalitz in Illinois, meeting "Chicago hoodlums" to discuss the takeover. Other memos describe key DI employees working at the Riv, although lacking "full control." Their "primary objective now," said G-men, was protection of their loan to the failing casino. Moe and his partners were often seen in the Riviera's counting room, between casino shifts. If state authorities were nervous, they had cause to be. Informants told the FBI that Moe and company "are greedy to the point where their singular purpose is controlling the industry and making as much money as possible."

Confusion still surrounds Moe's bid to run the Riv. Ed Reid claims Sidney Korshak supported the move in 1959 — a year *before* Moe's license application — by booking clients Tony Martin, Dinah Shore, and Debbie Reynolds in the Riviera's showroom. Reynolds did not mind working for mobsters. "I don't say I respect how they got their money," she explained. "It's none of my business anyway. That was for Eliot Ness to handle. But no one got killed who wasn't supposed to be. We were never frightened or anything of that sort." In February 1961, G-men reported that DI employees still held "command positions in the hotel," but that

Chicago hoodlums had "some type of financial interest and control." Hank Messick wrote that Moe and company departed from the Riviera with their "goal achieved," after the place was sold to "certain nominees."

* * *

Moe played a more straightforward role at the Stardust, brainchild of Tony Cornero. After California lawmen sank his gambling ships, Cornero tried his luck with mainland casinos, but Mickey Cohen blocked that move and bombed Cornero's mansion in Beverly Hills. Undaunted, Cornero paid $500,000 for forty acres on the Vegas Strip and launched construction of a huge hotel-casino he originally called Tony Cornero's Starlight, changed to Star*dust* a year later.

Historian Steve Fischer puts Cornero's first contact with Moe Dalitz in March 1955, when the DI gang forked over $1.25 million to secure a partnership with Cornero in the name of United Hotels. Two more loans followed, totaling $4.3 million — and still the Stardust money pit proved bottomless.

Part of the problem was Cornero's concept. He designed the Stardust as a "grind joint" for low-rollers, with 1,000 rooms renting at five dollars per night. It was a vision that concerned proprietors of swanky "carpet joints" along the Strip. Dalitz reportedly complained to Meyer Lansky, but he was willing to live and let live for a piece of the action.

Tony applied for a gaming license in April 1954, listing himself as owner of the Stardust with eight partners and 1,138 stockholders. In May 1955 the GCB refused to license a casino with more than fifty investors. John Tuohy blames Dalitz for obstructing Tony's application, claiming that Moe refused Cornero's demand for $500,000 in monthly casino rent and schemed to seize the Stardust after Tony was bankrupt.

In June 1955 Cornero withdrew his application, substituting Milton Farmer with eight partners. The board approved Farmer's license, despite testimony that Cornero owned 51 percent of the Stardust and would remain "in the driver's seat." Two weeks shy of the Stardust's scheduled July 31 opening, Tony found that he needed another $800,000 for supplies, payrolls, and a casino bankroll. He turned, once again, to Moe Dalitz.

Cornero met Moe at 9:30 A.M. on July 31, but he received no sympathy or cash. By 10:30 Tony was trying his luck at a DI crap table, drinking and losing heavily. Varied reports of his last fling cite losses ranging from $10,000 to $37,600. At 11:17 A.M., while Moe watched from the sidelines, a cocktail waitress delivered the ultimate insult, handing Cornero a $25 bar tab. Tony exploded, raved hysterically — and crumpled to the floor, stone dead.

Tony's liquor glass was whisked away and washed, while someone at the DI phoned a Los Angeles mortician to claim the corpse. Cornero's physician signed the death certificate, advising DI security guards not to bother Clark County's coroner. Local authorities learned of Tony's death at 1:15 P.M. Deputy coroner Glenn Bodell complained that DI management had given him a "runaround." Eight hours after he died, without an autopsy, Tony was buried in L.A. Rumors persist that his final drink was poisoned, and that Dalitz got away with murder once again.

Stardust directors named Tony's brother, Louis Stralla, to serve as the resort's president and general manager, claiming the Stardust would open for Christmas. Tony's widow, jailed in January 1956 for brandishing a pistol at the L.A. airport, claimed she had been threatened by "the syndicate," which craved her Stardust stock. At last, in January 1958, headlines declared that the Desert Inn's owners would run the Stardust on behalf of new owner Rella Factor, who purchased the Stardust for $4.3 million.

Rella's husband was John Jacob Factor, a rabbi's son whose family traveled from Poland to St. Louis in 1904, then settled in Chicago. Half-brother Max kept heading westward to California, founding the cosmetics firm Max Factor & Company. While Max revolutionized movie makeup, John cut hair and earned his nickname "Jake the Barber." Preferring fraud to honest work, he logged his first indictment in 1919, followed by more in 1922–23. When none of those cases sent him to prison, New York mobster Arnold Rothstein fronted $50,000 for the largest stock fraud in British history. He robbed investors of $9.5 million before reporters exposed him in 1930.

Back in the States, Factor listed himself as a "visiting" Englishman, but immigration officers had his original entry documents. When a British court convicted Factor of fraud *in absentia*, Chicago's U.S. commissioner ordered him deported. Two days before a scheduled hearing on Factor's appeal, Chicago kidnappers allegedly snatched his son Jerome, releasing him only when friendly Mob leaders paid a $50,000 ransom. Many historians believe Jerome's kidnapping was a fraud; in any case, what happened next was certainly a scam designed to keep Jake safe in the U.S. — and to eliminate one of the old Capone gang's main bootlegging rivals.

On June 30, 1933, gunmen grabbed Jake the Barber from a Mob speakeasy. Twelve days later he returned, naming his kidnappers as members of a gang led by Roger Touhy. G-man Melvin Purvis charged Touhy and three others with *two* kidnappings, Factor's and that of Minnesota brewer William Hamm Jr., ransomed for $100,000 twelve days before Factor's alleged disappearance. In fact, Hamm was abducted by a different gang, a fact that prompted jurors to acquit Touhy in November 1933. Purvis forged ahead with the Factor case, convicting the framed defendants in 1934. Thus Touhy's gang was crushed, while Factor's British fraud conviction seemed to be forgotten.

In August 1942 Factor was indicted for a $459,000 whiskey swindle. Sentenced to ten years in February 1943, he served five and was discharged from parole in 1954. Four years later, his conviction was too much for GCB members to stomach. Construction forged ahead on the Stardust, but Factor clearly would not be allowed to run the joint.

Moe Dalitz filled the void. Early in 1958 Sidney Korshak hosted a meeting in Beverly Hills. Dalitz attended with Sam Garfield, Morris Kleinman, Meyer Lansky, Doc Stacher, and Longy Zwillman, plus Chicago delegates John Battaglia and Marshal Caifano. Factor missed the meeting, G-men noting that "Factor and Dalitz, while friendly on the surface, actually dislike each other intensely." Before the group dispersed, it was agreed that Moe would lease the Stardust for $100,000 per month, in the name of a firm called Karat Incorporated.

Karat's incorporation papers show that it was organized in April 1957, by DI attorney John Donnelly and four other San Diego residents. Operating from the New Frontier in Vegas, Karat advertised its purpose as the purchase, sale, and operation of Nevada resorts. Karat issued 10,000 shares of common stock, sold for $100 each. Dalitz, holding 22 percent, served as president. Vice-President John Drew was something of a mystery, while secretary/treasurer Al Roen and board member Bernie Rothkopf were familiar faces from the DI.

The Stardust finally opened on July 2, 1958. It featured a 16,500-square-foot casino, a 105-foot swimming pool, and the world's largest electric sign, with 7,100 feet of neon tubing and 11,000 light bulbs. Albert Parvin decorated the lobby and 1,065 hotel rooms, which rented for six dollars nightly. George Jessel charmed a crowd including Texas Senator Lyndon Johnson, Bob Hope, Jack Benny, Carol Channing, Milton Berle, and Ethel Merman. An anonymous promotional brochure called the Stardust "the end product of John Factor's dream [which] fulfills this life-long ambition."

Those visibly in charge included casino director Mike Benedict and manager Silvio Petricciani. Television star Ed Sullivan agreed to play four weeks at $25,000 per week, then sold a Connecticut farm to a corporation owned by Dalitz and his partners. Morris Kleinman vacationed on the farm in 1958, while Moe's company claimed a $109,000 capital loss and Sullivan declared a $70,000 capital gain. An FBI bug caught Moe's complaint that "the whole deal was so fucking fouled up that we are not going to get mixed up in a deal like that again."

* * *

The question persists: who *really* owned and ran the Stardust? Clearly, Dalitz and his partners started out leasing the premises from Jake and Rella Factor, but Ed Reid and Ovid Demaris claim that Moe "pulled a switch" on the Factors in December 1959, selling off all assets to his United Hotels Corporation. On paper, thereafter, Dalitz, Morris Kleinman, and Sam Tucker each owned 22 percent; Ruby Kolod held 8 percent; Wilbur Clark had 5.5 percent; John Drew claimed 5 percent; Tom McGinty owned 4.5 percent; Allard Roen had 4 percent; Milton Jaffe and Bernie Rothkopf had 2 percent each; and Cornelius Jones brought up the rear with 1 percent.

Nonetheless, Reid and Demaris maintain that Tony Accardo and Sam Giancana ruled the Stardust for Chicago until 1966, through emissaries John Rosselli and John Drew. Rosselli told Jimmy Fratianno, "I'm now the man in Vegas. I got the Stardust for Chicago." Fratianno said Rosselli claimed to pocket $25,000 per month from the Stardust, out of $400,000 in untaxed monthly "skim." Referring to his Chicago overlords, Rosselli claimed that "Moe's their man," then backpedaled, acknowledging that Dalitz had "a fifty-fifty deal" at the Stardust. According to Rosselli, John Drew ran Chicago's action at the Stardust, while Dalitz sent Yale Cohen "to watch his end." Reid and Demaris also say Sam Giancana was a frequent Stardust visitor — though he was banned from all casinos after June 1960 — and they describe the spectacle of Giancana ordering Morris Kleinman to leave the casino and "never come back."

That showdown smacks of fiction, but Cohen and Drew were certainly present. Yale Cohen, an Ohio native born in 1912, had five convictions from the 1930s but was unknown in Vegas prior to 1958, when he arrived to work for Dalitz at the Stardust. In December 1960, FBI files named him as a partner, with George Gordon and others, in Newport's Beverly Hills and Yorkshire Club casinos.

John Drew was more mysterious. Gus Russo calls Drew "a former Capone crew member," while Giancana biographer William Brashler dubs him "a Chicago bookie." Ex-G-man Bill Roemer claims Drew ran the Bank Club in Reno before migrating to Vegas, and credits him with recommending Dalitz to run the Stardust. Deanna DeMatteo says that Drew's brother served as a Fremont Casino "box man" (collecting cash from gaming tables), while brother-in-law Harry Flynn held a similar post at the DI. During Drew's Stardust tenure, a Chicago newspaper accused him of running illegal crap games in the Windy City. Nevada's GCB summoned Drew for an inconclusive grilling on that subject, then allowed him to retain his license.

In fact, "John Drew" did not exist until July 1933, when he obtained a Wisconsin birth certificate by filing a "declaration of self," claiming that he was born at LaFarge in November 1901. Before that move, he had been Jacob Stein, the same New York attorney twice convicted of liquor violations and disbarred during Prohibition. Four months after his rebirth on paper, Stein/Drew became the first president of Molaska Corporation, serving silent partners Moe Dalitz, Sam Tucker, Chuck Polizzi, and Meyer Lansky.

So much for the supposed Chicago Irishman. At Drew's 1958 Nevada license hearing

Allard Roen testified that Drew was hired because "he is a colorful character" and because his "outsider" status would somehow stop the Stardust from luring high-rollers away from the Desert Inn.

John Rosselli named Robert Stella Sr. and Allan Sachs as two other "Chicago men" at the Stardust. He was correct in Stella's case, but Sachs, though trained as a dealer at Chicago's Jockey Club, moved on to work for Dalitz and company in Havana and at the Royal Nevada in Vegas, then joined the Stardust as a floorman in 1958. Soon, he owned 2 percent of the resort. Most media profiles describe him as a Dalitz protégé.

Even observers who contend that Giancana and his minions ran the Stardust sometimes contradict themselves. Bill Roemer, while calling the Stardust Chicago's Vegas "flagship," wrote in 1990: "Without any question [Dalitz] was the most powerful man in the Sin Capitol of the U.S.A. If Babe Ruth had been the Sultan of Swat, Moe Dalitz was the King of Skim." Lansky biographer Robert Lacey agreed, reporting that Moe's group "took care of their own concerns" in Las Vegas without submitting to control from either New York or Chicago.

Still, there was ample skim to go around. In December 1960, an informant told G-men that Dalitz, Drew, Tony Accardo, and Murray Humphreys had "recently" met in Chicago with "two unidentified individuals from Cleveland ... one of whom was probably Morris Kleinman." As a result of that meeting, Bureau analysts surmised, Chicago's Outfit received shares "in a three-way deal which was not clear to the informant, but which apparently involved the Riviera, Desert Inn, and Stardust." Years later, Bill Roemer declared, "It soon became quite clear to agents like myself that Chicago had reached an accommodation with Moe Dalitz and the New York families in order for them to run the Stardust, the Desert Inn, and the Riviera.... [T]he deal that granted autonomy to the Chicago Outfit, we learned, was cut in early January 1961 when Dalitz and his partner Morris Kleinman came to Chicago to confer with Tony Accardo and Sam Giancana." Aside from mistaking the date, Roemer failed to explain why Chicago should negotiate shares in two casinos which it "owned" from the time they opened.

One documented point of contact between Dalitz and the Chicago Outfit was Silver State Warehouse, a firm organized in 1955. According to FBI reports from 1963, Silver State's corporate papers listed John Rosselli, Wilbur Clark, Ruby Kolod "and others" as principal stockholders. Discussions among the Desert Inn's officers, overheard by FBI eavesdroppers, branded Rosselli "one of the strong-arm boys" and noted that any time his name was mentioned "there is something rotten in Denmark"—hardly the respect owed to a secret overlord.

The confusion served Moe Dalitz well. He had learned to let impetuous Sicilians claim the headlines and endure the heat, while he toiled quietly and made his millions, spared from public scrutiny. Doc Stacher said it all when he described the Stardust conference of early 1958 to author Dennis Eisenberg: "Our lawyers set it up so that nobody could really tell who owned what out there."

*   *   *

In November 1960 an informer told G-men, "There is presently underway some sort of national organization composed of the younger, aggressive element of sons and relatives of the older top hoodlums. These younger men are all 'clean' in that they have no criminal records, and the only derogatory information concerning them is their family connections." The spy had no specific details, but he had "heard enough conversation to be convinced that they 'have seen the handwriting on the wall' and know that the Government is out to stop all forms of illegal gambling. They hope to concentrate their efforts on getting into legal businesses, including gambling in the west. He believes that they are also interested in real estate as a future major source of revenue."

In fact, that trend had started in the 1940s. Allard Roen, with his Duke diploma, was a prime example. Asked in 1955 why he should choose to work at the DI, Roen replied, "I feel that many of the biggest fortunes in our country were originated by men who ignored the laws of the time to take advantage of the natural laws of supply and demand. These included fur trappers, land poachers, cattle rustlers, early railroad barons and bootleggers, among others. But time and a new life within the law and the raising of families placed their descendants among the blue bloods of the nation's society."

While Moe Dalitz would never be mistaken for a paragon of Judaism, he took pride in his heritage. When he arrived in Vegas, Jewish life revolved around the Temple Beth Shalom, opened in 1946 at 13th and Carson. In the mid–1950s Moe and Irwin Molasky joined others — Lloyd Katz, Harry Levy, David Zenoff — to finance relocation of the synagogue to 16th and Oakey, considered in those days a ritzy neighborhood. Ruby Kolod endowed a children's center for the temple.

Moe had a temper when his race was criticized. Vegas reporter John Smith told the story of a casino manager at the Sahara, dubbed "Jimmy Jacobsen" — who hated Jews, constantly asking subordinates if they were "kikes." Dalitz sent two sluggers to counsel Jacobsen. "Moe sent us with a message for you," one goon said. "He hears you've been making nasty remarks about Jews. Moe doesn't like that. In fact, he told us that if you make another one, we're to break your arms and legs." The other added, "If you don't believe us, make a remark now." The bigot promptly fled — both the Sahara and Las Vegas, never to return.

* * *

Heat generated by the Kefauver Committee swiftly dissipated under President Dwight Eisenhower and Vice President Richard Nixon. During the 1956 presidential campaign, Howard Hughes loaned $205,000 to Nixon's brother Donald, ostensibly to support a failing restaurant chain. Two months later the IRS reversed its denial of tax exemption for the Hughes Medical Foundation, making exemption retroactive to the foundation's launch in December 1953. The "loan" was never repaid. Hughes told friends, including Sam Giancana, that Nixon was "eating out of his hand."

Another blip in 1956 involved Murray Chotiner. Robert Kennedy, serving as counsel for Joe McCarthy's Senate committee, subpoenaed Chotiner to explain his representation of New Jersey mobster Marco Reginelli. McCarthy intervened to save Chotiner, and Nixon was appropriately grateful. While GOP leaders forced Nixon to repudiate Chotiner — a circumstance which Nixon dubbed "a tragedy" — the men remained close friends.

Moe had other friends in Congress, as well. Lyndon Johnson served as U.S. Senate majority leader from 1955 until he became Vice President in 1961. Two years before that promotion, Johnson was a guest of honor at the Stardust's grand opening. LBJ confidante Robert "Bobby" Baker forged a close link to the Mob through his involvement in Dominican casinos and through friendship with a cast of characters including Meyer Lansky, Sam Cohen, Ed Levinson, and Miami-Vegas front man Benjamin Sigelbaum.

* * *

While Dalitz and his partners built an empire in Nevada, the Mafia seemed intent on spoiling everything. Soon after the November 1956 election, the largest Mob meeting in two decades convened at a midtown Manhattan hotel. Police bugged the banquet room and planted one of their own inside as a waiter. Forty-two syndicate leaders turned out for the meeting, with Dalitz among them. According to NYPD, the main order of business was an effort to retire Mob "prime minister" Frank Costello. Costello resisted, but the vote went against him. He agreed to step down if the Mob guaranteed his safety.

Meanwhile, Costello partner Phil Kastell had spent $11 million to build the Tropicana in Vegas, but GCB agents forced him to sell off his interest before it opened in April 1957. One month later, gunman Vincent Gigante bungled a murder attempt on Costello, leaving Costello with a scalp wound and a legal headache. Police found a note in Costello's pocket reading, "Gross casino win as of 4/26/57 ... $651,284"—the exact amount earned by the Tropicana on April 26. Handwriting experts traced the note to casino manager Louis Lederer, subsequently bought out of the Tropicana by Ed Levinson with $80,000 borrowed from Sam Garfield.

Frank Costello, following an attempt on his life in 1957 (Library of Congress).

The Costello hit, most Mob-watchers agree, was planned by rival Vito Genovese. Costello ally Albert Anastasia went berserk, assassinating Genovese subordinate George Scalise on June 17, but Anastasia had grave problems of his own. Aside from bitter enmity with Genovese, the former Lord High Executioner of Murder Inc. demanded part of Lansky's gambling action in Havana. So, most Mob-watchers agree, his fate was sealed.

The first step, says Hank Messick, was securing an ally for the "Jewish boys" inside the Mafia. Tampa mafioso Santo Trafficante Jr. reportedly met Meyer Lansky and Charles Tourine in Sam Tucker's office at the Nacional in Havana, swearing allegiance "to the will of Meyer Lansky and the organization he represents," signing a copy of the oath in blood.

Back in New York, Anastasia called for a meeting of 100 leading mafiosi on October 28, to rubber-stamp his plan for war against the non–Italian Mob over control of Cuba and all rackets nationwide. Four days before that scheduled conference, Trafficante met Anastasia at the Park Sheraton Hotel, then hastily departed

Albert Anastasia, the Mafia's "Lord High Executioner," executed by unknown gunmen (National Archives).

after receiving a phone call from Florida. Next morning, October 25, two gunmen caught Anastasia in the Park Sheraton's barbershop and riddled him with bullets.

Anastasia's meeting proceeded without him. Instead of plotting war against the larger Mob, the conference — convened outside Apalachin, New York, on November 14, 1957 — served as a platform to justify Anastasia's murder. Vito Genovese argued the case, claiming that Anastasia had sold Mafia memberships to unqualified members and that he had killed George Scalise without provocation. Before the assembled mafiosi could absorb Vito's spiel, however, they were rudely interrupted. State police swept the estate, bagging fifty-nine prominent mafiosi, while an uncertain number escaped. Those arrested included Genovese, Joe Bonanno, Carlo Gambino, Joe Profaci, Santo Trafficante, Cleveland's John Scalish, and Joe Civello from Dallas.

Apalachin took the feds completely by surprise. J. Edgar Hoover had assigned agents "to determine and document the nonexistence of organized crime," but now that effort was wasted. Robert Kennedy, pressing for investigation of the Mafia, discovered that "the FBI didn't know anything, really" about the Apalachin delegates, which struck him as "rather a shock." Attorney General William Rogers said Hoover had to be dragged "kicking and screaming" into the manhunt. Hoover created a new "Top Hoodlum Program," demanding that each Bureau office compile a list of ten local mobsters — no more, no less — for intensive surveillance.

Bill Roemer called Moe Dalitz "probably the number-one target of the Top Hoodlum Program" in Nevada, but agents fumbled the ball. They sought a line on Moe's parents, mistakenly calling them "Morris and Anna Dalitz," but failed to track his movements. A terse note from Hoover chastised his minions for "a glaring omission" in a March 1958 report on Moe, citing "a meeting of hoodlums in Las Vegas during January [1958] at which time Dalitz conferred with Abner Zwillman ... and an individual later identified as Sam Garfield. There is no indication that the purposes of this meeting have been fully explored and no leads have been set out to secure additional information."

While Hoover flogged his agents, he simultaneously fought a stubborn rear-guard action against federal Mob investigations. By 1959, while Hoover declared his intent "to keep such pressure on hoodlums and racketeers that they can't light or remain anywhere," Agent William Turner reported that L.A.'s Top Hoodlum Program was "dead in the water." Bill Roemer saw Chicago's THP staff cut from ten agents to five. "Mr. Hoover seemed to lose interest," Roemer said. "Organized crime was no longer his priority."

One theory has it that Hoover feared corruption of the Bureau if his agents came to grips with millionaire mobsters. Another story, floated by Anthony Summers, claims that Meyer Lansky blackmailed Hoover, using photographs of the director engaged in homosexual activity. A simpler explanation may be Hoover's longtime friendship with known mobsters. He gambled at their racetracks and casinos, stayed for free at their hotels, and profited from timely tips on stocks, oil leases, real estate, and other ventures. Profits aside, mobsters were anti-communists, bare-knuckle capitalists, and sporting men — the very people Hoover most admired in life.

* * *

Robert Kennedy did not share Hoover's admiration for the Mob. Despite his father's rum-running background, Bobby viewed the Mafia as a pervasive "enemy within." A year before the Apalachin meeting he had toured the nation, collecting evidence of labor racketeering, with special emphasis on the Teamsters. In Washington, he argued for creation of a Senate panel to investigate the problem.

In January 1957 a unanimous vote created the Senate Select Committee on Improper Activities in the Labor or Management Field — better known as the McClellan Committee, after chairman John McClellan of Arkansas. Kennedy served as chief counsel and persuaded brother John participate. The panel served 8,000 subpoenas and interviewed 1,526 witnesses, publishing 20,432 pages of testimony.

Phase one of the investigation focused on Teamster president Dave Beck, documenting his receipt of kickbacks and embezzlement of union funds. Beck resigned in September 1957, replaced by Jimmy Hoffa. Two months later, the AFL-CIO expelled the IBT. The investigation's second phase focused on Hoffa. Chairman McClellan branded Hoffa "the source of the cancer" infecting the Teamsters, and Bobby Kennedy emerged as Hoffa's personal nemesis. Their mutual hatred endured to the end of Kennedy's life and sent Hoffa to prison.

McClellan's probe inevitably touched the Dalitz brothers. Bobby Kennedy fumbled his first sally in July 1958, referring to the Michigan Industrial Laundry owned by "Mr. Lu Gailex," but he secured testimony from Detroit auto dealer Ray Tessmer, whose employees tried to

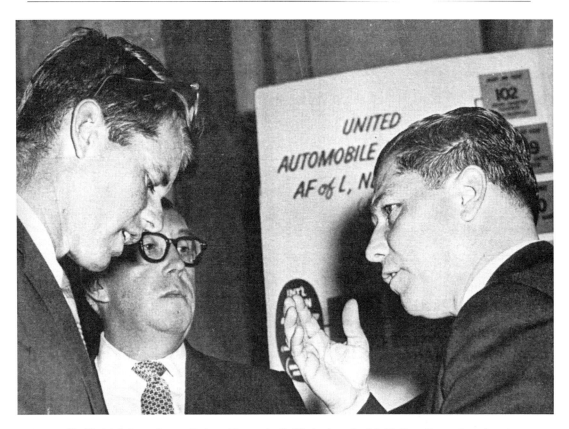

Jimmy Hoffa (right) confronts Robert Kennedy (left) during the McClellan Committee hearings. The third man is unidentified (Library of Congress).

unionize in December 1957. Tessmer dreaded paying higher wages, and his problem vanished after a January 1958 lunch date with Richard Taylor, sales manager for Michigan Industrial, and Joe Lehr, a partner in the Star Coverall Supply Company. Tessmer agreed to let Lou Dalitz wash his mechanics' coveralls, whereupon Tessmer's employees suddenly lost interest in collective bargaining.

Nancy Dawson, president of Dawson Industrial Laundry, followed Tessmer to the witness stand. She had attended a meeting between Tessmer and Lehr, where Tessmer dropped his contract with Dawson in favor of Michigan Industrial. Dawson said the agreement included "some kind of arrangement between Mr. Dalitz and Mr. Lehr concerning a Pontiac dealership.... I believe it was Mr. Dalitz [who] wanted to take the account." Before her testimony, Dawson had received a phone call warning her, "If you keep your mouth shut it will be all right. There won't be any trouble." Joe Lehr admitted introducing Tessmer to "Mr. Dick Dalitz," but testified that their conversation never touched on union matters.

On August 5, Kennedy broke the story of Moe's involvement with the Teamster sweetheart contract hatched in 1949. William Balkwill, from Detroit's Institute of Laundering, described how Dalitz introduced him to Joe Holtzman, supervising a subsequent $17,500 payment to Hoffa that aborted impending strikes. Jack Bushkin, present at that meeting, claimed his Fifth Amendment privilege, while Kennedy produced three checks written by one Benjamin Dranow in Las Vegas, in March 1955. Dranow — a Hoffa aide convicted of tax evasion and mail fraud — had bounced one rubber check for $500 at the Flamingo, then wrote two more for $1,100 and $1,500 at the DI. Bushkin paid Dranow's debts and received an interest in Globe Linen Supply, where Kennedy claimed Bushkin "bought out the interest of Mr. Moe Dalitz in that company."

* * *

McClellan's hearings failed to end Mob infestation of the Teamsters, the Longshoremen, or affiliated unions. G-men caught Hoffa red-handed passing a $2,000 bribe to committee attorney John Cheasty in March 1957, but jurors acquitted Hoffa four months later. In 1958 prosecutors indicted Hoffa aide Frank Fitzsimmons for taking kickbacks. A Detroit judge dismissed that charge after Hoffa made a contribution to the judge's re-election campaign.

In August 1958 Hoffa established a cosmetic "anti-racketeering mission" within the IBT, chaired by former Ohio senator George Bender. While serving as a congressman in 1954, Bender accepted a $40,000 bribe to quash contempt charges filed against Ohio Teamsters Bill Presser and Louis Triscaro. After the charges were dropped, Teamsters bankrolled Bender's successful Senate campaign. Bender met Hoffa at "an Italian banquet" in Akron, and Hoffa paid him $5,000 per month to "clean up" the union with little effect.

* * *

Despite their busy schedule in Vegas, Dalitz and his partners kept track of events in Ohio. Alan Balboni notes that Morris Kleinman and Ruby Kolod maintained "considerable contact" through the 1950s with Midwestern cronies who had not attained the DI gang's "relative respectability." A Cleveland FBI informant suffered a beating in March 1954, allegedly after receiving telephone threats from Dalitz himself. One call came from Chicago and another from Miami, but the victim swore he had spoken to Moe "on one or two occasions in the past ... [and] he was positive that it was Dalitz's voice on the phone."

The Cleveland Four suffered a grievous loss on July 17, 1956, when Lou Rothkopf died at his home in Ohio. Found dead in his garage, a victim of supposed "accidental" carbon monoxide poisoning, Rothkopf had been depressed since wife Blanche killed herself in June 1955. Semi-retired from Mob affairs, Lou wintered in Florida, dining there with Moe, Averill, Mike Coppola and Coppola's new bride in February 1956. Coppola paid $300 for the banquet, then beat his wife because the meal failed to lift Rothkopf's spirits. Rothkopf left an estate valued at $740,000, subject to a $578,000 tax lien which the IRS settled in 1960 for $70,560. Media reports describe a "large bequest" to nephew Bernie in Las Vegas. Tom McGinty filled Rothkopf's seat at the Syndicate table.

FBI reports from 1956 declare that Mob mule George Gordon had "left Las Vegas to operate gambling activities in Ohio, Kentucky, and Florida for a group headed by Morris 'Moe' Dalitz." Shondor Birns, paroled in 1956, joined in another battle to dominate Cleveland's numbers racket. October 1957 found Birns on trial for bombing black rival Donald King's home. Before the trial, where a hung jury freed Birns, King suffered a shotgun blast to the head. He survived that attack—and a subsequent prison term for manslaughter—to become millionaire fight promoter Don King.

A sniper fired at Birns outside his home in March 1959, and suspect Clarence "Sonny" Coleman—a numbers racketeer and former army marksman—received near-fatal gunshot wounds in April. Coleman named Birns as the shooter, then hedged before a grand jury and scuttled the indictment.

* * *

Matters were equally unsettled in the West, where Mickey Cohen staged a comeback after his parole in 1955. Mickey operated Michael's Greenhouse as his new command post, supervised a casino in the Ambassador Hotel, and met with Chicago Mob attorney George Bieber in Palm Springs. In August 1956 feds claimed that Cohen and bodyguard John Stompanato had tried to blackmail an heir to the Woolworth's fortune, but the victim refused to press charges.

Wherever he went, Cohen spawned lurid headlines. Divorced from wife Lavonne, he proposed to stripper Candy Barr, but her Texas drug arrest spoiled the wedding. In her absence, Mickey negotiated terms for his biography with author Ben Hecht, then borrowed $27,500 from friends with pledges of repayment from future royalties. Celebrity attorney Melvin Belli loaned Cohen $3,000 and paid his way to a Miami convention of the American Bar Association. A Cincinnati tree surgeon paid Cohen $2,350 to promote his twelve-year-old daughter's singing career. In May 1957, appearing on Mike Wallace's television show, Mickey declared, "I killed nobody that didn't deserve killing."

The IRS finally nailed Cohen again, with a September 1960 indictment on thirteen counts of tax evasion. T-men (Treasury agents) believed that Cohen spent an average $200,000 per year, but they could only document $393,513.10. It was enough, resulting in conviction on five counts in May 1961. Cohen received a record fifteen-year sentence but delayed incarceration until spring 1962 with serial appeals. A cellblock beating in August 1963 left him partially crippled.

Moe Dalitz was probably happy to see Cohen go. Unlike Mert Wertheimer, who died from leukemia in July 1958, Mickey had caused more problems than he solved as West Coast front man for the Mob. Moe preferred stable friends like Doc Stacher, who leased his Moulin Rouge nightclub to Dalitz "and other gamblers" in 1956, or Lew Wasserman, who purchased Universal Studios from Decca Records two years later. Gene Butler, ex-husband of Barry Goldwater's daughter Joanne, recalled that Moe was mentioned often in the Goldwater household as a man who could "fix things" in Southern California.

* * *

Business and politics mixed just as well in Arizona, where voters sent Barry Goldwater to the Senate in 1953. Goldwater won a second term in 1958, despite exposure of his close friendship with murdered mobsters Gus Greenbaum and Willie Bioff, although both acquaintances required some explanation.

Goldwater attended Bioff's funeral in 1955, but he denied knowledge of Willie's true identity. Still, reporters learned that Bioff had known Goldwater since November 1952, that he loaned Goldwater $10,000 for a California farm investment, that he had toured Arizona with Goldwater aboard the senator's private plane, and that the Bioffs had vacationed with Goldwater's family a month before the fatal Phoenix bombing. Goldwater changed his tune as that news emerged, claiming that he had used Bioff to obtain information on labor racketeering, for the McClellan Committee.

Harry Rosenzweig also downplayed his ties to Bioff, telling reporters that "he had loaned Bioff small sums of money but that Bioff had never loaned him any money." Further investigation revealed three checks written by Bioff to Rosenzweig Investment, including one for $5,000 cashed ten days before Bioff's murder. A month before that, Rosenzweig had booked rooms for the Bioffs and Goldwaters in Vegas, at the Riviera.

Senator Goldwater also attended Gus Greenbaum's funeral, while denying knowledge of Greenbaum's Mob ties. Brother Robert Goldwater denied meeting Greenbaum before Gus assumed command of the Riviera, and likewise denied any knowledge of loans from his bank to Ben Siegel, though Robert attended the Flamingo's opening. Greenbaum had "comped" the Goldwaters at both casinos on various occasions. Rosenzweig, who joined Goldwater at the Flamingo's premier, served as an unpaid appraiser of Greenbaum's estate.

Left: Detroit mafioso Joseph Zerilli (National Archives). *Right:* "Black Bill" Tocco joined Joe Zerilli in Arizona business ventures (National Archives).

Friends from Detroit kept Moe Dalitz up to speed on other Arizona operations.

In July 1955, Joe Zerilli and Black Bill Tocco founded the Arrowhead Ranch, north of Phoenix, on 3,900 acres purchased for $2.6 million. To move their produce, Zerilli established a local fruit brokerage house. Four years later, Zerilli and Tocco sold the farm to Del Webb for $4 million. In 1966 Webb sold Arrowhead to the Goldmar Corporation, named for owners Robert *Gold*water and Joseph *Mar*tori. Eight years later the Phoenix Legal Aid Society sued Goldmar, charging that the company held Mexican migrant workers as "virtual slaves." That lawsuit was later dismissed without going to trial.

Pete Licavoli's luck soured in July 1958, with his conviction for income-tax evasion. Licavoli's lawyer begged for leniency, describing Pete as a "devoted family man and a diligent, hardworking, self-educated businessman." Reporters noted that Pete "appeared somewhat stunned" when Judge Theodore Levin sentenced him to thirty months in prison and a $10,000 fine.

* * *

In March 1954 a federal grand jury examined the Miami rackets, noting that local sales of wagering stamps had declined from 800 in 1953 to a single stamp purchased in the new year. G-men observed that "well-known gambler" Lou Rothkopf occupied the penthouse of the Seabrook Hotel, in Miami Beach, while Moe Dalitz went yachting with Longy Zwillman. Agents shadowed Moe around Miami through the winter season of 1954–55, then warned headquarters that "a group of Cleveland gamblers and racketeers, including Moe Dalitz, were reported to have been approved to operate the gambling in Miami during the winter season of 1957–1958." Sam Tucker had a $55,000 home on Biscaya Island, while Morris Kleinman spent $140,000 on his digs at Bay Harbor — plus another $35,000 for construction of a private putting green next door.

Just when the Mob needed a conduit for funds in Florida, the Bank of Miami Beach opened in January 1955. Founder Ben Danbaum was an ex-policeman from Omaha who made his fortune organizing armored-car deliveries of cash. Before founding the BMB, Danbaum sold his security firm to Ben Gaines, later a partner with Sam Tucker in Miami's Skyways Motel and the Sahara Motel in Miami Beach.

It was a short boat ride and even shorter flight from Florida to Cuba, where Fulgencio Batista's government made U.S. mobsters feel at home. Gamblers ranked high on Batista's list of most-favored entrepreneurs, and Moe Dalitz gave Meyer Lansky a run for his money in Havana.

In August 1955 Wilbur Clark's Casino International was organized in Cuba, with its stock divided equally among Clark, Dalitz, Kleinman, Tucker, and McGinty. McGinty served as president, with Tucker listed as secretary/treasurer and casino manager. In

Hymie Martin supervised Cleveland's gambling rackets in Florida (Cleveland Public Library).

November the company signed a sub-lease agreement with Inter-Continental Hotels Corporation of Cuba, a subsidiary of Pan-American World Airways, to run Meyer Lansky's old casino at the Hotel Nacional. Play began on January 19, 1956, with Moe, Tucker, McGinty, and DI shareholder Robert Kaye on hand to greet celebrity guests. Hank Greenspun's *Sun* reported that the "temporary" casino cost $100,000, while the DI partners planned to spend $450,000 on new construction.

Eleven weeks later, Mohawk Securities was organized in Panama. Gambler George Francis paid $450,000 for half of Mohawk's stock; the rest was equally divided among Dalitz, Clark, Kleinman, Tucker, and McGinty. All stock in Wilbur Clark's Casino International immediately transferred to Mohawk, and since Americans owned only half of Mohawk its income was tax exempt in the U.S., immune to IRS audits. Mohawk set up accounts at the Bank of Miami Beach and at Union National Bank in Newark. The BMB account received deposits from Vegas and from Miami's Isle d'Capri casino. In September 1958, Miami Customs agents caught Jake Lansky returning from Cuba with $200,000 in cash and $50,000 in checks, earmarked for Mohawk's BMB account. During its three years of operation, the Nacional drew $1.53 million from the BMB. Sam Tucker collected the satchels filled with hundred-dollar bills.

Business was good for Dalitz in Havana. Future campaign rivals JFK and Richard Nixon both enjoyed Cuba's nightlife. In 1956, after a night of gambling at the Nacional with director Alfred Hitchcock, Lew Wasserman remarked on Cuba's political unrest and asked Moe, "Why are you guys here? You own Las Vegas and here you risk losing it all." Moe replied,

"Sambo [Tucker] loves to fish, and this is the best fishing in the world. But, then, there was nothing to do at night, so we built the casinos."

G-men tracked the Cuban action from afar. They noted Moe's flight to Havana in July 1955 and five months later claimed that he "had also indicated an interest in gambling activities in Puerto Rico." In December 1956 agents spotted Moe's yacht at Miami's Isle d'Capri, noting that he was "spending quite a bit of time in Havana." A memo from December 1957 claimed that "the 'Jewish Boys' were ... going to have a meeting at Havana ... similar to the Apalachin ... meeting. Moe Barney Dalitz and Longy Zwillman ... were or had been in Miami Beach, and were going to the Hotel Nacional in Havana, date unknown." Days later, agents reported "considerable competition by various groups" for a gambling concession at the new Hilton Hotel, noting that one group "appeared to be headed by Moe Dalitz and Morris Kleinman."

Those were thrilling days, but Dalitz and his partners knew they were running out of time. Batista had released Fidel Castro in May 1955, whereupon Castro fled into exile and plotted Batista's downfall. Batista, barred by law from succeeding himself as president, arranged the 1958 election of hand-picked successor Carlos Rivero Aguero, but the semblance of democracy was too little, too late.

Dalitz wanted out before the axe fell, but he needed an excuse to leave while Cuba's casinos and brothels were earning the Mob an estimated $100 million yearly. On April 25, 1958, Nevada's Tax Commission "discovered" that eight licensees from the DI group had $400,000 invested in Cuban gambling. As the *Sun* observed, that was "hardly enough to bankroll one of the good-sized casinos" in Vegas, but state authorities worried that "the gambling element in Cuba, many of them ineligible to hold Nevada licenses, has become an issue between the revolutionary parties and the Cuban government, lending to the situation an international aspect which though incidental could have serious repercussions here." State licensees were given a choice: get out of Cuba or surrender their Nevada licenses.

For Moe, the choice was simple. All he needed was a buyer for the Nacional, and Mike McLaney fit the bill. An ex-cop and sometime pro golfer, McLaney launched various projects with loans from the Bank of Miami Beach. On September 30, 1958, McLaney met Dalitz and Sam Tucker in New York, and agreed to buy the Nacional from Mohawk Securities. Lou Chesler and Carroll Rosenblum, owner of the Baltimore Colts, shared in the $800,000 purchase price.

Batista fled to the Dominican Republic on January 1, 1959. Castro closed Havana's casinos and Cuba's national lottery, both viewed as incompatible with socialist reform. Jake Lansky, Santo Trafficante, Mike McLaney, and other gamblers remained in Cuba, hoping Fidel would change his mind—and he did, after several thousand casino employees protested the loss of their jobs. Castro aide Pastora Núñez rescinded the government's closure notice on condition that discharged workers would receive seven weeks' back pay. The next morning, an airplane flew over Miami Beach, trailing a banner that read CASINOS REOPEN IN HAVANA.

In retrospect, it seems that Castro tried to make a go of it with Lansky and the rest. He employed Philadelphia native Frank Sturgis (né Fiorini) as his liaison to Havana's gamblers. Years later, Sturgis told author Michael Canfield, "I met ... Santo Trafficante, I met the Lansky brothers, I met ... Charlie Terrini [*sic*]. They call him Charlie the Blade."

Under Castro's watchful eye, American mobsters resumed gambling. In January 1960 Fidel expropriated 70,000 acres owned by U.S. sugar companies. In June, when three foreign oil refineries declined to process Russian crude, Castro nationalized the plants. One week later,

The Nacional hotel-casino in Havana (Library of Congress).

on July 5, Fidel nationalized all U.S. commercial properties in Cuba. In August 1960 Castro nationalized all American-owned industrial and agrarian enterprises, followed by all U.S. banks in September and all commercially owned real estate — including Lansky's Riviera and 165 other enterprises — on October 24. American embargoes followed, which remain in force today.

Meyer Lansky left an estimated $17 million behind when he fled Cuba, midway through 1959. Brother Jake and Santo Trafficante were among those jailed by Castro pending negotiation of ransom for their release. Sometime in 1959, Lansky placed a $1 million bounty on Castro's head. Norm Rothman heard about the contract in Havana and discussed it with Frank Sturgis, who in turn recruited Marita Lorenz for a bungled attempt to poison Fidel. Rothman also met with Trafficante, John Rosselli, and the Mannarino brothers to discuss elimination of "The Beard." The CIA pitched in, but Castro outlived them all.

* * *

While his Mob colleagues plotted Castro's death, Moe Dalitz looked around the Caribbean for alternative casino sites. Texan Bobby Baker had a foothold in the Dominican Republic, through the Intercontinental Hotels Corporation, with casinos financed from 1955 onward by Ed Levinson and Miami gambler Ben Sigelbaum. Lyndon Johnson joined Baker for the first casino's grand opening in Santo Domingo, and while dictator Rafael Trujillo welcomed bribes, his regime's brutality and increasing isolation from civilized states reminded Moe too much of Batista's last days.

In Haiti, François Duvalier used voodoo and brute force to dominate an equally corrupt regime, where gambling was permitted at the tyrant's pleasure. Jake Kosloff, onetime lessor of the Royal Nevada in Vegas, ran a casino in Port-au-Prince with Cliff Jones, but a rebel bombing in June 1959 made them eager to sell. Dalitz considered the prospect, but Ambassador Gerald Drew warned that Haitian politics were "unstable" and thus queered the deal.

Only the Bahamas remained as a potential island paradise for gamblers. A 1954 FBI memo noted that "a British group" had contracted with Indiana oilman William Dunn to take over Butlin's Island "and run it with wide-open legalized gambling." An informer told G-men there "was some talk" that Moe Dalitz might be involved in building the casino. That project never gelled, but one year later, in August 1955, mobsters got their break with passage of the Hawksbill Creek Act.

That law was the brainchild of Wallace Groves, a Virginia native convicted of mail fraud and conspiracy in 1941. Paroled three years later, he resurfaced on Little Whale Cay, northwest of Nassau, in 1954. Groves befriended Stafford Sands, a Bahamian legislator who sponsored a 1939 statute permitting "certificates of exemption" for gambling. In January 1950 Sands led a new Development Board to promote tourism. Groves proposed a "free port" on barren Grand Bahama island, run by a private agency with virtual immunity from government supervision. The Hawksbill Creek Act let Groves buy 211 square miles of Grand Bahama at $2.80 per acre and to acquire the remaining 319 square miles almost as cheaply. He became the uncrowned "King of Grand Bahama," dredged a harbor, launched construction projects with duty-free materials, and generally acted with what a later commission of inquiry called "almost feudal powers."

Kentucky gambler Ed Curd recognized the Bahamas' potential. Facing a tax-evasion charge in 1952, he fled to Canada and joined Gil Beckley in a bookie operation. The Mounties got wise five years later, and Curd spent two years island-hopping in the Caribbean, then surrendered to the IRS in December 1958. A guilty plea earned him six concurrent one-year sentences, discharged in September 1959. Curd migrated to the Bahamas and established L&W Realty. When the gamblers arrived in force, Curd, Groves, and Sands welcomed them with open arms.

* * *

Foreign adventures notwithstanding, it was business as usual for the Mob in Kentucky. And the first order of business was suppressing independent numbers racketeers like Melvin Clark.

Clark had survived the first attempt on his life and beat the subsequent murder rap in 1948. By 1954 he was back in business, running numbers in Newport and Cincinnati, taking more heat from Screw Andrews. In July 1955 Andrews shot Clark outside the Alibi Club. At trial, defended by a law partner of Governor Happy Chandler, Andrews won acquittal from an all-white jury on a plea of self-defense. The feds had better luck in 1956, convicting Screw of operating slot machines without the mandatory gaming stamps, but he emerged from prison to resume his war against black independent operators. A series of bombings in early 1959 consolidated Screw's control of ghetto rackets, while Screw looked around Campbell County in search of new prospects.

While Andrews served Mike Coppola, Moe Dalitz kept a low profile. In 1958 G-men reported that "none of the original Cleveland group ... any longer had financial interests in gambling establishments in Northern Kentucky." Still, partners at the Beverly Hills Club included Dalitz cronies George Gordon, John Croft, Al Goltsman, and Yale Cohen. Agents dubbed Gordon "a sort of traveling representative for interests represented by Morris B. Dalitz." He was "frequently in and out of Las Vegas," lodging at the DI "where he is in frequent contact with Dalitz and other Desert Inn owners." He also traveled to Miami, Cleveland, Chicago, L.A., and Detroit, with agents noting that "[h]e is regularly in contact with the [DI] while he is on the road."

While G-men tracked Gordon, mobsters faced a new nemesis in Newport. Hank Messick was born in 1922, earned a degree in journalism from the University of Iowa, and taught for several years before he felt the urge to "get out and get some real experience." That impulse led him to North Carolina and a job with the weekly *Waynesville Mountaineer.* Messick caught his first whiff of the Mob in 1952, when a drunken high-school stabbing caused police to jail moonshine peddler David "Dog" Underwood. From there, the trail led back to Newport, where Underwood bought his supplies from Screw Andrews. In 1958, newly hired by the Louisville *Courier-Journal,* Messick got his chance to see the underworld at work, first-hand.

Gil Beckley, once America's top layoff bookie (National Archives).

He arrived in Newport in September and toured local casinos, identifying three factions active in Little Mexico: Cleveland controlled the largest clubs; Screw Andrews ran the numbers game and prostitutes; and so-called "independents" led by Sleepout Louie Levinson collaborated both with Cleveland and with Meyer Lansky. A local grand jury report, released in October 1958, was considered a "shocker" because it acknowledged "a laxity in law enforcement with regards to the operation of taverns, prostitution, and gaming," but no indictments resulted.

In 1958 Andrews briefly closed his brothels, in a fruitless bid to pacify reformers. A year later, "United Effort Day" saw Newport's pastors hit the streets, patrolling bars and casinos, calling for impeachment of corrupt officials. The next grand jury acknowledged evidence of gambling, its members concluded that "Mankind, having been born in sin, will ever be prey to the temptations of sin."

That attitude was great for business. On August 5, 1960, Morris Kleinman purchased a cashier's check for $299,682.07, made out to himself, at the Bank of Las Vegas. Four months later, on November 30, George Gordon cashed the check in Newport, bearing Kleinman's endorsement.

Hank Messick survived one high-speed chase but refused to take the hint. Soon afterward, a stranger warned Messick that "the big boys" had convened in Lou Levinson's office to discuss his fate. A majority thought Messick should be fitted for a concrete "Newport nightgown," but one delegate recalled the Mob's ban on killing journalists. According to the stranger, "orders have gone out to leave you alone. The younger men wanted you hit, but the older ones argued that it would create too much heat."

Presidential politics finally tipped the balance in Newport. Robert Kennedy, campaigning for his brother John, secured a promise from Kentucky governor Bert Combs to close Campbell County casinos if reformers gathered sufficient evidence. A few days later, Judge Paul Stapleton ordered Sheriff Norbert Roll to examine the Snax Bar casino. Roll reported that "a thorough investigation" revealed no gambling, but reporters found the Snax Bar running wide-open an hour later. Judge Stapleton ordered a raid, which brought attorney Charles Lester to his chambers, inquiring, "How long are you going to keep annoying my clients?" Stapleton's answer — "As long as necessary" — set a new tone for law enforcement in Newport.

In October 1960 G-men seized 420 slot machines en route from Newport to England, where casino gambling had been legalized. Judge Edward Hill ordered the slots destroyed and convened a special grand jury to indict Sheriff Roll for malfeasance.

* * *

Throughout the latter 1950s, Moe Dalitz pursued diverse legitimate investments. G-men tried to track his money, with mixed results. They failed to secure financial records for U.S. Industrial Glove in Detroit, but reported its net worth from 1955 as $22,849. They had better luck with Moe's personal finances for 1959, revealing $142,122.38 in various bank accounts. Moe declared a $25,000 salary from the DI Operating Company, $12,550 from Michigan U.S. Industrial Glove and Laundry, and $2,600 from U.S. Industrial Glove. Four enterprises — Detroit's Bernardine Realty, the DI Operating Company, Las Vegas Bowl Inc., and U.S. Industrial Glove — paid Moe $12,664.90 in interest. Partnership income of $3,847.26 from Bowl Amusement Company, in Vegas, was offset by losses from A&M Enterprises and the Nevada Building Company. Moe bought fifty shares of Mohawk Securities for $4,500 and sold them for $138,000, then bought Turbo stock for $500 and sold it for $14,933.38, reporting long-term capital gains of $75,803.85. On the debit side, he listed farm losses of $8,597.04 and losses on the DI Ranch of $2,855.91.

Moe's ranch kept G-men hopping, trying to connect the dots. Memos noted that Moe had purchased the "old Nordin Ranch" in Washington County, Utah, "for use as a hunting lodge." Agents visited the spread "under pretext" in January 1958, reporting that Moe owned three acres and was negotiating purchase of twenty-seven more from a local Indian tribe. He had built an airstrip and renovated ranch buildings to sleep twenty guests. He kept horses and grazed 400 head of cattle at the ranch, co-owned by an unnamed local hunting guide.

Other businesses scrutinized by the FBI included M.B.D. Inc., founded in August 1956 with offices housed at the DI. Moe was the president, wife Averill vice president, and Vegas resident H.J. McDonald served as secretary/treasurer. In May 1957 M.B.D. Inc. became Motor Sailer Inc., with Dalitz as the sole stockholder. Incorporation documents described the firm as a "general brokerage commission, forwarding and export business," created to "buy and sell and deal in any and all kinds of commodities," as well as "listed and unlisted stocks, bonds, and securities on commission."

Throughout 1958–60 G-men eyed Moe's links to other companies. They studied Bernardine Realty in Wyandotte, Michigan — named for vice president Bernardine Cinnamon, whose husband Jack served as president — but Michigan's Corporation and Securities Commission found no listing for the firm. Agents *did* find Sam Garfield, owner of the defunct Garfield

Gas and Oil Company, holding stock in Cleveland's Monmouth Producing and Refinery Company, and linked Dalitz to the Cleveland Retail Credit Men's Company (Maurice Maschke president and treasurer).

Mohawk Securities tied Moe to Newark's Union National Bank, where Tom McGinty and Allard Roen funneled $1 million into Morrell Park, a Philadelphia housing development. Builders broke ground in 1959 and had completed 1,500 homes by December 1963. Priced between $10,990 and $12,350, all were swiftly occupied. Morrell Park's design was so unique that the American Conservation Association featured it in a 1964 book titled *Cluster Development*. Author William Whyte filled 130 pages without once naming McGinty, Roen, or their partners.

Martinolich Construction was another firm whose finances required some explanation. Wilbur Clark owned half the company until 1955, when he bought the rest. During 1952–55 Martinolich borrowed $450,000 without interest from Refrigerated Transport, owned by Anthony Martinolich (Clark's partner in Martinolich Construction), his son, and DI lawyer John Donnelly. Anthony and his wife owned 60 percent of Martinolich Shipbuilding, which made repeated loans to Martinolich Construction, the largest for $300,000. Martinolich Shipbuilding dissolved in 1960, although Clark "and others" retained a ship's charter used for exporting slot machines to Germany. In 1954, when Moe Dalitz expanded the Colonial House in Las Vegas, Martinolich Construction did the work, financed by a $200,000 loan from Refrigerated Transport. Six years later, when Martinolich Shipbuilding dissolved, it received four $100,000 promissory notes from National Steel & Shipbuilding (directed by San Diego financier Arnholt Smith). The first note was paid, while Martinolich discounted the second at 15 percent, then assigned the third and fourth notes to Dalitz for $100,000—a 50 percent discount. Moe later sold one note for $97,500 and the other for $93,400, turning a profit of $90,900 on what a federal tax court later called "a sort of 'Tinker to Evers to Chance' financial baseball."

Aside from gambling, Moe appeared to love construction most. In 1955 his Paradise Developments constructed Vegas Bowl—a bowling alley with a restaurant, bar, and slot machines. Irwin Molasky estimated that Paradise sold an average one house per day during 1957–59, at $30,000 to $40,000 each. Other projects included a home for Variety Club Tent No. 39 (which Moe often served as "chief barker"), and the Las Vegas Convention Center.

Moe's interest in construction was not confined to the Strip. In July 1954, John Gluskin of Masonic Lodge 32 leased four lots at the corner of Fremont and Third Streets. Six days later he assigned the lease to Stardust attorney David Goldwater, who surrendered it in October to the Pulliam Company, a partnership doing business as the Nevada Building Company. Moe Dalitz was one of the partners. In February 1955 the lease passed to the Three-O-One Corporation, whose president was Willie Alderman. Three-O-One's vice-president was Allard Roen, while Moe Dalitz and Morris Kleinman completed the board of directors. In October 1955 Three-O-One leased the land back to Nevada Building and Moe began construction of an office building. An $850,000 loan from the Teamsters Union facilitated expansion in April 1961.

* * *

The central jewel in Paradise Development's crown was Sunrise Hospital, on Maryland Parkway. It was not the first Vegas hospital, but it *was* the first designed to operate for profit. Irwin Molasky says that he and Merv Adelson conceived the idea in 1956, because physicians demanded it. "The doctors wanted out of politics," Molasky said, "and also they wanted to practice with modern facilities." Incorporation papers for Sunrise Hospital Inc. were filed in August 1957, signed by Molasky, Adelson, and future Nevada Supreme Court justice David Zenoff. S.H.I. authorized 1,500 shares of capital stock at $100 per share.

As Molasky told it, original financing came from a local savings and loan company, "[b]ut we ran out of money and had to take in some investors"—specifically, Moe Dalitz and Allard Roen. As a for-profit hospital, Sunrise was barred from receiving federal funds. The answer to that problem was a new partnership, Sunrise Hospital Inc., with Molasky as president, Merv Adelson as vice president, and Dalitz as second vice president. Partners Nathan Adelson and Eli Boyer, Moe's accountant, completed the lineup. They created a network of subsidiaries: Sunrise Hospital Pharmacy Inc., Sunrise Hospital Clinical Laboratory Inc., and Sunrise Hospital X-Ray Laboratory Inc.

Sunrise opened on December 15, 1958, with sixty-two beds. Senator-elect Howard Cannon cut the ceremonial ribbon, with investor Roy Cohn present, while Averill Dalitz and Evelyn Roen played hostess. The *Sun* declared that Moe's new hospital was "rated among [the] best," but it still had a long way to go. In April 1959 S.H.I. assigned its accounts to Congress Factors, a corporation based in Los Angeles. Milton Dranow—brother of Benjamin Dranow, whose 1955 Vegas gambling losses were covered by Detroit's Jack Bushkin—signed the agreement as Congress Factors' vice president. In September 1959 a new firm called A&M Enterprises (Adelson and Molasky) recorded a deed of sale for desert acreage adjacent to Sunrise, in return for "valuable consideration." As author Wallace Turner notes, the absence of federal stamps on the paperwork suggests that no money changed hands. That same day, A&M borrowed $1 million from the Teamsters at 6 percent interest, using the Sunrise property and hospital equipment as collateral. Three months later, Milton Dranow canceled the assignment of accounts to Congress Factors. Attorney David Goldwater filed the paperwork with Parry Thomas at the Bank of Las Vegas.

Now that Jimmy Hoffa had a stake in Sunrise, he took steps to guarantee the hospital's success. Hoffa decreed that members of the IBT and Culinary Union must obtain their medical care from Sunrise if they wished to use union insurance. Hoffa, in turn, collected $6.50 per month from employers to cover each worker. Irwin Molasky described the arrangement as "an early form of managed care." With Teamsters money in the bank, Moe and his partners expanded Sunrise to 688 beds, adding adjacent medical-professional buildings. The Variety Club, with Moe in charge, donated a $25,000 fluoriscon image intensifier.

Still, it was not all smooth sailing for Sunrise. Hank Greenspun initially praised the hospital, then changed his mind in 1959, reporting that Sunrise had opened with thirty-nine building code violations. That scandal prompted dismissal of Bill Rardon, Clark County's director of building and safety, who claimed his objections to Sunrise were overruled by commission chairman Harley Harmon. Rardon said, "Harley told me they have a million invested and have already announced their opening date. Then he dictated a letter on his own office typewriter allowing the hospital to open regardless of the violations." Sunrise sued the *Sun* for libel, but the case was never tried.

* * *

Commerce and controversy took their toll on Moe's personal life. He dined with son Andrew and ex-wife Toni during visits to Detroit, and sometimes took Andrew to ball games, "but not very often," as Toni recalled. "Just keeping in touch." One such occasion was in April 1958, when G-men overheard Moe telling friends that he was in town to visit his father, whom the agents claimed was "near death."

Moe's ex-wife Toni with adopted son Andrew (Toni Clark Drago).

Andrew's new life included photograph shoots and fashion shows with Toni. In March 1954 he obtained Social Security number 374–36–8653 to legitimize his earnings. Lou Dalitz took offense to Andrew joining Toni on the catwalk. He phoned her home, angry and worried that the work would make Andrew a "sissy." "What do you think you're doing?" Lou demanded. "How can you *possibly* have your son do fashion shows?" Toni deflected the outrage, replying that Andrew enjoyed the jobs and money that he earned, despite the fact that he did "very, very little" fashion work.

Out west, informers told G-men that Moe "enjoys living in the open and will take off for two or three days at a time, at which time he sleeps outside and travels by horseback or jeep." He hunted deer and cougar at the DI Ranch, where employees were surprised to see

Moe perform "some of the menial tasks" himself. Averill and Suzanne often accompanied Moe to Utah, where one spy opined that he was "using the ranch to get away from business pressures in Las Vegas."

* * *

Those pressures increased with the advent of Alexander Guterma, nicknamed "the Mad Russian." In April 1955 Denver stock promoter Albert Hayutin announced an offer of shares in Garnak Drilling, an oil company owned by *Gar*field and partner Irving Paster*nak*. Two days later, Guterma wired Hayutin a proposal to underwrite Garnak's stock through his own McGrath Securities firm. Guterma soon acquired Garnak in exchange for shares in Shawano Corporation, a worthless Florida firm. Garfield, Pasternak, and Guterma sold the Shawano shares for a reported $6 million to suckers nationwide.

That windfall certainly encouraged Garfield to sing Guterma's praises, but Dalitz may have known the Mad Russian beforehand. Other possible contact points include Guterma's Isle d'Capri hotel, in Florida (where Morris Kleinman kept a house and Dalitz parked his yacht between sojourns to Cuba), and Las Vegas (where Guterma gambled often at the DI).

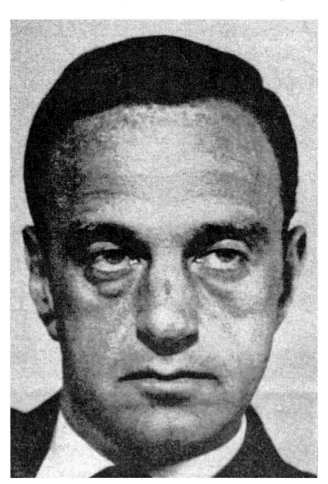

Cash from the Isle d'Capri passed through the Bank of Miami Beach for deposit with Mohawk Securities in 1956, by which time Guterma was in business with the DI partners in United Hotels.

That firm was born in April 1956, to sell stock in the DI hotel. United Hotels absorbed the Isle d'Capri, in exchange for 275,000 of the new corporation's 5 million common shares, valued at ten cents par. In a similar trade-off, the DI Operating Company received 3,285,051¾ common shares, plus 1,402,143 preferred shares valued at three dollars par. Guterma later denied any leadership role in United Hotels. "They just elected the directors and ran things," he said. "That's all there was to it."

Two contradictory accounts explain what happened next. DI attorney John Donnelly claimed that he approached the Securities Exchange Commission to discuss the pending sale of stock and was warned of unspecified "problems" with the venture. By the time he alerted Dalitz, it was too late to stop Guterma. Another version claims that an informant tipped

Roy Cohn, a friend, partner, and later mortal enemy of Dalitz (Library of Congress).

the SEC to what was happening and federal inquiries warned the DI group of trouble in the wind. Unfortunately, nothing could prevent Guterma from selling his shares to the public. Suddenly, Dalitz was awash in "partners" from all corners of the nation who claimed shares of the DI.

How could Dalitz be deceived by such a scheme? In 1963 he told Wallace Turner, "I was afraid of [Guterma]. He talked too fast. The only reason I gave that bastard any consideration is that Sam Garfield went to grade school with me and brought him to me." Hank Messick spoke for those who thought Moe's gang was using Guterma. In May 1959 they created United Resort Hotels, chartered in Delaware. FBI memos say Dalitz, Kleinman, and Tucker owned 70 percent of the new firm, while John Drew held 5 percent and the rest was "spread among lesser Desert Inn Hotel operators." New York attorney Lawrence Wien handled the transaction, which included buying back Guterma's scattered shares for $257,000, then shifting ownership of the DI's physical plant into a partnership with Sunrise Hospital and leasing it back to the DI Operating Company. Thus, the Cleveland partners "sold" the DI to themselves, collecting $2,875,000 in cash and dividing the $7 million balance between two mortgages. The DI lease, with options for renewal, spanned sixty-three years. In effect, nothing changed for Moe except his lightened tax burden, increasing depreciable assets from $3.6 million to $9.8 million. The partners withdrew $2 million from United Resort Hotels in 1960 alone, taxable at 25 percent rather than the normal 52-percent corporate rate.

Guterma's federal indictment did not spring from his United Hotels adventure, but rather from United Dye & Chemical. Guterma discovered that firm in 1955, used it to buy the Bon Ami soap company, looted Bon Ami of $3 million by 1957, then sold it. Next, Guterma merged United Dye with Hendridge Oil, another company controlled by Sam Garfield and Irving Pasternak. He swapped 575,000 shares of United Dye, valued at $18 million, for an equal number of Hendridge shares worth $519,000, hyping the stock though a bank in Tangier. Guterma and Virgil Dardi made $5 million before United Dye crashed, with the price of its shares plummeting from $15 to less than one dollar.

Indictments followed, and Guterma turned state's evidence in 1959. In 1960 a federal grand jury charged Dardi, Garfield, Pasternak, United Dye investor Allard Roen, and a host of others with conspiracy and sale of unregistered stock. Roy Cohn, another Garfield business partner whose biographer claims he met Garfield and Roen "as extensions of his friendship with Moe Dalitz," pulled strings to help the defendants and was indicted for perjury. Cohn, the guest of honor at Moe's 1960 New Year's Eve party in Vegas, described Dalitz as "a four-star general in the syndicate, only a cut below Meyer Lansky." Their acquaintance came via Averill Dalitz. "I naively thought that Dalitz didn't mind me spending so much time with Averill," Cohn told author Sidney Zion. Later, a prosecution witness in Cohn's case quoted Moe as saying he "would spend five years in jail to put Roy Cohn there for one day."

* * *

Charles Russell broke with tradition in 1958, seeking a third term as Nevada's governor. Although supported by "McCarran's Boys," he faced opposition from Democrat Grant Sawyer, who spent 1950–58 as Elko County's district attorney. Attorney Hyman Raskin, serving Joseph Kennedy, invited Sawyer to the Riviera, where co-owner Ross Miller handed Sawyer $1,300 in cash. More money soon followed, from casinos where Dalitz and others had soured on Russell. Sawyer won, and a friend later said that the Riviera donation "made Grant governor, no question."

Still, he did not seem particularly grateful. In 1959 state lawmakers passed a Gaming Control Act, severing the Gaming Control Board from Nevada's Tax Commission, created a new Gaming Commission to supervise licensing, and barred casinos closed for illegal actions from seeking injunctive relief. In June 1960 Nevada created its "Black Book," naming eleven mobsters whose mere presence inside a casino warranted license forfeiture. Of the eleven, nine were infamous mafiosi, including Sam Giancana, Lou Dragna, John Battaglia, and Mike Coppola.

The Black Book's leading sponsor, honest lawman William Gallagher, was fired a short time later, seemingly for his refusal to accept a bribe. Morris Kleinman invited Gallagher to the DI and flashed a roll of bills — "at least five thousand dollars," Gallagher declared — with the announcement that he planned to stake his newfound friend at the craps table. Gallagher assumed that he was meant to have a "lucky streak," return Kleinman's five grand and take his "winnings" home, but he declined to play. Soon afterward, his superiors dismissed him and he wound up running a small liquor store that suffered four robberies during its first three years. Overall, the Black Book had little impact on Nevada gambling. Only fifty-one persons were banned between 1960 and 2007.

Governor Sawyer's cleanup program struck some observers as a sham. In Reno, during 1960, veteran lawbreaker Lincoln Fitzgerald received approval to buy a third casino after GCB chairman R.J. Abbaticchio Jr. called him "a square gambler and businessman." In Vegas, the GCB let Frank Soskin buy 1 percent of the Desert Inn despite his history of illegal gambling. Such records were so common, the board's chief investigator said, that they hardly mattered.

It was also during 1959 that Jimmy Hoffa made the first of many Teamster loans to Dalitz and his partners in Las Vegas. Questioned about those loans, Hoffa replied, "Well, let me tell you this. Moe Dalitz was an officer in the U.S. Army. He's a casino owner approved by the Gaming Commission in Nevada. He's been on committees representing the voters under the governor of Nevada. So if Jimmy Hoffa is associating with a hoodlum, what the hell are they doing? You got to say that the Army, the Gaming Commission, and the governor are all associating with hoodlums. So who's to say who's a hoodlum?"

The GCB *did* question Moe, in August 1960, concerning his acquaintance with the Lansky brothers, Longy Zwillman, Lucky Luciano, Joe Adonis, Doc Stacher, Marty O'Boyle, Mickey Cohen, and John Rosselli. Jake Lansky, Moe explained, had been a floor boss at the Nacional in Havana, where he "was a salaried employee only, and had no financial interest in the hotel." As for the rest, "[h]e stated that he had met these people in the past and knows who they are, but has no contact with them at the present time. He came in contact with many of them while he was stationed at Governors Island, New York, during the war." Despite contradictory testimony in 1951 and 1953, no perjury charges resulted.

Longy Zwillman, at least, was out of the picture. In February 1959, Zwillman allegedly drank half a bottle of bourbon, then hanged himself with an electrical cord in the basement of his home. Ignoring bruises on his wrists that indicated he was bound, police declared the death a suicide. Skeptics suspect that Meyer Lansky and/or Vito Genovese killed Zwillman, fearing that he might spill gangland secrets at an upcoming appearance before the McClellan Committee. In April and June 1960, G-men reported that Moe Dalitz flew to New York for meetings with Zwillman's unnamed successor.

* * *

Even before the Stardust opened, Moe planned to expand it, and his opportunity lay right next door. In 1953 Frank Fishman had announced construction of the Royal Nevada, but he soon ran out of cash. Sale of adjacent property to Tony Cornero kept Fishman's dream afloat until April 1955, when the Royal Nevada opened as the "Showplace of Showtown, USA." It was bankrupt by New Year's Eve 1956, and a $10,000 loan from Dalitz failed to halt the downward spiral. Its casino closed, while the hotel struggled on. Moe bought the property in 1959, expanding Stardust occupancy to 1,300 rooms.

Next came a $1.2 million Teamster loan for the 241-acre Stardust Golf Course and Country Club and the adjacent Paradise Palms housing project. That money flowed through Star Investment, a partnership including Dalitz, Allard Roen, Merv Adelson, Irwin Molasky, and Bernie Rothkopf. G-men kept track of Moe's progress, claiming that "as of 1958, Moe Dalitz was associated in Las Vegas with John Roselli [sic], who was engaged in various criminal activities" They also counted seven pistols registered in Moe's name, declaring that he "therefore should be considered armed and dangerous."

A staple of the Stardust's entertainment fare was sex. In 1960 Dalitz summoned friend Frank Sennes from the Moulin Rouge to make the Stardust sizzle. With Al

Abner "Longy" Zwillman died in a suspicious "suicide" (Library of Congress).

Roen and Irwin Molasky, Sennes flew to Paris and persuaded choreographer Donn Arden to prepare a Vegas-style version of his *Lido de Paris*. It featured three elevators, sixty skyloft lines for airborne acrobats, and a basement filled with props costing $450,000. Director Margaret Kelly dressed her "Bluebell Girls" in topless costumes that cost $1,500 each. Sheriff Butch Leypoldt threatened raids until Dalitz invited him for two performances — one with the dancers wearing bras, and one without. Leypoldt decreed that nipples were "not offensive to an adult's taste," and the show went on, sold out each night between its October 1960 premiere and its closure in 1991.

G-men kept watching, noting Moe's April 1958 hunting trip with Bing Crosby on a ranch outside Elko, Nevada. They logged Moe's phone calls to Chicago's Commercial Salvage Company in March 1959, followed by a DI visit from the Duke and Duchess of Windsor. April 1959 found Moe and Averill dining at the Variety Clubs International banquet. In May, Moe and the DI's other officers were back to hear Crown Prince Bernhard of the Netherlands address a NATO banquet held in conjunction with the World Flight Congress. Moe and Wilbur Clark comped Prince Bernhard at the DI while he enjoyed the local sights. In December 1960 agents spied Roy Cohn at the DI with an unnamed "wealthy oil man," whom they called "a close personal friend of Dalitz, [who] is given 'top priority' at the hotel."

In May 1959, while Wilbur Clark toured Europe, longtime DI secretary Frosty Jensen called to warn him of a plan to strip his name and smiling image from assorted items of resort paraphernalia. The next day, May 4, Dalitz stormed into Jensen's office and fired her, where-upon she toppled over lifeless from a heart attack. Clark flew home for the funeral, joining honorary pallbearers Morris Kleinman, Tom McGinty, Allard Roen, Ruby Kolod, Bernie Rothkopf, and Parry Thomas, while Moe helped carry Jensen to her final rest.

The Rev. Billy Graham visited Las Vegas in 1960, to preach and accept a jeweled wrist-watch from Wilbur Clark. On December 13 Graham wrote Clark a thank-you letter, gush-ing that "to meet a living legend is a treat to anyone, and especially to me." He went on: "I appreciated the hospitality ... and the explanation of gambling which was most enlightening. I also appreciated your coming to the service in spite of the wintry weather. I am convinced that such a spiritual emphasis in Las Vegas was not only pleasing to our Lord but instructive and enlightening to the citizens of your fabulous city." Graham signed the letter, "Most cor-dially yours, Billy."

Sam Giancana was less cordial on a visit to the DI that same year, presumably before the Black Book banished him in June. Various authors claim that Momo glimpsed singer

Left to right in front: Moe Dalitz, Elvis Presley, Juliet Prowse, Wilbur Clark, Toni Clark, and unidentified companion (UNLV Wilbur Clark Collection).

Phyllis McGuire in the casino, fell instantly in love, and ordered Dalitz to "eat" her $100,000 gambling debt. Moe's compliance, the authors submit, is more proof of his domination by Giancana and the Chicago Outfit.

Unfortunately for the legend-makers, it appears that the incident never happened. McGuire denied the story in an interview with Dominick Dunne, insisting that she never lost more than $16,000 on any occasion and complaining that Antoinette Giancana's description of the incident "wasn't accurate." Moe gave McGuire a blackjack table for her home, and Bill Roemer reports that after the supposed casino disagreement "she and Moe became close. Very close."

Dalitz kept his cool, as when commenting for the *Saturday Evening Post.* "Let's say gambling isn't moral," he said. "Neither is drinking to excess. I think Las Vegas has given people lots of fun. Sure, some will get hurt. But listen, they can go to Atlantic City and get into more danger in a crap game than here, where there's supervision."

* * *

In May 1960 Sam Cohen, Morris Lansburgh, and Daniel Lifter applied for permission to buy 87.75 percent of the Flamingo from Albert Parvin for $10.5 million. GCB investigators found the trio "most cooperative." Authorities approved the sale in July and Meyer Lansky received a $200,000 "finder's fee."

The biggest controversy in Las Vegas during 1960 involved segregation. African Americans in Dixie launched demonstrations against whites-only cafés that year, but Vegas had its own color line, known in some quarters as "the Mississippi of the West." Black entertainers were welcome in casino showrooms, but they could not sleep in the hotels. Likewise, residents of the city's Westside ghetto were confined to menial casino jobs, barred from working as dealers, cocktail waitresses, or any other job that might offend racist high-rollers.

Dr. James McMillan rallied his Vegas NAACP chapter and threatened protest marches on the Strip unless racial restrictions were lifted. Alan Balboni writes that Moe was "shocked" by the demand; he joined Mayor Oran Gragson and fellow casino moguls in asking McMillan to drop his crusade. McMillan — Nevada's first black dentist — was pragmatic. As he said in 1997, "The mob owned the joints. They were the ones who could say yes or no. I don't know what Moe Dalitz owned. But he was the power." Some sources credit Governor Sawyer for resolving the crisis, but those in the know recognized Moe's pivotal role in dismantling local apartheid. Michael Green, in his analysis of Jewish impact on Las Vegas, dubbed Moe the "key figure" in desegregation, while historian David Schwartz writes that the color bar was dropped specifically "at the behest of Moe Dalitz." Moe chose wisely once again, as new legions of black gamblers and hotel guests put millions in his pocket.

* * *

The biggest news of 1960 was the U.S. presidential race. Joe Kennedy had groomed son John for the White House since World War II, but brother Bobby's clashes with Jimmy Hoffa and others at the McClellan hearings threatened JFK's hopes by creating gangland animosity.

In December 1959 ex-congressman Allan Hunter met Hoffa in Miami to discuss the IBT's "program for political action" in 1960. Afterward, Hunter wrote a "Dear Dick" letter to Richard Nixon, outlining Hoffa's complaints over "nuisance suits" filed by the Justice Department. Word came back that Hoffa could help the GOP by urging Teamster locals to endorse Nixon's candidacy.

The Kennedys, meanwhile, were busy mending fences with the Mob. JFK visited the

Sands in February 1960, for a bash arranged by brother-in-law Peter Lawford and Frank Sinatra's "Rat Pack." There, Kennedy received a satchel containing $1 million in cash and met Judith Campbell, a good-time girl whose lovers included Sinatra and Sam Giancana. Their affair continued into 1962, while Campbell simultaneously entertained Giancana. Her other Mob contacts included John Rosselli and Skinny D'Amato.

Around the time JFK was partying in Vegas, his father dined in Manhattan with Rosselli and Mario Brod, a labor attorney with ties to the Mob and CIA. Historian Richard Mahoney claims that other unnamed gangsters also made the meeting. Joe consoled them with a promise that "it was Jack running for president, not Bobby, and that this was business, not politics."

Sam Giancana needed more convincing. He met Joe Kennedy in Chicago, and followed up with other meetings at Lake Tahoe's Cal-Neva Lodge. As a result, Giancana convinced Tony Accardo to support JFK's candidacy, while Murray Humphreys opposed the move, still smarting from FDR's betrayal in the 1930s.

Lyndon Johnson also coveted the Democratic nomination, doing his best to secure gambling donations with a visit to the DI in April 1960. Loyal Democrat Wilbur Clark considered himself a close friend of Johnson *and* JFK, extending hospitality to both candidates, but it had been a decade since Clark called the shots around the DI on anything that mattered.

JFK's first hurdle was the May primary in West Virginia, where the Ku Klux Klan distributed anti–Catholic propaganda. FBI bugs caught Skinny D'Amato boasting that he spread $50,000 in payoffs around the state, while candidate Hubert Humphrey complained to the press, "I don't think elections should be bought. I can't afford to run through this state with a little black bag and a checkbook." Kennedy swept West Virginia and rolled on to capture the nomination in July. Before JFK's first-ballot triumph, Jimmy Hoffa met with Texas governor John Connally and vowed to support Lyndon Johnson if LBJ secured the nomination, but Kennedy's eleventh-hour choice of Johnson as his running mate killed that dream.

On September 7 the IBT's board of directors endorsed Nixon. Hoffa toured the country speaking on Nixon's behalf and delivered a secret $500,000 campaign donation from Louisiana mafioso Carlos Marcello. When Hoffa's endorsement proved embarrassing, a Nixon aide told journalists, "You may be assured that neither the vice-president nor the Republican Party will ever ally themselves with men like Mr. Hoffa." However, within weeks of Marcello's donation, Nixon killed a Florida land-fraud indictment targeting Hoffa. Tom Zander, an investigator with the Department of Labor, later told Gus Russo, "Anybody who wanted to pay for it had a connection to Nixon. The locals gave massive amounts of untraced money to Nixon. They got away with murder."

Hoffa remained a Nixon man until the bitter end, hiring private detectives to tap JFK's phones and bug the homes of his known mistresses. Sam Giancana was more realistic, telling friends, "We'll contribute to Nixon, too.... We'll hedge our bets, just like out in California when Nixon was running for senator.... You don't know what the hell Jack'll do once he's elected. With Nixon, you know where you stand."

Moe Dalitz missed the election in Vegas, having flown off to Detroit for his father's funeral. Barnet Dalitz died from a stroke on October 31, and while Jewish law normally mandates burial within twenty-four hours of death, Moe did not reach Detroit until November 3, remaining for a week under the scrutiny of G-men. His absence from Vegas coincided with a gathering of mobsters from Detroit, Cleveland, New York, and L.A. at the DI. According to feds who observed their two-week session, the mobsters convened "to force an accounting of" a $250,000 shortage in the DI's insurance fund and "had given the Desert Inn until

11/21/60 to make up the shortage." Journalists published conflicting reports of the meeting. Victor Riesel claimed the delegates "discussed the protection of their $20 billion a year empire during the new administration." Ed Reid and Ovid Demaris moved the gathering to the Jackpot Motel and described its result as the elevation of Nicholas "Peanuts" Danolfo from his job as "host" at the DI to a more prestigious but unspecified position.

The nation voted on November 8. With 69 million ballots cast nationwide, it was the largest vote in U.S. history — and the closest decision since 1916. Kennedy carried the day by a margin of 119,450 popular votes. Analysts opined that a shift in 28,000 Texas votes and 4,500 in Illinois would have tipped the balance for Nixon. The furious vice president sought a federal investigation, but Ike talked him out of it, warning that too close a look "will tear the country apart."

The question for historians is not *whether* Kennedy won the election, but rather *how* he won. Sam Giancana delivered 80 percent of Chicago's critical wards, and later told Judith Campbell, "Listen, honey, if it wasn't for me your boyfriend wouldn't even be in the White House." Well satisfied with his achievement, Giancana, told friends, "We'll all get our payoff in the end."

Seldom has any prophecy gone more awry.

9

Camelot

The Mob had every reason to expect peaceful coexistence with JFK, but brother Bobby was another story. All accounts agree that Papa Joe chose Bobby to be Attorney General. The president-elect protested, fearing claims of nepotism, but Joe Kennedy insisted, saying, "He's a lawyer, he's savvy, he knows all the political ins and outs and can protect you."

Despite some raised eyebrows in Congress, Bobby was approved to join his brother's cabinet. It was the worst news possible for leaders of the Mob.

* * *

Immediately after his appointment, Robert Kennedy proclaimed "a very serious situation that's facing the country at the present time." The threat, he declared, was a "private government of organized crime, resting on a base of human suffering and moral corrosion."

Kennedy's first stumbling block was Hoover's FBI. In 1961, when Bobby asked New York's FBI office to update him "on what's been happening with organized crime," agent-in-charge John Malone could not oblige "because we've been having a newspaper strike." When Kennedy staffer George Robert Blakey asked G-men about organized crime, "They told me that the Mob does not exist. It was just a loose association of gangs. They are not organized." Hoover insulted RFK at every opportunity and once described him to Richard Nixon as a "sneaky little sonofabitch."

Despite that opposition, Bobby compiled a list of 4,300 targets for prosecution, with Jimmy Hoffa at its head. IRS agents delved into gangland tax records, while the Justice Department's Organized Crime and Racketeering Section grew from seventeen attorneys to sixty-three.

The results were dramatic. In 1960, anti–Mob prosecutors spent 61 days in court, 660 in the field, and 100 before grand juries. Three years later, Kennedy's lawyers spent 1,081 days in court, 6,177 in the field, and 1,353 before grand juries. Under Eisenhower, Mob investigations had declined from 10,041 in 1953 to 1,039 in 1955 and 125 in 1960. Kennedy indicted 121 mobsters in 1961, 350 in 1962, and 615 in 1963. His prosecutors convicted 73 gangsters in 1961, 138 in 1962, and 288 in 1963.

Bobby's targets blamed Papa Joe, insisting that the new crusade was a vendetta aimed at settling scores with prohibition-era enemies. Most mobsters shared the view of Boston's Vincent Teresa, who complained that the Kennedys accepted Mob money and favors, "[t]hen they turn around and say they're great fighters against corruption. They criticize other people for being with mob guys. They're hypocrites."

But they were hypocrites with power, and the Mob would suffer while they held the reins in Washington.

None suffered more than Jimmy Hoffa and his Teamsters. Kennedy's Justice Department indicted 201 IBT members and co-conspirators during 1961–63, convicting 126. Thirteen grand juries convened to investigate Hoffa in 1961, while Jimmy fought a mail-fraud indictment held over from 1960.

That case ended with a mistrial, but Kennedy was relentless. In May 1962 a Tennessee grand jury indicted Hoffa for receiving $1 million in kickbacks through a trucking firm established in his wife's name. Jurors deadlocked two days before Christmas 1962, but Judge William Miller convened a new grand jury to investigate alleged jury-tampering. That panel indicted Hoffa in May 1963. One month later, a Chicago grand jury charged Hoffa and seven others with embezzling $1 million from the IBT pension fund. Hoffa was convicted, and five months later he received another five-year sentence in Chicago.

* * *

In April 1961 immigration officers arrested New Orleans mafioso Carlos Marcello and put him on a plane to Guatemala. Louisiana pilot David Ferrie flew Marcello home on June 1, prompting an indictment for illegal reentry and a new deportation order in July. Prosecutors next indicted Marcello and his brother for falsifying passports and other documents.

In June 1961 a New Orleans grand jury indicted Gil Beckley and twelve other gamblers for using interstate phone lines to operate their bookie syndicate with outposts including Miami, Las Vegas, and Newport, Kentucky. All won acquittal at their trial in May 1963. Pete Licavoli faced the McClellan Committee in Washington but refused to provide even his name or date of birth. That defiance sent him to jail for six months, after which he returned to business as usual in Tucson. Sam Giancana sued the FBI for its lockstep surveillance and won: Judge Richard Austin ordered G-men to remove four of the five cars staking out Momo's home and to remain at least one foursome behind him on the golf course.

* * *

The feds got a break in June 1962, when inmate Joseph Valachi beat another convict to death in Atlanta's federal prison. Valachi believed that his victim was a hitman sent by fellow inmate Vito Genovese to kill Valachi over some supposed infraction of the Mafia code. Now, facing life imprisonment, Valachi offered himself to the Federal Bureau of Narcotics as an informant.

And what a story he told.

Beginning with prohibition, Valachi outlined the Mafia's history from the Castellammarese War onward. In September 1963 he testified before the McClellan Committee and told America that mafiosi called their network *Cosa Nostra* ("our thing"). Overnight, a sensation was born.

How accurate was Valachi's information? By his own admission, Valachi knew nothing of Mob activities outside New York. His ignorance was so profound, in fact, that by his own admission he had "never heard of" Iowa or Nebraska. Years later, Joe Bonnano compared Valachi's revelations to the ramblings of a "New Guinea native who had converted to Catholicism describing the inner workings of the Vatican." Chicago's Virgil Peterson called Valachi's testimony "oversimplified and unrealistic," warning that acceptance of his tale would be a "great error."

The Mafia existed, to be sure, but G-men and journalists alike exaggerated its influence.

Left: Joe Valachi mixed fact and fable in his Senate testimony (Library of Congress). *Right:* Angelo "Gyp" DeCarlo lamented the power of Jews in organized crime (National Archives).

One of their favorite quotes, from a bug planted in Angelo DeCarlo's headquarters, had the mafioso telling a friend, "There's only two Jews recognized in the whole country today. That's Meyer and ... Moe Dalitz, but [Dalitz] ain't got much recognition." Typically omitted from such publications are the *other* statements by DeCarlo, taped over a two-year period. In May 1961 DeCarlo told Anthony Boiardo, "You see, if you want to kill a Jew, you're supposed to let the Jews know. When Willie [Moretti] killed Charlie the Jew — oh, there was a helluva beef." An FBI memo from August 1963 described another conversation in which "DeCarlo deplored the fact that the Jews wield so much influence in Las Vegas, giving the Italians only a few crumbs."

* * *

In February 1961 G-men suggested charging Moe Dalitz with bribery, labor racketeering, and Mann Act violations (transporting women across state lines for "immoral purposes"), but Hoover scotched the plan. Instead, he hoped for a federal grand jury on skimming, where Moe would face a triple threat: admit embezzlement and go to jail; deny it and face perjury charges; or plead the Fifth and face revocation of his gaming license. Hoover's marginal note on the memo inquired, "Can we do something here as harassment?"

They could, indeed.

Agents trailed Moe around the Desert Inn, reporting his movements and phone calls. They noted his "intense conversation" with George Gordon in February 1961 and questioned him in June about a fishing trip with Phil Harris. Two weeks later G-men named Moe "one of 42 prime targets for early prosecution under the Criminal Intelligence Program." A July memo placed Moe and Meyer Lansky on a list of ten mobsters marked for "intensified investigations." In August Hoover chastised his Vegas agent-in-charge, whose last report was "not in full accordance with instructions set out," demanding data "as an aid to conducting a grand jury probe" of Moe's activities. Three weeks later Hoover announced a "crash program" to put Moe away.

None of it worked.

In July 1961 G-men requested Hoover's permission to bug the DI. Hoover approved, but hotel security frustrated his men until early 1962. Their bug, under a conference table in the DI's executive office, began transmitting on March 22. A memo dated March 26 described it as the only surveillance device on the premises, broadcasting at a projected cost of $4,557 per year.

The first significant transmission occurred on March 27, when the bug caught DI executives "counting money and attempting to divide it up among several individuals." G-men noted division of skim as follows: $33,195 to "M.D." (Dalitz), $28,520 to "M.K." (Kleinman), $13,300 to "Ruby" (Kolod), $13,040 to "Sam" (Tucker), $9,400 to "T.J." (McGinty), and $5,615 to "Wilbur" (Clark). Those present debated whether "Chicago" should receive $10,000 or $15,000.

Agents had Chicago's Murray Humphreys on tape, stating that the Outfit owned 35 percent of the DI and Stardust, saying, "We're right at the point where we can hit [Dalitz] in the head." But with his next breath he seemed grateful for his share, reluctantly conceded by "a Jew guy." A January 1962 memo reports Sam Giancana speaking "very derogatively of 'the Jews,'" who were "taking advantage of a situation in Las Vegas" that barred mafiosi from legal gaming. The same memo says that "no factions [are] contending for power" at the DI.

An FBI report from January 1963 claimed $280,000 skimmed in recent weeks from the Flamingo, Fremont, Sands, and Horseshoe in Vegas. Another memo said that DI skimmers stole $100,000 monthly, 10 percent of it going directly to Dalitz. Hoover's "Skimming Report" of May 1963 leaked to Mob leaders, and wiretaps were discovered at the Sands two months later, along with a bug in Carl Cohen's bedroom.

The DI filed suit in November 1961, to block an IRS "fishing expedition with respect to the customers of the hotel, thereby causing incalculable damage to the company." The petition alleged that IRS agents sought to "harass and annoy hotel owners despite full payment of taxes." Five months later the DI bug heard Sam Tucker declare, "I've got an FBI guy here in my pocket who's been calling me for a week." That agent had approached Tucker in Indianapolis, recalling a 1959 meeting in Newport. "Luckily," Tucker said, "the guy copped out and I was saved." G-men, disturbed by intimations of corruption in their ranks, proposed to harass Tucker with phone calls "since this has obviously had a disturbing effect."

In June 1962 a federal judge ordered the DI to surrender credit card records for all customers. While Moe's attorneys fought that order, the IRS proposed a new tax on Keno winnings. Moe called the move "a bad situation" and proposed contacting "the horse-racing lobby" for legal assistance. When the IRS pressed for details on casino IOUs, Allard Roen told Tucker that a judge on Nevada's appellate court would "understand our situation." In April 1963 the IRS served Moe with notice that disallowance of various deductions had increased his 1962 taxable income by $1,377,645.82. When one of Moe's partners observed that "there is a lot of intrigue going on around here that neither of us know anything about," Dalitz replied, "Yeah, isn't it fun?"

The "fun" seemed never-ending. In April 1963 DI executives denounced federal harassment of their customers as "legalized blackmail," spawned by RFK's failure to jail Jimmy Hoffa. T-men were also sniffing around the Bank of Las Vegas, where Parry Thomas did "everything possible to protect individuals in the gaming industry." Ruby Kolod warned his partners against coddling the IRS, saying that "jails are full of people who cooperated with these guys." G-men who approached Kolod described him as his "usual obnoxious, nasty, uncooperative self," noting that he "was brought up as a hoodlum and had never learned to act any other way."

* * *

Moe made himself scarce in those days, traveling as widely as his fortune and duties allowed. In July 1961 he received passport No. B195021, preparing for a tour of England, France, Italy, Switzerland, and Hong Kong. G-men noted his departure for New York in December, suggesting that he "may contact" Gerardo Catena in transit, then logged his flight to Paris and "Nairobe, South Africa." Another FBI memo notes Moe's January 1962 departure with Averill and Suzanne for a tour including stops in Paris, "various points in Italy," and other unspecified countries.

When G-men learned that Moe would visit New York in May 1962, en route to Ireland, they proposed to bug his hotel suite and "guaranteed full security." Prior to takeoff, Moe exchanged his round-trip ticket for a one-way booking and flew on from Dublin to London, then surfaced on June 2 in "Monte Carlo, Italy." An unexplained "emergency call" brought him back to Vegas ahead of schedule, while Averill and Suzanne returned aboard the S.S. *France.*

Moe's interests in Europe included a new yacht, the *Moby Dick,* under construction in Norway. Dalitz planned to moor the boat in Greece for two years before sending it on to the States. He also had business in Turkey, where unnamed contacts had invited him to run three large hotels. Moe described Istanbul as "a playground," telling his DI partners that "he had received the whole story on gambling" in Turkey, but he did not "exhibit excessive enthusiasm." France seemed more promising, and Moe considered purchasing a hotel on the Riviera during early 1963 but never followed through.

Moe's sharpest foreign focus lay south of the border, around Acapulco. He kept a smaller yacht, the *Stardust,* anchored there for fishing trips, spent considerable time in Mexico throughout 1962–63, and built a $100,000 house. In December 1962 the U.S. embassy in Mexico City asked G-men for a background dossier on Moe. Agents reported that Dalitz had "recently relinquished management of the Desert Inn and is reported to be interested in trying to open up organized gambling in Acapulco."

The media got wind of Moe's Mexican travels in January 1963, whereupon he told his partners, "We can take the sting out of it by handling it quickly.... I'll explain that my wife likes Acapulco and she wants to settle there. I can afford to build this house I am building down there and I have no right to tell her she can't have it if she wants it."

The Averill cover worked to a point—an FBI memo from August 1961 deemed Moe "extremely attentive and solicitous to his wife and [he] affords her every luxury money can buy"—but it fell apart when the couple divorced on September 11, 1963. The file, sealed by court order, listed Dalitz as the judgment debtor. Part of Averill's payoff was the Acapulco house.

* * *

The pressures of work, his disintegrating home life, and incessant federal investigations prompted Dalitz to consider retirement. In June 1962 G-men told Washington "it appears possible that Dalitz anticipates leaving Las Vegas and possibly residing on a permanent basis in Mexico or some other locality." Moe expressed a desire to sell off his share of the DI and Stardust, seeking to "lay low and pass out of the limelight" so that "things may cool off and pass over," but he complained that "I can't leave it to some fucking new guy." In April 1963 agents claimed that George Gordon was being groomed to replace Moe, despite insistence from Moe's partners that Gordon "will never be as effective an executive as Dalitz."

In fact, Moe remained at the helm, while agents noted that "on occasion [he] drinks to excess." Reporter Ed Reid describes an interview in 1963 where Moe allegedly broke down: "'Why, why,' he implored, his arms rising in supplication, the tears streaming from his hard little eyes, 'why are they persecuting me?' 'Who?' [I] inquired. 'Them. All of them! I've fought hoodlums all my life. What are they trying to do to me?'"

Some of "them" were trying to put him in prison. The FBI harassed him constantly, taking "extensive motion pictures" of Dalitz around the DI, staging "pretext visits" to the Utah ranch. "If I could only get my name off that Top Forty [list]," he said in July 1962, "I've got a lot of people rooting for me.... That's the whole fucking thing." In February 1963 he told Sidney Korshak, "FBI agents were in here a while back and tried to ask me some questions. I told them to put them right back in their fucking pocket because I was not going to answer anything. They said, 'We would like you to at least hear the questions.' I said, 'You are not going to read them because I don't want to hear them.'"

Despite that lack of cordiality, G-men deleted the "armed and dangerous" notation they had appended to Moe's dossier in 1958. Seven guns were registered in Moe's name, but agents claimed that most were rifles used for big-game hunting. In fact, all seven were pistols. Nonetheless, agents reported that Dalitz "has never been known to personally carry a sidearm. He has never used any threatening language nor given any indication of being physically dangerous."

One witness who might have disputed that claim was heavyweight boxing champion Charles "Sonny" Liston. On October 25, 1963, while Moe and a companion lunched at Hollywood's Beverly Rodeo Hotel, Liston rolled in looking for trouble. He approached Moe's table with the comment that Dalitz "ain't such a tough guy away from Las Vegas." Moe's unknown response made Liston raise his fist, as if to strike. Author Don Remnick claims it was "a joke," but Moe replied in deadly earnest. "If you hit me, nigger," he declared, "you'd better kill me. Because if you don't, I'll make one phone call and you'll be dead in twenty-four hours."

Liston gaped, then turned and fled — not only the hotel, but California, hurrying home to Las Vegas. He did not box again until February 25, 1964, when contender Cassius Clay defeated Sonny in the seventh round. Liston died at home on December 30, 1970, from an apparent overdose of heroin.

* * *

While Moe had America's heavyweight champ on the run, other African Americans were spoiling for a fight in Las Vegas. James McMillan had retired as head of the Vegas NAACP in 1961, and his successor waited two years before launching a new civil rights drive. The DI bug relayed discussions of plans to picket Strip hotels, but Moe was in Europe and missed the meeting. His partners still balked at hiring black dealers, and refused to "lower their standards" by firing white employees to create new slots for blacks. The pickets failed to materialize, and DI leaders voted to coordinate policy revisions through the Nevada Resort Hotel Association — which FBI memos describe as "completely dominated" by Moe Dalitz.

Amidst his travels, Moe found many projects in Nevada to consume his time. The DI was expanding to include Goldwater's of Las Vegas — later renamed DI Distinctive Apparel when Barry Goldwater sought to mask his Vegas connections — while Moe examined other prospects. In 1962 he debated the $9 million purchase of 254 acres near Reno, to launch a new Vegas-style Strip, but decided against it. Likewise, a plan to buy land at Lake Tahoe fell through after Moe decided the proposed 230-room hotel would not support a casino. Owners of the new Landmark Tower in Vegas asked Dalitz to lease the casino and restaurant, but he demurred.

One project that *did* fly was a tomato farm outside Vegas. Moe projected a $1 million return on $35 in seeds, but construction cost $365,000. Still he forged ahead, telling his partners the farm should produce 2 million pounds of tomatoes by February 1963, for an estimated $500,000 profit. FBI eavesdroppers found Moe's partners "lukewarm" on his plan to buy acreage at Lake Mead for construction of lakefront homes, but Dalitz carried the day. In June 1963 newspapers announced that Paradise Homes had paid $5 million for 1,400 acres, planning construction of 4,500 homes at a cost exceeding $100 million.

The owners of Paradise Homes were never publicly identified, but Irwin Molasky told Wallace Turner they were "about the same" as the partners in A&M Enterprises. Sam Garfield did not make the list, and Eli Boyer was relegated to serve as financial advisor, while Dalitz, Allard Roen, Merv Adelson and Molasky divided ownership. The firm's first big deal with the Federal Housing Administration, in 1962, involved renovation of the failing Desert Gardens apartment complex to create Desert Palms. Casino employees filled Desert Palms, while the DRAM group moved on to build Paradise Palms, a housing tract near Sunrise Hospital with homes priced from $22,900 to $42,500. FHA records showed 492 units sold by early 1964. A major selling point for Paradise Palms was the nearby Stardust Golf Course, created with a $1.2 million Teamster loan to Star Investment.

Another Paradise project, described in 1962 newspaper spiels as the "downtown of tomorrow," was the Las Vegas Commercial Center on Maryland Parkway. Moe's builders broke ground in 1963 for a complex including shops, professional offices, and restaurants. Later they tacked on the Ice Palace, a skating rink and sometime rock-concert venue.

* * *

After cold cash, celebrity was the lifeblood of Vegas, and most of the stars knew Moe Dalitz. Honored DI guests included British royalty and Vice President Johnson. Peter Lawford joined Frank Sinatra and Dean Martin at the DI in May 1961, "inquiring as to the health of his good friend Moe Dalitz," but their relationship soured in January 1963, after Lawford "ran wild" with unauthorized charges during an eight-week engagement. Groucho Marx and Jack Benny demanded payment "under the table" to outwit tax auditors. G-men tracked Moe to a Desert Inn party in December 1961, accompanied by Betty Grable and three unidentified beauties.

Moe enjoyed the ladies, as did fishing partner Phil Harris. Harris produced and directed his own DI stage show in April 1962, but G-men were more interested in his travels with Dalitz. They tracked Moe and Harris to San Diego in February 1962, where they enjoyed "quite a party" with unidentified female companions, then sailed off to Mexico. Five months later, agents snapped photographs while Moe and Harris golfed at Pebble Beach. Before that outing, the DI bug recorded plans to import prostitutes for the players. Those present "discussed the qualities of various girls" and dropped one from the stable who had charged $300 on the last go-around but proved "unsatisfactory." Again, G-men considered Mann Act charges against Moe and Harris, but the outlaw bug precluded prosecution.

While Phil Harris was fun, Eddie Fisher proved to be a headache. His relationship with Moe began when Fisher squired actress Stefanie Powers to Vegas and brought her mother along to chaperone. Fisher says, "I fixed her up with Moe Dalitz, the most charming mobster I've ever known.... I never knew what happened between him and Stefanie's mother, but that was the end of our chaperone." Eddie described Dalitz as being "like a father to me — as long as I was at the Desert Inn. But the day I signed with the Riviera was the day he stopped talking to me. When I opened at the Riviera they threw a big party for me, and Sidney Korshak forced Moe to come and shake my hand in public. But Moe didn't love me anymore."

Their trouble actually started when Sam Giancana assumed control of the Villa Venice Supper Club in Wheeling, Illinois. Giancana wanted Fisher, Frank Sinatra, and Dean Martin for the club's grand opening in 1962, which pulled Fisher from the DI lineup and "disturbed Dalitz considerably." Fisher also objected to playing a small unknown venue, and his manager phoned Dalitz, saying, "Moe, we don't want to go to that fucking hotel.... This man's career is at stake." Dalitz surmised that Giancana planned "to dump this place and get a whole lot of acts in there and build up a good financial picture," suggesting that he would "gladly pay up to $20,000 if he could figure out some way to get out of the deal." Finally, however, he agreed to "do a favor for our friends in Chicago."

Phyllis McGuire served as an intermediary in those negotiations, but caused her own furor at the DI. FBI transcripts from June 1962 find Allard Roen telling Sam Tucker that "everything was going very well except he had had a run in 'with these guys you know.' He stated half the trouble is with the McGuire sisters. They wanted to leave and 'it all boils down to what happened in the casino last night.'" The trouble involved a pit boss who "made a decision on something he didn't look into far enough," Roen said. "I'll get it straightened out, but the only thing I'm worried about now is let's assume they want to quit. I'm not going to stand in their way and then I'm going to have trouble with Moe. You know how he yelled about the other thing."

* * *

The McGuire incident prompted more FBI speculation concerning Moe's presumed bondage to the Mafia. A conversation between Giancana and Kansas City mafioso Nicholas Civella included Civella's claim that Moe "was under Giancana's control," but an October 1962 memo found Dalitz "at frequent odds" with Giancana. One month later agents called Moe "one of Giancana's 'people' in Las Vegas," yet they recorded Moe's comment that John Rosselli was "nothing but trouble." After an April 1963 incident with Rosselli at the DI, "Dalitz made the observation that he had been trying for years to keep 'these people' out of here and if it hadn't been for him they would have taken the place over long ago."

Nonetheless, one month later Moe paid Rosselli $6,000 for defective ice machines at the DI, explaining that "in matters of this nature it is not simply a matter of price, but on occasion it is better for everyone concerned 'to do it one way rather than another way.'"

Such expressions led G-men to brand Moe "a physical coward," proclaiming that "Dalitz and associates are victims of the greed of the Chicago Crime Syndicate and Miami's [DELETED] and Alfred Polizzi."

A case in point, according to authors Ed Reid and Ovid Demaris, occurred either in autumn 1960 or January 1961. Chicago enforcer Marshal Caifano, banned from Nevada casinos in June, showed up at the DI where Morris Kleinman confronted him. Reid and Demaris say Kleinman called Caifano "a dumb dago," whereupon Caifano chased Kleinman back to his office before he was nabbed by security guards. While some authors portray the incident as proof of Kleinman's domination by the Mafia, retreating from Caifano simply made good sense. Guards at the El Rancho had ejected Caifano on June 17, 1960, and their hotel burned down that very night.

* * *

Amidst his travels and business deals, Dalitz made time for charity. In June 1961 he chaired a committee that raised $300,000 for construction of a local YMCA. The same month saw Moe elected as vice president of the Donna Kutzen Youth Foundation, which promoted sports to curb juvenile delinquency. In November 1961 Dalitz solicited donations for the United Fund, which he served as vice chairman. Simultaneously, Moe donated $8,500 to Clark County's schools, the first installment of a $25,000 pledge earmarked for teacher salaries and special education scholarships in 1961–62.

Dalitz also led the fundraising drive for Guardian Angel Cathedral, described by author Alan Balboni as "an example of both the nonsectarian nature of Dalitz's generosity and his vision of Las Vegas as a resort city." In September 1962 the DI bug caught Moe explaining the project to Sam Tucker: "We are trying to be civic minded here for Christ's sake!"

* * *

Hank Greenspun had secured a $250,000 Teamster loan in 1958 to build the Paradise Valley Golf Course, which soon faced competition from Moe's course at the Stardust. Greenspun alleged that state engineer Edwin Muth denied him permission to drill for water, then granted the Stardust approval in January 1961, around the same time Moe was named chief barker for the local Variety Club. Dalitz resigned within days, and while the *Sun* described his move as "unexplained," Moe told the competing *Review-Journal* that Greenspun's "hate campaign" had driven him from office. He was quitting, Moe said, to spare the Variety Club and other charities from "the embarrassment of being attacked" by Greenspun.

Moe resumed his chief barker's post in January 1962, while the *R-J* opined that Greenspun "didn't think that Mr. Dalitz was too bad when he worked for him as a publicity agent at the Desert Inn.... Could it be that the *Sun* publisher has never forgotten that Dalitz fired him? Could it be that Dalitz and his partners refused to go along with a golf course deal or other business propositions the *Sun* publisher wanted them to enter into? ... Apparently ... Dalitz became evil only when he would have no part of certain business deals."

In January 1962 Moe and his partners organized the Nevada Resort Hotels Association to address "problems of mutual interest." Ex-GCB member George Ullom resigned his post as Vegas city manager to head the NRHA for $200,000 per year, whereupon Greenspun called him "a liaison man for the Sawyer administration and sinister elements in Las Vegas gambling." Hank's candidate for governor that year was Republican Rex Bell. Moe and the NRHA sought primary opponents for Bell, but the main contender demanded $50,000 "on the line" before he would commit. Meanwhile, Dalitz funneled cash to Sawyer's camp, reminding his associates that "we always take care of that."

Moe returned from Europe in July to help with the campaign. He called an *R-J* reporter "to discuss strategy," specifically urging the newsman "to answer pro-Bell articles" published in the *Sun*. Speaking to Dalitz in the DI's bugged office, a partner said, "We're going to be killed if we lose this one." Moe agreed, saying of Sawyer on July 3, "We can't let him lose."

The next day, Bell suffered a fatal heart attack. Mayor Oran Gragson announced his candidacy, followed swiftly by Greenspun. It was no contest for Dalitz, who sought a "calm governor" committed to defense of gambling. FBI memos report that Dalitz was "going all out" to beat Greenspun. Moe said, "I called Reno and talked to people I know and they feel about like I do, but there is so many new people in the state who don't know about this fucker.... I'd personally rather live in the slums of Hong Kong than in Nevada with Greenspun as governor."

One irony of Greenspun's attacks on Dalitz was the *Sun*'s defense of Jimmy Hoffa. Hank's campaign vows to "sanitize" Nevada gaming rang hollow when he praised Hoffa as "a man with a mission" and "very positive ideas," cheering Jimmy's "wry barbs" against the FBI. Mayor Gragson blasted Greenspun as a "Hoffa tool" who had also banked $190,000 in advertising revenues from the DI and Stardust while working secretly to "sell out" Nevada's gamblers. "There wasn't anything 'tainted' about this money as long as Mr. Greenspun was collecting it," said Gragson. As for Moe's donations to his own campaign, Gragson said, "I have nothing to hide."

"If he believes that," Hank retorted, "he's even more naïve than I thought." Greenspun declared that Dalitz had "brought harm to our state, onus to the gambling industry, and federal intervention into our affairs. If he leaves the industry, 95 percent of its problems would be solved." Gragson fired back, telling jovial crowds, "Mr. Greenspun believes that any money is tainted if it tain't his." Moe and the NRHA sponsored what Greenspun called a "smear campaign," releasing bulletins that Greenspun failed to pay his temple dues and had reneged on pledges to the Jewish Fund. Anonymous pamphlets compared Hank to his old rival Joe McCarthy, one claiming that "Greenspun by comparison would make Genghis Khan look like a Bible salesman."

Gragson trounced Greenspun by a two-to-one margin on primary day, prompting Hank's complaint to G-men that his loss was "influenced by money put into the campaign by Morris Barney Dalitz, leader of the hoodlum element in Las Vegas." Moe allegedly confirmed it in an interview with Ed Reid, saying, "Hank says it cost a quarter of a million? Hah! It cost almost twice that, but we got results! Why, we threw the money away like water, and I'm telling you in front of witnesses. Now go on, go on and print it!" Greenspun himself dismissed that comment as a joke, insisting that Moe was too wise to confess the "vast sums" spent on Gragson's behalf. Hank's warning that the DI crowd would dump Gragson before November's general election proved prophetic. One day after the September primary, DI and Stardust workers received bumper stickers supporting Grant Sawyer.

Aside from Sawyer, Dalitz campaigned for re-election of Senator Alan Bible (whom Moe called a "mere figurehead"), backed Ralph Lamb for Clark County sheriff, and supported *Review-Journal* editor Al Cahlan's bid to succeed retiring county commissioner Arthur Olsen. Cahlan's victorious opponent also pocketed DI donations. Moe explained his generosity to rival candidates by saying, "They can't get it [money] anywhere else." After the final votes were cast, Moe told his partners, "We have never been stronger in our influence of these people than at the present time."

* * *

Still, two days after November's election, Moe complained of "a wave of general harassment by the IRS and the FBI," coupled with Greenspun "firing at us from every direction." He told his partners, "We have suffered a barrage of attacks, but since we have done nothing wrong, we have nothing to fear. None of us are going to be governors or senators. We are going to be just what we are. So let's just live our lives and do it peacefully and don't let these fuckers upset you."

Investigators focused chiefly on the Vegas skim, which Moe dismissed as fantasy. He told

Wallace Turner, "Our costs of operating and cost of entertainment and high wage rates make us glad to make expenses, much less take any money off the top." "You know who does the most policing?" Moe asked another interviewer. "We do! We've helped many a competitor financially." Ex-state legislator Stan Irwin, ensconced as the Sahara's entertainment director, assured journalists, "We have no gangsters here. We have qualified businessmen who are in a recognized industry — gaming."

Moe was aware of leaks at the DI, although he never tracked them down. In July 1962 he ordered "a big check-up of the security guards," suspected of squealing and closing their eyes to a series of hotel burglaries. Four months later he ordered meetings held outside the DI's office, saying, "Each time will be a different place. The reason is very obvious. We want the meetings to be very private." The feds, he warned, "mean you no good and will fuck you if they can."

* * *

In December 1960 FBI eavesdroppers heard Murray Humphreys say that Sam Giancana "wants to buy [the Stardust] and make it a capital gain on his side of the fence and we'd be in on it legit." Giancana's June 1960 Black Book listing rendered that fantasy moot, but Dalitz and Kleinman flew to Chicago in January 1961 for a meeting with Humphreys, Giancana, and Tony Accardo. According to Bill Roemer, the conference was held to let Chicago and New York mobsters swap shares of the Desert Inn, Stardust and Riviera. Author Connie Bruck claims that the meeting gave Chicago hoods their first-ever piece of the DI, Riviera and Fremont, while making the Outfit "a bigger partner than it already was" in the Stardust.

In any case, their first roadblock was Jake Factor, who remained the Stardust's landlord. In early 1962 newspapers reported Factor's acceptance of a $14 million offer from Moe's United Hotels, but Moe complained in March that investors "are being pushed around by Factor and he is dictating terms of the new contract." Hank Greenspun's Sun announced the final sale in August 1962, prompting Dalitz to scold Factor for leaking the story. G-men found Moe "still considering" the deal in November, and the sale — to Lodestar Corporation, with three DI secretaries listed as directors — was not finalized until December. Corporate spokesmen announced that Dalitz and his partners would "lease" the Stardust from Lodestar.

Factor's final surrender resulted from pressure on various fronts. Sidney Korshak briefed Moe on Chicago's role, saying Factor gave up the Stardust after consulting Murray Humphreys. Around the same time, police discovered Sam Tucker's new office in Chicago, at 134 North LaSalle Street.

John Tuohy claims that Outfit bosses Accardo, Humphreys, and Paul Ricca gained five points each in the Stardust from Factor's sellout, while Kansas City's Nick Civella banked a $6,000-per-month "broker's fee." If so, no such arrangements were discussed in the DI's bugged conference room. Eleven weeks before the final sale, Dalitz discussed Chicago's mobsters with Tucker and George Gordon. "I was seen with them," he said, "but I didn't think it was a good idea to tie everybody in the mob up." Tucker mentioned "those Detroit guys I see around here," prompting Moe to reply, "They want to move in here and we can't have that. I don't want to make an issue of Rosselli.... We didn't want him in here. We've got real men." In February 1963 Moe said, "I think we made a wonderful deal on the Stardust. We have a good package over there. We have gathered up all the loose ends."

Except for John Drew. In April 1963 G-men reported that Drew was drinking heavily and had been warned that "if he didn't straighten out, he was finished." Nonetheless, by April 24 Drew was "in trouble again with Dalitz," for losing $150,000 of the casino's money at poker. Threats to "get rid of Drew completely" prompted immediate repayment of $55,000. A week later, Moe announced that IRS agents "have a case on John Drew," who risked indictment for obstructing justice by asking one T-man to scuttle the case. As far as Drew's authority around the Stardust went, G-men heard Wilbur Clark declare that "Johnny Drew ... is only on paper anyway."

* * *

If *some* "Detroit guys" were unwelcome in Vegas, Dalitz still cherished his partners in Motown and Cleveland. FBI monitors listened while Moe, Kleinman, and Tucker discussed "matters in Cleveland" in October 1962 and seven months later heard Moe praise his "friends in Detroit."

Chief among those friends was Jimmy Hoffa, whose IBT pension fund bankrolled Moe's projects in Vegas and elsewhere. In February 1963 G-men recorded Moe's side of a phone conversation with Hoffa, discussing a new business prospect:

> I am sending that man in to see you.... He has got some ideas that he wants to put forth to you and they are good because he explained them to me.... Now you know that the name of this company is the Re-Insurance Investment Company.... They are the mother company and it is listed on the American Board.... We want it.... You helped us and we want to help you.

Memos note that certain IBT officials needed $5 million in casualty insurance to obtain mandatory bonds, and Moe offered the proposed transaction in lieu of loaning Hoffa the money himself, which he felt "would be declaring war on the Department of Justice."

In other Motown business, G-men noted Moe's membership in "a prominent Jewish social club" composed of "wealthy Jewish people." Dalitz also owned an ice skating rink, with an unidentified partner. His most vexing connection involved Jack Cinnamon, former president of Bernardine Realty, who died in September 1962 and left his finances in disarray. When a jointly owned supermarket went bankrupt, creditors sued Cinnamon's estate. Dalitz expected a subpoena to testify and promptly left for Mexico, but he was ultimately served with orders to appear in January 1963. The DI bug recorded his concern that "both sides would probably want to go into the whole history of the deal and that he would have no alternative but to take the Fifth Amendment."

In Cleveland, meanwhile, G-men monitored Morris Kleinman's sale of stock in the Ice Capades, which made $3 million on an initial $323,000 investment. The DI bug broadcast details of Kleinman's will, which included a $50,000 bequest to George Gordon and an unspecified sum for a Cleveland orphanage. Mushy Wexler spent $1 million to rebuild the Theatrical Grill after a 1960 fire, rebounding with reviews that ranked it among Cleveland's best restaurants. Shondor Birns was in trouble as usual, implicated in the theft of Canadian securities with broker Melvin Gold. In July 1963 Gold turned up in his car's trunk, strangled, shot, and beaten. Gold's wife told police he had vanished en route to a meeting with Birns, but Shondor produced a schoolteacher half his age who swore that he had spent the murder night with her.

* * *

California remained a region of peril and promise for Moe Dalitz and his partners in the early 1960s. Mickey Cohen's replacement was Harry Gross, an ex-Brooklyn bookie who moved west in 1958 and was jailed the following year for killing his wife's grandfather. Paroled soon after Cohen's conviction, Gross kept a low profile and managed Mob affairs until 1972, when he was arrested again.

The heat that concerned Dalitz most was a federal grand jury convened to investigate Doc Stacher. Moe expected a subpoena but it never arrived. Carl Cohen and Ed Levinson were less fortunate. Summoned to testify in summer 1962, they refused to answer any questions and were slapped with contempt charges. Judge Thurmond Clarke came to their rescue, dismissing the charges and denying bids to make them answer, based on revelation of illegal bugs at the Sands and other Las Vegas casinos. The IRS indicted Stacher for tax evasion in 1964, and he was deported in lieu of trial.

An FBI memo from January 1962 noted that Moe and four unidentified partners had purchased parcels of land in the Rancho Guajome sector of San Diego County, near Carlsbad. Allard Roen later said that he scouted the location during 1958, while visiting the Del Mar racetrack. Four years later he paid $2 million for 2,000 acres, while Paradise Homes bought another 2,000. The DRAM partners initially bought 200 acres for $540,000, then added another 800 for $2,675,000. Whatever the original investment, Dalitz had ambitious plans for the property they renamed Rancho La Costa. Starting with a golf course and clubhouse, they proceeded to construct palatial homes and a resort hotel, a lavish country club, and the nation's only health spa formally approved by the American Medical Association. "We figured," Roen said, "to capitalize on the fad for losing weight."

La Costa's acreage was jointly held by three corporations: Rancho La Costa Inc. and Lofty Inc. were registered in Nevada; Planet Inc. was registered in California but operated from a Las Vegas office. La Costa's sole stockholder was the Star Investment Company, a five-man partnership whose 1,000 shares were divided among Dalitz, Adelson, Molasky, Bernie Rothkopf, and Vegas resident Harry Lohn.

Financing came from various sources, including the Teamsters Union and Arnholt Smith's U.S. National Bank. Attorney John Donnelly coordinated the cash flow through firms including the Bagshaw Corporation, Planet Inc., and Star Investment. Moe hired Wallace Groves from the Bahamas to promote sale of La Costa homes and condominiums. G-men began investigating La Costa in December 1964, after newspapers revealed a $4 million Teamster loan bankrolling the project. Over the next quarter-century the IBT pumped more than $97 million into La Costa.

In 1961 *Los Angeles Times* editor Frank McCulloch assigned Jack Tobin to investigate land sales in the Santa Monica Mountains. Tobin found Moe Dalitz and Sidney Korshak among the buyers, bankrolled by Teamster money. That story was still in the works when Tobin met Robert Kennedy at a party hosted by *Times* publisher Otis Chandler. Tobin mentioned his findings to RFK, who "got red faced and violent. His voice rose. He said, 'You'd better lay off that!'" The next day, Kennedy's press secretary called McCulloch to say that Justice was on the verge of indicting Hoffa for his California land deals. It never happened, and McCulloch published Tobin's series despite protests from Washington.

* * *

Little had changed in Kentucky since the Kefauver hearings, but Newport gave Robert Kennedy his first real victory against the Mob. State attorney John Breckenridge joined the crusade, while former Cleveland Browns quarterback George Ratterman carried the ball in Campbell County, campaigning for sheriff to clean up Newport.

Nervous gamblers hatched a plot to discredit Ratterman in May 1961, luring him to a Cincinnati hotel where he was drugged, driven back to Newport, and placed in bed with stripper April Flowers at mobster Tito Carinci's suite in the Glenn Hotel. Detective Pat Ciafardini arrested Ratterman and Flowers on a prostitution charge. Ratterman proclaimed his

George Ratterman (right) addresses a TV audience while Hank Messick looks on (National Archives).

innocence and Robert Kennedy ordered an FBI investigation. Prosecutors dismissed Ratterman's charge, then indicted Carinci and sidekick Thomas Paisley for conspiring in a frame-up. Jurors acquitted both defendants in June.

Two days before Carinci's acquittal, Hank Messick took his wife to dinner at the Beverly Hills Club and saw bingo cards stamped "PROPERTY OF THE DESERT INN, LAS VEGAS, NEVADA." Soon afterward, Moe Dalitz joined Morris Kleinman, Sam Tucker, Lou Levinson, Red Masterson, Gil Beckley, and John Croft for a meeting at the Beverly Hills. Two days later, Chief Gugel and Chief of Detective Leroy Fredricks quit the police force in a failed conciliatory gesture to reformers.

A new grand jury convened in Newport in August 1961. Eight days later the IRS raided Screw Andrews's Sportsman's Club, bagging 200 gamblers. Three safes yielded guns, gambling records, and $79,500 in cash. On August 31 the grand jury indicted fifteen gamblers, including Red Masterson and ex-mayor Robert Siddell. A second flurry of indictments in September named nineteen more defendants including Mayor Mussman, Chief Gugel and his son, Detective Ciafardini, and three of Newport's four city commissioners. Governor Bert Combs signed orders barring Gugel and Fredricks from public office for the next four years. In October police nabbed April Flowers in Cincinnati, sharing a room with Charles Polizzi

Jr. Chuck's son told officers that April would cooperate, explaining that he had been chosen to protect her from the Newport crowd "because my old man has a lot of clout."

Ratterman won by a landslide and celebrated his inauguration as sheriff by joining the state police and T-men on further raids. A new grand jury charged Tito Carinci, Charles Lester, Marty Buccieri, and three Newport cops with conspiracy to violate Ratterman's civil rights. At trial in 1963, Lester and Buccieri received one-year prison terms, while Carinci and the rest were again acquitted. IRS agents finally nailed Carinci for tax evasion. A December 1961 grand jury indicted Screw Andrews and seven others on thirty-five charges. Jurors convicted all eight defendants in July 1962, whereupon they received five-year terms. Gil Beckley took the hint and moved his headquarters to Florida.

Newport was out of business—Sam Tucker told Hank Messick, "We don't want to be where we're not wanted"—but the Mob taint lingered on. In 1951 Dalitz had denied any ongoing interests in Kentucky, but the DI bug caught Moe, Tucker, and Kleinman discussing the Beverly Hills Club in October 1962. Seven months later Moe complained that the club cost $1,000 per month for its skeleton maintenance staff. When it was finally sold to new owners, Alvin Giesey served as trustee for the sale.

* * *

Gil Beckley was not the only mobster who found Florida's climate hospitable in 1961. Tom McGinty had moved down from Cleveland, Sam Tucker spent much of his time in Surfside, and Morris Kleinman left Vegas for Bay Harbor Islands, using George Gordon to ferry his cash because "I wanted it near to hand." Moe Dalitz kept the *Howdy Partner*, moored at Miami Beach. Solly Hart, former Cleveland roommate of murder victim Morris Komissarow, ran the Mob's message center in North Miami Beach.

When Mexican gamblers approached Morris Kleinman in December 1962, seeking advice on the prospects for floating casinos, Kleinman replied that his colleagues "were doing it in Florida." Kleinman explained that Tom McGinty had "two or so" boats filled with slot machines anchored offshore, earning $6,000 per month.

Cleveland's leading front man in Florida was Hymie Martin, whose continuing reward for silence in the William Potter homicide included control of the numbers rackets in Dade and Broward Counties. In March 1963, he visited fixer Bill Dorn, complaining that he had paid $100,000 to Broward politicians and was not getting his money's worth. Dorn suggested abolishing the county vice squad and installing a relative of Dorn's as Broward's new chief criminal investigator with a stipend of $100 per week. Within two weeks the vice squad was disbanded and Dorn's nominee took charge of gambling investigations, while Hymie saved $500 a week in bribes.

* * *

The loss of Cuba still rankled Mob leaders. A summary of the DI bug for August 26, 1962, found Dalitz reminiscing about his days at the Nacional in Havana and being "very, very critical of the Castro regime."

In Florida and elsewhere, Cuban exile groups grew ever more extreme and violent after the bungled 1961 Bay of Pigs invasion. In April 1963 a pamphlet circulated in Miami's Cuban neighborhoods declared: "Only through one development will you Cuban patriots ever live in your homeland again.... [I]f an inspired Act of God should place in the White House within weeks a Texan known to be a friend of all Latin Americans."

While Cuba was closed to the Mob, the Bahamas beckoned. Legal gambling would flourish in due time, but meanwhile there was banking to consider, offering a money-laundry service much closer to home than the classic Swiss numbered accounts.

John Pullman pioneered the trend in June 1961, establishing his Bank of World Commerce in Nassau. Original stockholders included Ed Levinson, Nig Devine, Miami's Ben Sigelbaum, and Nevada's ex-lieutenant governor Cliff Jones. Alvin Malnik, one of the BWC's three directors, partnered with Sam Cohen to buy land in Pennsylvania's Pocono Mountains. Several authors labeled Malnik "heir apparent" to Meyer Lansky's empire. Thus it came as no surprise that early BWC depositors included Lansky, Moe Dalitz, Morris Kleinman, Doc Stacher, and Vincent Alo. The IRS later indicted Malnik for tax evasion, despite FBI interference, but he beat the rap at trial with co-defendants Ed Levinson, Nig Devine, and Cliff Jones.

In July 1963 the Bank of Miami Beach changed hands again. Its new owners, Philip Simon and Benjamin Cohen, borrowed heavily from the newly formed Five Points National Bank, created by former BMB head Martin Von Zamft. Five Points closed its doors in January 1966, by which time Von Zamft and others faced investigation for embezzlement. Jurors convicted eleven defendants at trial in 1968. One of them, William Marmonstein, was the brother of Cleveland's Max Marmonstein, linked to the Cleveland Four in Kefauver testimony.

Meanwhile, attorney and CIA contract agent Paul Helliwell established Nassau's Mercantile Bank of the Americas in January 1962, then changed its name to Mercantile Bank and Trust in November. Business was slack until October 1964, when the firm was renamed Castle Bank and Trust. Chicago attorney Burton Kanter, listed with Helliwell as a co-owner, was also a registered agent of the La Costa Land Company, formed to promote sales at Rancho La Costa.

When the IRS obtained a list of 308 Castle depositors, those on the roster included Moe Dalitz, Morris Kleinman (contributor of $600,000 start-up capital for Castle), actor Tony Curtis, *Playboy* publisher Hugh Hefner, and *Penthouse* rival Bob Guccione. T-men traced a $70,000 cashier's check from Castle to Stardust manager Yale Cohen. They launched an investigation of the bank in 1962, dubbed "Operation Tradewinds," but it made slow headway for the next decade.

Establishment of Bahamian money laundries paralleled the advance of legalized gambling. Millionaire Huntington Hartford bought Hog Island, northeast of Nassau, in the late 1950s and renamed it Paradise. He built a hotel but found his gambling license stalled by Stafford Sands. Al Malnik solved that problem in 1961, with a bid to buy Paradise Island. Mary Carter Paint furnished the cash and purchased 1,300 acres on Little Hawksbill Creek to build the Queen's Cove housing subdivision. In January 1963 Sands regained his seat on the Bahamian Executive Council. Ten weeks later he applied for a gambling license in the name of Bahamas Amusements, with 500 shares of Class A stock and 500 Class B. Lou Chesler claimed 498 Class A shares, while Mrs. Wallace Groves secured 498 of the Class B, leaving the last four shares to "friends." Sands drafted their application for a gambling license, which was granted on April 1. Before that vote, five of the six counsel members landed lucrative "consulting" jobs with Bahamas Amusements. Chesler and Groves also contributed generously to the ruling United Bahamian Party, while Sands banked $10,000 per month in "legal retainers."

A footnote to the Paradise Island sale involved Richard Nixon, who visited Paradise with Bebe Rebozo in 1962, following his defeat in California's gubernatorial race. During their visit, Nixon and Rebozo enjoyed the red-carpet treatment from Sy Alter, described by G-

The first hotel-casino on Paradise Island (Library of Congress).

men as a "mob guy" linked to Lansky "from the old days." Alter also did business with Rebozo's bank in Key Biscayne, where Bebe told his staff, "Alter is a friend of ours. Treat him well." Six years later, Bahamian cash helped finance Nixon's second presidential campaign.

* * *

The trouble spawned by Moe's dealings with Alexander Guterma continued through the early 1960s. In 1961 a federal grand jury indicted Sam Garfield, Allard Roen, Irving Pasternak, and three others. Prosecutor Robert Morgenthau was also gunning for Roy Cohn, which gave Moe Dalitz and his partners hope.

Garfield and Roen claimed they paid Cohn $50,000 to scuttle the indictment. Subsequently, Cohn had "caused Dalitz to return from a trip to Paris" and met him in New York, urging Moe to use his influence on Garfield to prevent further cooperation with the feds. Failing that, Cohn warned, he would "take Dalitz and the Las Vegas people down with him." Moe said, "I talked to Roy about it when I was in New York and I told him what I thought about it and he said, 'Those fuckers Roen and Garfield, look what they are doing to me. They are going to put me in jail.' He said, 'I'm supposed to be your friend, your people.' I said, 'You started the whole ball rolling with [DELETED].' I said, 'Any time you think you can compel or threaten me Roy, I want you to know something. You're not going to get away with it.' I told him, 'You sonofabitch, anything you say I'll deny it.'"

Behind the scenes, Dalitz put out feelers to Herbert Miller Jr., chief of the Justice Department's Criminal Division, offering to "trade Las Vegas for Roy Cohn," but Miller refused. Garfield explained to friends at the DI, "Roy sent this fellow to see me and he said, 'I think you ought to sit down and talk to him.'...I said, 'That dirty cocksucker, I've done some business with him and I got my check to show what I gave him.'"

The United Dye trial was the longest ever held in federal court. Dalitz traveled widely to avoid subpoenas, ducking G-men in New York en route to foreign lands. On March 13, Garfield collapsed and was hospitalized with a bleeding ulcer. Six days later, Garfield, Roen, and defendant Allen Swann pled guilty and turned state's evidence. Roen stood firm where Dalitz was concerned, telling prosecutors "he will go to jail before he will tell them anything about him," but he freely implicated others, helping jurors convict four defendants on February 4, 1963. Guterma drew a sentence of four years and eleven months.

Still, Morgenthau pursued Roy Cohn. An eighteen-month grand jury probe climaxed with Cohn's September 1963 indictment for perjury and conspiracy to obstruct justice. Cohn claimed a "perfectly routine and peripheral relationship" with Garfield and Roen, insisting that he merely recommended an attorney when the SEC began dissecting United Dye. Garfield and Roen stuck to their tale of a $50,000 bribe. Cohn later divided the blame for his "persecution" between Morgenthau and Moe Dalitz, referring again to his friendship with Averill, "who had divorced Dalitz some time before the case. I was high on his private-enemy list because of my regard for his former wife." In fact, while they were separated, Moe divorced Averill eight days *after* Cohn's September 3 indictment. Cohn's first trial ended with a hung jury in April 1964. A second panel acquitted him in July.

In April 1965, Nevada's Gaming Control Board ruled that "administrative action [was] unwarranted" against Al Roen on his guilty plea, since he was "only a nominee" in United Dye stock sales and confessed no role in planning the fraud. Still, his two-year probation and $10,000 fine soiled Roen's image. He was no longer the DI's golden boy, and Moe soon eased him out of management into a fringe advisory role. By that time, new trouble had found Moe and his partners in Vegas.

* * *

Mob money draws jackals. In April 1963 G-men recorded Moe's discussion of an unnamed man who claimed he could save the casino $200,000 in return for a $10,000 payoff. Moe ordered the stranger checked out and rejected his offer, calling it extortion and remarking that the man might prove dangerous.

Meanwhile, two of his own subordinates were snared in crude extortion plots. The first involved Ray Ryan, a gambler and friend of John Drew. In 1963 Chicago mafiosi Marshall Caifano and Charles Del Monico approached Ryan, claiming they had saved him from a kidnap plot and offering to continue their "protection" for $60,000 per year. Drew offered help but accomplished nothing. Ryan subsequently met Caifano and Del Monico at the DI, where their threats caused him to bolt and call the FBI. G-men arrived to find another Chicago killer, Felix Alderisio, trying to dissuade Ryan from squealing. Prosecutors indicted Caifano and Del Monico for attempted extortion in early 1964. At their trial, Drew refused to testify despite subpoenas from the prosecution *and* defense. Jurors convicted Caifano and Del Monico, while acquitting co-defendant Allen Smiley. Nevada attorney general Harvey Dickerson asked the GCB to revoke Drew's license, charging that his Fifth Amendment plea "purports two things — that Drew was involved in the extortion case, or, that if he testified, he would have to reveal facts which would incriminate him with some criminal act which might lead to an indictment." The GCB, in its wisdom, refused.

Felix Alderisio figured more prominently in a second extortion case, this one involving Ruby Kolod. DI transcripts for May 1963 reveal Moe Dalitz's concern about Alderisio — whom he dubbed "a real bad guy" — spending time with Kolod in Vegas. Moe could not understand why Kolod and Alderisio were in "constant contact," warning that Alderisio might cause "considerable trouble." Further, Moe did "not believe Kolod is smart enough to talk to these guys and at the same time protect himself."

Those words proved prophetic. Even as Moe spoke, Kolod was immersed in a shady oil deal with Willie Alderman and Denver attorney Robert Sunshine, formerly an owner of the Royal Nevada. The mess began in 1960, when Kolod and Alderman invested $68,000 skimmed from the DI in oil leases promoted by Sunshine. Sunshine hit dry holes, whereupon Kolod and Alderman demanded a refund. When Sunshine refused, Kolod said his lawyers would arrive in Denver soon, expecting cash.

The "lawyers" who showed up in July 1961 were Alderisio and triggerman Americo DePietto. Alderisio announced, "We're here to kill you." Sunshine persuaded Alderisio to call Kolod, whom they found sharing a New York hotel room with Alderman. Kolod agreed to let Sunshine pay off his debt at $2,000 per month and welcomed Sunshine back

Ruby Kolod (Las Vegas Historical Society).

to the DI, where Sunshine lost $21,000. "Hell," Kolod told Alderisio, "we'll be collecting from this sucker for the rest of his life."

Already strapped for cash, Sunshine began embezzling from his clients—$90,000 in all before he was caught and arrested. He sang immediately for the FBI, whereupon prosecutors charged Kolod, Alderman, and Alderisio with extortion. Celebrity attorney Edward Bennett Williams defended Kolod but jurors convicted the defendants in April 1964: Alderisio received 4½ years in prison, Kolod got four years, Alderman got three years. Sunshine received a sentence of 1½ to 5 years for embezzlement.

On April 22, 1965, the GCB issued an emergency order suspending Kolod's gaming license. Black Book listings followed for all three defendants, but Kolod and Alderman were removed from the list in May. Two months later, Hank Greenspun chided the GCB for being "a little hasty" with Kolod, suggesting that his conviction occurred "not because of the evidence that a crime had been committed, but because Kolod was a gambler." Vegas judges William Compton and John Sexton blocked further efforts to ban Kolod from gambling, despite GCB assertions of his ongoing ties to "unsavory characters" and Kolod's refusal to sell stock in a California racetrack, held in violation of Nevada law. Ruby overstepped his bounds in November 1965, suing the state for a $2.2 million "violation of his civil rights."

Greenspun, having overcome his hatred of the DI gang, found it "appropriate to mention Ruby Kolod, a man who has been castigated by many" at Christmas 1966. "Irrespective of anything else," he wrote, "there are many Las Vegans who say Ruby Kolod is a good man. We are among them." Kolod's case was still in limbo when he died in August 1967. Pallbearers for his funeral included Dalitz, Kleinman, Tucker, Alderman, Nig Devin, George Gordon, and Peanuts Danolfo.

* * *

The Camelot anti–Mob crusade accelerated during 1962–63. Author John Davis writes that "[g]iven another five years in office, the Kennedys could conceivably have exterminated the Cosa Nostra entirely, or at least crippled it beyond repair." Whether that judgment is correct, the world will never know. By summer 1963 they were running out of time.

Various factors led to the events in Dallas, Texas, on November 22, 1963. Robert Kennedy's racket-busting overlapped machinations against Fidel Castro in Cuba. After the Bay of Pigs fiasco, JFK threatened to "splinter the CIA into a thousand pieces and scatter it into the winds." The Kennedys likewise made no secret of their plan to fire J. Edgar Hoover after JFK's re-election. Lyndon Johnson's head was also on the chopping block, thanks to scandals surrounding Bobby Baker and Texas financier Billy Sol Estes.

High-ranking mobsters spoke freely of their wish to see the Kennedys eliminated. The following threats are a matter of record:

August 1962: Jimmy Hoffa met Louisiana Teamster Ed Partin at IBT headquarters in Washington, to discuss plans for killing Robert Kennedy. Hoffa proposed "the possible use of a lone gunman equipped with a rifle with a telescopic sight ... an assassin without any identifiable connection to the Teamster organization or Hoffa himself." He also noted "the advisability of having the assassination committed somewhere in the South," where "segregation people" would be blamed.

September 1962: Still furious at Bobby Kennedy for ordering his deportation, Carlos Marcello cursed the attorney general in Sicilian, saying, "*Livarsi na petra di la scarpa*" ("take the stone from my shoe"). Marcello then said, "Don't worry about that little Bobby sonofabitch. He's going to be taken care of." According to witness Edward Becker, Marcello "clearly stated that he was going to arrange to have President Kennedy killed in some way." The best "insurance," Marcello said, would be "setting up some nut to take the fall for the job, just like they do in Sicily."

September 1962: While discussing Teamster loans with Cuban-exile financier José Alemán, Santo Trafficante steered the conversation to JFK, saying, "Have you seen how his brother is hitting Hoffa, a man who is a worker, who is not a millionaire, a friend of the blue collars? ...Mark my words, this man Kennedy is in trouble and he will get what is coming to him." When Alemán predicted Kennedy's re-election Trafficante said, "No, José. He is going to be hit."

July 23, 1963: Hoffa told attorney Frank Ragano, "Something has to be done. The time has come to use your friend [Santo Trafficante] and Carlos [Marcello] to get rid of him. Kill that sonofabitch John Kennedy." When Ragano relayed the comment to Marcello and Trafficante they stared at him until Ragano changed the subject.

November 9, 1963: Miami police informant William Somersett met Joseph Milteer, a wealthy racist, and secretly recording their conversation. Milteer predicted that JFK would be slain "from an office building with a high-powered rifle," and that police "will pick somebody up within hours afterwards, just to throw the public off."

November 21, 1963: Anti-Castro exiles told an FBI informant, "We now have plenty of money — our new backers are the Jews — as soon as they take care of JFK."

Hundreds of books describe Kennedy's murder in Dallas. This much is certain: At least three shots were fired at JFK in Dealey Plaza, with the fatal head shot striking at approximately 12:30 P.M. Dozens of witnesses claimed a gunman fired from a "grassy knoll" in front of the president's limo, a judgment confirmed with 95-percent certainty by analysis of audio recordings fifteen years later. Meanwhile, shots from *behind* the car wounded JFK, Texas governor John Connally, and a bystander. Forty-five minutes after the assassination, a gunman killed Dallas patrolman J.D. Tippit. Officers caught the alleged gunman, Lee Harvey Oswald, in a nearby theater at 2:00 P.M. They charged him first with Tippit's slaying, later claiming that he also shot the president. Their suspect's answer to that charge: "I'm just a patsy."

Between January 1954 and July 1956 Oswald and his mother occupied an apartment on Exchange Place, in the French Quarter of New Orleans. Police described Exchange Place as "the hub of the most notorious underworld joints in the city," where Marcello mobsters operated brazenly. In 1955, at age sixteen, Oswald joined the Civil Air Patrol and met instructor David Ferrie. In April 1963 Oswald established a one-man Fair Play for Cuba Committee in New Orleans, strangely sharing quarters with anti–Castro activists Ferrie and Guy Banister. In August, witnesses saw Oswald with Ferrie and CIA contract agent Clay Shaw. Days later, when Oswald was jailed for brawling with Cuban exiles, Marcello aide Nofio Pecora paid his bond.

Across the street from Oswald's supposed sniper's nest in the Texas Book Depository, sheriff's deputies arrested two men for "behaving suspiciously" at the Dal-Tex Building. Both were taken off in squad cars, whereupon one vanished utterly, forever unidentified. The second introduced himself as Jim Braden, explained that he entered the Dal-Tex Building to find a pay phone, and was freed without submitting fingerprints. FBI agents questioned him on January 29, 1964, reporting that "Braden has no information concerning the assassination and both Lee Harvey Oswald and Jack Ruby are unknown to him." It was another case where G-men dropped the ball.

"Jim Braden" was born Eugene Brading in 1915. His rap sheet began with a burglary conviction at nineteen, followed by five arrests in the 1940s. In 1951 jurors convicted him and accomplice Victor Pereira of swindling a widow out of $50,000. While appealing that 12-year sentence, Brading paid a fine for vagrancy in Dallas.

Top: President Kennedy's limousine speeds away from Dealey Plaza after the ambush of November 22, 1963 (Library of Congress). *Bottom:* Eugene Brading, aka Jim Braden, linked "coincidentally" to both Kennedy assassinations — and to Moe Dalitz (National Archives).

LAPD files list Brading as an associate of Jimmy Fratianno, Joe Sica, and other gangsters. He also partnered with two California felons in Miami's Sunbeam Oil Company, described as "a pure front for con-men schemes."

In September 1963 Brading legally changed his name "for business reasons," without informing parole authorities. One day later he received permission to visit Houston oilman D.D. Ford "in connection with Tidewater Oil Company litigation." Braden spent ten days in Texas but never met Ford. On the day he left Houston, Lee Oswald passed through town en route to Mexico. Back in L.A., Braden's third spouse discovered he had siphoned $40,000 from her bank account, and she secured an annulment on grounds that Braden had never divorced two previous wives. At the same time, records show Braden operating from Room 1706 at the Pere Marquette Building in New Orleans. David Ferrie's office was Room 1707.

Braden's parole officer approved another Texas trip in November, unaware that Braden was traveling with convicted swindler Morgan Brown. They reached Dallas on November 21 and registered at the Cabana Hotel. Braden claimed that he "planned to see Lamar Hunt and other oil speculators while here." Lamar was a son of billionaire Haroldson Hunt, whose friends included J. Edgar Hoover, Carlos Marcello, Meyer Lansky, Frank Costello, and Dallas mafioso Joe Civello. Jimmy Hoffa had resolved labor problems at Hunt Oil, and bookie Frank Erickson once collected a $40,000 gambling debt from Haroldson Hunt. Lamar's brother Nelson Hunt paid $1,465 for a full-page ad in the *Dallas Morning News* on November 22, 1963, branding JFK "Wanted for Treason." Coincidentally, mobster Jack Ruby also visited Hunt Oil on November 21, allegedly escorting one of his strippers to a job interview. Brown and Braden were back at the Cabana by midnight, when Ruby met Chicago colleague Lawrence Meyers at the hotel.

Braden and Brown had booked their room through November 24, but Brown checked out at 2:00 P.M. on November 22, while Braden was in custody. Two months later, Braden became a charter member of Moe Dalitz's La Costa Country Club. He subsequently married a rich Dallas widow, then dumped her when she ran out of money. His next wife, a Mexican citizen, gave him a Learjet and bankrolled jaunts from California to Holland, Spain, and Switzerland. Federal agents watched his movements, dubbing Braden a "personal courier" for Meyer Lansky.

* * *

Any risk from Oswald vanished on November 24, when Jack Ruby shot him in the basement of Dallas police headquarters. Ruby claimed he killed Oswald to spare Jackie Kennedy from testifying at Oswald's murder trial. G-men believed him, unaware of a note Ruby passed to lawyer Joe Tonahill, reading: "Joe, you should know this. [Dallas attorney] Tom Howard told me to say that I shot Oswald so that Caroline and Mrs. Kennedy wouldn't have to come to Dallas to testify. OK?"

Several witnesses placed Ruby in Dealey Plaza when JFK was shot. Journalist Seth Kantor met Ruby at Parkland Hospital on November 22, though Ruby later denied it. That night, Ruby was filmed among reporters at a police press conference. When D.A. Henry Wade referred to Oswald's role in the "Free Cuba Committee"—an anti–Castro group—Ruby corrected him: "That's Fair Play for Cuba, Henry."

Nor were Ruby's suspicious actions confined to the days around JFK's murder. During October and November 1963 he made 171 long-distance phone calls to Mob-connected friends. Those who spoke to Ruby included LBJ aide Bobby Baker, gambler Lewis McWillie in Nevada, Teamster bondsman Irwin Weiner in Chicago, Jim Braden's partner Victor Pereira, Miami Teamster boss Murray Miller, Puerto Rican Teamster chief Frank Chavez, Mickey Cohen's ex-fiancée Candy Barr, IBT enforcer Robert Baker, and Oswald benefactor Nofio Pecora. Ruby visited Las Vegas on November 16–17, 1963 and cashed a check at the Stardust. His address book contained the name of Stardust point-holder Milton Jaffe. John Rosselli told columnist Jack Anderson that Ruby was "one of our boys."

Some of the tangled threads from Dallas and New Orleans met in Rome, behind the corporate façade of Centro Mondiale Commericale. CMC's directors included CIA contract agent Clay Shaw, owner of the International Trade Mart in New Orleans. Shaw also sat on the board of a CMC subsidiary called Permindex. Author William Torbitt claims that Bronfman family attorney Louis Bloomfield founded Permindex and held 50 percent of its stock. Other investors included Moe Dalitz, Joe Bonnano, and Cuban ex-president Carlos Prio

Jack Ruby kills Lee Harvey Oswald on live TV (Library of Congress).

Socarrás. Swiss authorities dissolved their branch of Permindex in 1962, after proving the firm delivered $200,000 to right-wing terrorists bent on killing French president Charles de Gaulle.

* * *

Jimmy Hoffa telephoned Frank Ragano within minutes of JFK's death, asking, "Did you hear the good news?" Santo Trafficante dined with Ragano that evening, remarking, "Isn't that something? They killed the sonofabitch. This is like lifting a ton of stones off my shoulders. We'll make money out of this and maybe go back to Cuba." Three days later, Hoffa told Ragano, "I told you they could do it. I'll never forget what Carlos and Santo did for me." On November 24, Hoffa told a Nashville reporter, "Bobby Kennedy is just another lawyer now."

Ralph Salerno, former head of NYPD's Organized Crime Unit, opined, "The bullet that killed John Kennedy killed Bobby Kennedy's dream to destroy the organized-crime society." Without JFK, Salerno said, "the leadership was not there. The driving force was not there, and the commitment in government at a very high level was not there." Two weeks after Dallas, RFK told an aide, "Those people [the FBI] don't work for us anymore."

Two hours after Oswald's death, Hoover told LBJ, "The thing I am concerned about is having something issued so we can convince the public that Oswald is the real assassin." Hoover coordinated leaks suggesting that Oswald shot Kennedy "in his own lunatic loneliness."

On November 29, LBJ appointed a commission to halt the incipient "rash of investigations" in Dallas, New Orleans, and elsewhere. Its chairman was Earl Warren, chief justice of the Supreme Court. Other panelists included Representative Hale Boggs of Louisiana, Senator John Cooper of Kentucky, ex-CIA chief Allen Dulles, Representative Gerald Ford of Michigan (known as "Hoover's man" in Congress), JFK advisor John McCloy, and Senator Richard Russell of Georgia (a 1920s member of the KKK). Together, they produced a report branding Oswald and Ruby "lone gunmen."

First, though, there was much to manipulated, fabricated, and ignored. The Warren Commission buried testimony from inconvenient witnesses, published frames from Abraham Zapruder's film of JFK's last moments out of sequence, and rewrote the laws of physics to support their "magic bullet theory." Dulles urged his colleagues not to worry, telling them, "Nobody reads. Don't believe people read in this country."

Even LBJ did not believe the panel's findings. In 1973 he told *Atlantic Monthly*, "I never believed that Oswald acted alone."

* * *

Three days after LBJ created the Warren Commission, John Rosselli escorted Judith Campbell to Moe's New Year's Eve party at the DI Country Club. Dalitz seemed not to recognize Campbell, repeatedly asking her name while Rosselli and Campbell refused to answer. In her words, "it became quite a game." Still grieving for Kennedy, Campbell got drunk and quarreled with Rosselli, whereupon Moe kissed her cheek and said, "Come on, now, don't get so mad." Campbell slapped Moe's face, prompting a stunned Rosselli to remark, "You must be crazy." Next morning, Rosselli told Campbell, "Nobody smacks Moe Dalitz across the face. Christ, don't you know anything yet? Haven't you learned anything?"

G-men continued their surveillance of Dalitz into 1964. A February memo logged numerous sightings around the DI, reporting that Moe was "friendly with agents and talks freely about innocuous matters but has evaded answering direct questions" concerning suspected crimes. Agents restored the "armed and dangerous" tag to Moe's dossier in March but never seemed to take it seriously. An April memo noted Moe's "diminishing interest" in the DI and Stardust, adding that "no information has been developed indicating he is violating any law within the purview of the FBI."

Perhaps they meant no violation they could prosecute with evidence collected from illegal bugs and wiretaps. In any case, the Vegas FBI office put Moe's file on "P*" status — pending for six months, when surveillance would be reconsidered. Headquarters canceled any further Mexican investigations on July 31, and the Vegas Bureau closed Moe's file on November 10, 1964. Hoover countermanded that order ten days later, writing:

> The Bureau does not approve the closing of this matter in view of the fact that subject has long been one of the top hoodlums directing Las Vegas operations and allegedly may be the front for various other top hoodlums throughout the United States and elsewhere. You should continue to investigate his activities in accordance with current instructions. Dalitz is a top leader of the hoodlum element and ... he continues to make his headquarters in Las Vegas and allegedly is in close contact with numerous national and international hoodlums such as Meyer Lansky, Doc Stacher, Sam Giacana [*sic*] and others.

Two weeks later, Hoover flew to Chicago for the Sword of Loyola awards banquet, where he was honored for "exhibit[ing] a high degree of courage, dedication, and service." Seated with Hoover at the head table — and underwriting the full $50,000 ceremony — was Mob attorney Sidney Korshak.

10

Yechus

Having received their orders to continue watching Dalitz, G-men faced the tiresome chore of keeping up with him. Moe traveled frequently through 1964–69, including jaunts to visit "friends" in Cleveland and Toledo, Miami, New York and Detroit. He hunted at the DI Ranch and teed off at the Bob Hope Pro-Am Golf Tournament at Palm Springs. Ranging farther afield, he spent most of summer 1964 in Europe, with stops in Naples, Cannes, Seville, and Gibraltar, where the *Moby Dick* was moored. November found him in Gibraltar once again, then back in Spain. Moe visited Jamaica during January 1965, returned to Gibraltar in May, docked his yacht at Cannes in August, then moved on once more to tour England, Spain, and the Bahamas. Flying home, he was observed by G-men in Detroit, meeting unnamed individuals "associated with organized crime."

March 1966 took Moe back to London, followed by flights to Tokyo and Hong Kong. Customs agents searched him in Chicago, on his return from the Far East, and found a list of bank accounts: Bank of Las Vegas, $28,154.76; Bank of Nevada, $25,000; First National Bank, $13,991.54; Nevada Bank Commission, $25,000; Nevada State Bank, $51,860.59; Valley Bank, $26,446.25. Another note, of unknown significance, read "Crown album number B338."

Moe's link to Mexico endured. G-men noted his sale of the Acapulco house in July 1967, but his visits continued. Frank Sinatra joined Moe to promote local gambling, but it was never legalized. In June 1968 Moe flew to San Diego, retrieved one of his boats, and sailed along the Pacific coast of Mexico and Central America, passing through the Panama Canal on his way back to the Caribbean and Florida. Come December, G-men reported that Moe was bound for the Caribbean once more, "to look after his yacht."

Although he never found the DI bug, Moe knew that he was being watched. Conversations taped in April 1965 include discussion of an unnamed DI employee whom Moe suspected of talking to G-men. When Attorney General Ramsey Clark challenged illegal FBI bugging in October 1966, Hoover blamed Robert Kennedy and commanded removal of memos on Moe to his "June Mail" file, created to conceal reports derived from illegal sources.

* * *

Feds had their best luck watching Dalitz in Nevada, but they hit roadblocks there as well. In 1964 the IRS requested tax records from Moe and Wilbur Clark but were denied access by attorney John Donnelly. On August 22, Clark announced that he was selling his interest in the DI to Dalitz, Kleinman, and Tucker. Shareholders Tom McGinty, Bernie Rothkopf, and

Bobby Kaye also sold their stock back to the parent corporation, while Allard Roen remained as general manager. Moe reigned as president of both the DI and Stardust.

G-men noted John Rosselli's DI meeting with Ruby Kolod and Willie Alderman in January 1965, observing that Rosselli "very rarely" spoke to Moe. In February a federal judge ordered Dalitz and Clark to surrender their records for IRS inspection, specifically detailing the entanglement of Martinolich Construction and Shipbuilding with Refrigerated Transport and Arnholt Smith's National Steel and Shipbuilding. April 1965 brought Clark a $1,636,938 tax bill dating from 1959, while John Drew stood accused of evading $152,000 in taxes at the Stardust during 1958–61.

Clark seemed unfazed by his latest troubles. In August 1965 he opened the Wilbur Clark Crest Hotel, adjacent to California's Disneyland. The celebration featured fireworks and cocktails for guests including Eli Boyer, John Donnelly, Hank Greenspun, Milton Jaffe, Morris Kleinman, and their wives. Less than four weeks later, Clark was dead, stricken by a heart attack on August 27. Senator Alan Bible mourned the loss of "a pioneering and public-spirited leader," while Mayor Gragson dubbed Clark "one of our finest citizens." Ex-sheriff Butch Leypoldt, now a member of the Nevada Gaming Commission, remembered Clark as "an asset to the gaming industry." Pallbearers at Clark's funeral included Governor Sawyer and Lieutenant Governor Paul Laxalt, Senators Bible and Howard Cannon, Rep. Walter Baring and Attorney General Harvey Dickerson, four district judges, Mayor Gragson and Sheriff Ralph Lamb, Allard Roen and Parry Thomas, Dalitz and Kleinman, Tucker and McGinty, Clifford Jones and Carl Cohen, Ruby Kolod and Bernie Rothkopf, Bobby Kaye and Eli Boyer, Merv Adelson and Irwin Molasky, Frank Sennes and Cornelius Jones, John Drew and Sidney Korshak, Milton Jaffe and Kirk Kerkorian, Peanuts Danolfo and Pete Bommarito.

Clark's passing forced others to consider their mortality. Morris Kleinman devised a family trust, duly approved by the Nevada Gaming Commission with Kleinman and Sam Tucker named as trustees, to transfer $1 million in casino stock to his wife and children upon his death. Moe Dalitz found his antidote for grief in work, opening the Stardust Raceway — with himself as president — three weeks after Clark's funeral.

John Rosselli ran afoul of Sheriff Lamb in December 1966, after Lamb heard rumors that Rosselli was extorting cash from various casino owners. Lamb and Undersheriff Lloyd Bell found Rosselli with Dalitz and Peanuts Danolfo in the DI coffee shop, sending a rookie deputy to demand that Rosselli accompany him to headquarters. Rosselli brushed the rookie off. Lamb entered, cursing Rosselli as he neared the mobster's booth, seized his tie, dragged him across the table, and began to pummel him. Danolfo rose to fight, but Moe held him back. Lamb hauled Rosselli out, telling the rookie to take him downtown and "treat him like a bank robber." That included chemical delousing, a humiliating gesture that reduced Rosselli's stature in Las Vegas.

When not preventing brawls, Moe occupied himself with real estate, philanthropy, and politics. Gus Russo reports that partners Merv Adelson and Irwin Molasky donated the first tract of land for the University of Nevada–Las Vegas, while Moe contributed $1,000 to launch UNLV's football team in 1965. Such moves paid dividends in years to come, as Paradise Developments erected dorms and other campus structures. Paradise also built Sin City's first modern shopping center, the Boulevard Mall, in 1966.

The same year found Moe abandoning Governor Sawyer. Incensed by Sawyer's handling of Ruby Kolod in the Sunshine case, Dalitz sought a more pliable governor and found him in Paul Laxalt, who served as Ormsby County's D.A. in 1952–54, then won election as lieutenant governor in 1962. In 1964, while working for Barry Goldwater's presidential campaign,

Laxalt met actor Ronald Reagan, who coincidentally sought California's governorship in 1966. Dalitz protégé Lew Wasserman bankrolled Reagan's campaign, while Ruby Kolod was Laxalt's fundraising chief and premier contributor. Laxalt's largest corporate donations flowed from the DI-Stardust conglomerate.

Laxalt's campaign reunited Moe Dalitz with Hank Greenspun. Authors Jerry Simich and Thomas Wright claim that the alliance had "more to do with common enemies than common interests," but it marked the launch of an enduring friendship. Twenty years later, *Sun* reporter Wade Cavanaugh described Moe and Greenspun as "gin rummy buddies at the country club." Following Laxalt's election in 1966, Vegas G-men reported that Moe "had 'put' the Governor of Nevada in office and had made a deal with him ... to 'whitewash' the probe by the Gambling Commission [*sic*] into casino operations."

By summer 1966 the DI partners needed friends in office more than ever.

* * *

Moe's latest trouble with the feds sprang from IRS investigations of his Martinolich dealings. G-men learned of the approaching storm in September 1965, when Dalitz attorney Edward Bennett Williams subpoenaed records of surveillance on his client. Hoover ordered his Special Investigative Division to determine whether any information fueling the IRS probe came from "tainted" FBI sources, while assistant director Cartha DeLoach opined that Williams was embarked on a fruitless "fishing expedition."

On October 13, 1965, a federal grand jury in Los Angeles indicted Moe and Eli Boyer for attempting to evade income taxes from 1959. Specifically, the pair stood accused of wrongfully declaring profits from a stock sale as long-term capital gains, rather than ordinary income, which slashed their tax bill. Moe surrendered on October 14, was fingerprinted, and posted $1,000 bond. He pled not guilty at his arraignment, where his bond was also refunded over government protests.

The charges alleged that Moe and Boyer met in L.A., in December 1958, where Boyer delivered 5,000 shares of Turbo-Dynamics stock to Moe, then falsely recorded the date of the transfer as October 1. Moe and Boyer also arranged for Turbo-Dynamics to issue a four-month $50,000 loan to a Panamanian firm called Atlantida S.A. Boyer put the T-D stock in escrow as collateral, then negotiated an extension of the Atlantida loan in April 1959, guaranteed by another firm, Memco Oil. Boyer failed to report the T-D shares as income on Moe's 1958 tax return, thus dodging payment of $6,678.59. T-men said Boyer made matters worse in November 1963, by falsely denying participation in the Turbo-Atlantida loan.

In Las Vegas, both the *Review-Journal* and Greenspun's *Sun* ignored Moe's indictment. They also missed a sideshow to the main event, involving Roy Cohn. Cohn had obtained a $400,000 loan from Atlantida, used to buy a controlling interest in Lionel Toys. When T-men questioned the low-interest loan in October 1965, Cohn complained to Missouri Senator Edward Long, a friend of Cohn who owed his 1960 Senate appointment to LBJ aide Bobby Baker. Now, as chairman of a Subcommittee on Administrative Practice and Procedure, Long prepared for war against the IRS — or more specifically, its efforts to investigate the Mob. Long told reporters that Cohn's case gave him a chance to "prove what I have charged the IRS with — an abuse of raw naked power."

As chief counsel, Long chose Bernard Fensterwald, an attorney who lived in Long's apartment building and shared office space with Cohn. An embittered crusader fired from the Kefauver Committee, Fensterwald had hoped a $5,000 donation in 1960 would land him a job with JFK's administration. He blamed Robert Kennedy when that scheme failed, and became a strident critic of the Camelot crime war, joining Cohn as an observer at Jimmy Hoffa's jury-tampering trial. While Long prepared his inquisition, Long's son-in-law obtained a job with one of Cohn's four banks at $12,500 per year. He averaged one day per month in the office before his promotion to serve as chairman of the board, with a $5,000 raise. Long's Tower Loan Company also received seven unsecured loans from Cohn's banks.

Long's hearings failed to save Jimmy Hoffa from prison, but Hoffa remained free on bond pending appeal of dual convictions in 1964. The Supreme Court upheld Hoffa's jury-tampering conviction in December 1966. Legal motions from attorney Morris Shenker stalled the inevitable until March 1967, when Hoffa entered federal prison.

Meanwhile, Nevada belatedly tackled casino skimming, spurred by a *Cleveland Plain Dealer* article describing a "secret" IRS probe based on testimony from Ruby Kolod's Denver trial. Moe Dalitz, George Gordon, and Cleveland mafioso John Scalish were named as suspects, while evidence showed

Moe Dalitz arrives for casino skim hearings, 1966 (Cleveland State University Library).

Kolod financing his oilfield speculation with undeclared DI cash. A simultaneous series in the *Chicago Sun Times* charged that six Las Vegas casinos — the DI, Stardust, Flamingo, Sands, Fremont, and Horseshoe — lost an average $70,000 to $100,000 per month through skimming.

Governor Sawyer ordered an investigation on July 15, 1966, commanding that Gaming Commission chairman Milton Keefer "develop through any legal means the truth or falsity" of the published charges. While the probe was in progress, Sawyer urged Washington to "immediately prosecute federal violations" by any known skimmers.

The Gaming Commission began by grilling Dalitz, Kleinman, Tucker, Allard Roen, Yale Cohen, Milton Jaffe, John Donnelly, and DI slots supervisor Max Kaplow. Reporters noted the preponderance of Cleveland witnesses, but Chairman Keefer insisted, "There's no significance to that fact, and I hadn't kept track." Deputy state attorney general Don Winne told reporters, "We wouldn't have spent this much time on it without finding something," yet outsiders remained skeptical. The commission's final report accused G-men of waging "a morally reprehensible program of domestic espionage" under Bobby Kennedy, resulting only in "indictments by newspapers." As evidence, the panel cited 206,844 unannounced "obser-vances" of casino activities during 1961–66, with spot-checks on 313 gaming tables where the cash drop was "accidentally" understated by only 1.8 percent.

Governor Sawyer sent a copy of the report to Washington, with a letter denouncing the federal campaign of "espionage and harassment against our gambling industry." Lieutenant Governor Laxalt predicted that "people outside the state will call it a whitewash," but casino owners were delighted. Dalitz told reporters, "I was sure there were no undisclosed interests, no skimming, and that's it." Ed Levinson — soon to be indicted with three others and fined for skimming at the Fremont — agreed, saying, "I didn't think they'd find any skimming or undisclosed interests."

Moe still faced trial on federal tax evasion charges. A change of venue placed his fate and Eli Boyer's in the hands of Judge Roger Foley, a JFK appointee who discouraged federal casino raids in 1961. In September 1966 Foley gave prosecutors thirty days to answer a list of ques-tions from Moe's defense team, concerning bugs installed at the homes of either defendant. FBI headquarters admitted bugging the DI executive office from March 1962 through mid–August 1963, but denied that any transcripts were furnished to IRS agents.

Judge Foley scheduled trial for April 1967, then postponed it. On February 7, 1968 Eli Boyer changed his plea to guilty and paid a $1,000 fine. One month later, Foley dismissed Moe's case, leaving prosecutor Charles McNelis to explain that "[t]he interest of the govern-ment would best be served by dismissal of all counts against Mr. Dalitz." Specifically, as noted in FBI memos, the Boyer plea bargain waived publication of the Bureau's illegal DI transcripts. Boyer, his duty done, embarked upon a six-month all-expense-paid trip around the world. On December 11, 1968, the Gaming Control Board approved Moe's expansion of control at the Stardust to 85 percent.

* * *

In January 1965, George Gordon met John Scalish in Cleveland, delivering $58,900 ear-marked for mobsters in Detroit and Miami. Gordon and Scalish discussed a "misunderstand-ing" between Moe Dalitz and Detroit's Joe Zerilli, which prompted Zerilli to accuse Dalitz of ducking their scheduled appointments. Scalish warned Gordon that an unnamed third party "did something" for Moe in the 1930s and was "using that favor to work himself into the business."

Despite the brief unpleasantness with Joe Zerilli, Dalitz maintained his standing in Detroit. He met with local mobsters in September 1965, observed by FBI agents, and mourned old friend Joe Massei's passing in May 1971.

Farther east, a strange situation arose with hitman Harold Konigsberg, who claimed service as Moe's chauffeur in 1940. If true, that put Kayo behind the limo's wheel when he was only eleven years old, but siblings described him as a gangster from the age of five, "an illiterate amid a family of studious children, a malevolently wild creature in a house full of Sabbath keepers." New Jersey prosecutors called Konigsberg the Mob's "smartest hit man" and "king of the loan sharks," while *Life* magazine dubbed him "the most dangerous uncaged criminal on the East Coast." Convicted of murder in 1963, Konigsberg sent his wife to Dalitz for help when their savings ran out. Moe obliged with $5,000 per month until his own death. No other evidence exists linking Moe to Konigsberg, but the marathon series of payments suggests an enduring obligation.

When Miami G-men prepared a list of local "gamblers, hoodlums and members of the Cosa Nostra" in October 1964, they included Moe's name. A year later, they spotted him with Jake Lansky at Miami's Doral Hotel and trailed him to the Bayshore Golf Club, where he teed off with Lansky "and others." February 1966 found Moe back in Miami, sailing aboard the *Golden Fleece*. In October 1966 agents declared that George Gordon "was reportedly transferred to Miami from Cleveland by the Dalitz crowd because of heavy gambling losses" and was put to work in the *bolita* racket.

By the time Gordon moved to Miami, variations on the numbers racket earned an estimated $1 billion per year in Florida. Hymie Martin controlled 80 percent of the Gold Coast action, banking $350,000 on an average Saturday. Morris Kleinman grudgingly admitted shifting cash from Vegas to Miami but denied that any of it went to Martin.

Al Polizzi was close by, if Martin needed any help. In 1964 Senate investigators branded him "one of the most influential figures of the underworld in the United States," who was "associated with international narcotic traffickers and illicit gambling activities." He also traded real estate and backed construction projects with partner Bebe Rebozo, who founded the Key Biscayne Bank in 1964. Richard Nixon swung a golden shovel at the bank's groundbreaking ceremony and later held Account No. 1.

In 1968 Rebozo chose Polizzi's construction firm to build El Centro Commercial Cubano, a shopping center in Miami's Little Havana district, bankrolled by government loans obtained with help from Senator George Smathers. Construction cost $673,839, and Rebozo hired ex-Havana mayor Edgardo Buttari to recruit merchants, each eligible for loans up to $25,000 from the Office of Economic Opportunity. A year after El Centro was completed, Rebozo sold it to Canadian buyers at a $200,000 profit.

In October 1968, Congress passed a bill creating the Biscayne National Monument (now a national park). The project involved buying various Florida islands spanning 207 square miles of Atlantic coastline. Most owners happily sold at inflated prices, but Al Polizzi resisted leaving his sanctuary on Gold Key. Accordingly, the island was deleted from Washington's must-have list and remained with the Polizzi family.

A cloud formed on the Mob's bucolic Florida horizon in 1965, when the *Miami Herald* hired Hank Messick to cover its crime beat. Messick covered gambling and prostitution, then launched a "Know Your Neighbor" series that profiled transplanted mobsters including Meyer Lansky, Sam Tucker, Morris Kleinman, Hymie Martin, Vincent Alo, Gil Beckley, Ed Curd, Pittsburgh's Gabriel Mannarino, Chicago's David Yaras (a friend of Jack Ruby), and others. Moe Dalitz featured prominently in the articles addressing Lansky and Moe's Cleveland partners, drawing links across the decades to Molaska Corporation and Bill Potter's assassination. The exposés, running from September through December 1965, prompted raids and grand jury investigations in Dade, Broward, and Palm Beach Counties. Broward police promised a "constant crackdown" on vice, while Sheriff Martin Kellenberger denied the existence of any rackets in Palm Beach.

Dade County authorities likewise denied any knowledge of Hymie Martin. Sheriff T.A. Buchanan told the *Herald*, "I can't say I know anything about him." Miami's police chief said, "I imagine Intelligence might know something about him," but Lieutenant H.C. Surlley, commanding that division, asked reporters, "Does he live here?" In Miami Beach, the police chief shrugged and said, "I really don't know. What's his specialty?" The helpful *Herald* ran photographs of Hymie and his house to guide investigators, but he remained unmolested.

Florida governor Haydon Burns had vowed in October 1965 to "take whatever action is fitting and appropriate" against organized crime, but he spent most of his tenure trying to preserve segregation. Successor Claude Kirk declared a statewide "war on crime" in 1967, inviting Messick to join the state's team. Messick agreed but grew suspicious when Kirk hired right-wing security consultant George Wackenhut to lead the crusade. According to Messick, Wackenhut ignored gambling in Broward County, while welcoming Bahamian huckster Stafford Sands as a corporate client. When Wackenhut hired Sands's daughter in Miami, Messick resigned.

* * *

In January 1964 the Monte Carlo Casino opened at Freeport, with Eddie Cellini in charge. Eddie and brother Dino were Buckeye natives who learned their gambling skills in Ohio, serving Moe Dalitz and Meyer Lansky in Kentucky. Dino later worked at the Nacional in Havana, remained with Mike McLaney's team until Castro pulled the plug, and briefly managed a

Bebe Rebozo, friend of Richards Nixon and various mobsters (Library of Congress).

Haitian casino until Eddie got the Monte Carlo gig, whereupon Dino headed a new school for dealers in London. Meanwhile, Stafford Sands applied for more gambling permits in Freeport.

The Mob's Bahamian conquest proceeded smoothly, but the ruling United Bahamian Party grew too greedy. In 1966 leaders of the underdog Progressive Liberal Party — representing the country's black majority — found unexpected friends in the U.S. They visited New York for lessons in casino management from Lansky associates and talked politics with Angus Stevens, a former aide to Florida's attorney general whose business partners included Al Malnik. On another Florida visit, PLP officers lodged at the Coral Gables Holiday Inn, whose owner was a business partner of Sam Tucker. Mob money fattened the PLP's coffers while news leaks bared UBP corruption. Mike McLaney furnished the helicopter used by PLP chairman Lynden Pindling for island campaigning, telling reporters that he expected "kindness to bring back kindness." Wherever he spoke, Pindling called for costly reforms funded by tourism.

Pindling won the premier's post in January 1967, then created a Royal Commission of Inquiry to examine charges of rampant corruption. He belatedly expressed misgivings about Mike McLaney, who was called to testify at length. Witness Dusty Peters, public relations director for Grand Bahama Amusement, admitted prior involvement with Mohawk Securities, owned by Dalitz and his DI partners. Lansky bookmaker Max Courtney told the panel he had been invited into the Bahamas because his list of clients included wealthy gamblers "from the ex–Vice-president [Richard Nixon] on down."

Pindling's investigation failed to drive the Mob from the Bahamas. Several would-be rivals of Mary Carter Paint withdrew their bids on Paradise Island in March 1967, and Mike McLaney took a lashing in the commission's final report as "a thoroughly dangerous person who is likely to do nothing but harm to the Bahamas," yet it hardly mattered. Eddie Cellini remained in charge of Mary Carter's casinos through November 1969, when he was finally banned from the islands, while brother Dino—likewise expelled from England—booked junkets to London's Colony Club and Portugal's new Casino Estoril.

In January 1968, presidential hopeful Richard Nixon attended the grand opening of Mary Carter's Paradise Island Casino. Chairman James Crosby donated $100,000 to Nixon's campaign and placed the casino's yacht at Nixon's disposal. In June, after selling its paint division for $10 million, Mary Carter was reborn as Resorts International, with Crosby still in charge.

Every empire needs protection, and Resorts International had International Intelligence, alias Intertel. First on board was Robert Peloquin, a veteran of Robert Kennedy's Hoffa squad, later head of the Justice Department's first Organized Crime Strike Force. Assigned to fight the Mob in Buffalo, Peloquin filed a "clean" report on Emprise Corporation, then retired with colleague William Hundley to private practice. Resorts International installed Peloquin as president of Intertel while Hundley served as secretary and general counsel. James Golden—formerly Nixon's Secret Service bodyguard, then security chief of Nixon's 1968 presidential campaign—became vice president. Field agents included recruits from the FBI, CIA, IRS, Scotland Yard, Britain's MI-5, and the Canadian Mounties.

With such talent on board, Intertel clearly knew how to spot mobsters. Peloquin himself, in 1966, had branded Mary Carter's Freeport operation "ripe for a Lansky skim." Still, a curious myopia paralleled receipt of paychecks from Resorts International. Peloquin claimed his men had purged "the Mafia" from Freeport, but he lamented Eddie Cellini's departure, telling reporters, "I found Edward Cellini to be an outstanding individual." Author Gigi Mahon reports that Eddie Cellini earned $450,000 from Resorts International during 1968–70.

While casinos fleeced the tourists, Bahamian bankers served more affluent clients. Swiss banks were still useful—an FBI memo notes that "[a]s of August 1967, Lansky and several associates including [Moe] Dalitz reportedly controlled the International Credit Bank, Geneva"—but banking close to home was more convenient. In November 1965 Bahamian legislators banned disclosure of information protected by the Bank and Company Secrecy Act, forcing IRS agents to swap data outside the islands or face prison time. In January 1972 an IRS informant hired a woman to distract Castle Bank vice president Michael Wolstencroft during a Florida a visit. While Wolstencroft and his date dined out, the informant stole Wolstencroft's briefcase and photocopied a list of 308 depositors. Most were familiar to T-men—including Dalitz, Kleinman, and Richard Nixon.

Kleinman was particularly close to Castle's leaders. Documents filed with the Bahamian Ministry of Finance in July 1970 reveal that Castle founders Paul Helliwell and Burton Kanter each owned 16.66 percent of the bank, while a firm called Fomentos—controlled by Kleinman—owned 33.66 percent. Two months later, Helliwell and Swiss banker Settlor Bossard founded the $10,000 Gizella [Kleinman] Family Trust. The trust's first purchase was a 50-

percent share of Doral Property, a twenty-acre tract in Dade County, Florida. Helliwell and Burton Kanter divided the other 50 percent. Helliwell and Kanter also managed another Kleinman trust that pursued real estate transactions through their Mercantile Bank.

In January 1972 Castle Bank received $135,000 from Sheridan Ventures, run by Kleinman's nephew. Kleinman subsequently added $200,000 to his Mercantile account and received $22,500 for a matured certificate of deposit at Castle. Mercantile Bank hit the skids in 1972, and its owners scrambled to save their most valued depositors from any harm. Kanter ordered Kleinman's funds transferred to Castle before the collapse, with Helliwell warning Castle's president, "If you don't do it, Kanter will wind up face down in the Chicago River."

* * *

Nevada's public reputation suffered during 1965–66 from extortion trials, skim hearings, and the Dalitz-Boyer tax indictments. Civic leaders scoured the landscape for a savior. What they found, instead, was an eccentric who could buy and sell them all.

Howard Hughes was a Texan, born in 1905, who inherited his father's mechanical skills and his mother's obsession with germs. In 1932 he launched Hughes Aircraft, and seven years later purchased Trans World Airlines for $7 million. Longy Zwillman furnished Hughes with liquor during prohibition, and Hughes maintained his Mob alliances thereafter. In May 1966 a federal court ruled joint ownership of TWA and Hughes Aircraft a conflict of interest, compelling Hughes to choose between the two. Hughes sold his TWA stock and became a billionaire. Federal law required him to reinvest that windfall within two years or face heavy taxation. Hughes looked around for something to buy and saw the neon glimmer of Las Vegas.

Enter Robert Maheu, once a Chicago G-man under suspected JFK conspirator Guy Banister, then a central figure in the Mob-CIA plots to kill Fidel Castro. In 1966 Hughes hired Maheu as a general fixer, paying him $520,000 per year. One of Maheu's first assignments was to find "a person who had connections with certain people of perhaps unsavory background" in Vegas. He mentioned John Rosselli's name and was surprised to learn that Hughes had known Rosselli "for many years."

And Rosselli, of course, knew Moe Dalitz.

Before dawn on November 27, 1966, Hughes and his entourage occupied the DI's top two floors. His crew frisked visitors, covered windows with blackout drapes, replaced penthouse elevator buttons with key-operated locks, and installed an air-filtration system designed by Hughes. In private conversations with Dalitz, Hughes ranted about germs, radicals, and the blight of Fidel Castro's Cuban regime, calling it "a cancer in the heart of the Americas."

Billionaire Howard Hughes failed to "clean up" Las Vegas (Library of Congress).

Moe and his partners were not thrilled to have Hughes as a guest. Hughes spent no cash in the casino and was hogging space reserved for high-rollers. Matters went from bad to worse when Maheu told Dalitz that Hughes intended to remain through Christmas and beyond. Moe later said, "We had already confirmed many reservations for those two floors in anticipation of Mr. Hughes moving, as he had promised." Ruby Kolod confronted Maheu with an ultimatum: "Get the hell out of here, or we'll throw your butt out." Hughes shrugged and told Maheu, "It's your problem. You work it out."

Maheu reached out to Jimmy Hoffa through attorneys Edward Bennett Williams and Ed Morgan. Hoffa asked Dalitz to let Hughes remain at the DI. Six years later, Moe falsely claimed that he honored Hoffa's request because they "were practically raised in the same neighborhood" in Detroit. In mid–January 1967 tension spiked once again. When Dalitz repeated demands that Hughes leave, Maheu urged his employer to "buy the damned place." Hughes agreed.

What happened next depends on who was asked. Maheu claims that he turned again to Ed Morgan and John Rosselli, who "smoothed the way" despite Moe's reluctance. Moe described a meeting with Hank Greenspun, where Dalitz told his former adversary, "Boy, if ever a man was ready to sell something, I'm ready to sell this place." Greenspun offered Morgan's help "to find a buyer." Yet another version, advanced by Rosselli, has Maheu consulting contractor Del Webb, who steered Maheu to Parry Thomas and his Bank of Las Vegas, later renamed Valley Bank. Gaming Control Board files from this era state that Valley Bank "is run by E. Parry Thomas ... but is directly controlled by Moe Dalitz."

Negotiations for the DI tested Moe's patience to the limit. As he said in 1973, "The deal kept changing daily. We agreed on a price at one time and [Maheu] says, 'I think that will conclude the sale; if you will do such-and-such and such-and-such, I think we can get that through.'" Repeatedly, Moe and his partners acquiesced, but each time Maheu "tried to complete the deal that way, he was told that it wasn't good enough." Finally, on March 22, Maheu wrote that "[s]everal of the partners went up in smoke. One of them told me, 'We've had it with Hughes. We're going to come up there in the next thirty minutes and throw his ass out of there.'" Maheu begged for an hour to change Hughes's mind, thus closing the deal.

In fact, Hughes did not *buy* the Desert Inn. He only bought control of the hotel and casino for fifty-five years, while leaving Dalitz and his Desert Inn Associates as owners of the land and buildings. The lease cost Hughes $13,250,000. On top of that, he agreed to pay the DI partners $1,115,000 per year through 1981, then $940,000 per year from 1982 through 2022, for a total of $55,265,000. Ed Morgan received a $150,000 "finder's fee" for his role in the negotiations, passing on $50,000 to John Rosselli and $25,000 to Hank Greenspun.

Hughes had his casino, but he still required a gaming license. On March 24 Texas attorney Richard Gray filed an application for Hughes as the DI's sole operator. Such applications require fingerprints, recent photographs, comprehensive financial statements, and a detailed personal questionnaire — none of which Hughes provided. Still, an "emergency hearing" was scheduled for March 30. On March 27 a Hughes aide visited Governor Laxalt, delivering a letter from Hughes that promised $6 million for construction of a new Las Vegas medical school. Laxalt read the letter to his legislature, dismissing suggestions of a bribe with claims that "the announcement speaks for itself." On March 31 the Gaming Commission unanimously approved Hughes's application. He took control of the DI at midnight on April Fool's Day.

Despite his years of gambling, Hughes was clueless on the subject of casino management. Maheu turned once again to Dalitz. Moe said, "I was asked to be available for any assistance I could give them pertaining to casino policy and so forth, and I volunteered this on a no-pay basis." When questioned on his generosity Moe said, "I felt they were an asset to Las Vegas. I felt it was a good thing for Las Vegas when they moved here, and I was glad to be on their team, so to speak." Maheu regarded Moe as "very helpful," calling him a "hard-nosed businessmen who let nothing escape his attention," thus ensuring "a highly successful operation." Maheu further claimed that Hughes held Moe "in the highest esteem," adding that "many contacts I made with Mr. Dalitz were made at the specific suggestion of Mr. Hughes, wherein Mr. Hughes wanted the benefit of his thinking."

G-men were typically confused, filing a memo in March 1968 that claimed Cleveland mobsters were "completely out of the Desert Inn picture," then noting "rumors" of Moe's continuing involvement since he was "seen frequently" at the DI and "seems to have free access to anyplace he wants to go." On June 28, 1967, agents watched Moe enter a DI cashier's cage and retrieve an envelope, contents unknown.

* * *

Such observations raised the specter of continued skimming. In April 1967 a federal grand jury convened to investigate embezzlement at the Fremont and Riviera. In May the panel indicted Ed Levinson and six others for tax evasion. Levinson and co-defendant Joel Rosenberg pled guilty in 1968, paying small five-figure fines.

That embarrassing case prompted Governor Laxalt to place even more trust in Hughes. Laxalt played tennis with Maheu, claimed access to FBI files proving Hughes "clean of any criminal associations," and called Hughes's link to John Rosselli, "merely opportunistic." Still, Laxalt recognized that Nevada had problems. "We had whores all over," he said. "We had people like Moe Dalitz in Las Vegas and the attitude was that if he kept his nose clean he could stay." In fact, Laxalt was a friend of Moe's. On another occasion he said, "My general opinion of him as a citizen of Nevada is favorable. He's been a good citizen."

Laxalt's response to the Fremont-Riviera indictments was a "task force" on skimming, created in October 1967. Reporters noted that the group began work "with a touchy attitude," announcing that it was "not an 'anti-skimming' group" but would "seek cooperation of the casinos via an exchange of letters." Members planned to visit sixteen casinos chosen as a "cross section" of the gambling industry, but no site would be toured without advance permission from the licensed owners. The panel's see-no-evil attitude was guaranteed by Laxalt's choice of members: Stardust partner Alvin Benedict; Frank Mooney, from the Fremont; John Meier from Hughes Tool; Keith Hannah from Maheu Associates; Bob Miller from the Silver Slipper; and Leon Nightingale from the Cal-Neva Lodge.

* * *

Despite Moe's ongoing involvement at the DI, changes *were* made — not always for the better. Hughes hated children and immediately axed the DI's annual Easter egg hunt. Next went the stage show *Pzazz*, a victim of an ex-playboy's aversion to nudity. A racist who believed that African Americans had "set back civilization a thousand years," Hughes sought to cancel the Davis Cup tennis championship from fear that black star Arthur Ashe would lure "hordes of Negroes" to the DI. Bob Maheu quelled that spasm of paranoia, but he could not save the Tournament of Champions, despised by Hughes because he dreaded players rummaging around in filthy holes to find their golf balls. Dalitz shifted the tournament to his Stardust golf course, then westward to La Costa.

Before the ink was dry on the DI contracts, Moe struck a long-term bargain with attorney Ed Morgan. "I explained to him that other deals would materialize," Moe said, "and that if I had an opportunity I would like to have him involve himself as my legal adviser in some other deals that I'd been contemplating."

First up was the Sands, run by vice presidents Jack Entratter and Carl Cohen. Dalitz "heartily approved" of Hughes buying the resort and recommended leaving its current "array of talent" in place. Hughes paid $14.6 million for the resort on July 22, 1967 and assumed control on August 1. Parry Thomas made $275,000 on the deal, while Ed Morgan received $225,000 and passed $95,000 to John Rosselli. Hughes Tool spokesmen told reporters, "We plan no change in operation of the Sands." There was one new addition, though: Lou Rothkopf's nephew Bernie joined the staff as managing director, later president.

Hughes focused next on the New Frontier. Detroit mobsters Michael Polizzi and Anthony Zerilli (son of Joseph) owned 30 percent of the joint and had arranged a $6 million Teamster loan to cover its debts in April 1964. Hughes paid $14 million for the resort, with Parry Thomas handling the finances, and Nevada granted Hughes his third gaming license after a midnight telephone conference. He took control on September 22, and paid John Rosselli a $25,000 finder's fee, with a long-term lease on the hotel's gift shop.

In 1969 Hughes focused on the Landmark, designed to be the tallest building in Vegas. Moe Dalitz surveyed the design and predicted that the casino would lose $5.5 million in its first year. Hughes forged ahead regardless, paying $17.3 million, and opened the resort in July. Over the next twelve months the Landmark lost $5.7 million.

In June 1970 Hughes eyed the Golden Nugget, downtown, and penned a warning memo to Maheu.

> Re. the club being a gathering place for North Las Vegas's less respectable citizens, all the more reason for us to control this very dangerous gathering place ... to the result that it no longer continues to be a gathering place for the less desirable element.... I am determined we under no circumstances bring Moe or any of his group in to run it under our control. This is the very last thing I feel we should do. So please don't discuss the Nugget with Moe or any of his group at this time.

Hughes never got the Nugget, but he seemed intent on buying everything else in Nevada. Biographers Donald Barlett and James Steele calculate that Hughes spent $178,000 each day that he lived in Nevada, a total of $65 million in Vegas alone. By 1970 Hughes was the state's largest employer, signing paychecks for more than 8,000 workers.

And all the while, his gaming empire hemorrhaged cash.

How much he lost may never be known. Maheu cites losses of $8.4 million for 1969, while Gus Russo puts the total at $50 million over three years. While most Nevada casinos posted profits of 15–20 percent on their owners' investments *despite* covert skimming, the Hughes casinos earned only 6.15 percent in 1968, declining to 1.63 percent in 1969, and lost $10 million overall in 1970.

All this, despite Moe Dalitz and his "hard-nosed" stewardship at the DI; despite former Lansky-allied Flamingo manager Chester Sims doing his best for Hughes at the Frontier; despite Carl Cohen and Bernie Rothkopf at the Sands. Maheu later explained that "Johnny [Rosselli] told me who to hire to run the casinos and pit crews."

* * *

The Cleveland partners lost another of their own in March 1970, when Tom McGinty died in Florida, but business precluded mourning. In August 1970 Merv Adelson and Irwin Molasky announced that their Realty Holdings firm — including Dalitz as a partner — had signed to buy the Bonanza Country Club in Vegas. They renamed it the Las Vegas Country Club, closed it to the public, and sold the mortgage to forty equity members. Moe later claimed that shares were sold below cost, to create a "family-based" country club and "enhance Las Vegas's growth potential."

Image — the Hebrew *yechus* — was increasingly important to Moe Dalitz as he aged. Some guests at his casinos visibly enhanced Moe's reputation — like Greek operatic soprano Maria Callas and her friend Mary Carter from Texas, whom Moe "treated royally" in 1968 — while others placed his image at risk. Boston mobster Willie Fopiano complained that Dalitz "tried to act like he was overjoyed to see me when I looked him up, but he didn't want me around at all. Whenever he ran into me he'd give my hand a quick shake and say 'Nice to see you, nice to see you' — and back away even while he was saying it!" Small wonder, considering Fopiano's suspected involvement in a 1969 murder and countless other Mafia-related felonies.

Future mogul Steve Wynn was one Vegas player favored by Moe and his friends in high places. In January 1969 Parry Thomas arranged for Wynn to buy Best Brands, a local liquor distributor, for $65,000. A casino operator told reporter John Smith, "I got a call one day from Moe Dalitz. It was about Steve Wynn. Moe said Parry Thomas had asked him to ask me, as a favor, to give the kid some of my liquor business. So, I did. For a while, he was fine. The deliveries were made on time, but it wasn't long before he lost interest." Wynn ran Best Brands into debt over the next three years then sold it for $121,000.

* * *

While Howard Hughes bought up the lion's share of Las Vegas, the Stardust gave Dalitz more headaches. Politicians still turned out for Stardust events — including Lieutenant Governor Edward Fike, state senator Chick Hecht, Mayor Oran Gragson, and vice presidential candidate Edwin Muskie — but rumors of Mob domination endured. G-men continued their surveillance on John Drew and reported that he had been banned from gambling in the club's casino.

Who better to remove the millstone from around Moe's neck than Howard Hughes?

In March 1968 Hughes offered $29 million for the Stardust. Moe wanted $35 million. Governor Laxalt convened the Gaming Control Board, saying, "Plainly and simply, we want to find out if we are on the brink of a monopoly." Hughes, as usual, was unavailable for questioning, but Maheu told the GCB his boss would "have no further interest in acquiring other major hotels in Las Vegas" after the Stardust. Hank Greenspun rushed to Carson City, urging authorities to approve the sale. "It is within our grasp now," he said, "to look the world straight in their national magazines and law enforcement and say, 'We have achieved a clean, decent society.'"

Those who examined Greenspun's motives found that he had sold his local TV station to Hughes for $3,625,000 in 1967, and banked a $25,000 "finder's fee" from the DI lease. Greenspun had also received a $4 million loan from Hughes Tool at 3 percent interest, and enjoyed a unique advertising contract with Hughes-owned casinos: he received a $500,000 cash retainer, but instead of deducting fees for specific ads from that balance, he billed Hughes again as each ad ran, collecting another $488,000.

On March 17, Hughes penned a memo to Maheu, complaining of Moe's demand for $35 million. Moe stood firm, but Morris Kleinman sold his Stardust shares to Dalitz, prompting G-men to report that Kleinman was "out of Las Vegas" entirely. Moe now owned 88 percent of the resort's preferred shares and 73.334 percent of its common stock, with the remainder divided among partners Al Benedict, John Donnelly, John Drew, Milton Jaffe, Cornelius Jones, and George Stillings.

In April 1968, Justice attorney James Coyle met lawyer Richard Gray in Vegas, then drafted a memo opposing the Stardust sale. Undeterred, Hughes forged ahead, raising his offer to $30.5 million. On April 30 the state approved his license for the Silver Slipper but deferred a verdict on the Stardust. Governor Laxalt wrote to Attorney General Ramsey Clark, warning that blockage of the sale "jeopardized the employment of 2,000 people in the Stardust enterprise" and threatened "permanent damage" to Nevada's economy. If Justice moved against Hughes, Laxalt "would be faced with no alternative other than to intervene and oppose the action with all the resources of the state."

Moe sought a few days' relaxation at the DI Ranch in Utah. Riding along through the desert on June 14, he fell from his horse and ruptured a kidney, lying in the sun for several hours before help arrived. Aides flew him to California, where surgeons removed the kidney. Moe emerged from the hospital in good spirits, still an avid horseman — and found that nothing had changed in Vegas. Following a July 2 meeting with Maheu and Gray, James Coyle noted that Hughes planned to leave the old Stardust management intact. "The people are there," Coyle said, "and that's one reason we're interested in it."

Hughes withdrew his Stardust bid on August 15, 1968. Furious, Moe consulted Ed Morgan, who urged him to sue. Moe agreed, telling Morgan, "See if you can get us a deal that we can live with, that we can straighten out the obligations that we've incurred, and we'll settle it that way." Maheu and Gray agreed to a $3 million loan with the prevailing interest rate, but Moe complained that "we should get the very lowest possible rate of interest." Gray agreed to 3 percent, prompting Moe to say, "It was all very, very pleasant. There was no argument about it, nobody tried to gouge, nor did anybody try to welch out."

Moe's fuzzy feelings extended to Morgan, whom he said "was very solicitous of getting as good a deal as he could for us, and I felt that we should be liberal with him." Moe offered Morgan his choice of a $500,000 fee or a share of the Stardust. Morgan took the cash, passing $100,000 to Maheu. No one suggested that Morgan's $100,000 yearly retainer from Hughes Tool might constitute a conflict of interest. Nor were any questions raised when Morgan collected another $100,000 from Dalitz, for arranging yet another multimillion-dollar sale of Strip real estate to Hughes.

In October 1968, Del Coleman agreed to buy the Stardust for $15 million, pending approval of a gambling license. Coleman was a friend of Sidney Korshak and had hired Ruby Kolod and George Gordon to secure control of the Seeburg Corporation's vending-machine empire in 1956. Twelve years later Coleman teamed with Albert Parvin to create the Parvin-Dohrman Corporation. Moe closed the deal on January 23, 1969, accepting half the price offered by Hughes the previous year. Sid Korshak received a $500,000 finder's fee for introducing Coleman to Dalitz. In May 1969 FBI agents reported that "Dalitz is no longer affiliated with any gambling enterprise in Las Vegas and contemplates traveling throughout the United States and Europe," while maintaining a year-round home at La Costa.

Once again, they were mistaken.

Parvin-Dohrman's purchase of the Stardust left most of the club's staff intact. Yale Cohen continued as president, Frank Sennes remained as entertainment director, and Al Sachs stayed on as casino manager until May 1970, when he advanced to general manager. Mark Swain, a DI publicity staffer from 1949 until his shift to the Stardust as sales director, soon became vice president of sales and public relations for all three Parvin-Dohrman casinos. Peanuts Danolfo found himself in a vice presidential office, while mobsters Phil Ponti and Bobby Stella Sr. kept the skim flowing.

Left to right: Moe Dalitz, Herb Tobman, and Senator Paul Laxalt (Las Vegas Historical Society).

* * *

Robert Kennedy announced his presidential candidacy in March 1968, declaring, "I do not run for the Presidency merely to oppose any man, but to propose new policies. I run because I am convinced that this country is on a perilous course and because I have such strong feelings about what must be done, and I feel that I'm obliged to do all I can." Kennedy's main issue appeared to be U.S. withdrawal from Vietnam, but author Charles Higham reports that "even after he left the post of Attorney General, he was aggressively exploring the Hughes-Moe Dalitz–Sam Giancana–CIA–Mary Carter Paints–Nassau connection."

And, by extension, the men who had murdered his brother.

Jimmy Hoffa's obsession with Kennedy endured beyond Dallas. Author Walter Sheridan reports that Puerto Rican Teamster boss Frank Chavez flew to New York in 1964, planning to kill RFK, but was dissuaded by associates who thought the slaying would seal Hoffa's fate. In March 1967 Chavez left San Juan once again, vowing to kill Kennedy and prosecution witness Ed Partin if Hoffa went to prison. Hoffa himself allegedly persuaded Chavez to desist, and Chavez was murdered before year's end. Then, in May 1968, a federal prisoner told G-men that he heard Hoffa discussing "a contract to kill Bob Kennedy" with New York mafioso Carmine Galante. Hoffa refused an interview.

On June 4, 1968, Kennedy won California's Democratic presidential primary election. At 12:15 A.M. on June 5, he addressed cheering supporters at the Ambassador Hotel in L.A., then left to exit through the hotel's kitchen. In the crowded pantry, gunfire suddenly erupted, killing RFK and wounding five bystanders. Friends of Kennedy seized the apparent killer, Sirhan Bishara Sirhan, and wrenched a .22-caliber revolver from his hand.

The case seemed open-and-shut — but was it?

Coroner Thomas Naguchi reported that RFK was hit by three bullets, while a fourth passed through his coat. All four came from *behind* Kennedy and to his right, with the gun's muzzle "held at a distance of between one inch and six inches from the coat at the time of all firings." The fatal head shot, striking behind RFK's right ear, was fired from a range of one inch or less. Meanwhile, all witnesses to the assassination testified that Sirhan approached Kennedy *from the front,* firing from three feet or more.

The number of shots fired was also in question. Sirhan's gun held eight rounds, all of which were fired. Surgeons removed two slugs from Kennedy and five from other victims, while LAPD reported that the eighth bullet pierced a ceiling panel and was "lost." Meanwhile, published police and FBI photographs depicted at least at least four more bullet holes in pantry walls. LAPD criminalist DeWayne Wolfer later acknowledged those photographs, saying, "We wouldn't photograph just any hole. I mean, there were too many holes to photograph."

In short, at least twelve shots were fired on June 5 from an eight-shot pistol, which Sirhan never reloaded.

At Sirhan's murder trial DeWayne Wolfer testified that all slugs from the Ambassador shooting matched Sirhan's revolver. He identified the gun by its serial number: H18602. Sirhan's weapon actually bore the serial number H53725. When confronted with the discrepancy, Wolfer called it a "clerical error," claiming that he accidentally cited the serial number of an identical revolver used for tests at the hotel. The second gun had been destroyed, but *did* the bullets match Sirhan's?

Not according to criminalist William Harper, who examined two of the recovered slugs in 1970. While denied access to Sirhan's pistol, Harper concluded that the bullets came from different weapons. Other experts who examined the bullets also found "significant differences" among several slugs and refused to rule out a second gunman. In 1975, experts at Chicago's American Academy of Forensic Sciences test-fired Sirhan's pistol. Panel member Herbert MacDonnell said, "The bullet removed from Kennedy's neck could not have come from Sirhan's revolver."

If a second gunman fired at Kennedy in the Ambassador's crowded pantry, who was he? Published conspiracy theories focus on a private security guard named Thane Eugene Cesar. Cesar walked beside RFK as Kennedy entered the pantry, holding Kennedy's right arm to guide him through the crowd. After the shooting, multiple witnesses described seeing Cesar with his pistol drawn. Cesar's clip-on necktie wound up on the floor beside Kennedy, as if the senator had clutched it while falling.

Cesar told conflicting stories about the shooting. On June 5, he told LAPD that he started to draw his gun "but it was too late." Six days later he told G-men he was knocked down before he could draw. On June 24 Cesar told police he drew his gun *after* he fell. Witness Don Schulman told journalists, "A Caucasian gentleman stepped out and fired three times — the security guard — hitting Kennedy all three times."

Cesar denied firing his pistol, supposedly a .38-caliber revolver, and LAPD accepted his word. However, Cesar *also* owned a .22 revolver "similar" to Sirhan's. Cesar told police that he sold the .22 "somewhat around" February 1968, but journalist Theodore Charach traced the buyer to Arkansas and found the sales receipt dated September 6, 1968. LAPD found no

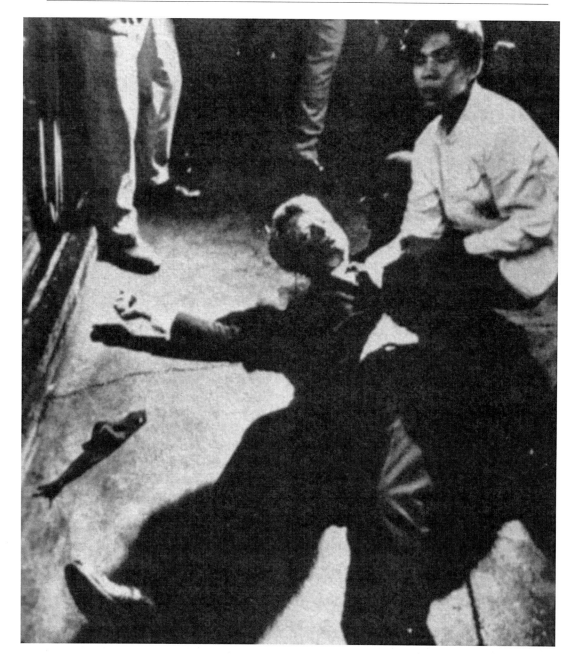

Robert Kennedy lies dying. Thane Cesar's tie is seen beside his right hand (National Archives).

criminal record for Cesar, but author Alex Bottus claims Cesar was arrested several times in Tijuana, Mexico. Each case, Bottus writes, was "fixed" by bookie John Alessio, owner of Tijuana's Agua Caliente racetrack and "protégé" of sometime Dalitz business partner Arnholt Smith.

Sirhan told anyone who asked him that he murdered RFK because of Kennedy's support for Israel — yet he also had Mob connections. During 1965–67 Sirhan was often seen at the Del Mar and Santa Anita racetracks. At Santa Anita, he met Henry Ramistella (alias Frank

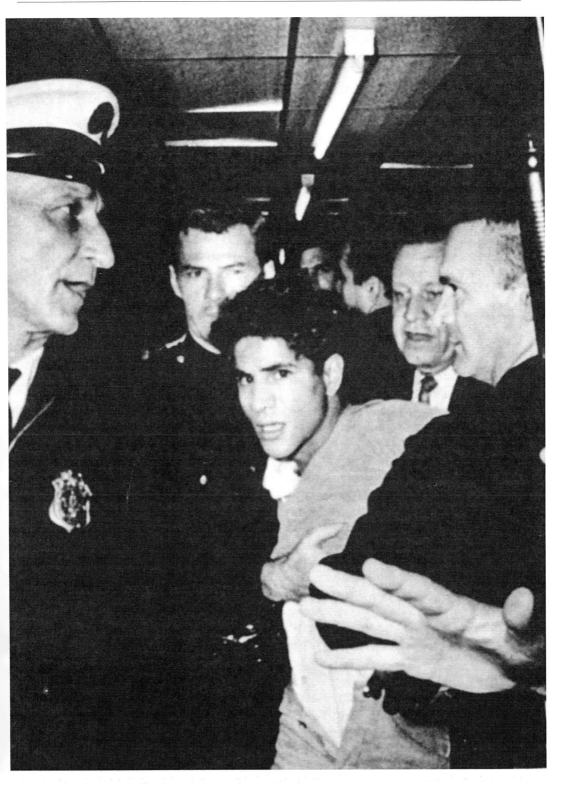

Sirhan Sirhan (center), captured at the scene of RFK's shooting (Library of Congress).

Donnarauma), a New Jersey native with multiple narcotics arrests. Ramistella hired Sirhan to work at the Corona Breeding Farm in 1966, and later got Sirhan a job at Santa Anita. Ramistella's pseudonym, misspelled "Donaruma," also appeared repeatedly in Sirhan's semi-coherent diary. G-men searched for Ramistella after Kennedy's assassination but did not find him until April 1969, when he denied any knowledge of the crime.

Another character with Mob associations, enigmatic JFK assassination figure Jim Braden, was in Los Angeles the night Bobby Kennedy died. Interviewed by police at Rancho La Costa, Braden acknowledged spending the night of June 4–5 at the Century Plaza Hotel, less than fifteen minutes from the Ambassador, but said he was watching TV with his wife when the shooting occurred. Braden's spouse contradicted him, saying they separated in February 1968 and she was not in California during June. Deputy Chief Robert Houghton, in charge of LAPD's "Special Unit Senator" created to investigate the murder, ignored that discrepancy and called Braden's presence in L.A. a "historical coincidence."

Sirhan, though penniless, had no shortage of legal talent on tap. One volunteer was Russell Parsons, who represented mobsters before the McClellan Committee and called chief counsel Kennedy "a dirty sonofabitch." Parsons also served client Mickey Cohen, seeking termination of Cohen's criminal probation — an act that scuttled Parsons's mayoral campaign in L.A. In autumn 1968 Parsons told Sirhan that Dalitz-Hoffa attorney Edward Bennett Williams had agreed to join the defense, whereupon Sirhan replied, "Beautiful."

Williams changed his mind, leaving attorney Grant Cooper to lead the defense team, but Cooper's advent was delayed by his commitment to client John Rosselli. In October 1967 federal prosecutors indicted Rosselli for failure to register as an alien. Two months later another panel indicted Rosselli, Maurice Friedman from the New Frontier, and three other defendants for running a card-cheating scam at the Beverly Hills Friar's Club. G-men recall that L.A. district attorney Evelle Younger "put pressure on us to pull in our horns" and wrote to Nevada's Gaming Commission on Friedman's behalf, seeking to block revocation of Friedman's license. Friedman subsequently comped Younger at the New Frontier, bragging to friends that the letter had cost him $2,000. The Friar's trial opened in June 1968, sidelining Cooper until jurors convicted all five defendants.

During that trial, feds caught Cooper with a stolen grand jury transcript. In January 1969 Cooper told Sirhan's judge that he could "not conceive" being indicted. Thirty-three years later, new attorneys filed a habeas corpus motion on Sirhan's behalf, charging that the feds had pressured Cooper into betraying his client at trial. Jurors convicted Sirhan in April 1969 and he received a death sentence six days later. Cooper subsequently pled guilty to possession of stolen documents and paid a $1,000 fine.

Evelle Younger's career in law enforcement was curious. FBI files report that he flew to Mexico aboard a private plane in February 1969 for a vacation at the Acapulco Towers, built by bookie Moe Morton (who sold a yacht to Moe Dalitz for $60,000 around the same time). While there, Younger allegedly received $50,000 in cash from an associate of Sam Giancana. Younger soon quashed subpoenas from Hollywood Park officials, seeking data on Morton's record. In 1970 Younger was elected state attorney general, aided by a $3,000 donation from Sidney Korshak and a $45,000 "loan" from Arnholt Smith that was never repaid. Where predecessor Thomas Lynch had initiated thirty-one Mob prosecutions in 1970, Younger filed none in the next seven years. Instead, he scuttled ongoing investigations of Arnholt Smith, his sidekick John Alessio, and a $26 million fraud case involving the Baptist Foundation of America. When asked about Mob ties in 1979, Younger replied, "I never said I was tough on crime."

* * *

Memos from Dalitz's FBI dossier, filed in May 1968, describe investigations of illegal gambling operations in Arizona, California, Illinois, Kansas, Michigan, Missouri, Ohio, Oklahoma, and Texas, but Bureau censors have blacked out so much of the various documents that Moe's name never appears and we are left to speculate in vain about his link to those activities.

One memo that escaped the censor's pen — from June 1965 — reports that Moe was "not held in high esteem by certain individuals associated with organized crime ... in Los Angeles." Still, he had friends where it counted — at the helm of the Teamsters pension, and at Arnholt Smith's bank. During 1967–69 Moe received $27 million from the Teamsters to expand and beautify La Costa, while IBT president Frank Fitzsimmons and vice president Jackie Presser became regular visitors. Another part-time tenant was IBT pension controller Allen Dorfman — of whom Jimmy Hoffa said, on his way to prison in 1967, "When this man speaks, he speaks for me."

La Costa's list of residents and visitors read like a social register of both the upperworld and underworld. In July 1968 Dalitz and Allard Roen welcomed Jimmy Hoffa's wife, Bahamian fixer Wallace Groves, and Allan Korshak of the California Life Insurance Company to discuss national expansion of the "managed care" insurance system pioneered at Sunrise Hospital. Gus Russo claims that meeting also arranged a $1 million payoff to presidential candidate Richard Nixon. Bugsy Siegel colleague Allen Smiley visited La Costa with John Rosselli to see Sidney Korshak. G-men also spotted Detroit mafioso Anthony Giacalone at Korshak's La Costa home in 1969. Gene Butler, Barry Goldwater's ex-son-in-law, said the family was treated "like royalty" at La Costa and never charged for anything.

Moe and his guests enjoyed themselves at La Costa. The Tournament of Champions, played on what was then America's largest golf course, drew thousands of visitors yearly, supervised until 1971 by U.S. Marines bused in from Camp Pendleton. La Costa got a break from state surveillance in 1972, when Robert Houghton — head of California's Criminal Intelligence and Investigation Division — decreed that maintaining informants "was not a productive project." More specifically, he said, "The boss [Evelle Younger] doesn't think that is a good thing to do." Simultaneously, La Costa sought annexation to Carlsbad-by-the-Sea, a tiny retirement community. G-men opined: "It is believed that the real reason for having this annexation take place is that surveillance by the San Diego Sheriff's office will be restricted." Moe won that bid in November 1972 by a narrow vote of 41–39.

Arnholt Smith soon ran afoul of the feds. He had supported Richard Nixon since 1948, including a $250,000 donation in 1968 and rumored arm-twisting that produced another $1 million from wealthy cohorts. During the same period Smith dealt with Moe Dalitz through Martinolich Shipbuilding, loaned money to La Costa, and welcomed DI attorney John Donnelly to Westgate Corporation as chairman of the firm's audit committee. In 1967 Attorney General Thomas Lynch linked Smith to the "efficient organization and communication between various factors making up the total of organized crime," but Evelle Younger replaced Lynch in time to squelch that investigation before it produced indictments.

Smith ran out of luck in 1973, when his embezzlement of $400 million caused the U.S. National Bank to collapse. Smith resigned as chairman in May, on the eve of multiple indictments, while the *New York Times* branded USNB vice president Lewis Lipton "well-connected in the Southern California underworld." Smith pled guilty to embezzlement in 1975 and received a two-year suspended sentence.

* * *

There was trouble in Arizona, as well. On July 3, 1968, snipers fired blasts into the Tucson home of Sam Giancana's daughter. Police suspected members of the Bonnano family until July 21, when a bomb exploded at Pete Licavoli's ranch. One night later, two explosions rocked Joe Bonnano's home. Over the next twelve months, fifteen more bombings jarred Tucson, inspiring speculation on Mafia feuds.

Authorities finally captured three suspects, whose raids were directed by G-man David Hale, hoping to start a full-scale gang war. FBI headquarters suspended Hale, but he had nothing to fear. One witness against him died in what Tucson police called a suicide. A judge convicted the confessed bombers on misdemeanor charges and fined them $260 each. No charges were filed against Hale, who quietly resigned and found a corporate executive job, suggesting that the Bureau granted him a glowing reference.

Arizona congressman Sam Steiger tackled Dalitz's old friends at Emprise Corporation in 1970, delivering four separate speeches on the company's Mob ties and shady dealings. Steiger's reports named Moe and Sam Tucker, Mushy Wexler and Anthony Zerilli, Black Bill Tocco, and New England mafioso Raymond Patriarca as cronies of late Emprise founder Lou Jacobs. In the midst of his campaign, Steiger said that Barry Goldwater and Harry Rosenzweig asked him to "go easy."

* * *

In August 1968 Republicans chose Richard Nixon as their presidential candidate. Howard Hughes chipped in $100,000 to help Nixon win "under our sponsorship and supervision." James Crosby sent $100,000 from the Paradise Island casino and squeezed a like amount from his gambler associates. Overall, investigators estimate that Nixon received at least $1 million in secret contributions, much of it from old friends in the Teamsters Union.

All this, despite Nixon's acceptance speech at the GOP convention, in which he told cheering delegates, "I pledge to you that our new Attorney General will be directed by the President of the United States to launch a war against organized crime in this country."

Howard Hughes expected payback for his campaign contributions, and he got it when Justice withdrew objections to his purchase of the Landmark Tower in January 1969. Hughes beat the monopoly complaint by calling the Landmark a "failing company" and gave Nixon another $50,000 in February 1969, drawn from a safe-deposit box at the Frontier. In June 1970, after Nixon received another fifty grand from the Silver Slipper, Justice approved Hughes's purchase of Harold's Club in Reno.

Friends in Washington could not reduce the mounting losses in Las Vegas. As his madness deepened, Hughes lost interest in Nevada and fled on November 26, 1970. G-men reported that Hughes had flown from Nellis Air Force Base in a private jet bound for Paradise Island, where he took up residence at a hotel owned by Resorts International. On December 4, Hughes fired Bob Maheu and replaced him with Intertel agents who evicted Maheu from his home at the DI, seized his yacht and a second home — most everything, in short, but the clothes on his back.

Paul Laxalt was concerned about "rumored" links between Meyer Lansky and Resorts International. Still, he told reporters, "Mr. Hughes's involvement here has absolutely done us wonders.... People come here now feeling they can come here in respectable, safe circumstances."

* * *

President Nixon nurtured a façade of honesty — as long as it did not interfere with profits.

Soon after his election Nixon sold his 185,891 shares of Fisher's Island, Florida, as he explained it, "to avoid even the appearance of impropriety." Bebe Rebozo handled the sale, demanding three dollars per share — a 300 percent increase over what Nixon paid in 1962 — and he was reportedly furious when Nixon settled for merely doubling his money.

Meanwhile, Nixon sold ambassadorships to the highest bidder, collecting at least $1.8 million from would-be diplomats who wanted taxpayers to fund their luxurious sojourns abroad. After his re-election in 1972, Nixon appointed thirteen non-career diplomats who gave the GOP $706,000; another $607,000 came from two applicants whom Nixon rejected.

Nixon often used the IRS against his enemies, demanding audits on 575 political opponents in 1972 alone, but he resented T-men chasing mobsters. His concern may be explained by Jimmy Hoffa's claim that the Government Accounting Office missed 80 percent of Nixon's campaign contributions in 1968. Was it mere coincidence that new Attorney General Mitchell canceled Operation Snowball — an IRS investigation of illegal campaign contributions by thirty-one Los Angeles-area firms — soon after Nixon's inauguration? Or that Donald Alexander, named to serve as IRS commissioner in April 1973, pulled the plug on Operation Tradewinds in the Bahamas? Alexander — dubbed "a financial crook's delight" by author Alan Block — scuttled 488 pending tax-evasion cases, lobbied for revision of IRS Form 1040 to delete questions concerning foreign bank accounts, effectively ceased prosecutions under the 1971 Narcotics Traffickers Tax Program just as major cocaine cartels invaded the U.S., and gutted the IRS Intelligence Division, prompting many veteran agents to resign. By 1979 a Ford Foundation study of offshore banking estimated that "up to $20 billion annually" went untaxed.

Nixon's friendship extended beyond "normal" white-collar criminals to known mafiosi and their relatives. Salvatore "Sonny" Provenzano, brother of Genovese family capo Tony Pro, was photographed with Nixon in 1971 and joined him for golf three years later, at Rancho La Costa. New Jersey's Angelo DeCarlo used Frank Sinatra to deliver a $100,000 campaign contribution in 1972. Sinatra chipped in another $50,000 of his own — and Nixon commuted DeCarlo's sentence in December 1972. A Justice Department official told Dan Moldea, "The whole goddamn thing is too frightening to think about. We're talking about the President of the United States ... a man who pardoned organized crime figures after millions were spent by the government putting them away, a guy who's had these connections since he was a congressman in the 1940s. I guess the real shame is that we'll never know the whole story; it'll never come out."

And then, there was Jimmy Hoffa.

Most scholars agree that Nixon won the IBT's 1968 endorsement with a promise to liberate Hoffa. Paul Laxalt also rose to Hoffa's defense, with a 1971 letter to Nixon that read:

> Dear President Dick:
>
> The other day I had an extended discussion with Al Dorfman of the Teamsters, with whom I've worked closely the past few years.... This discussion, which described in detail the personal vendetta that Bobby Kennedy had against Hoffa, together with other information provided me over the years, leads me to the inevitable conclusion that Jim is a victim of Kennedy's revenge.

FBI files indicate that Dorfman himself met Attorney General John Mitchell in 1970, gave him $300,000 in cash, and obtained a receipt. According to G-men, "The money was paid to obtain the release of James Hoffa from jail." In December 1971 Nixon's secret microphones caught him telling Henry Kissinger, "We're going to give Hoffa an amnesty but we're going to do it for a reason." Nixon mentioned "some private things" which IBT president Frank Fitzsimmons did in 1968 "that were very helpful." The plan was to guarantee long-term Teamster support by freeing Hoffa, while preventing Hoffa from unseating Fitzsim-mons. On December 23, 1971, Nixon commuted Hoffa's sentence, but barred him from union politics until March 1980. On July 17, 1972, the IBT Executive Board convened at La Costa and unanimously voted to endorse Nixon's re-election bid. Before year's end the union donated at least $1 million to Nixon's campaign.

On another front, author James Neff reports that "[f]rom 1971 to 1974 two IRS agents met secretly with Fitzsimmons ... in Washington, Miami, Las Vegas, Los Angeles, and at the La Costa resort.... Fitzsimmons pretended to be candid ... [as to] why [he] was informing, claiming to want to rid the Teamsters union of mobsters and racketeers. But the only names he coughed up were allies of Jimmy Hoffa." Coincidentally, in 1973 Attorney General Richard Kleindienst denied FBI requests to extend surveillance on IBT-Mob connections.

* * *

In 1971 IRS agents charged Meyer Lansky, Sam Cohen, Morris Lansburgh, and five others for skimming $36 million from the Flamingo during 1960–67. Lansky skipped to Israel, then returned to plead ill health and ultimately saw his charges dropped, while Cohen served one year and Lansburgh did five months.

Journalist Nicholas Gage reported that 70-odd Lansky associates were under active investigation, including Moe Dalitz and Sam Garfield. Dalitz still spent much of his time at the DI, although Hughes spokesmen claimed that "he and his people are being weeded out."

Paul Laxalt left office in January 1971 with a "gut full of politics" and a failing marriage, to enter the casino business. The first step, according to his ex-sister-in-law, was a Palm Springs meeting attended by "every hood in the nation." To build the Ormsby House in Carson City, Laxalt secured three loans totaling $9.3 million from a Chicago bank. Bernard Nemerov, a friend of Jimmy Hoffa's at the Riviera, invested $50,000. Vegas G-man Joseph Yablonsky claims that "Nemerov was there to get the skim out." In 1974, when Laxalt changed his mind and sought a seat in the U.S. Senate, Moe Dalitz and selected friends gave $50,000 to launch his campaign. Laxalt won—and Moe claimed full credit. "Laxalt is my boy," he declared. "I put him there."

Frank Fitzsimmons succeeded Jimmy Hoffa as president of the Teamsters Union (Library of Congress).

John Rosselli's Friar's Club conviction left a vacancy in Vegas. His replacement was Anthony Spilotro, a protégé of Felix Alderisio whom Illinois' Crime Commission called "one of the most dangerous gang terrorists in the Chicago area." As "Tony Stuart," Spilotro assumed control of the gift shop at Jay Sarno's Circus Circus, then pocketed $700,000 when Sarno sold the resort in 1974. Spilotro then opened a jewelry shop, The Gold Rush, which served as a front for bookmaking and burglaries. In February 1974, when the feds accused Spilotro, Alderisio, and three others of embezzling $1.4 million from the Teamsters pension fund, Tony chose Jerris Leonard — Richard Nixon's former assistant attorney general for civil rights — to defend him.

Dalitz despised Spilotro but he got along famously with Kirk Kerkorian. Their mutual friends included mafioso Charles Tourine and Paul Laxalt — who visited Washington twice in 1970, pleading for SEC leniency on behalf of Kerkorian's International Leisure Corporation. Kerkorian also spent time at La Costa and in Acapulco, where Moe was a frequent visitor. Kerkorian bought the Flamingo from Sam Cohen in 1967, then acquired control of MGM Studios in 1969 and steered the firm into gambling. In 1971 he announced plans to build the world's largest resort on the Strip. To realize his dream — the future MGM Grand — Kerkorian bought twenty-six acres from the Realty Holdings firm of Moe Dalitz, Merv Adelson, and Irwin Molasky. When reporters questioned his relationship with Dalitz, Kerkorian replied, "What's wrong with Moe?" Bernie Rothkopf helped Kerkorian lay out the MGM's 140-yard-long casino and subsequently left his post at Caesar's Palace to serve as the MGM's president.

While the MGM was under construction, billionaire brothers Jay, Robert and Donald Pritzker — owners of the Hyatt hotel chain — announced plans to buy the Four Queens in Vegas. Donald Pritzker met Moe Dalitz in Honolulu on May 14, 1972, to discuss a Teamster loan and went home to Chicago elated. The IBT signed off at 4 percent interest, saving the Pritzkers some $8 million, then purchased $30 million in Hyatt stock.

* * *

In January 1971 federal agents raided the Stardust, seizing credit card receipts for 1966–69. They scrutinized those records to determine how much credit Al Parvin's Recrion Corporation had granted to out-of-state gamblers, and while no indictments resulted, Parvin saw the writing on the wall. In 1972 he sold the Aladdin to friends of Mob attorney Morris Shenker from St. Louis and Detroit. Shenker banked a $500,000 finder's fee, while Vito Giacalone, a friend of Anthony Zerilli, established himself as Detroit's man in Vegas. The Teamsters subsequently loaned nearly $100 million to remodel the Aladdin.

Enter Allen Glick, a Pittsburgh native who bought the Hacienda in 1972, using money from a realty firm that soon went bankrupt. A few months later he received $30 million from the IBT to beautify the resort. In March 1973 Glick met Allen Dorfman at La Costa, to discuss purchase of the King's Castle at Tahoe. Dorfman agreed to let Glick control the hotel, while Edward Buccieri — formerly convicted of the Ratterman frame-up in Newport, lately employed at Caesar's Palace — ran the casino. Nevada's Gaming Commission refused to license a casino with Buccieri in charge, so Glick revised his plan and created Argent Corporation (*Al*len *R. G*lick *Ent*erprises). In May 1974 Glick bought Al Parvin's Recrion with $62.7 million borrowed from the Teamsters, thus acquiring the Stardust and Fremont.

As with Howard Hughes, gaming officials touted Glick and Argent as symbols of the new "clean" Nevada — but nothing changed. Al Sachs and Herb Tobman, Stardust managers under Recrion, remained at their posts. So did Yale Cohen, Phil Ponti, and Bobby Stella. Tobman, who became the Stardust's president in 1974, dated his first meeting with Moe Dalitz from 1970. "I was in awe of meeting him," said Tobman. "As far as I'm concerned he was a great man." Glick himself knew even less about casino management than Hughes. John Rosselli told Jimmy Fratianno, "This guy don't know what's going on. He made a deal with Lefty Rosenthal, who runs all of Glick's gambling operations." Rosenthal, driven from Miami by Hank Messick's exposés — could not be licensed in Nevada but Argent paid him $250,000 a year to manage the Stardust's casino. Each time officials noticed him he changed job titles, but his focus never varied. "Glick is the financial end," Lefty told *Business Week* in 1975, "but policy comes from me."

And the policy was all-out skimming. Employee Carl Thomas testified that an average $400,000 per month was skimmed by Rosenthal and company, while Glick spent most of his time on La Costa's golf course. Glick later said he was oblivious to the pervasive criminality surrounding him but disclosure statements from the American Stock Exchange reveal that Argent advanced $10 million in Teamster money directly to Glick and his various subsidiary firms while bypassing mandatory reporting procedures. When those handouts were finally revealed, Argent admitted that the "loans" to Glick were unsecured and never were repaid.

* * *

Moe Dalitz dealt with Argent from a distance, keeping track of its affairs through his partners and protégés. His interests were diverse and constantly expanding, as were his excursions into charity. Las Vegas grew by leaps and bounds, owing a major share of its new landscape to the DRAM partners at Paradise Development.

Banker Parry Thomas boasted $270 million in assets by the early 1970s, including an $8.4 million interest in the Riviera and a fleet of oil tankers registered in Liberia. In 1975 he told Irwin Molasky, "I want an image and a name to be seen from miles around." As Molasky explained it, "He wanted prestige and he wanted a modern branch downtown." Paradise Development obliged, erecting a seventeen-story behemoth that ranked as the tallest building downtown.

Farther west, in 1969, Molasky and Merv Adelson bought half of a new film production company for $450,000. They called it Lorimar — named for Adelson's ex-wife Lori plus the last initials of its owners: Mo*lasky*, A*delson*, and TV producer Lee *Rich*. Lorimar produced such TV hits as *The Waltons, Eight Is Enough, Dallas, Knots Landing*, and *Flamingo Road*. Its big-screen offerings included *Being There, Cruising*, and *An Officer and a Gentleman*. An FBI memo from February 1966 says of Adelson and Molasky: "Neither are known to have arrest records, but there is no question as to their close association with the hoodlum element."

Which, in Hollywood, never did any real harm.

Nor were Mob ties a problem in Acapulco, where Moe Dalitz remained a frequent visitor. His former home was gone, but he found space at the Acapulco Towers, owned by friend Moe Morton. Morton hatched his plan to build a Mob retreat in 1966, paving the way via his wife's school ties to former Mexican president Miguel Alemán. Alemán won election in 1947 with aid from Meyer Lansky, then became Mexico's President of Tourism for life. John Rosselli told his goddaughter, "The Acapulco Towers was built with Vegas skim money" — and Mob ties extended from there. In 1968 Morton and Sid Korshak formed the Simo Corporation and persuaded ten rich friends to pay $50,000 apiece for "private time-shares" in the Acapulco Towers.

Each investor owned 5 percent of the resort, leaving the other half for use by wealthy tourists. Agents of the Illinois Racing Board, dispatched to investigate Moe Morton in 1970, compiled a list of celebrity guests including *Playboy* publisher Hugh Hefner, actors Tony Curtis and Kirk Douglas, plus "numerous influential businessmen" who "were all friends and all

Prince Rainier and Princess Grace of Monaco were sailing with Moe Dalitz when his son died in a plane crash (Library of Congress).

knew each other." One of those—Getty Oil executive Stuart Evey—met Moe Dalitz at the Acapulco Towers, reporting that Moe often flew south with Allard Roen to meet "friends from the Midwest and East Coast."

Between November 1969 and March 1970, Racing Board agents shadowed Morton through a series of meetings with Dalitz, Meyer Lansky, Del Coleman, Mob attorney Moses Polakoff, Philadelphia mafioso Angelo Bruno, and Canadian mobster Ben Kaufman. When not engaged in meetings at the Acapulco Towers, gangsters rode taxis to the nearby "residence of Leo Berkowitz who has ties with these individuals in Canada." It may be mere coincidence that Acapulco's Leo Berkowitz shared the birth name of Cleveland mobster Chuck Polizzi.

At home in Vegas, Moe Dalitz never failed to open his wallet for worthy causes. In 1970 he received Israel's City of Peace Award for "distinguished service to the people and state of Israel." Nevada Supreme Court justice David Zenoff chaired the testimonial dinner, while those in attendance included Senators Alan Bible and Howard Cannon, governor-elect Mike O'Callaghan, and other state officials.

Tragedy struck Dalitz on August 24, 1972, when son Andrew crashed his single-engine airplane at Capital City Airport in Lansing, Michigan. Andrew and two business colleagues had flown to Benton Harbor and were returning home to Detroit when they stopped in Lansing for fuel. Witnesses reported that the plane took off successfully and reached 200 feet before it plummeted to earth, killing all aboard. Investigators blamed a "too-steep takeoff" for the accident. Andrew's funeral was delayed for five days while authorities searched for Moe.

They found him sailing the Mediterranean aboard a yacht owned by Prince Rainier and Princess Grace of Monaco. By the time Moe finally arrived, ex-wife Toni says, his friends had sent so many wreaths that "the place looked like a flower garden — which I kind of resented because I thought, these people don't even know [Andrew]."

* * *

On February 8, 1973, Frank Fitzsimmons convened an IBT executive meeting in Palm Springs, then adjourned to La Costa. An undercover agent, present at the gathering, reported that Fitzsimmons and his aides were joined by Chicago mafiosi Tony Accardo, Marshall Caifano, Tony Spilotro, and La Costa resident Lou Rosanova. Simultaneously, Nixon aides H.R. Haldeman, John Dean, and John Ehrlichman met at La Costa to discuss the mushrooming Watergate scandal. On February 12 Nixon invited Fitzsimmons to join him aboard Air Force One for a flight to Washington. En route, according to author William Balsamo, Fitzsimmons told Nixon, "You'll never have to worry about where the next dollar will come from. We're going to give you $1 million up front, Mr. President, and there'll be more that'll follow to make sure you are never wanting." Days later, Attorney General Richard Kleindienst cut off various court-authorized FBI wiretaps on Teamster officials.

Nixon hung tough as Congress began impeachment hearings in May 1974, but exposure of the "smoking gun" White House tapes in August prompted his resignation. On September 8, successor Gerald Ford issued a blanket pardon for any and all crimes committed by Nixon since birth.

* * *

While the Nixon administration unraveled, it seemed that the feds had lost interest in Moe Dalitz. Marion Phillips, director of the California Justice Department's Organized Crime Unit, placed Moe on a list of "LCN members" in 1968, but admitted that Moe had not taken the Mafia's "blood oath." An FBI memo from March 1969 advised headquarters that agents in Vegas "will continue to follow and report the activities of the subject," but nothing came of their efforts. In January 1970 the Bureau prepared a "correlation summary" of files on Moe spanning four decades, noting that "this summary is not suitable for dissemination." The first page lists fifty-six alleged pseudonyms with several more blacked out, but some of those included — "Mae Dalitz," "One Dalitz," and so forth — are obvious typographical errors.

More telling than the summary itself is an appended 217-page list of files on Dalitz, each marked with the order "DESTROY." We may only surmise how much data was shredded and burned when the Bureau purged files.

11

Makher

As the FBI lost interest in Moe Dalitz, the rival Drug Enforcement Administration noticed him for the first time. The incident occurred on the Arizona-Mexico border.

Nogales, in Sonora, nearly doubled its population during 1970–74, from 53,000 to 100,000 inhabitants. Sweatshop factories shipped all manner of products across the border, but the main exports were drugs and illegal immigrants. DEA agents were surprised to find Dalitz entering Arizona in 1974, in a large recreational vehicle owned by a couple whose names remain classified.

Moe told the agents he was on vacation with friends, but had been turned back from the Mexican interior for want of a tourist card. One agent told author Michael Wendland, "The whole story stinks. For one thing, Dalitz, is a very, very wealthy man. He doesn't vacation in motor homes. He goes in style, Learjet all the way. For another, he's not stupid. Everyone knows you need a tourist card to go to the interior. And a tourist card is easy as hell to get. So he doesn't have one? All he has to do is ask, and he would get one."

* * *

When Howard Hughes fled Vegas, he left a mess behind. Hughes Tool and its successor, Summa Corporation, posted losses of $79.6 million for 1971–74, topping $100 million in 1975. One casualty was the Desert Inn, languishing from neglect and mismanagement. Summa executives refused to authorize renovations without direct orders from Hughes.

Moe lobbied vigorously for repairs and improvements, fuming when Clark County's Health Department condemned ninety of the DI's rooms in October 1974. Moe threatened litigation but never filed. It remained for Hughes's death to break the deadlock, whereupon Summa announced plans to expand the DI from sixteen acres to 165, at a cost of $54 million. The final vote by Summa's board scaled back that vision to accommodate renovations costing $49,978,000. By 1978 most of the original DI had vanished, replaced by new buildings and supervised by manager Burton Cohen.

* * *

While Dalitz fought to save the DI, Jimmy Hoffa schemed to regain control of the Teamsters Union. He planned to challenge Fitzsimmons for the presidency in 1976, prompting a union official in Washington to tell *Newsweek* magazine, "Fitz has been worried as hell ever since Nixon resigned." The struggle centered on Detroit Local 299, run by Hoffa supporter Dave Johnson. Saboteurs burned Johnson's yacht in 1974, while unidentified thugs beat one of his organizers in a Detroit parking lot. In July 1975, after Fitzsimmons put his son Richard in charge of Local 299, bombers destroyed Richard's car.

Despite that violence and his own ongoing backstage machinations with mafiosi, Hoffa told *Playboy* magazine: "I don't believe there is any organized crime, period. Don't believe it. Never believed it. I've said it for the last 40 years. Hoover said it! Supposed to be the greatest law enforcement man in America, with the means to find out. He said there was no Mafia, no so-called organized crime."

Hoffa left home for the last time at 1:15 P.M. on July 30, 1975, allegedly to meet Detroit mobster Anthony Giacalone and New York mafioso Tony Provenzano at a suburban restaurant, then vanished. Police found his car on July 31. A trucker reported seeing Hoffa leave the restaurant with several men in a Mercury Marquis Brougham later traced to Joe Giacalone (Tony's son), who claimed he loaned the car to Hoffa's foster son, Chuckie O'Brien (son of former Dalitz paramour Sylvia Pagano). DNA testing of hair and blood traces found in Giacalone's car placed Hoffa in the vehicle despite O'Brien's persistent denials, but no charges have been filed.

Ten weeks after Hoffa's disappearance, Frank Fitzsimmons went golfing again at La Costa. His party included Tony Provenzano, Allen Dorfman, Jackie Presser — and Richard Nixon, gracing Moe's resort with his first public appearance since his resignation. Fitzsimmons presented Nixon with a trophy, prompting Nixon to remark, "That's nice. Where's the union bug?"

Despite the laughter all around, Nixon was closer to the truth than he supposed. Jackie Presser had become an FBI informant two years earlier, as part of an arrangement to spare father Bill from prison on fraud charges. A transcript of one conversation between Presser and Cleveland G-man Patrick Foran reveals the depth of FBI's ignorance on organized crime.

> FORAN: Who's the main man in Vegas?
>
> PRESSER: You don't know? You don't know who runs Vegas?
>
> FORAN: Well, we've heard rumors, of course, but none of them have panned out.
>
> PRESSER: You got agents from one end of that town to the other. I'm dealing with a bunch of damn morons. How the hell did I get myself messed up with you clowns?
>
> FORAN: Just answer my question.
>
> PRESSER: I don't know what to say. I guess I better start with the basics. Have you ever heard of an organization called *La Cosa Nostra*?
>
> FORAN: Stop being a smart-ass. Just give me the name of the guy in charge.
>
> PRESSER: The guy's name is Moe Dalitz.
>
> FORAN: Who?
>
> PRESSER: He is the main overseer in Vegas for the various crime families. Everything goes through him if it involves casino operations.... You'd have trouble getting anything on Moe.
>
> FORAN: Oh? Why is that?
>
> PRESSER: 'Cause he owns the sheriff in Vegas. I think the sheriff's name is Lamb or something like that. Yeah, Sheriff Lamb, that's his name. Anyway, Lamb provides Moe with all his protection.
>
> FORAN: But I still don't see the connection between Moe Dalitz and Frank Fitzsimmons.
>
> PRESSER: That's because you were always looking for Hoffa. You guys have been handing out the same line of bullshit for so long, you've begun to believe it yourselves. If you want to keep believing that Hoffa ran the show, that's okay with me.... Why not just stick with [Las Vegas Teamster Local 995 secretary-treasurer] Dick Thomas and his land developments? He's tight with Moe.
>
> FORAN: Dalitz?
>
> PRESSER: Yeah. Don't you see the connection? Christ, I got to do everything, including your thinking for you.

FORAN: Enlighten me.
PRESSER: Thomas was the go-between for Moe and [Kansas City mafioso Nick] Civella. He
        was Civella's bagman before they promoted him.

G-men listened, but nothing suggests that they ever truly understood.

* * *

Jimmy Hoffa's death was not the only Mob-related murder making headlines in 1975. On
June 18, 1975, Sam Giancana admitted an unknown acquaintance to the basement kitchen of
his home. The visitor shot him once from behind with a .22-caliber pistol, then pumped six
more shots into his mouth and throat, symbolically muting a squealer.

John Rosselli dined with Santo Trafficante in Fort Lauderdale on July 16, 1976. Twelve
days later he borrowed his sister's car for an errand and never came home. Rosselli surfaced
on August 7, when fisherman snagged an oil drum weighted with chains in Dumfounding
Bay, near Miami. Inside the drum they found Rosselli's strangled and dismembered corpse.

While no one mourned Rosselli's passing in Las Vegas, other deaths around Miami forced
Moe Dalitz to confront his own mortality. George Angersola died in January 1975, followed in
May by Al Polizzi. The worst loss was Sam Tucker, gone to his reward on June 17, 1978. Sam
Cohen's passing, in December 1980, carried off the last known member of the Purple Gang.

* * *

The March 1975 issue of *Penthouse* featured an article titled "La Costa: The Hundred-Mil-
lion Dollar Resort with Criminal Clientele." Co-authors Jeff Gerth and Lowell Bergman were
virtual unknowns at the time, though Bergman later emerged as one of America's top investigative reporters. Their *Penthouse* story was an unexpected bombshell.

On the surface, there was nothing new or revolutionary in the Bergman-Gerth report.
It cited Moe's background, his transformation to a civic leader in Las Vegas, and his launching of La Costa in the 1960s. As for the resort itself, Bergman and Gerth related well-estab-
lished links to Frank Fitzsimmons and the Teamsters, Richard Nixon and his Watergate
conspirators, Arnholt Smith and John Alessio, Meyer Lansky and Tony Spilotro. "Alliances
between crime and wealth are an American tradition," Gerth and Bergman wrote. "With so
much crime at the top, it is hardly surprising that many people see corruption as our dominant characteristic. The La Costa playground is a power center for the organization and pro-
liferation of that corruption."

In May 1975 Moe filed a libel suit against Bergman and Gerth, *Penthouse*, and publisher
Bob Guccione, seeking $630 million in damages. Co-plaintiffs included Allard Roen, Merv
Adelson, Irwin Molasky, Rancho La Costa Inc., and four associated firms. Attorney Roy Grutman, chief counsel for *Penthouse*, mounted a twofold defense. He declared that Moe, his partners, and their corporations were "public figures" of such notoriety that special standards must
apply to proof of damages from libel, and that *Penthouse*'s exposure of La Costa was protected
under California's Civil Code as a matter of public interest. To support those arguments,
Grutman assembled a collection of thirty books, 3,000 official documents, hundreds of magazine articles, and "mountains" of press clippings. Moe fired back with an affidavit that read:
"I have never had any involvement in organized crime. Mob money did not build La Costa.
There is a certain type of 'reporter' or 'crime writer' that makes a living out of organized crime
fantasies of this sort, created out of rumor and innuendo. To the extent that they have used
my name from time to time to fill a few of the pages of their books, they have created a completely fictional character that has no resemblances to me."

Moe's lawyers offered Gerth and Bergman an easy way out of the lawsuit. Both were dropped as defendants after they produced a letter reading: "We feel it right to acknowledge the positive information we have received about you in recent years and, accordingly, to express regret for any negative implication or unwarranted harm that you believe may have befallen you as a result of the *Penthouse* article."

The opposing sides squared off before Judge Thomas LeSage in L.A., on November 13, 1975. Grutman presented his mass of documentary evidence and evoked a smile from Moe as he told the court, "If these men are not found to be public figures, then reporting on organized crime in this country is dead. 'Dalitz' is a generic term in the world of crime and his face has launched a thousand investigations." Round one went to *Penthouse*, when Judge LeSage ruled that "the evidence is overwhelming that the corporate plaintiff, La Costa, and the individual plaintiffs are public figures, and that the La Costa story is a matter of general or public interest." La Costa lead attorney Louis Nizer appealed and resumed collecting testimonials on behalf of his clients.

The strangest by far was an affidavit submitted by Robert Blakey in February 1976. A former member of Bobby Kennedy's staff and author of federal racketeering legislation in 1970, Blakey gave Moe Dalitz a clean bill of health, while condemning *Penthouse* and its methods. "I have been a fascinated observer of the growth of the unfortunate mythology that has developed around this subject," Blakey said. "I view this present libel suit, therefore, as presenting a unique opportunity for judicial analysis and public instruction in the distinction between myth and fact." Concerning FBI charges that Moe handled much of the Vegas skim, Blakey said, "Dalitz was one point of suspicion, but nothing was, in fact, proved against him in a court of law, and no action has ever been taken against him by the relevant Nevada gambling control authorities."

Sheriff John Duffy of San Diego County joined Blakey in defending Rancho La Costa. His affidavit denied any knowledge of Dalitz, but acknowledged personal acquaintance with plaintiffs Adelson, Molasky, and Roen. La Costa, Duffy said, had been "routinely scrutinized" by sheriff's officers "for many years." They deemed it "luxurious and dignified," run "in a responsible and normal manner." The *San Diego Union* noted that Duffy's surveillance had missed Meyer Lansky's visits to La Costa.

Moe had other problems that winter, including a rumored contract on his life from L.A.'s Mafia. Attorney Ed Becker traced the stories to Jimmy Fratianno, who claimed he was supposed to "do a job" on Moe, but that the contract was rescinded. Vegas reporter John Smith claims G-men visited Moe's Utah ranch and found a pile of cigarette butts near a tree overlooking the house, as if Moe was under surveillance. The mystery remains unsolved, and Fratianno later claimed that Moe contributed $20,000 toward L.A. *capo* Dominic Brooklier's legal defense against racketeering charges in 1978.

Another threat from L.A. involved the Mafia's attempt to extort money from Dalitz in 1977. Details remain vague, but Fratianno claimed that Michael Rizzitello confronted Moe at the Las Vegas Country Club that September, demanding $1 million in cash. "The idea," Rizzitello said, "was for me to grab him and he'd run to Chicago for protection." Similar approaches were made to Sid Korshak, Benny Binion, and Cleveland pornography king Reuben Sturman. None of them paid off, and Rizzitello overreached himself in January 1978, trying to squeeze $7,500 out of undercover G-men posing as porn dealers. Convicted on eleven racketeering counts in November 1980, Rizzitello drew a four-year prison term.

La Costa caught a break in March 1976, when a Supreme Court ruling narrowed guidelines for defining public figures. Judge LeSage revised his November decision on April 5, deciding that only Moe and Allard Roen qualified as public figures under the new rules. Adelson, Molasky, and their five corporations were thus restored as plaintiffs. That decision trimmed La Costa's damage claim to $490 million and left a jury to decide the case.

The *Penthouse* lawsuit revived FBI interest in Moe. In November 1976 Director Clarence Kelley demanded "additional details" on Dalitz, "including subject travel itinerary, if available." An internal memo ranked Moe "second only to Meyer Lansky" as a "representative of hidden interests" in Las Vegas during the 1950s and 1960s, but any new data was blacked out by censors before the files were released a quarter-century later. Today, we have only Kelley's observation of November 19: "In view of the above, no request is being made re. investigation."

Officials in San Diego were unnerved by the *Penthouse* story and subsequent media coverage, prompting Sheriff Duffy to deliver a speech on November 18, 1975, titled "What? Organized Crime in San Diego County?" In May 1976 a grand jury opened hearings with forty-four witnesses. Those questioned included Irv Roston, executive vice president of the La Costa Land Company, but the panel dropped plans to subpoena the four DRAM partners. The panel's verdict: "From the lengthy testimony heard by the Grand Jury, it could only conclude that there was at this time no known influence by organized crime in San Diego County."

Legal maneuvers in La Costa's case dragged on for three more years. Roy Grutman followed Nizer's lead in hiring former G-men to investigate the opposition. One of them, Bill Roehmer, interrogated Meyer Lansky. Lansky admitted visiting La Costa once, to see "a sick friend," then flared: "Listen, I'd rather be counted a pal of Moe Dalitz than that fucking Guccione who peddles slime and pornography to the youth of the country." Both sides were paying through the nose, meanwhile — including $250 per hour from *Penthouse* to Jimmy the Weasel, for his 1,000-page deposition detailing Moe's gangland connections.

In May 1978 Evelle Younger issued an unexpected report from California's Organized Crime Control Commission. Timed to boost Younger's gubernatorial campaign, the report stressed Mafia domination of illegal gambling, loan-sharking, stock fraud, and pornography. Even so, two names stood out from the crowd of ninety Italian felons. The report named Sidney Korshak as "the key link between organized crime and big business," and quoted the Illinois Racing Board's description of Moe Dalitz as "an organized crime figure ... sometimes referred to as one of the architects of the skimming process that developed in Las Vegas in the early 1960's." The document noted Moe's role as director of an unnamed "resort community near San Diego," adding that "[h]e is also involved in a partnership which has invested between $10 to $15 million in San Joaquin Valley wine grape vineyards."

The *Penthouse* case went back to court in October 1979, before Judge George Dell. Dell denied Allard Roen's motion for reinstatement as a plaintiff, then sank La Costa's case — for the moment — with an eight-point ruling which again declared that Adelson, Molasky, and their various firms were indeed public figures.

California's Court of Appeals reversed that ruling in June 1980. The case was remanded for trial, with opening statements scheduled for February 1981. In December 1980 *Penthouse* served a subpoena for any and all FBI records dealing with Dalitz, Roen, Adelson, Molasky, and their several corporations spanning the years 1958–78. Specifically included on the list was a report titled "A History of the Las Vegas Group Behind the Rancho La Costa Operation."

* * *

Reporters were trouble wherever they nosed into Mob affairs, and Phoenix was no exception. The local fly in the underworld's ointment was Don Bolles, with the *Arizona Republic*. In

1965 his probe of bribery and kickbacks in Arizona's Tax and Corporations Commissions earned Bolles a Pulitzer Prize nomination. Two years later Bolles targeted Ned Warren, self-styled "godfather" of Arizona land fraud. Authorities estimate that customers lost $500 million to Warren and his shady salesmen during 1966–76, yet Ned remained at large. In 1969 Bolles focused on the Jacobs brothers and their Emprise network's Mob connections. Four years later, Bolles wrote a series titled "The Newcomers," emulating Hank Messick's "Know Your Neighbor" series with profiles of transplanted mobsters. In January 1976, after Governor Raul Castro named power broker Kemper Marley to a seat on Arizona's Racing Commission, Bolles exposed Marley's longstanding ties to organized crime and forced his resignation.

Bolles drove to the Clarendon Hotel on June 2, 1976, to meet an informant who promised incriminating data on real estate deals involving Barry Goldwater and Harry Rosenzweig. Bolles had identified his source to colleagues as a "sleazy bastard" named John Adamson. When Adamson failed to appear, Bolles returned to his car at 11:35. Before he could leave, a remote-control bomb exploded, severing both of his legs and one arm. The first pedestrians to reach Bolles heard him gasp, "They finally got me ... the Mafia ... Emprise ... Find John Adamson." Bolles died on June 12, and Adamson soon found himself charged with murder.

Trouble began on June 14, when Phoenix district attorney Moise Berger resigned amid complaints that a local "power coalition" blocked aggressive prosecution of felons. Berger told the *New York Times*, "You can't get work done. Cases get thrown out of court and you don't understand why. The lid is on ... all the way to the very top." Successor Donald Harris, expected to serve as a silent caretaker in office until the next election, surprised everyone with his own blast at local corruption, denouncing an alliance of the Mob and old-money elite that produced "decay from within." State attorney general Bruce Babbitt joined the chorus, saying, "Has the lid been on in Arizona? The answer is yes. What I mean is that there has been an atmosphere in the state for some time that anything done by people wearing coats and ties goes."

In October 1976, with jury selection in progress for Adamson's trial, Babbitt's office joined the defense in moving for a mistrial based on adverse publicity. When D.A. Harris objected, Governor Castro removed him and handed the case to Babbitt. Judge Frederic Heineman granted a mistrial, then ironically refused a change of venue. Arizona's supreme court overruled him, ordering that Adamson be tried in Tucson. His trial began at last on January 13, 1977 — and ended the following day, with another bombshell.

In a bid to save himself from execution, Adamson confessed the bombing and named two accomplices — plumber James Robison and Phoenix contractor Max Dunlap, a close associate of Kemper Marley. Marley had loaned Dunlap $1 million, which Dunlap never repaid. According to Adamson, Dunlap hired him to kill Bolles for embarrassing Marley. Adamson, in turn, hired Dunlap to plant and detonate the bomb. Police received corroboration from Neal Roberts, a Phoenix attorney who met with Dunlap on June 4 and arranged his legal defense in exchange for $25,000 from Marley. Roberts received immunity, while officers arrested Robison and Dunlap.

They did not arrest Marley or Barry Goldwater, although detectives investigated five calls made from Goldwater's office to Roberts in days surrounding the bombing. In subsequent court proceedings, witness Howard Woodall testified that James Robison told him Bolles was killed for uncovering proof of fraudulent loans involving Marley, Harry Rosenzweig, and the Goldwater brothers — but again, the investigation went nowhere.

If the Bolles murder was meant to silence media investigation of the Mob in Arizona, it failed monumentally. Almost before the smoke cleared, members of a nonprofit group called

Investigative Reporters and Editors swarmed over the state. The resultant series of articles, syndicated nationwide in March and April 1977, left no stone unturned. Successive reports linked the Goldwaters to mobsters including Moe Dalitz, Gus Greenbaum, Willie Bioff, and Clarence Newman; described the late Del Webb as "a business partner of organized crime figures for three decades"; and described how Rosenzweig had "nurtured prostitution and gambling in Phoenix for years, after establishing ties with mob-connected bookmakers and syndicate hoodlums who midwifed the birth of Las Vegas." Other targets included federal judge Walter Craig (described as the Mob's "friend at court") and restaurateur Herbert Applegate (who partnered with Pete Licavoli and Robert Goldwater, diverting $1.5 million from his Hobo Joe's chain to Licavoli's pocket and setting up a Phoenix "love nest" staffed with former *Playboy* bunnies).

Despite the heat surrounding Bolles's death, the only mobster seriously inconvenienced was Pete Licavoli in Tucson. The trouble arose from Licavoli's Vesuvio Art Gallery, co-owned with wife Grace, where Pete displayed a portrait painted by sixteenth-century Italian artist Dominia Pulige. An undercover G-man saw the painting, recognized it as an item stolen during an Ohio burglary, and offered Licavoli a $500 down payment. When Pete accepted, he was slapped with charges of receiving stolen property, convicted in December 1976, and sentenced to eighteen months in prison on February 5, 1977. Appeals proved fruitless and he wound up serving thirteen months.

Kemper Marley sued the IRE for libel in 1981, calling Barry Goldwater and Governor Babbitt as character witnesses. Jurors rejected Marley's seven-figure bid for damage to his reputation, but awarded him $15,000 for "emotional distress."

Meanwhile, Max Dunlap and James Robison faced trial in July 1977, naming Neal Roberts as the plot's mastermind, but John Adamson's testimony persuaded jurors to convict them, resulting in death sentences for both defendants. Arizona's supreme court reversed both convictions in February 1980, finding that defense attorneys should have been allowed to question Adamson more forcefully. At Dunlap's bail hearing, in April 1980, Adamson pled the Fifth Amendment 167 times in response to defense allegations of perjury during court proceedings in 1976–77. Judge Robert Myers granted Dunlap's plea for bail over Attorney General Bob Corbin's fierce objections, whereupon Corbin "temporarily dismissed" all charges against Dunlap and Robison. In June 1980 Corbin filed new murder charges against Adamson. Arizona's supreme court ruled that Adamson's refusal to testify violated his 1977 plea bargain, thus voiding both his negotiated twenty-year prison term and any defense against double jeopardy.

Adamson faced trial in October 1980. Jurors convicted and condemned him. Max Dunlap sued Phoenix for $605 million in July 1983, prompting detectives to purge their files before a mistrial was declared in 1987. A federal appellate court overturned Adamson's death sentence in December 1988, ruling that Arizona's capital punishment statute was unconstitutional. Attorney General Corbin filed new murder charges against Robison in November 1989, followed by a fresh indictment of Dunlap in December 1990. Jurors convicted Dunlap of murder and conspiracy in April 1993, imposing a life sentence. Another panel acquitted Robison in December 1993. John Adamson left prison for the federal Witness Protection Program in August 1996. James Robison won parole in 1998, at age seventy-six. Max Dunlap remained behind bars as this book went to press.

An angle of inquiry neglected by police was raised in Adamson's 1977 confession. After the bombing, Adamson said Max Dunlap told him "that the people in San Diego would be glad to hear that Don Bolles was not coming over there because he was supposed to go over there to investigate a bank." Coworkers at the *Arizona Republic* knew nothing of any Bolles interest in San Diego — where Arnholt Smith's bank had recently collapsed — but another lead surfaced in 1993, when Neal Roberts testified at James Robison's second murder trial. In that proceeding, defense attorney Tom Henze asked Roberts whether he had visited La Costa in 1980 and while there bragged of planning Bolles's murder. "As multifarious as that question is," Roberts replied, "I deny all of it." Henze then asked, "Do you deny making a statement about your part in the murder?" Assistant attorney general Warren Granville interrupted, demanding a sidebar conference with Judge Norman Hall, who disallowed the question. Finally, Henze asked Roberts, "It was you, wasn't it, who actually introduced Adamson to Dunlap? And wasn't it you who told Adamson to sit on Dunlap's porch until he got paid for the bombing?" To which Roberts replied, "I can't recall. I'm afraid I don't remember. After all, it's been 17 years."

* * *

The Mob views politics as enterprise for profit, promoting its friends where feasible, donating to both sides in any major race as a matter of course. Ex-Texas governor John Connally, acquitted on bribery charges in 1975, announced his presidential candidacy in January 1979. Over the next twelve months he raised more campaign cash than any other candidate but found one of his donors an embarrassment. When reporters asked about a $1,000 donation from Moe Dalitz, Connally denied any knowledge of the contribution but declared that, if it had been made, "We'll refund the money." It was in fact returned, as a campaign aide told the press, "for reasons I'm sure can be understood." In the end, it did not matter. After losing the South Carolina primary in January 1980, Connally quit the race and endorsed rival Ronald Reagan.

Reagan began his political life as a New Deal Democrat, but switched to the GOP in the mid–1950s, when Robert Kennedy extended the McClellan Committee's crime investigation to include Lew Wasserman's Music Corporation of America. Eight years as California's governor secured Reagan's reputation as a darling of the far-right, enamored of sweeping tax breaks for his millionaire corporate donors. Best friend Paul Laxalt launched the Reagan for President Committee in March 1979 and served as Reagan's campaign manager.

Returning to the source that had served Republican hopefuls since 1960, Reagan addressed Jackie Presser's Ohio Conference of Teamsters in August 1980. Before that speech, the candidate spent forty-five minutes alone with Presser and IBT Central Conference director Roy Williams. One day prior to meeting with Reagan, Williams had appeared before a U.S. Senate committee investigating Mob infiltration of unions, where he pled the Fifth Amendment twenty-three times in response to questions about his association with mobsters including Carlos Marcello. One week before the Reagan-Presser-Williams meeting, Jimmy Fratianno told a federal grand jury in L.A. that Presser had admitted taking orders from Cleveland mafioso James Licavoli.

None of that fazed Reagan in his quest for cash. Jackie Presser's uncle, Allen Friedman, claimed that he delivered a suitcase filled with money to Edwin Meese III — a Reagan campaign aide and future U.S. Attorney General — on Presser's orders in 1980. Reagan, unaware of Presser's double life as an FBI informant, promptly named Jackie — an eighth-grade dropout under active federal investigation for fraud — as a "senior economic advisor" to his Washington transition team.

Paul Laxalt seemed content with his role as what *Forbes* magazine called Reagan's "trusted link to the outside world, including at times the world of business." Granted, the Ormsby

President Ronald Regan (seated) with "first friend" Paul Laxalt (Library of Congress).

House in Carson City had been nearly bankrupt when he sold it in 1976, but he still made a profit. Moe Dalitz contributed the legal maximum of $2,000 to Laxalt's Senate campaigns, as did Allen Glick, Lefty Rosenthal, Benny Binion, Morris Shenker, former Bugsy Siegel partner Sydney Wyman, and their myriad corporations. And unlike John Connally, Laxalt had no qualms about such donations. He told reporters, "A politician taking campaign money from gamblers in Nevada is like one taking campaign money from the auto people in Michigan." Moe's personal donations were "relatively small," Laxalt said, but they were gratefully accepted. "All the years I've been in Nevada politics," Laxalt explained, "he's been very honorable with me. We never had a social or business relationship. He has not asked me for the time of day." Laxalt was more emphatic with the *New York Times Magazine*, saying, "Moe Dalitz is a friend of mine. I'm not going to say to him now, 'Get lost, you're too hot.' I don't play it that way." This from the man whom the *Times* expected to "have a key role in Reagan's Washington," described by campaign aides as Reagan's "closest friend and most trusted advisor."

Reagan beat incumbent Jimmy Carter by 8.4 million votes on November 4, 1980. His first selection for a cabinet post was lawyer William French Smith as Attorney General. His legal skills aside, Smith also had connections where it counted. During the 1980 campaign L.A. Bistro owner Kurt Niklas saw Smith sharing a booth with Meyer Lansky. A month after Reagan's election, Smith joined Mob lawyer Sidney Korshak as a guest at Frank Sinatra's sixty-fifth birthday party.

* * *

Irwin Molasky once said that Moe Dalitz "tried to be low-profile, believe it or not," and while that was true in politics, Moe enjoyed his celebrity status in Las Vegas. He had worked long and hard to become a *makher*—a "big shot," in Hebrew—and he relished every moment of it.

Nineteen seventy-six was a banner year for Moe, beginning with daughter Suzanne's marriage to Blair Monteith on June 30 and continuing through November, with the American Cancer Research Center's announcement that Moe would be honored with its annual Humanitarian Award. Moe received the prize on December 15, at the MGM Grand, with proceeds from the gala used to establish the Moe B. Dalitz Fellowship Fund for Cancer Research. Nine days later, Moe celebrated his seventy-seventh birthday in grand style. Bob Hope turned out, describing Moe as "one of my dear friends," while comedian Danny Thomas told reporters, "I think his contribution to Las Vegas is incalculable."

Cancer research was only one of fifty-seven worthy causes favored with Dalitz donations during 1976. Most went unnamed, but Moe's association with the United Way of Southern Nevada was well publicized. On one occasion, when the charity's fundraising drive fell short of its goal, Moe turned up with an eleventh-hour bag of cash to put it over the top. In November 1979 he created the Moe Dalitz Charitable Remainder Unitrust, donating $1 million worth of securities to be divided at his death, with 50 percent to the United Way and 50 percent spread among fourteen other charities. Garth Winkler, executive director of the UWSN, told reporters that "The foundation is the trustee for the contribution and we have invested it. For the rest of his life, we will pay Dalitz 8 percent interest on the gift each year. This is a painless way to give money. Dalitz will get a substantial deduction off his income tax. The gift came from his estate, so he will probably miss paying an estate tax. And by giving the $1 million in securities, he skipped paying the capital gains tax."

Always thinking.

Dalitz campaigned against various diseases in his later years (Las Vegas Historical Society).

Moe Dalitz (holding monkey) at his 80th birthday party (UNLV North Las Vegas Library Collection).

In another venue, Moe's donations to the University of Nevada–Las Vegas won him recognition as a "Grand Patron of the Arts." In 1978 Paradise Developments applied to purchase 118 acres of land from UN-Reno. One of the university's regents, Chris Karamanos, revealed that he rented a restaurant from Irwin Molasky, suggesting a possible conflict of interest. UNR attorney Larry Leslie read aloud the relevant statute — barring public officers from having any interest in or benefit from public contracts — and told Karamanos to "draw his own conclusion." Deciding that the deal would cause no breach of ethics, Karamanos joined James Buchanan in support of the sale, while Dr. Louis Lombardi opposed it and Molly Knudtsen abstained. Afterward, Knudtsen asked if Moe Dalitz was a partner in Paradise Developments, to which Karamanos replied, "I believe he is."

Win or lose on land deals, Dalitz remained a local luminary, often referred to as "Mr. Las Vegas" or — invariably with a cautious smile and chuckle — as "the Godfather of Las Vegas." A lead editorial in the *Review-Journal*, published on November 21, 1979, hailed Moe as "an asset to Nevada." One month later, his eightieth birthday bash at Caesars Palace drew 600 guests, including state senator Floyd Lamb and comedian Shecky Greene. On March 24, 1980, Vegas mayor Bill Briare gave Moe a "Trendsetter" award. As Briare explained, "Because of Mr. Dalitz's foresight, Las Vegas has become the home of lavish spectacular shows." By then, even keen-eyed reporter John Smith admitted that Moe's "contributions to the growth of Las Vegas are priceless."

Or was it all too much of a good thing? After the fact, a Vegas pit boss who had once served Dalitz in Kentucky told Sally Denton and Roger Morris, "Moe started believing he really was Man of the Year like they kept callin' him. He forgot he was just a bootlegger and a killer."

Concerning the religion of his ancestors, Dalitz was generous but undemonstrative. Leo Wilner, executive director of Temple Beth Shalom in Vegas during 1966–84, said that Moe paid his fees on time but "wasn't one to come around the temple often." According to Wilner, Moe left Temple Beth Shalom in 1976 to join the Congregation Ner Tamid, a reform synagogue created the previous year.

Records from the Department of Commerce indicate that the last Dalitz laundry — U.S. Industrial Glove in Detroit — dissolved in May 1977. It should not be supposed, however, that Moe severed any ties to Motown or to Cleveland. Friends from both cities maintained their interests in Las Vegas and in Moe's well-being. On the local scene, Al Benedict still reigned as president of the MGM Grand, a post so influential that Governor Mike O'Callaghan named Benedict to serve on Nevada's state gaming policy committee in June 1977. Two years later, when Benedict stepped down as president at the MGM, Bernie Rothkopf moved in to fill the void.

* * *

More of Moe's friends were involved with Allen Glick's Argent casinos. Stardust president Al Sachs promoted Herb Tobman to executive vice president in October 1974, then resigned two months later, succeeded by Tobman. Tobman named Milton Jaffe vice president in May 1975, as Burton Brown left his job as president of Paradise Developments to become an Argent vice president. Glick promoted Lefty Rosenthal to president of Argent's executive committee in June 1975, Phil Ponto rose to direct all of Argent's casinos, Yale Cohen became the Stardust's new executive vice president, and Bobby Stella filled that post at the Fremont. Burton Brown became the Stardust's president in August 1975, as "informed sources" told the *Sun* that Tobman was leaving to pursue unknown ventures. In fact, it was simply the time-honored game of musical chairs.

Behind the scenes, Glick's empire was in turmoil. In March 1975 mafioso Nick Civella summoned Glick to Kansas City and informed him that he owed Civella's family $1.2 million for greasing the wheels on Argent's Teamster loans. Glick left K.C. with orders to "repay" the money and give Lefty Rosenthal a free hand in managing Argent's casinos, but Lefty's efforts to obtain a gaming license proved fruitless. Rosenthal appealed the denial of his application and won a fleeting victory before Judge Joseph Pavlikowski — until reporters learned that Stardust executives had thrown a free wedding reception for Pavlikowski's daughter in February 1974. Pavlikowski explained that the favor was granted by "previous management," but that carried no weight since Lefty had been on the Stardust's staff before Argent moved in. Final rejection of his license application left Rosenthal posing as the Stardust's entertainment director, but he continued to run all three Argent casinos.

In May 1976 a frightened Argent employee told GCB agents that the Stardust had an "auxiliary bank" whose contents were not tallied for taxation. Raiders served a search warrant on May 18 and seized $10,000. That same night, George Vandermark — hired by Glick as a "construction consultant" in November 1974, then placed in charge of slots by Rosenthal — fled to Mexico. Agents traced Vandermark to Mazatlan and lured him home with a promise of immunity from prosecution, but then his son was murdered and Vandermark fled once again. He has not been seen since, and G-men now presume him dead.

If anyone believed the problem had been solved, they were mistaken.

June 1976 brought more trouble at the Stardust. GCB investigators now believed that slot-skimming went far beyond theft of spare change, to include manipulation of the scales that weighed masses of coins each day. A statement published on June 12 suggested losses of $3 million to $7 million on Argent's watch, later inflated to $12 million. In July, Burton Brown and three other Argent executives resigned in what the *Sun* called a "major shakeup." Six weeks later the U.S. attorney's office announced a grand jury investigation of Stardust skimming.

In February 1977 Al Sachs resurfaced as president of two casinos, the Sundance and the Aladdin — already under FBI investigation for hidden ownership by members of Joe Zerilli's Mafia family. State authorities revoked the Aladdin's gaming license in June 1978 but allowed the casino to stay open pending sale to new owners. In December the GCB rejected a bid from Del Coleman and Ed Torres, then approved a $105 million offer from the National Kinney Corporation. Kinney withdrew its bid in February 1979, citing conditions imposed by the Teamsters Union as holders of the Aladdin's mortgage.

While Sachs left the Aladdin without any charges filed against him, Herb Tobman found himself named as a defendant in a federal lawsuit against the Southern Nevada Culinary and Bartenders Pension Fund, which he served as a trustee. Specifically, the feds accused Tobman and company of making "questionable" loans to various firms owned by lawyer Morris Shenker, whose longstanding Teamsters-Mob ties were a matter of record. Tobman denied any impropriety, and that case blew over, leaving Tobman free to wheel and deal on higher levels in the years ahead.

Meanwhile, the Stardust skimming probe continued. In January 1978 Glick and Rosenthal received subpoenas demanding all Stardust employee tip records for 1974–77. That same month, a grand jury indicted two Fremont employees for embezzling $50,000 in a past-posting scam (illegally accepting bets after a race has started, when information about its outcome may be available). Two months later, the GCB slapped Argent with an order commanding Glick to show cause why his license should not be revoked. Nick Civella next offered to let Glick out of their deal with his life plus $10 million. G-men heard mobsters discussing the buy-out on a tapped phone line, then launched sweeping raids to seize more evidence. The GCB revoked Glick's license and threatened a $12 million fine, soon whittled to $500,000. Beset from all sides, Glick surrendered on September 21, announcing that Argent would sell its three casinos to Tropicana landlords Ed and Fred Doumani.

Governor Robert List was caught in fallout from the Argent case. Elected after serving eight years as state attorney general, List had returned a $15,000 campaign contribution from Argent and another $10,000 from the Aladdin during his 1978 campaign, while Democratic rival Bob Rose insisted that the $25,000 he got from Argent had "no strings attached." List was barely in office when he accused *Valley Times* publisher Bob Brown of attempted blackmail, claiming Brown had offered to withhold damaging stories about List if List, in turn, would support Lefty Rosenthal's bid for a gaming license at the Stardust. List refused and Lefty never got his license, but Brown helped Rosenthal skim $200,000 through advertising kickbacks from his newspaper. Brown pled guilty to criminal charges in 1983 and testified against others, before a heart attack killed him in June 1984.

In May 1979 Al Sachs announced his application for a gaming license, prior to assuming control of the Stardust and Fremont with his A.D.S. Management Corporation (co-owned by Herb Tobman). One month later, an FBI report declared that the Fremont, Stardust, Dunes and Tropicana were all Mob-controlled "to some degree." In July, Sachs and Tobman merged the Sundance with A.D.S. Management. Nine days later they created a new firm, Trans-Sterling, to manage the Fremont and Stardust. The Gaming Commission launched an investigation of Trans-Sterling's owners in August 1979. GCB chairman Roger Trounday worried about the Sundance, built on land owned by Dalitz and paying him monthly rent, but Sachs saw no problem. "I think he's a nice man and has done a lot for me," Sachs told reporters. "I think he's a friend but we have no special relationship." Jimmy Fratianno briefed state agents on Sachs's Mob connections, but commission chairman Harry Reid dismissed that information, claiming that investigators "went to the FBI and nothing could be confirmed." The Gaming Commission approved Sachs's license on November 15, incorporating "several conditions" to monitor his relationship with Dalitz.

Clark County launched a parallel probe of Sachs in October 1979, considering his fitness for a liquor license. Such investigations normally required three months, but officials imposed a November deadline. The investigation was still incomplete when the licensing board mustered a unanimous vote of approval. Sachs and Tobman assumed control of the Stardust and Fremont on December 5, 1979. Allen Glick made $66 million on the sale, financed through Valley Bank. One week later, the *Wall Street Journal* named Sachs as the target of a federal probe into Mob infiltration of Vegas casinos.

* * *

That probe, predictably, focused on Mafia or "LCN" control. J. Edgar Hoover's death had not cured the FBI's ethnic blind spot where organized crime was concerned, leaving agents convinced that a handful of Italians ran all rackets nationwide. Even members of the Mafia began to think so, seduced by what *Time* magazine called "*The Godfather* syndrome." Michael Rizzitello's futile bid to squeeze $1 million from Moe Dalitz was a case in point, but others failed to learn from his example.

Tony Spilotro threw his weight around in Vegas, sampling the local skim and pulling burglaries, traipsing in and out of court often enough to keep his name in headlines. Frank Rosenthal told author Nicholas Pileggi that "[a]ll Nevada — Moe Dalitz, my own wife, for God's sake — all thought Tony [Spilotro] was the boss of Las Vegas. But the truth is, he wasn't." Clearly, Dalitz *did not* share that delusion when he blocked Spilotro's application to join the Las Vegas Country Club in August 1976 and ordered employees to stop paging Spilotro on the premises. Spilotro heard the wake-up call and smoothed things over by purchasing a $67,000 apartment at Moe's Regency Towers, where Dalitz, Irwin Molasky, Hank Greenspun and other Vegas luminaries resided. Thereafter, reporter John Smith maintains, Spilotro and Dalitz were "quite at ease with each other."

Whatever Spilotro might think of himself, the real power in Vegas remained in Moe's hands. A federal report from 1977 declared that "Spilotro has become the most powerful man in Las Vegas, next to Moe Dalitz," while Lefty Rosenthal himself admitted that "Moe Dalitz had the first count for the Midwest and Cleveland. And the bosses back home, the guys who were in the Nevada Black Book, had to stay home and take the word of their front men on the count." An FBI memo from 1978 confirmed that view, stating: "The individual who oversees the operations for the LCN families in Las Vegas is Moe Dalitz. Dalitz makes certain that there is no cheating with regard to the skim money taken out of the casinos and further, that there is no fighting among families for control of various casinos."

Despite his power and celebrity, however, Moe faced opposition from state gaming authorities in the late 1970s. The first problem arose in November 1978, when the GCB debated a license application from Cecil Simmons, desirous of purchasing the Old Vegas casino. Simmons had borrowed $30,000 from Dalitz in 1975, and the board was concerned about ongoing ties. Simmons's lawyer referred to Moe's prior licensing and his many civic honors, but GCB member. Jeff Silver replied, "When a person who would be on a post office wall in other communities is honored by high officials, it is a sorry, sorry case for society. This is a sickness in our society today. We pay homage to power and money." Chairman Roger Trounday urged public officials to "look behind" the awards heaped on persons with "that kind of reputation."

Ten months later, Moe hit another roadblock with the Sundance. Sachs and Tobman owned the casino, but Dalitz owned the land beneath it, purchased by his Three-O-One Corporation in the 1950s. That link caused problems for Trans-Sterling's bid to buy the Stardust and Fremont. In September 1979 chief GCB investigator Bob McGuire said of Dalitz, "I don't see how we can license him. On the one hand, he is 'Mr. Nevada,' and you probably can't find anything he's done wrong in fifteen years. On the other hand, he has a history of organized crime links." Ten days later, Moe and attorney Devoe Heaton asked Nevada's Public Employees Retirement System for a $27 million loan to demolish and rebuild the Sundance, creating downtown's tallest building. Upon completion, Moe would lease the Sundance to Trans-Sterling. Gaming Commission chairman Harry Reid opined that Moe might not require a license to collect rent from the new Sundance, if he had no part in its daily operation.

Prominent Las Vegans celebrate the opening of the Sundance casino. Left to right: Mayor Bill Briare, Moe Dalitz, Al Sachs, Councilman (later mayor) Ron Lurie, and Herb Tobman (Las Vegas Historical Society).

Two months after Moe filed his PERS loan application, Roger Trounday told the *Review-Journal*, "I have some concerns about Moe Dalitz's involvement in gaming. Somewhere down the road I'm going to take a hard look at those [Sundance] financial transactions and agreements." On June 17, 1980—two weeks before the Sundance's grand opening—the GCB convened a special meeting and recommended a "landlord suitability probe" on Dalitz. Harry Reid found Trans-Sterling's lease "well within the letter of the law," but questioned Moe's guarantee of $5 million for casino operating expenses. Reid told reporters that he would have opposed any license application including Moe's name, except for his (Reid's) personal friendship with Herb Tobman. Sachs and Tobman received unanimous approval on June 19, while Reid hedged on Dalitz. "He is so intertwined in this operation," Reid said, "if it wasn't for him, this place wouldn't exist." Reid could not "put a finger on what's wrong," but said, "I have some real concerns ... until the investigation is completed."

Moe spared Reid the headache by withdrawing his license application, although he remained as landlord of the Sundance. The new casino opened on July 2, with Al Sachs proclaiming "another growth cycle downtown." President Don Pulliam ran the resort for Trans-Sterling, while Gil Cohen—son of longtime Dalitz employee Yale Cohen—left his post as Stardust hotel manager to fill an identical slot at the Sundance.

* * *

Dalitz owed his latest embarrassment in equal parts to *Penthouse* magazine, Evelle Younger's California crime report of May 1978, and the FBI. The 1975 *Penthouse* article and Moe's resultant libel suit had resurrected stories of his Mob involvement from the 1920s to the birth of modern Las Vegas, with echoes audible from the Strip to Carson City. Jimmy Fratianno told Ovid Demaris that Moe built the Sundance "on orders from Chicago," and most G-men agreed. A report from September 1979 cautioned that sale of the Stardust and Fremont to Trans-Sterling would make Paradise Developments "one of the largest casino operators in Nevada." Twelve days later, another memo announced an investigation of Dalitz and Paradise for suspected wire fraud, linked to the collapse of Arnholt Smith's bank, but no charges resulted.

The main Bureau thorn in Moe's side was Joseph Yablonsky, new agent-in-charge of Vegas. Known as "The King of Sting" for his crafty moves against mobsters, Yablonsky was four years away from retirement when director William Webster chose him to lead the Las Vegas field office. Harry Claiborne—longtime attorney for crooked cops and gamblers—was the newest federal judge in town, appointed in 1978. The following year, Claiborne ironically accused Vegas G-men of prosecuting only "little fish" in racketeering cases, then called members of the Justice Department's Organized Crime Strike Force "rotten bastards" and "a bunch of crooks." Hank Greenspun cheered him on, while mobsters from the Strip to Glitter Gulch sat back and laughed.

Yablonsky hit town in January 1980, quickly perusing FBI files that suggested wholesale skimming from at least five major casinos. He established a hotline for tipsters, then followed with "Operation Yobo," a sting operation targeting corrupt officials. Five grafters took the bait, including state senators Floyd Lamb and Eugene Echols, two Clark County commissioners, and a Reno city councilman. All five were convicted, while Yablonsky negotiated with fugitive pimp Joe Conforte to testify against Judge Claiborne. On another front, Yablonsky lectured civic groups on the subversive impact of corruption. In one such speech, he estimated the casino skim at $170 billion, saying, "So long as Las Vegas's vaults are filled with ready cash the city will be a magnet for gangsters and weak politicians."

Such public declarations, backed by prosecutions, won Yablonsky no friends in Las Vegas. Hank Greenspun led the attack, branding Yablonsky "an enemy of the *Sun*" who "came to Las Vegas with a preconceived notion that everyone in Nevada is evil." When Yablonsky lunched with a friend at the Riviera coffee shop one afternoon, he saw Dalitz, Tobman, Morris Kleinman, and Alvin Baron (assets manager of the Teamsters pension fund) seated in a nearby booth. Spotting Yablonsky, Tobman rose and "swaggered over" to his table, where he "hissed" at Yablonsky's companion, "I guess you don't mind who you're seen with." Yablonsky recalled that Tobman "had a lot of chutzpah. Dalitz and his friends were used to having their way in town."

Nor was their influence restricted to casinos. On arrival in Vegas, Yablonsky had joined the director's board of Temple Beth Shalom, where Tobman was also a member. Despite that initial acceptance, Yablonsky and his wife soon found themselves ostracized at the synagogue. "The Jews treated me worse than anyone else," he later said. "I was in a subculture that was totally different from anything I had ever experienced. In a community that worships the almighty buck, where Moe Dalitz was a patron saint, there's a strange assimilation that takes place and your values get distorted — or else." Tobman was probably responsible for most of that reaction at the temple, and reporters who claim that Moe Dalitz left Temple Beth Shalom to get away from Joe Yablonsky are mistaken. Former synagogue director Leo Wilner says Moe left Beth Shalom in 1976. His move to Congregation Ner Tamid, therefore, occurred four years *before* Yablonsky settled in Las Vegas.

Yablonsky responded to the snubs and smears with an investigation of Trans-Sterling's casinos. Paul Laxalt voiced his first protest to the *Miami Herald*, complaining that Nevada had "far more bureau agents than we need" and that they trampled "on people's private rights." Yablonsky heard the squeal and guessed its source. Years afterward, a Vegas casino boss told Sally Denton and Roger Morris that Dalitz and his friends were "turning on the Washington juice like never before." Yablonsky branded Laxalt a sellout who was "in the pocket" of organized crime throughout his political career. "Particularly with Dalitz," the G-man added, "who he's never forsaken, according to remarks he's made. In fact, I think it was a *Los Angeles Times* reporter, when he was exploring [Laxalt's pursuit of] the Presidency, [who] asked, 'Would you invite Moe Dalitz to lunch at the White House?' and he said 'Yes.'"

In fact, Moe did not have to wait. By January 1981 he had a friend-of-a-friend in the Oval Office.

12

Twilight

When Ronald Reagan took office as president on January 20, 1981, Moe Dalitz had eight years, seven months, and eleven days to live. Moe did not know it at the time, but everyone around him realized his health was failing. Trouble with his sole remaining kidney caused high blood pressure, and cancer had begun to germinate inside him, still unrecognized. At eighty-one, he must have felt the precious hours slipping through his hands, but there was still more work to do.

* * *

Reagan's romancing of the Mob did not go unobserved. Journalist Ryan Emerson told readers of his *Organized Crime Review:* "About six months before the presidential election I received word that certain individuals within the Reagan camp were negotiating with key people in Las Vegas, Nevada, who were involved in the casino industry, the Teamsters Union, and organized crime. The basis for the discussions was the acute desire of the Teamsters Union to obtain relief from the aggressive probes by the United States Department of Justice organized crime strike forces and the Federal Bureau of Investigation. There was also a continuing grave concern about the FBI's productive court-ordered wiretaps that had revealed hidden interests in many Las Vegas hotels and casinos by some of the country's most powerful organized crime figures."

Reagan's early appointments signaled his intent with respect to organized crime. William French Smith became Attorney General and in May 1981 introduced new regulations curbing public access to government documents under the 1966 Freedom of Information Act, while Associate Attorney General Rudolph Giuliani scuttled corporate criminal cases filed by the feds under Jimmy Carter.

Next to Justice, mobsters were most concerned with Reagan's Department of Labor. Ray Donovan won confirmation to head that department in February 1981, with Senator Orrin Hatch describing Donovan's nomination as "one of the most rigorously scrutinized in our country's history." Donovan quickly slashed his department's staff and budget, reducing labor-racketeering prosecutions by 30 percent, while simultaneously cutting back enforcement of the Occupational Safety and Health Act against big-money employers nationwide. Senator Hatch seemed startled when news of Donovan's Mob ties surfaced in December 1981, prompting Hatch to call Donovan's "policy of inaction and ineptitude" a "travesty." In September 1982 special prosecutor Leon Silverman declared the allegations against Donovan — including murder of two witnesses in a New Jersey racketeering case — "disturbing" but found

Jackie Presser (right) shakes hands with Secretary of Labor Ray Donovan. The man in the center is unidentified (National Archives).

"insufficient evidence" to prosecute. Donovan resigned in March 1985 and was subsequently indicted with six others for conspiring to defraud New York City's Transit Authority of $7.4 million. During the trial, which ended with acquittal of all defendants in May 1987, President Reagan described Donovan as "a man of great integrity."

Two years before Donovan left Labor, Reagan found room for another crony in the department. Roy Brewer met Reagan in Hollywood during the 1940s, when Brewer's IATSE

Ronald Reagan and George H.W. Bush maintained Teamster support in their 1984 re-election campaign (Library of Congress).

was engaged in a struggle with the AFL's Conference of Studio Unions. The AFL-CSU appealed to Reagan and SAG for support against Brewer's thugs, but Reagan declined to help and Brewer's brawlers crushed their opponents. A proud "close friend" of Reagan through the years, in 1983 Brewer found himself appointed to lead the Federal Service Impasses Panel, created to resolve disputes between the U.S. government and unions representing federal employees. Jackie Presser's uncle, Allen Friedman, summarized the changing atmosphere in Washington when he remarked that Teamsters "didn't dominate [President Carter's] White House labor policy as we had under Nixon and as we were about to under Ronald Reagan."

* * *

Two weeks before Reagan's inauguration, Nevada's Gaming Control Board announced the exposure of credit scams at the Desert Inn and Sahara casinos, ostensibly masterminded by East Coast bookie Anthony Caputo. According to the state, Caputo and other high-rollers had been granted extensive credit, gambled with house money, then left the resorts without paying their debts. The DI acknowledged losing $684,500, while GCB agents placed total losses for the two casinos closer to $1.5 million. In February 1981 the GCB recommended fines of $75,000 for the DI and $37,500 for the Sahara. DI executives stalled payment with appeals, compelling GCB chairman James Avance to say that he was "not for sale," despite attending a March 1984 world-premiere show with Summa executives at the DI.

The most shocking event in living memory, for most Las Vegans, occurred in November 1980, when fire swept through the MGM Grand, killing eighty-five people and injuring more than 700. Investigators discovered eighty-three separate building code violations, and a local judge chose private attorney Lou Wiener as a "special prosecutor" to investigate rumors of criminal negligence, but Wiener died in 1996 without submitting a report. Meanwhile, the MGM reopened in July 1981, with Al Benedict as chairman of the board, assisted by director Bernie Rothkopf.

Moe Dalitz made unexpected and unwelcome headlines in 1981, when *Forbes* magazine inaugurated yearly lists of the 400 richest Americans. *Forbes* set the bar at $100 million, without regard to the source of an individual's wealth. Research consumed a year and climaxed in August 1982, with advance copies of the magazine's September 13th issue. The final list included corporate CEOs, celebrities (Bob Hope and Yoko Ono), a mental-ward resident (H. L. Hunt III), two fugitives from justice (swindlers Marc Rich and Robert Vesco)—and two "alleged" mobsters. *Forbes* estimated Moe Dalitz's net worth at $110 million, while Meyer Lansky trailed slightly with $100 million and a note that the true tally "may be far higher."

A suggestion of Moe's wealth in Vegas may be derived from Nevada's tax assessment rolls, published annually. The rolls for 1980–81 reveal that Moe owned land and buildings valued at $783,220. Two of his partnerships, Paradise Homes and Realty Holdings, held property valued at $1,262,385 and $5,817,070, respectively. In 1983–84 the rolls listed property worth $1,086,498 held by Dalitz personally, while Paradise weighed in with $1,705,770 and Realty Holdings claimed property worth $6,742,730. All that without the income generated by La Costa, Lorimar, Moe's monthly rent from the Sundance, his stock portfolio and California vineyards, interest on his bank accounts—or any sources unreported to the government.

Moe knew that he had to spend money to make money, and political donations were as critical as any other business investment. Nevada politics had grown increasingly expensive by the 1980s, with candidates demanding more and more cash from casino coffers. State attorney general Richard Bryan received fewer contributions than Governor Robert List in 1982, yet he somehow spent $1.27 million *more* than List and beat the incumbent governor by 28,000 votes. In Vegas that year, John Moran spent twice as much as rival John McCarthy to retain the sheriff's office. Mob informant Frank Cullotta claimed that Tony Spilotro gave Moran $40,000 in return for a promise of immunity; Moran denied it. In most Nevada races, Dalitz publicly contributed the maximum $1,000 permitted by law. Similar donations flowed from Herb Tobman, Bobby Stella, and Stardust casino manager Louis Salerno, among oth-

Moe Dalitz (center) with protégés Herb Tobman (left) and Al Sachs, targets of the Trans-Sterling skim investigation (Las Vegas Historical Society).

ers. Grateful recipients in 1981–82 included Senator Howard Cannon and Nevada's two congressmen, Harry Reid and James Santini.

* * *

No one owed more to Dalitz than Paul Laxalt, and no one in public office worked harder to repay those favors. Immediately after his election, President Reagan named Laxalt as chairman of the Republican National Committee, effectively placing him in charge of the nation's dominant party. Laxalt used that power, and his personal friendship with Reagan, to plead Nevada's case at every opportunity.

In early 1981 Laxalt met repeatedly with Attorney General Smith, seeking relief from what Laxalt called Nevada's FBI-IRS "infestation." Specifically, he wanted Joe Yablonsky reassigned to someplace far away, where Vegas power brokers would be safe from stings and wiretaps. Smith listened but declined to interfere with individual Bureau assignments. Laxalt threatened hearings by the Senate Appropriations Committee but failed to produce them. In October 1982 Laxalt came back to Justice, bringing Hank Greenspun with him. Greenspun brandished 800 complaints against Yablonsky, some allegedly from disgruntled G-men, and demanded an investigation of Yablonsky's "criminal misconduct." Deputy Attorney General Edward Schmults dismissed Greenspun's charges as "preposterous," sparking a new round of virulent *Sun* editorials. Governor List led his own angry delegation to Washington, including Senators Laxalt and Cannon, congressman James Santini, Gaming Commission chairman Carl Dodge, and GCB chairman Richard Bunker. FBI director William Webster declined to meet the group but warned Yablonsky, "They really want your head out there."

Review-Journal columnist Ned Day supported Yablonsky, complaining in print about Greenspun's "singularly vicious, months-long campaign ... intent on discrediting and humiliating" the agent. "Why is there no journalistic outrage at the malodorous campaign of vilification aimed at Yablonsky?" Day asked. "The hypocrisy, unbridled silliness, and self-aggrandizing power plays ... could break the heart of a ten-dollar hooker who thought she'd seen everything."

Judge Roger Foley disagreed. After a Reno newspaper reported that Yablonsky's G-men kept a photographic "rogue's gallery" of prominent Nevadans "with creative captions underneath," Foley ordered an unprecedented raid on the FBI's office. Some photographs were found, but no disciplinary action resulted from Foley's strange move. In the wake of that raid, even *Valley Times* editor Bob Brown was moved to inquire, "Will the lynch mob get Joe Yablonsky?"

Not quite, but his days with the Bureau were numbered. Administrative rules required all agents to retire at age fifty-five. Yablonsky turned that corner on December 29, 1983, and left the FBI on December 30. Whereas many his predecessors had retired to soft jobs in casino security, Yablonsky found himself blackballed statewide and effectively banished.

* * *

Yablonsky left Nevada still believing that Attorney General Smith was "basically honest, although he was not hip to the jive as far as organized crime and all that other stuff." For once in his career, Yablonsky had misjudged his enemies.

Ronald Reagan himself set the tone of his administration's ambiguous stance on organized crime. On one hand, he embraced corrupt labor unions and promoted their spokesmen to influential posts, while on the other he declared all-out war on the Mob. To judge the president's intent, observers were required to look beyond his campaign rhetoric and analyze his actions.

Reagan's outspoken disdain for "big government" never effected military spending or covert CIA activities, but it struck at the heart of federal law enforcement. His first budget imposed an FBI hiring freeze coupled with dramatic staff reductions and a 33-percent cutback on investigations of organized crime. The White House also indicated that no further undercover operations against mobsters or white-collar criminals would be authorized in fiscal 1982. Congress blocked Reagan's attempt to abolish the Treasury Department's Bureau of Alcohol, Tobacco and Firearms — created to punish liquor violations, bombings, and federal weapons violations — but the president hamstrung investigations and enforcement by the IRS, the SEC, and the Justice Department's Organized Crime Strike Forces. Reagan also threw his weight behind a bill proposed by Senator Howard Cannon, seeking repeal of "wasteful and inefficient" federal taxes on legalized gambling.

The only Mob activity that seemed of any great concern to Reagan was drug trafficking. Once again, however, what he *said* and what he *did* were very different things. In January 1982 Attorney General Smith announced a sweeping reorganization of federal law enforcement designed to crush drug traffickers. He removed the DEA from Treasury and assigned it to Justice, then fired Director Peter Bensinger and replaced him with assistant FBI director Francis Mullen — who had played a key leading role in suppression of FBI files during Ray Donovan's 1981 confirmation hearings. Reagan also proposed budget cuts of 6 percent for the FBI and 12 percent for the DEA. Similar cuts hampered the Coast Guard's anti-drug patrols. While Smith promised a "vigorous" war on organized crime without extra funding, Delaware's Senator Joseph Biden Jr. noted a 60-percent reduction in criminal cases prosecuted by U.S.

attorneys. Even the American Civil Liberties Union, reviled by Reagan chief-of-staff Ed Meese as a "criminal lobby," branded Reagan's war on drugs a "fraud in terms of being serious proposals to reduce crime."

In October 1982 Reagan staffers rallied for a banquet advertised as a "Tribute to Raymond J. Donovan," still under fire at that time for his ties to the Mob. Celebrants including Attorney General Smith, CIA director William Casey, and presidential chief-of-staff Ed Meese paid $50 per plate and proudly donned buttons reading "I'm a friend of Ray Donovan." The very next morning, blind to irony, Reagan held a press conference to advertise his "New Program to Combat Drug Trafficking and Organized Crime." Declaring that "the time has come to cripple the power of the mob in America," Reagan announced plans for a dozen special task forces including 900 new agents, 200 new U.S. attorneys, and a 400-person support staff, bankrolled with a minimum $130 million. The effort would be patterned, Reagan said, after a special anti-drug task force already being supervised in Florida, by Vice President Bush.

The *New York Times* dismissed Reagan's "war on crime" as political rhetoric, timed to boost Republican candidates in mid-term elections. Reagan countered with a plea to Congress for 155 million crime-fighting dollars squeezed from the budgets of various federal programs, then sent Attorney General Smith to plead for another $130 million in December. Skeptical senators noted that Reagan's first two years in office had purged 19,609 employees from the ATF, Coast Guard, Customs, DEA, FBI and IRS. While Smith praised Reagan's "unprecedented steps to combat the widespread lawlessness in America," a report from the General Accounting Office revealed that illicit drugs were cheaper and more plentiful than ever before. Between 1979 and June 1982, heroin prices had dropped from $2.25 per milligram to $1.66; the same dose of cocaine now cost 52 cents, down from 65 cents in 1980. Worse yet, the purity of both drugs at street-level had *increased*, proving that huge supplies were readily available. According to the GAO, Reagan's anti-drug campaign had wasted $66 million in Florida alone, through chaotic mismanagement. Florida congressman Claude Pepper surveyed George Bush's strike force and said, "I can't see a single thing it has accomplished. The lack of coordination among the various agencies charged with waging the war on drugs is disgraceful." An anonymous Coast Guard lieutenant branded the Florida campaign "an intellectual fraud."

Still, Reagan waffled on organized crime. In July 1983 he attended a convention of the Mob-infested International Longshoreman's Association, expelled from the AFL in 1953. Reagan praised ILA president Thomas Gleason — a target of investigation for three decades — as a man of "integrity and loyalty." Ten days later, Reagan declared yet another war on gangsters, calling for a "frontal assault" that would "break the power of the mob in America." This time his solution was a Commission on Organized Crime, led by federal judge Irving Kaufman. Congress granted the panel full subpoena power, whereupon Attorney General Smith claimed the prerogative to veto any summons at his sole discretion. Ed Meese recommended San Diego Sheriff John Duffy as a commission member, but Duffy withdrew when the media exposed his friendship with Rancho La Costa's partners. Duffy protested being "dragged through the mud" and told reporters, "I don't think Moe Dalitz is a mobster, but that's not an endorsement."

The commission's 1986 report was a disjointed document. More than half of the panel's members wrote individual opinions, one complaining that "dark places" had been overlooked, while another said, "Poor management of time, money, and staff has resulted in the commission's leaving important issues unexamined. The true history of the commission ... is a saga of missed opportunity." Sidney Korshak went unmentioned in the report. When Dan Moldea questioned that omission, one commissioner told him, "Korshak did come up in a couple of interviews and in one of the staff reports.... Several of us wanted to highlight him ... [b]ut it was just not meant to be. There were forces that didn't want Korshak touched. So the commission just rounded up the usual suspects." Another panel member described a tense nine-hour meeting that preceded release of the final report. According to that source, "Leaving Korshak out of the final report was no accident. A conscious decision was made to leave out any reference to him, and we were told about it at that meeting. It was too late to do anything about it. We really never had a chance to see the final version of the report before it was released."

Finally, the commission's report was more surprising for what it *did* say than for what it ignored. The panel found that ILA boss Thomas Gleason, praised by Reagan for his "loyalty and integrity" in 1983, had been a servile tool of the Gambino Mafia family since 1963. The commission painted a similar portrait of White House advisor Jackie Presser, who ascended to the Teamster presidency three months before Reagan launched his second war of words against the Mob. The panel said that "[w]hile the precise current relationship, if any, between organized crime and the current IBT president, Jackie Presser, is not known to the Commission, Presser's past activities indicate that he has associated with organized crime figures and that he benefited from their support in his elevation to the IBT Presidency." Reagan's ongoing ties to Presser and his union, the commission feared, might "lead to an erosion in public confidence and dampen the desire to end racketeering."

* * *

In April 1981 Justice filed suit against the Teamsters for mismanaging its pension fund. Accusations of malfeasance included huge loans to the Dunes and Aladdin casinos in Vegas, as well as to Rancho La Costa and the La Costa Land Company—all rated as firms with "a serious negative cash flow problem."

Throughout the latest round of Teamster prosecutions, Ronald Reagan continued to behave as if the IBT was squeaky-clean. On June 1, 1982—ten days after IBT president Roy Williams was indicted—Reagan addressed a Teamster convention in Vegas, telling the crowd, "I hope to be in team with the Teamsters." On June 12 Williams joined other union leaders at the White House for discussion of Reagan's tax-cut proposals. In May 1983 Reagan telephoned Jackie Presser to congratulate him on replacing Williams. In August 1983 columnist Victor Riesel reported that Presser was in "almost daily touch" with Labor Secretary Ray Donovan, supplementing that contact with frequent calls to the Oval Office. In September, Donovan joined Secretary of the Navy John Lehman and other White House aides for a Washington reception honoring Presser. Two weeks later, Cleveland jurors convicted Presser's uncle, Allen Friedman, of embezzling $165,000 from the union, but October 1983 found Presser closeted in the West Wing for a ninety-minute conference with Ed Meese.

* * *

The *Penthouse* lawsuit seemed eternal, but the plaintiffs could afford to take their time. In February 1981 they fattened their war chest by selling 3,300 acres in San Diego County to Canadian buyers for $110 million.

Attorneys for *Penthouse* and La Costa finally squared off for trial before Judge Kenneth Gale, in Los Angeles. Roy Grutman described Gale as "one judge who got around": while running a Utah dance club, Gale had married one of his teenage performers, then moved on to practice law in Vegas, where he counted union racketeers and Jimmy Fratianno's wife among his clients. From Nevada, Gale had emigrated to San Pedro, California, specializing in labor law among that seaport's mobbed-up unions. His appointment to preside over the *Penthouse* case was dreadful news for the defense.

Louis Nizer opened the proceedings on November 30, 1981, extolling plaintiffs Adelson and Molasky as "men of impeccable character all their lives." Roy Grutman called them "fronts and figureheads" who got lucky "when Mephistopheles came into their lives and they met Moe Dalitz." *Penthouse* attorneys got their first taste of Gale's bias when he refused to let jurors peruse the magazine's issue containing the disputed article. Gale's reasoning: *Penthouse* was "nauseous" and likely to disgust 60 percent of average Americans.

Merv Adelson appeared as La Costa's first witness and spent five days on the stand, assuring jurors that "there is no cover to be taken off at La Costa. La Costa is completely open." He admitted that Allen Dorfman had been placed on La Costa's board of directors as a condition of the resort's Teamster loans, but denied any impropriety. Banker Arnholt Smith had received a free "presidential membership," proposed by an unnamed principal at the resort, but Adelson insisted that he only met Smith once or twice. Likewise, he granted that various Teamster officials — including Frank Fitzsimmons and Tony Provenzano — "may have" received free memberships, but it was strictly business. Adelson hedged on cross-examination, when the defense listed prior articles about La Costa, contending that the Gerth-Bergman article had surprised and traumatized him. When Adelson denied any dodgy business practices, *Penthouse* attorneys produced his federal tax bill for 1969–70, including a $1.2 million penalty for falsely claiming that his La Costa stock was worthless. Outside of court, Adelson told reporters, "My practice is not to associate with mobsters. If somebody tells me he's a mobster, I won't associate with him. You can only go by the feeling you have from the meeting you have with them."

On December 8 *Penthouse* attorneys informed Judge Gale that Sheriff Duffy had purged his department's files on La Costa in 1976. Gale found the accusation "incredible," despite reports in the *San Diego Union* that Duffy received his largest 1970 campaign contribution from La Costa. San Diego's deputy D.A. claimed that he needed 500 hours to locate files subpoenaed by the defense. The import of those documents was borne home by a recording of Adelson discussing Moe Dalitz with one of La Costa's publicists. Merv admitted that Moe "has been under investigation for many, many years, for a long, long time. I imagine the files on him are this thick by this time. There's no sense kidding ourselves."

On December 28, Moe Dalitz took the witness stand. Reporters called it a "surprise move," but Moe could hardly have remained a silent watcher in the courtroom if his partners hoped to win. Spry and alert, he sparred with Grutman over three days of cross-examination. "I don't know what you mean by organized crime," Moe said at one point. "My interpretation of organized crime may be different than yours." Pressed to explain, he finally described a mobster as "a person who lives outside the law completely." Moe admitted knowing Sam Giancana "from 1953 on," but said, "I was mainly interested in customer relations. I met many people there of all caliber.... If I shook hands with the Duke of Windsor, it didn't make me a duke." He also claimed to be a "boyhood friend" of Jimmy Hoffa, while denying that he had exerted any influence over the Teamster Union's loans. Moe acknowledged FBI wiretaps at the DI, while saying, "There was never any unpleasantness between Bobby Kennedy and myself. I know that Bobby Kennedy did not hate me."

Grutman missed his chance to nail Dalitz for perjury concerning Moe's supposed childhood acquaintance with Hoffa, but he extracted admissions of *other* friendships, including ties to Bugsy Siegel, Willie Alderman, Jake Guzik, Tony Accardo and Meyer Lansky. Moe initially denied any contact with Lansky since the 1950s, then contradicted himself by saying that Lansky refused to invest in La Costa because "he thought we were going to go broke." Backtracking to the 1930s, Grutman asked about Molaska, prompting Moe's denial that Lansky was a partner in the firm. Grutman produced an interview from 1975, wherein Moe admitted Lansky's participation, but Dalitz called it "a mistake," explaining that he had confused Meyer with his father-in-law, Moses Citron. Finally, Grutman challenged Dalitz to explain a previous remark, in which he said, "If [Lansky] had any laundered funds he would not have put them in [Rancho La Costa]. He didn't like the deal." After a momentary stall, Moe snapped, "All right, all right, I said it."

Ex-plaintiff Allard Roen took the stand in January, proclaiming that La Costa was "basically like any other" resort. Authors Gerth and Bergman, Roen said, were "attributing things that could not be at La Costa." Roen denied waiving charges for any "serious" criminals, then admitted comping fellow stock swindler Sam Garfield, Lou Rosanova, San Francisco Teamster boss Rudy Tham (convicted of embezzlement in 1980), and Yale Cohen from the Stardust (with five convictions in the 1930s). "If we are talking about someone who may have had a conviction one time or so, I may know," Roen quibbled. "If we are talking about someone who had a great crime, I don't know."

Irwin Molasky and his wife followed Al Roen to the stand, repeating tales of emotional suffering caused by the *Penthouse* story. Susan Molasky told the jury that the article had left her husband "shaken, dazed and shattered." In short, she said, he was "not the man I married." Next came ex-Nevada governor Mike O'Callaghan and sitting Vegas judge Thomas O'Donnell, called by Molasky as character witnesses. O'Callaghan called Molasky "a very honorable man," while O'Donnell declared that the *Penthouse* article had tarnished Molasky's "excellent" reputation.

The best defense against a libel charge is truth. Ex-presidential aide John Ehrlichman admitted plotting Watergate cover-up strategy at La Costa in 1973, but claimed he chose the resort for its proximity to San Clemente and because "it was the closest one with tennis courts." Former U.S. attorney James Lorenz testified that La Costa had a "bad reputation" as "a meeting place for organized crime" in the early 1970s, then admitted that he called it "a legitimate community" in 1979. Robert McGuire, a former L.A. policeman later employed by Nevada's Gaming Control Board, described GCB informant Eugene Conrad's La Costa meeting with mobsters Lou Dragna and Lou Rosanova in 1973. Conrad himself testified that Moe Dalitz had joined him and Rosanova in La Costa's cocktail lounge. In case jurors had missed the point, *Penthouse* lawyers introduced a 1963 congressional report that called Rosanova "a top chieftain of Cosa Nostra." Ray Miller, a former undercover officer for Orange County's district attorney, described Rosanova's meeting with Frank Fitzsimmons and Allen Dorfman at Palm Springs, in 1972, days before a second meeting convened at La Costa.

Jimmy Fratianno was a major player in the *Penthouse* trial, banking $250 per hour as he prepared to testify for the defense, with another $125 per hour for his lawyer. Aside from his thousand-page deposition, Fratianno was also the subject and primary source for Ovid Demaris's 1980 bestseller *The Last Mafioso*, wherein Fratianno frequently mentioned Moe Dalitz, his partners, and La Costa. *Penthouse* subpoenaed 150 hours of taped Fratianno interviews in January 1982, and Demaris grudgingly delivered transcripts. Testifying in February, Demaris granted that it was standard procedure for journalists to contact their subjects before publication, but he noted that "it went the other way" with mobsters, since "you didn't want to tip them off." Judge Gale ordered that observation stricken from the record.

Fratianno was next up, admitting involvement in seventeen murders. His direct examination reiterated all that he had told Demaris and the *Penthouse* legal team, capped by a claim that Fratianno, Sam Giancana and others had met at La Costa to plot the slaying of TV star Desi Arnaz. On cross-examination Fratianno wavered, confessing that the meeting had actually taken place at San Diego's Del Mar Hotel. Next, La Costa's lawyers focused on his *Penthouse* deposition, wherein Fratianno denied ever visiting La Costa and claimed he knew nothing about it. Fratianno replied, "You can go through that deposition and maybe there's 150 lies there. I admit 90 percent are lies." As for his Demaris interviews, Fratianno said, "To my knowledge, everything I said was true."

That claim revived La Costa's demands for the actual tapes, still withheld by Demaris. At 11:00 A.M. on February 24, Gale's clerk phoned Demaris with an order to produce the tapes by 1:30 P.M. or face arrest. Demaris protested that he could not book a flight in time to make the deadline, whereupon Gale's clerk informed him that a private plane was standing by. Demaris caught the flight but did not recognize his benefactor until they touched down in L.A., where Irwin Molasky introduced himself. Demaris later filed an affidavit refuting Judge Gale's public claim that he "elected" to fly with Molasky. Jurors heard the tapes on February 25, including Fratianno's confirmation that the Arnaz murder plot was hatched in San Diego, but Gale barred Fratianno from returning to explain his lies.

Time and time again, Roy Grutman voiced complaints about Gale's pro-defense bias, once storming out of court and twice, drawing contempt citations. Gale insulted defense attorneys in front of the jury, accusing lawyer Michael Aguirre of using "the poorest logic I've ever heard," and excluded defense witnesses ranging from real-estate appraisers to Sheriff Duffy, Evelle Younger, and Vegas G-men who investigated skimming at the DI. When Grutman tried to introduce documentary evidence, Gale whined, "I could spend the rest of my life reading this. What do you want me to do, try every article, too?"

Gale's attitude was partially explained on March 24, 1982, when Jimmy Fratianno broke the news of his prior "close relationship" with Gale. As Fratianno told it, Gale had been his friend and legal counselor in Vegas. Gale belatedly acknowledged knowing Fratianno for a decade but denied they were friends. Gale said that he had represented Fratianno's second wife before they married, and had once inquired about early parole for Fratianno, but insisted that he dropped the matter after learning that Fratianno was a mobster. *Penthouse* attorneys called for a mistrial, Gale denied the motion, and *Penthouse* appealed to California's Supreme Court, which declined to intervene.

Gale instructed the jury on April 19, prior to closing arguments. Louis Nizer summed up for the plaintiffs, blasting *Penthouse* as a "filthy sheet" that fostered a "plague of sensationalism, of excoriating people falsely, of destroying people to make a buck." La Costa's Teamster loans were "honorable," Nizer said, and every cent had been repaid. Roy Grutman summarized the evidence of Mob involvement at La Costa, while downplaying Fratianno's fabrications. On April 22, after ninety-seven days of testimony from 100 witnesses, jurors retired to consider their verdict. Deliberations continued until May 13, when the panel returned with a verdict absolving *Penthouse* of libel. Irwin Molasky fumed that the verdict "struck a blow for yellow journalism."

That should have been the end, but Judge Gale was not finished yet. On July 9, 1982 he rejected the jury's verdict, branding it a "miscarriage of justice," and ordered the trial to start over from scratch with new jurors. California's Court of Appeals temporarily removed Gale from the case on August 5, pending hearings on his fitness to continue. The state supreme court rejected *Penthouse*'s appeal in February 1983, then Judge David Eagleson (presiding over California's superior courts) removed Gale from the case without comment. Legal maneuvers consumed two more years, interrupted by Merv Adelson's divorce from wife Gail and the June 1985 announcement of his engagement to TV star Barbara Walters.

On December 5, 1985, the combatants announced a settlement, signing off on a statement in which each side absolved the other of any wrongdoing. *Penthouse* and La Costa agreed that "continued litigation will only further torture and cause more expense to all parties. Accordingly, we have now reached a point where it appears that if the case were to continue through yet additional court proceedings, whoever would ultimately win would enjoy a Pyrrhic victory at best." La Costa's owners praised Bob Guccione and *Penthouse* for their "many personal and professional awards and distinctions," while the defense wrote that "*Penthouse* ... did not mean to imply nor did it intend for its readers to believe that Messrs. Adelson and Molasky are or were members of organized crime or criminals. *Penthouse* acknowledges that all of the individual plaintiffs, including Messrs. Dalitz and Roen, have been extremely active in commendable civic and philanthropic activities which have earned them recognition from many estimable people. Furthermore, *Penthouse* acknowledges that among plaintiffs' successful business activities is the La Costa resort itself, one of the outstanding resort complexes of the world."

In short, as author Michael Zuckerman observed, the epic libel suit had turned into a ten-year civics lesson, with estimates of the final price tag ranging from $14 million to $20 million. The FBI, meanwhile, kept watch on Adelson and Molasky. In 1984 G-men launched a new investigation into high-stakes betting by a group of New York businessmen dubbed the "Computer Group." Aided by front men in Vegas, the New Yorkers bet up to $250,000 on a single football game. A Nevada gaming veteran told Dan Moldea, "Adelson and Molasky became beards. They were moving money for the Computer guys. Instead of betting themselves, the Computers went to guys like Adelson and Molasky and said, 'We have some great games to bet on.'"

Perhaps, but the feds filed no charges. In May 1987 Merv Adelson and Barbara Walters hosted a charity weekend at La Costa. Their guest list included Donald Trump, Barry Diller of 20th-Century–Fox, *Dallas* stars Larry Hagman and Linda Gray, and ex-actor John Gavin (Ronald Reagan's ambassador to Mexico). Six months later the DRAM partners sold La Costa to a Japanese firm for $250 million. Allard Roen stayed on at the resort, later managing the nearby Lodge at Torrey Pines. Adelson and Walters separated in October 1990 and divorced in 1992.

* * *

More than reputations were at stake in Las Vegas and the Midwest, as authorities finally moved against mobsters who had looted Nevada's casinos. In November 1981 a federal grand jury indicted ten defendants for skimming at the Tropicana. They included Nick and Carl Civella, Joe Agosto, Billy Caldwell, Carl Caruso, Anthony Chiavola Sr., Angelo DeLuna, Charles Moretina, Donald Shepard, and Carl Thomas. All hailed from Kansas City except Chiavola, a Civella nephew who lived in Chicago. Nick Civella, already imprisoned for bribery, died in March 1983. Three other defendants—Agosto, Caldwell and Shepard—pled guilty prior to trial, with Agosto turning state's evidence. Caruso cracked and pled guilty during the trial, leaving jurors to convict the remaining defendants. Carl Civella received a thirty-five-year sentence; DeLuna got thirty years; Moretina got twenty; Chiavola and Thomas got fifteen years each, but Thomas shaved thirteen years from his sentence by agreeing to testify against the next batch of skimming defendants.

Things had started to unravel for the Argent skimmers in Las Vegas on July 4, 1981, when police caught Tony Spilotro's burglars looting a furniture store. Spilotro's second-in-command,

Frank Cullotta, entered the federal witness program in early 1982. A bungled car bombing in October 1982 failed to kill Frank Rosenthal but hastened his departure from Nevada. Key witness Joe Agosto died in August 1983, and while Hank Greenspun gloated that Agosto's passing "crippled the Mafia probe" in Las Vegas, Allen Glick stepped up to fill the void. On September 30, 1983, the feds indicted fifteen defendants for skimming the Stardust and Fremont. Argent defendants already on trial for crimes at the Trop included Carl Civella, Anthony Chiavola Sr., Angelo DeLuna and Carl Thomas. New defendants included Frank Ballistrieri, with sons John and Joseph from Milwaukee; Joe Aiuppa, John Cerone, Joe Lombardo, Angelo LaPietra and Tony Spilotro from Chicago; Anthony Chiavola Jr. and Peter Tamburello from K.C.; and Cleveland's Milton Rockman, brother-in-law of John Scalish and a former partner with Moe Dalitz in Buckeye Vending. Death spared co-conspirators Nick Civella, Allen Dorfman and Joe Agosto from further torment in court. Nevada governor Richard Bryan and congressman Harry Reid faced the press on October 12, boldly declaring that the charges cast no shadow on Nevada's reputation for honest gaming.

While politicians postured, the indicted mobsters scrambled to prepare for yet another trial. Vegas attorney and future mayor Oscar Goodman severed Tony Spilotro's case from the rest, while authorities dismissed Carl Thomas's indictment, adding his name to the list of prosecution witnesses including Glick, ex–Teamster president Roy Williams, and Cleveland mafioso Angelo Lonardo. Four defendants — Carl Civella, the Chiavolas, and Pete Tamburello — pled guilty prior to trial; two others, Frank Ballistrieri and Carl DeLuna, changed their pleas to guilty after the trial began. In January 1986 Judge Joseph Stevens acquitted John and Joseph Ballistrieri of all charges, citing lack of evidence. Two weeks later, jurors convicted defendants Aiuppa, Cerone, LaPietra, Lombardo, and Rockman. Frank Ballistrieri and Carl DeLuna got thirty-year terms on their guilty pleas; Aiuppa and Cerone received matching prison terms of twenty-eight years and six months; Rockman got twenty-four years; LaPietra and Lombardo drew sixteen years each.

Tony Spilotro's bid for a separate trial paid off—but not as he had hoped. His first trial ended with a hung jury in April 1986. Retrial was scheduled for June, but Tony missed the show. On June 21 police found Spilotro and his brother buried in an Indiana cornfield.

Few civic leaders in Vegas missed Spilotro, but they were distraught over the fate of Harry Claiborne, caught up in Joe Yablonsky's Operation Yobo. Days before retiring, Yablonsky persuaded fugitive brothel owner Joe Conforte to return from Switzerland, trading an eighteen-month prison term for full disclosure of the bribes Conforte paid Claiborne. Indicted before year's end, Claiborne faced trial in March 1984 on charges of bribery and tax evasion. Hank Greenspun charged to Claiborne's defense, accusing trial judge Walter Hoffman of "kissing the pimp's backside." Jurors deadlocked in April and Hoffman declared a mistrial, whereupon prosecutors dropped the bribery count but proceeded with retrial on tax charges. A second jury convicted Claiborne in August 1984, and he received a two-year prison sentence. Congress impeached him in April 1986, days before he entered federal prison with appeals exhausted. The Senate convicted Claiborne and removed him from office in October 1986. Paroled in 1987, Claiborne resumed legal practice in Nevada but never fully recovered. He shot himself in January 2004.

In general, however, non–Italian mobsters in the Reagan years had more to fear from Father Time than from the feds. Sam Cohen died in Miami at age eighty-four, in December 1980. Eighty-year-old Sam Garfield died in Carlsbad, California, six months later. Lung cancer killed Meyer Lansky, also eighty, at Miami Beach in January 1983. Chuck Polizzi hung on until April 1987 in St. Petersburg, Florida, then gave up the ghost at age ninety-two.

* * *

The Hebrew year 5744 — labeled *Tashmad,* or "disaster" — began on September 8, 1983, and ran for 385 days. There is no reason to suppose Moe Dalitz marked the dates or understood their ritual significance, but he observed the mounting turmoil as America prepared for yet another presidential race.

In November 1983 the *Sacramento Bee* published a feature on Paul Laxalt, quoting agents of the IRS and Nevada's Gaming Control Board who claimed the Mob had skimmed 20 percent of Laxalt's Ormsby House profits during 1971–76. Laxalt emulated Moe by suing the *Bee* and publisher C.K. McClatchy for $250 million in September 1984. McClatchy responded with a $6 million counterclaim, charging Laxalt with attempted censorship. The libel case dragged on until 1987, tainting yet another presidential year. Joseph Yablonsky, watching from the sidelines, told anyone who would listen that Laxalt had long been "a tool of organized crime."

In December 1983 Ronald Reagan announced his third attack on organized crime. "I've always believed," he declared, "that government can break up the networks of tightly organized regional and national syndicates that make up organized crime. So I repeat, we're in this thing to win. There will be no negotiated settlements, no détente with the mob. It's war to the end where they're concerned. Our goal is simple. We mean to cripple their organization, dry up their profits and put their members behind bars where they belong. They've had a free run for too long a time in this country." Four days later, reporter Ned Day told *Review-Journal* readers that Reagan's commission on organized crime was "waffling on dead center, not doing much of anything."

Moe Dalitz lost a longtime friend when Pete Licavoli died in his sleep at Grace Ranch, on January 11, 1984. Associates had questioned Licavoli's declining state since 1981, when he reported a theft of jewelry valued at $250,000, then found he had misplaced the pricey baubles at home. In April 1984 authorities charged son Michael and four others with sixty-one counts of theft and fraud in Las Vegas. Co-defendant Wilfred O'Brien was an estate coordinator for the Clark County public administrator's office who, with an investigator on his staff and their two wives, allegedly helped Licavoli steal $60,000 from the dead.

Paul Laxalt reprised his role as Reagan's campaign chairman in 1984, while his daughter landed a campaign "consultancy" post paying $3,000 per month. In September 1984 GOP sources announced that Laxalt was "no longer interested" in succeeding Reagan in 1988. Some blamed the Sacramento lawsuit and its aftershocks. As 1984 progressed, ABC and CBS planned exposés on Laxalt, using Joe Yablonsky on camera. Both networks received warning letters from Laxalt's attorneys, and the pressure went further at CBS, where Lowell Bergman was prepared to link Laxalt with Dalitz and other mobsters. A week before the story was supposed to air on *Sixty Minutes*, executive producer Don Hewitt dined with Lew Wasserman and Wasserman's wife in Manhattan. Lew assured Hewitt that Dalitz "hasn't done anything illegal since Prohibition," while Edie Wasserman described her beloved Uncle Moe as "a wonderful man." Bergman was furious next morning, when Hewitt related the conversation. Hewitt next called Nancy Reagan for advice. "Subsequently," Bergman told author Kathleen Sharp, "there were discussions with other friends of Hewitt." The story never ran, and while Bergman described the network's reasoning as "complicated," he was able to summarize it for Sharp: "At the time, Reagan was deregulating the broadcast industry. The story might boomerang on the CBS network. Why would they drop a turd on the carpet?"

Ronald Reagan's relationship with the Teamsters was also "complicated" in 1984. Jackie Presser announced his support for Reagan's re-election in March, complaining that the AFL-CIO's endorsement of Democrat Walter Mondale was "an embarrassing situation for all of labor." Three months later, the *Las Vegas Sun* reported that Presser was "keeping a low profile" to avoid embarrassing Reagan, but that did not prevent White House labor liaison Doug Riggs from telling a Teamster convention that the IBT "has an open door" to the Oval Office. Nonetheless, Reagan ducked the annual Ohio Conference of Teamsters which he had proudly addressed in 1980, sending George Bush in his place to praise the IBT as a "tremendous union." Ray Donovan and Reagan campaign manager Ed Rollins flew to Dallas on August 21, for a breakfast honoring Presser. Rollins told the cheering audience, "We want your endorsement again. We remember who our friends were and we hope that you remember what we've done for you when it comes to your endorsement."

* * *

Edwin Meese replaced William Smith as Attorney General in February 1985. He was more concerned with "smut" than tackling the Mob. His Commission on Pornography, chaired by federal judge Henry Hudson of Virginia, balanced its standard complement of lawyers and psychologists with members Ellen Levine (vice president of CBS Magazines), Diane Cusack (a member of the Scottsdale, Arizona, city council), right-wing radio evangelist James Dobson, and the Rev. Bruce Ritter (a Catholic priest accused of child molestation and embezzlement in 1989). Few scholars now regard the Meese Commission's 1,960-page report, published in July 1986, as either objective or credible.

Despite their superior's focus on porn, federal prosecutors still occasionally bestirred themselves to punish mobsters. President Reagan issued yet another call to arms in January 1986, telling the *New York Times*: "There's never been any question that the American people want the mob put out of business.... That's why this issue has always seemed to me a place of common ground for conservatives and liberals, Republicans and Democrats; a place where all Americans could align themselves against a dangerous and all too persistent domestic enemy." Ignoring his own ties to the Mob, Reagan proclaimed that efforts were "starting to pay off now.... We're hitting the mob where it hurts the most: in the pocketbook, using both new and old laws to confiscate its financial assets."

It was true, to a point, but the government's sights remained squarely fixed on Italian-American mobsters, joined in the spotlight by street-level drug dealers and thousands of users whose stiff prison terms meant nothing to smugglers in Latin America or Southeast Asia.

A case in point is the March 1986 federal indictment of fifteen defendants on charges including extortion, illegal gambling, labor racketeering, construction bid-rigging, and murder. Aside from Cleveland's Milton Rockman, slapped with one count of fraud, the rest might have come directly from the credits of a *Godfather* sequel, including Anthony Salerno, Matthew Ianniello, Louis and Vincent DiNapoli, John Tronolone, Alphonse Mosca, Neil Migliore, and so on. Jurors acquitted Rockman in May 1988, while convicting Salerno and eight other defendants on various charges.

* * *

The Argent prosecutions left Moe Dalitz unruffled, but there was cause for alarm when the feds turned a spotlight on his protégés at Trans-Sterling. G-men had begun investigating Al Sachs and company in August 1980, shadowing Phil Ponto from the Stardust as he passed packages to Joseph Talerico, a Teamster "business agent" from Chicago. Agents collared the pair in January 1982, but they were left with egg on their faces — or, rather, cookies and wine, the contents of Ponto's "suspicious" parcel.

Governor List, seeking re-election, blasted the FBI on January 5. "There's no evidence that they've uncovered anything," he told reporters. "They've got some people running around whispering in their ears." One day later, List announced that he would not return Trans-Sterling's large campaign donation "over hearsay accusations." Democratic rival Richard Bryan *did* return $10,000 from the Stardust, while assuring civil libertarians that "I do not want to prejudge Tobman or Sachs." GCB chairman Richard Bunker promised an "aggressive" but "cautious" probe of the new skimming charges. Meanwhile, the *Sun* revealed that Judge Claiborne had authorized an FBI bug at the Stardust. G-men concealed it in the hotel's Aku Aku restaurant, on a table reserved for Sachs and Tobman, casino manager Lou Salerno, and assistant manager Fred Pandolfo.

Despite the bungled cookie caper, Trans-Sterling was still in trouble. On August 10 the GCB ordered Fred Pandolfo placed on three months' leave, pending hearings on his suitability for casino employment. On October 20, citing complaints that included Pandolfo's receipt of a $60,000 interest-free loan from a gambler whom Pandolfo had favored with $20,000 credit, the board unanimously recommended his ouster from gaming. Meanwhile, Trans-Sterling posted losses of $6.7 million for the latest six-month fiscal period.

Cornered by charges that G-men had sandbagged state officials, FBI headquarters reluctantly submitted its Trans-Sterling evidence to Nevada's Gaming Commission. Aside from the Aku Aku transcripts, that haul included statements from Jimmy Fratianno and other informants, reports of physical surveillance, and an ex-GCB agent's claim that board member Richard Bunker concealed reports linking Al Sachs to the Mob in 1979. GCB chairman James Avance was adamant that mobsters had no "significant influence" over legalized gambling, but board member Patricia Becker disagreed, telling reporters it would be "naïve" to think the Argent trials had cleansed Nevada of its gangland taint.

On December 4, 1983, the Gaming Commission issued an "emergency order" suspending the Stardust's gaming license, with those of Sachs and Tobman, effective as soon as special caretakers were appointed. GCB spokesmen cited proof that fill slips had been used, as under Argent's reign, to siphon untaxed cash from gaming tables. State agents would monitor play at Trans-Sterling's casinos while the courts screened nominees to replace Sachs and Tobman. Trans-Sterling's executives advanced a conspiracy theory, wherein G-men themselves forged fill slips to bolster false allegations. On December 12 Judge Stephen Huffaker chose veteran gamblers Sam Boyd, Charles Ruthe and Perry Whitt to run the Stardust under state supervision, while auditors studied the books. Two days later, Sachs and Tobman filed suit to challenge statutes which permitted state authorities to suspend gaming licenses prior to conviction at trial. Sachs met privately with Gaming Commission members and dismissed claims of his Mob ties as "ridiculous." Unimpressed, the commission affirmed the Stardust suspensions. Boyd and company, doing business as Constellation Inc., took charge of Trans-Sterling's casinos on December 28. One day later, a court order barred them from cashing employee checks at the Stardust, Fremont, or Sundance, in order to "keep an arm's-length interest" from the money.

The new year brought *Tashmad* indeed for the Stardust. On January 4 state authorities slapped Sachs and Tobman with a nineteen-count complaint alleging 222 specific gaming violations, resulting in a $1.5 million skim during 1982–83. The GCB proposed a $3.9 million fine, then lopped $900,000 from that total without explanation. The fine broke down as $1.4 million from Karat Inc., $1.3 million from Trans-Sterling, $200,000 from Sachs, and $100,000 from Tobman. A further $200,000 was assessed to keep state agents at Trans-Sterling's casinos until they were sold. If Sachs and Tobman could not find "squeaky-clean" buyers before May 1, their three casinos would close.

Sachs agreed to the fines on January 8, without admitting guilt. Two days later, as the state revoked his gaming license and Tobman's, a grand jury indicted Lou Salerno, Fred Pandolfo, and seven subordinates on skimming charges. Sachs and Tobman were not charged, a circumstance that permitted Tobman to retain his seat on the Las Vegas Convention and Visitors Board. On January 17 Trans-Sterling's accountants refused to certify the company's financial statements for the past three years, based on uncertain losses from skimming.

Sachs and Tobman complained incessantly about Constellation's "mismanagement," alleging that income had dropped from $1.2 million in January 1983 to a mere $33,743 in January 1984. Further investigation bared the lie: Constellation posted a $700,000 profit in February 1984, compared to a $430,000 *loss* under Sachs and Tobman during February 1983. Vendors received payment for their goods within sixty days under Constellation, versus an average 130 days with Trans-Sterling. Ned Day's column revealed that the Stardust had been paying a Panamanian corporation $500,000 per year since 1960 to use the "Lido de Paris" logo. Tired of the sniping, Constellation moved to evict Sachs and Tobman from their Stardust lodgings on February 21, but friendly judge Thomas Foley blocked the evictions on February 23. Judge James Brennan overruled Foley on March 1, finding that he had no jurisdiction.

Al Sachs defaulted on payment of $13.2 million to Stardust bond holders in January 1984, then struck a deal with Valley Bank to pay those creditors when the casinos sold. Singer Wayne Newton offered to buy the Fremont in February, but Sachs and Tobman kept moving the goal posts, first announcing a price of $185 million, then bumping it to $200 million while claiming, "We have never asked for less." The snags were always someone else's fault. Trans-Sterling's lawyers sought dismissal of the skim indictments, citing FBI media leaks, but that bid was denied even as Nevada's supreme court dismissed Trans-Sterling's frivolous lawsuit against Constellation.

In May 1984 Wayne Newton announced that he had inked a deal to buy the Stardust and Fremont for $200 million. Two months later, Sachs and Tobman went back to court, asking a federal judge to block the sale on grounds that state gaming authorities had denied Trans-Sterling due process of law. GCB spokesmen condemned the "blatant attempt at forum-shopping," but acknowledged that Newton still had not submitted financial information required to complete his license application. The Fremont closed at midnight on July 19, then reopened eighteen hours later when Del Webb Corporation agreed to join Constellation as interim managers, for $120,000 per month. Constellation, thus inspired, announced intent to hike its monthly fee from $83,333 to $300,000. Herb Tobman scoffed at the mounting losses, telling reporters, "I've never given up a fight in my life." Wayne Newton folded in August, withdrawing his bid for the Stardust and Fremont.

Trans-Sterling's problems worsened in August 1984, as a grand jury considered more criminal charges. Judge Foley immunized Phil Ponto and Joe Talerico against prosecution, to compel their testimony, but both chose silence over shallow graves and were sentenced to ninety days for contempt. Similar terms were dished out to the Stardust's assistant casino manager, a baccarat floorman, and the Fremont's ex-casino manager. Through it all, Sachs and Tobman fought on, claiming that Constellation had "abused its position of trust" and misused hotel funds, yet the Stardust reported a $2.6 million increase in gambling revenue since Boyd's team had taken control.

July's deadline for sale of Trans-Sterling's casinos came and went with no progress in sight. Bill Boyd bought the Stardust and Fremont in October, closing the deal for $178 million. Delays in financing and state investigations stalled the hand-off until February 1985, when both resorts merged with Boyd's California Hotel and Casino Corporation. Trustee Victor Palmieri wound up with Trans-Sterling's promissory notes to the Teamsters but could not find a buyer until October 1985, when, as reporter John Smith explains, "Palmieri contacted Irwin Molasky—a man intimately familiar with the Teamsters pension fund—who, in turn, reached out for Steve Wynn." Wynn paid Palmieri $58.6 million for the notes and made a tidy 21-percent profit when they reached their full value in 1991.

Grand jurors returned a thirteen-count indictment against various Trans-Sterling subordinates in November 1984. The corporation and Karat Inc. posted $50,000 bond on December 15, to cover potential fines and court costs, with trial scheduled to begin in May 1985. That trial never convened, but in a separate case, Trans-Sterling was ordered to shell out another $44.2 million, including $24 million to the IRS, $13.2 million to public bond holders, $4 million to First Interstate Bank, and the $3 million in fines still owed to Nevada.

Herb Tobman turned the drama into farce during 1986, when he challenged incumbent Richard Bryan for the Democratic gubernatorial nomination. Tobman raised $90,000, ostensibly from individual ten-dollar donations, but his cause was hopeless. In September's primary Tobman polled 14,279 votes—a mere 15 percent of the total.

* * *

While the Stardust slipped beyond his reach forever, Moe Dalitz retained a vital interest in the Sundance. The initial hearing on his suitability to serve as landlord began in July 1980 but had reached no verdict by October 1981, when the *Sun* accused Governor Robert List of stalling to spare his re-election race from further controversy. At the two-year mark, GCB chairman Richard Bunker said, "The work has been assigned. It is progressing. It will be done when it gets done." Stuart Engs, a board member from Sparks, undermined that portrait of earnest effort when he asked a *Sun* reporter, "Who's Moe Dalitz?" Privately, a GCB investigator spelled out the state's plan in no uncertain terms: "Stall, and hope he dies."

But Moe revealed no inclination to oblige. In April 1983 he submitted a new application to take control of the Sundance from protégés Sachs and Tobman. Compelled to start from scratch, the GCB spun its wheels for another ten months, while the Sundance posted two-year losses of $20.5 million. In February 1984 attorney David Goldwater announced that Western Host Inc. had offered $34 million for the casino, leaving Dalitz to assume a $29 million loan from the Public Employees Retirement System. Western backed out of the deal in April, and Moe approached the GCB three weeks later, offering to personally buy out the stock of Sundance Associates. Chairman James Avance vowed that the board would complete its seemingly endless investigation of Dalitz by July 19, but told the *Sun*, "It's going to be a very difficult decision."

In fact, there was no decision. On July 11, board spokesmen announced that Moe would surrender management of the Sundance to El Cortez owner Jackie Gaughan, paying Gaughan $50,000 per month until he could locate a "viable buyer." John Anderson, boss of the Dunes and Maxim casinos, signed a letter of intent to buy the Sundance in October 1984, for $33 million. That deal fell through, as did the February 1985 offer from partners William Athan and William Fleischman. In December 1984 the M.B. Dalitz Revocable Trust assigned its interest in Sundance Associates to Sundance Hotel & Casino Inc., which amended the assignment one day later and delivered 50 percent of Sundance Associates to Moe himself, as trustee.

Three years later, in November 1987, Dalitz sold out to the Reno-based Fitzgeralds casino chain, which renamed the Sundance Fitzgeralds Las Vegas.

Between those events, Moe bid farewell to the Desert Inn. In April 1985 he attended the DI's thirty-fifth anniversary party, where the McGuire sisters sang "Happy Birthday." A year later, Summa Corporation began liquidating its Vegas assets, selling the DI and Sands to Kirk Kerkorian for $161 million. Local newspapers logged the end of an era, but an FBI report from 1987 repeated Jackie Presser's confidential statement: "The individual who oversees the operations for the LCN families in Las Vegas is MOE DALITZ."

* * *

The DRAM team made other changes in the latter 1980s. In 1986 Merv Adelson and Irwin Molasky bought the MGM studio lot from Kirk Kerkorian, then purchased nine TV stations and merged with Michael Garin's Telepictures syndication company to create Lorimar-Telepictures, reborn in 1988 as Lorimar Television. Warner Communications bought Lorimar in 1989, made Adelson a vice chairman and board member, then merged with Time Inc. to become one of the world's largest media-entertainment conglomerates.

Meanwhile, an FBI memo from February 1985 quoted Jackie Presser on the subject of money laundering in Hollywood. "[O]ne of the many ways of accomplishing this," G-men wrote, "is through the over-charging of legal fees and taking the overcharges and laundering those funds through West Germany. Source further advised that he does not know how or why the funds are passed through West Germany or where the funds go from that point, but did advise that it may only be coincidence, however, Lorimar Productions in Hollywood, California, receives funding from some source in West Germany."

Moe Dalitz left the rigors of show business to his junior partners, while he focused on securing his reputation for philanthropy. He donated $750,000 to build a new home for Congregation Ner Tamid, including a religious school that bears his name today. One month after breaking ground for the synagogue, in November 1982, Moe received a "Torch of Liberty" award from the Anti-Defamation League of B'nai B'rith. Mayor Bill Briare and sheriff-elect John Moran were among the celebrants attending that luncheon, where ADL associate national director Abraham Foxman told Dalitz, "Your presence here gives meaning to our resolve to fight bigotry and prejudice wherever it exists." In keeping with the spirit of Las Vegas, Moe received his plaque from comedian Joan Rivers, weeping as she honored "Mr. Las Vegas."

Despite his trouble with the GCB, Moe still retained the friendship of key Nevada officials. In March 1983 Nevada's Board of Finance approved a $4.4 million bond issue for the Sahara Nellis Apartments, built by Paradise Homes. Nine months later, the *Review-Journal* described Moe's Realty Holdings Group as the single largest landowner in Vegas. Columnist Ned Day opined, "When Dalitz chooses to exercise his power, when he calls in all those chips, he is probably the most powerful man in town. Few dare oppose him." Two who answered Moe's call that December were Governor Bryan and Senator Chic Hecht, turning out for Sunrise Hospital's twenty-fifth anniversary party. Moe stood smiling beside the governor as Bryan declared December 15 to be Sunrise Hospital Day.

There were sour notes along the way, of course. In March 1984 the *Review-Journal* covered a squall of controversy surrounding Burke Deadrich, hired in July 1982 as executive director of the nonprofit UNLV Foundation — created, in its own words, to support the "University of Nevada Las Vegas' development efforts, foster relationships with alumni, friends, corporations, and foundations to encourage their private financial support for all students, faculty, research, and innovative programs that distinguish UNLV as an exceptional univer-

Nevada governor Richard Bryan (right) presents Merv Adelson and his mother with an award honoring the Nathan Adelson Hospice (Las Vegas Historical Society).

sity." So far, so good, but Deadrich also drew a monthly paycheck as chief fundraiser for the Nathan Adelson Hospice, another nonprofit facility founded in 1978 and named for Merv Adelson's late father. Critics claimed a conflict of interest, since both charities competed for cash from the same donors. Furthermore, the hospice sat on land owned by UNLV, paying ten dollars per month on a fifty-year lease. Irwin Molasky served as co-chairman of the hospice, sat on the UNLV Foundation's board of directors, *and* donated office space to Deadrich at Paradise Developments headquarters. As usual, the controversy proved to be a tempest in a teacup, long forgotten by the time some bold (or suicidal) thief stole Moe's pearl-handled .38 revolver, engraved with his name, from a vehicle parked outside his home in March 1985.

The following year, a rare blood disease claimed the life of Moe's last significant female companion. Barbara Schick had earned her bachelor's and master's degrees in economics from the University of Nevada–Las Vegas, then remained on campus as director of UNLV's Center for Economic Education from 1972 onward. Around the same time, she met Dalitz and they became an "item." Despite an age difference of thirty-odd years, they clicked and appeared

Moe Dalitz with Barbara Schick and actor Lee Majors at a party in Las Vegas (UNLV North Las Vegas Library Collection).

to enjoy one another immensely. At her death, Moe paid UNLV $50,000 to put Schick's name on the department she had led for nearly fifteen years.

The local press had come to terms with Dalitz over three decades, progressing from the *Sun*'s harsh criticism during 1952–63, through cautious silence after Howard Hughes hit town, to open adulation in the 1970s and 1980s. Moe could literally tell the Vegas papers *anything*, and they would print it as established fact — a useful tool indeed for changing history. As early as December 1976 the *Review-Journal* published Moe's fable of meeting Jimmy Hoffa at Detroit's Central High — a school Hoffa never attended, which Moe left when Hoffa was four years old. The *Sun*'s two-part biography of Moe, published in June 1983, began as hagiography and veered off into fantasy. In that piece, Moe forgot about attending Bishop Elementary with members of the Purple Gang, claiming that he had gone instead to Irving Elementary. His move to Cleveland, Dalitz claimed, occurred after his father and his uncle built a nonexistent laundry there. Despite his brief role as a bootlegger, Moe told the *Sun*, "I didn't drink or smoke" — a lie the paper printed literally within one inch of a photograph showing Dalitz with a cigarette and cocktail glass in hand. Casting false modesty aside, Moe claimed that his original DI design inspired both the familiar logo of the McDonald's restaurant chain (actually launched in 1940) and the Gateway Arch in St. Louis (designed in 1947). Surely the *Sun*'s reporters should have known that Moe was slipping when he reminisced about the era "when I sold the Stardust to Hughes" — yet another event that never occurred.

The Las Vegas Sun ran this photo of Moe (right) and his father next to Moe's claim that he never smoked or drank liquor (Las Vegas Historical Society).

Above all, Moe repeated the essential message. "I was never a member of any gang," he claimed. "I never considered myself a gangster. I was always in the business that threw me into meeting all kinds of people."

None of it mattered, though. In Vegas, most reporters swallowed what Moe told them and regurgitated it in print as gospel truth, seasoned with adulation from the high and mighty. Those who could not bring themselves to play that game kept silent, for the most part. As Jack Sheehan, former editor of *Las Vegas Magazine,* observed in rejecting a proposed Dalitz exposé in 1985, "Moe scares the hell out of me."

And there was still good reason to be frightened in Las Vegas. Ned Day, the proverbial lone voice crying in Nevada's neon wilderness, survived a car bombing in 1986 and afterward described it as "the happiest day of my life." Day seemed to think himself invincible, saying, "If something happens to me, then *Sixty Minutes* and ABC's *20/20*— Geraldo Rivera and all those jerks — are going to be all over here like they were in Arizona when reporter Don Bolles got murdered." But he was wrong. Day died on September 3, 1987, while snorkeling in Hawaii. No one questioned the coroner's verdict of death by natural causes. Ironically, Day had mailed his last column home from the islands, asking the *Review-Journal* to keep it "as a potential historical record in the event that ... I sleep with the fishes tonight." Vegas reporter A.D. Hopkins later told authors Sally Denton and Roger Morris, "I know [Joe] Agosto, [*Valley Times* publisher Bob] Brown, and Day all officially died of heart attacks, but they all pissed off the same people and their deaths were mighty convenient."

* * *

Republican spokesmen had dismissed Paul Laxalt's presidential dreams in 1984, but Ronald Reagan forgot that in March 1986, while addressing a banquet in Laxalt's honor. Clearly look-

ing forward to the next election, Reagan told the crowd, "Look to the son of the high mountains and peasant herders ... to a friend, to an American who gave himself so that others might
live in freedom." In preparation for that race, Laxalt declined to seek a third Senate term in
1986, ceding his seat to Harry Reid.

In April 1987 Laxalt announced formation of a "presidential exploratory committee,"
telling reporters, "I have a full and keen realization of what it's like to run for the highest
office in the land." He also had an ugly libel suit in progress, dragging on since 1984 against
the *Sacramento Bee.* Ex-G-man Bill Roemer served a subpoena on Moe Dalitz for that case,
but Moe would not be called to testify. In June 1987, one day before FBI headquarters was
scheduled to surrender its files on Sidney Korshak, Laxalt settled his case in a style reminis-
cent of the *Penthouse* lawsuit. The *Bee* paid Laxalt's legal expenses and issued a statement
admitting that pretrial investigation failed to prove Laxalt's personal knowledge of skimming
at the Ormsby House, then C.K. McClatchy announced: "We have not retracted, we have
not apologized, and we have not paid any damages. Regardless of what the senator may say
to further his efforts in his campaign, we are not backing away from anything we say in the
news story." Later, McClatchy told Gus Russo, "Laxalt had Chicago money in his Carson
City casino, and he was being totally skimmed."

                                    * * *

By 1989 Moe Dalitz knew that he was running out of time. Weakened by cancer and degen-
erative kidney disease, confined to a wheelchair, his mobility was limited. Vegas reporter John
Smith called him "a forgotten man to all but his closest friends," but they were the people
who counted. Moe lost one of them, his sole remaining partner from the Cleveland Four,
when Morris Kleinman died in Florida on May 5, 1989. The former "Al Capone of Cleveland" was ninety-three years old.

Despite infirmity and his advancing age, Moe stayed in contact with his friends. As
singer Sonny King told newsman Smith, "When he knew he was dying, we would meet at
the country club for a drink or two, or sometimes three, with [Vegas golf pro] Charlie Baron."
After one such outing, good friend Marydean Martin — cofounder with ad man Jim Joyce of
Joyce and Martin Advertising, which landed its first contract with Sunrise Hospital in 1975 —
asked Herb Tobman when Moe had last gone on a picnic. Tobman replied, "I'd guess never."
Martin and some fellow Dalitz loyalists set up an excursion to the nearby mountains, where
Moe enjoyed himself immensely.

Still, his loyal friends and his millions could not halt the march of time.

Hank Greenspun, Moe's on-again, off-again rival and crony, died at home from cancer
on July 22, 1989. Less than three weeks later, Mob lawyer and former Dunes owner Morris
Shenker died in Los Angeles. It may have been a blessing in disguise for Shenker, who was
under indictment on multiple counts of tax evasion and conspiracy to commit bankruptcy
fraud. The headline for his obit in the *St. Louis Post-Dispatch* described Shenker as a "Businessman, Philanthropist."

Dalitz marked Shenker's passing from his penthouse overlooking the Las Vegas Country Club, where he spent his final days attended by two full-time nurses. Alan Balboni reports
that Moe's "reestablishment of positive relations with his daughter, Suzanne, was comfort-
ing," but it could not sustain him. He died at 1:00 A.M. on August 31, 1989, from what newspapers described as a combination of kidney failure and congestive heart disease.

The news made banner headlines in Las Vegas and cast ripples from La Costa to Detroit
and Cleveland. The *New York Times* recapped Moe's life in six short paragraphs, summed up

with the label "ex-bootlegger and owner of Las Vegas casinos." Closer to home, reporters scurried along the Strip, pleading for sound bytes. Herb Tobman called Moe "a legend in his own time," while Irwin Molasky deemed his late mentor a "very classy man." From Florida, Frank Rosenthal spoke up to say, "Moe was controversial but he helped a lot of people. I've known him for many years and would absolutely consider him my friend." Ex-governor Grant Sawyer said, "Moe Dalitz was probably as responsible for the successful gambling economy in southern Nevada as any one person. His conduct has always been exemplary. He was a stickler for observing the rules and regulations. In my opinion, he was a good citizen in every way." Ovid Demaris took a different view: "It's just another dinosaur dying." The *Sun*, which stalked and harried Moe for years at mid-century, now deemed him Sin City's "most distinguished citizen for four decades."

The eulogies continued on September 5, when 350 mourners crowded Congregation Ner Tamid for Moe's memorial service. Aside from Moe's various partners, those in attendance included Grant Sawyer, Vegas mayor Ron Lurie and predecessor Bill Briare, Sheriff John Moran and ex-sheriff Ralph Lamb, district attorney Rex Bell, and Republican National Committeeman Tom Wiesner. Rabbi Sanford Akselrod told the crowd that Moe "was not a particularly religious man, but he knew his roots and was proud to be a Jew." Daughter Suzanne Dalitz Brown capped the ceremony with childhood memories comparing Moe to "John Wayne in a dinner jacket, more god-like than father-like." Above all, she said, "He loved living and loved people. Moe Dalitz did not go gently into that big good-night. He fought desperately."

But the fight that began as a youth in Detroit was finally over.

From Ner Tamid Moe's relatives and closest friends moved on to Palm Valley Cemetery on Eastern Avenue, for a private graveside ceremony at the cemetery's Garden of Eternal Peace. An elegant reception followed at the Desert Inn, complete with gourmet fare and strolling violinists. Given his fondness for parties, Moe would have enjoyed it.

Indeed, he had enjoyed it all. From beginning to end, Moe told Sonny King during one of their last interludes at the Vegas Country Club, "I never had a bad day."

13

Kaddish

In life, Moe Dalitz had done everything within his power to avoid unflattering publicity. In death, he suddenly became fair game for anyone who owned a typewriter and an imagination.

Former G-man William Roemer fired the first salvo in *War of the Godfathers*, a 1990 book purporting to describe a battle for control of Las Vegas waged between Chicago's Tony Accardo and Joe Bonanno in Tucson. While the book's dust jacket billed it as "true crime," the first page of Roemer's introduction warned readers that "a number of important episodes ... have been fictionalized for several reasons, including protecting the sensitive nature of ongoing investigations and prosecutions and respecting the privacy of certain living characters." That said, Roemer proceeds to fabricate a tale loosely rooted in history, filled with events that never occurred.

He begins by discarding the premise detailed in his other three books, that Moe Dalitz was "owned" by Chicago. In *War of the Godfathers* we find Joe Bonanno telling his henchmen, "Dalitz is ours! He's with us!" and "With Dalitz we get Sinatra." Accardo grows suspicious, warning Gus Alex — the Outfit's Greek "fixer," successor to Jake Guzik — that Moe is giving Chicago "the runaround." Sidney Korshak fumes over Moe's crass betrayal, dating from 1983, when Meyer Lansky urged Moe to side with Bonanno. The action heats up in January 1986, when Bonanno meets with "Joe Zerelli" of Detroit to plot the final phase of his Las Vegas coup. "Zerelli" phones Moe to confirm his allegiance, but Chicago learns of the plot by torturing a fictional Bonanno ally named "Jack Holmes." Subsequently, on some unspecified date in "late 1986," real-life Chicago mobster Joseph Ferriola leads an ambush on Moe's limousine motorcade, wounding Dalitz and leaving seven other men dead on the Strip. While Moe clings to life at Sunrise Hospital, Gus Alex flies to Las Vegas and meets "Dr. Randolph Shulz," who directs him to Sunrise orderly "Ben Jackson." Jackson accepts $100,000 to poison Dalitz, who dies the following day. Roemer enters his own story as heroic G-man "Bill Richards" and cracks the case, tracing Moe's murder back to Chicago. It is, as Roemer modestly observes, "a tremendous task for a lone investigator."

Roemer was not content to simply murder Moe on paper, though. He rolled on from there to relate Ben Jackson's confession and sweeping federal indictments issued on February 14, 1990. In Roemer's fable the grand jury indicts Tony Accardo and nine other Outfit leaders; Gus Alex and Joe Ferriola are specifically charged with murdering Dalitz. Their trial convenes on November 1, 1990. Fictional "Judge John McGrath" dismisses Alex's charges, but Ben Jackson's testimony persuades jurors to convict seven other defendants. Accardo escapes, with a surprise acquittal, but the Outfit is crippled, so who really cares?

Some readers may have noted that Roemer's book was released on November 24, 1990, before the close of the mythical trial he describes. There were other discrepancies, too, beyond the glaring fact that Dalitz died from natural causes in 1989. One more example: Roemer claims that Frank Rosenthal's car bombing occurred *after* Moe's murder (instead of 1982), reports that the blast damaged Joe Bonanno's nonexistent "Star" casino (Lefty was bombed outside a Marie Callender's restaurant), and blames the bombing on Tony Spilotro (who died in June 1986). Joe Ferriola was already dead when Roemer's book hit stores nationwide, felled by a heart attack in March 1989 — twenty months *before* his alleged conviction for murdering Dalitz — but Accardo and his surviving minions had learned their lesson from Moe Dalitz and the *Penthouse* case. They filed no libel actions against Roemer or his publisher for charging them with crimes that never occurred.

No harm, no foul. Except...

The story should have ended there, but certain reviewers and "scholars" missed Roemer's up-front disclosure of public-spirited fraud. *Publishers Weekly* swallowed

Author Bill Roemer accused Tony Accardo (shown here at the Kefauver hearings) of "murdering" Moe Dalitz (National Archives).

the fairy tale hook, line and sinker, sketching details of the fabricated plot for would-be buyers and declaring that Roemer's "encyclopedic knowledge makes the book a unique contribution to U.S. crime history." *Library Journal* delivered a similar rave: "In 1986, the Chicago Mafia violently repulsed a bid by the Joe Bonanno crime family to wrest control of the Las Vegas underworld. It was a Pyrrhic victory; afterward most of the top Chicago mob figures were convicted of various crimes. The author, a former FBI agent who investigated the Las Vegas brawl, knows his subject. Although he employs fictional characters and invented dialog to dramatize these events, his account is probably reliable and generally readable."

Four years after Bill Roemer published his fable, author Bill Kelly revealed a different version in the August 1993 issue of *Detective Cases* magazine. According to Kelly, the mythical ambush occurred "almost fourteen years to the day of Bugsy Siegel's murder" — that is, sometime in June 1961— outside the Castaways hotel-casino, slated for demolition to make way for Steve Wynn's Mirage. In Kelly's tale, Moe survived four gunshot wounds *and* an attempt to poison him at Sunrise Hospital, to die of natural causes in August 1989. Aside from the fact that no such ambush ever occurred, Kelly is decades off on his casino history. The Castaways closed in 1987, and Wynn's Mirage did not open until November 1989, three months after Dalitz was buried.

It may be no surprise that a pulp "detective" magazine garbled the facts of Moe's life and death, but it was nothing short of shocking when Roemer's fabricated story found its way into a history of Jewish gangsters published in 1993 by Robert Rockaway, associate professor of Jewish history at Tel Aviv University. The myth endures.

A decade after Roemer's book appeared, author Cathie John used Dalitz as a character in *Little Mexico*, her novel of Newport, Kentucky. The story opens in September 1943, as Mob soldier Jimmy "The Shiv" Turelli receives orders to shut down "the mom 'n' pop operations" in Newport. As described by John, "Turelli left the back room at Meyer's Delicatessen with his marching orders from Moe Dalitz. Not exactly the ritziest of joints, but that's where the Big Four of the Cleveland Syndicate—Moe, Sam Tucker, Louis Rothkopf, and Morris Kleinman—held some of their business meetings. And this had been an important one. Sam even came all the way up from Kentucky to attend it." Turelli reflects that he "would rather be working for Italians, but Eliot Ness had busted up the Mayfield Road Mob, leaving the Jew boys to run this part of the country. So that's the way it goes in Cleveland."

Moe was also a presence — though less a prime mover — in best-selling author James Ellroy's novel *The Cold Six Thousand*, published in 2001. That story begins on November 22, 1963, moments after the JFK assassination, and follows ex-FBI agent Ward Littell through the next five years of America's hidden history. Dalitz turns up at odd times, advancing the plot with terse dialogue and timely donations of cash. Four years after Dallas, Moe declares his view of Howard Hughes's entourage: "Goyishe shitheels. Mormons are roughly synonymous with the Ku Klux Klan." In January 1964 he meets Carlos Marcello and Santo Trafficante for a "summit" at the Dunes. Cigars are banned, because "Moe Dalitz was allergic." Subsequently, in the DI counting room, Moe briefs Littell on the mechanics of skimming: "It's not that complicated. The count guys are in cahoots with the camera guys. The camera goes on the fritz, accidental on purpose, so the count guys can get the skim out and retally it. You don't need a college education." As couriers, he says, "We use civilians, exclusive. Squarejohns who owe casino markers. They run the skim and pay off their debts at 7½% of the transport." Moe hands Littell ten grand off the top, to bribe black activists, remarking, "Here, for your civil-rights deal. What's their fucking motto, 'We Shall Overcome'?"

* * *

Moe missed it all, and as his memory began to fade the death-clock ran for friends and enemies alike. No one gets out alive.

Kemper Marley died in La Jolla, California, from undisclosed causes, on June 25, 1990. He was one of Arizona's richest men. At his death, Marley left $1 million to the University of Arizona, which placed his name on a building devoted to agricultural studies.

Jimmy Fratianno was dropped from the federal witness program for violating its rules but continued to live in the spotlight, unmolested. Apparently dissatisfied with his portrayal in *The Las Mafioso*, Fratianno collaborated with author Michael Zuckerman on a second biography, *Vengeance is Mine*, published in 1987. By then, Alzheimer's disease had begun to erode his already selective memory. Fratianno died in his sleep on July 2, 1993.

Harry Rosenzweig outlived Fratianno by three months, dying in Phoenix on September 28, 1993. The *Jewish News of Greater Phoenix* called Rosenzweig "a legend in his time, not just for his leadership and accomplishments, but for his humanity as well. He was truly a mensch."

Phil Harris, Moe's old friend and fellow party animal, died from a heart attack at Palm Springs on August 11, 1995.

William Roemer died from lung cancer on June 14, 1996. His last detour into fantasy was the 1996 HBO movie *Sugartime*, wherein Roemer played a CIA agent who recruits Sam Giancana to kill Fidel Castro.

Barry Goldwater died from complications of a stroke on May 29, 1998. In his twilight years, he mortified old comrades by supporting legalized abortion and military recruitment of gays, while complaining that "a bunch of kooks" had seized control of the Republican Party.

Hank Messick, the reporter whom Moe once saved from a "Newport nightgown," died in Florida on November 6, 1999, from Sjögren's syndrome, a disease in which immune cells attack and destroy the exocrine glands that produce tears and saliva.

Al Sachs was frozen out of legal gambling after Trans-Sterling's collapse. He lived in affluent obscurity, dividing his time between Vegas and Malibu, California, until a heart attack killed him on February 17, 2002.

Lew Wasserman, Moe's former nightclub manager who rose to become Hollywood's "last mogul," died on June 3, 2002. Grandson Casey Wasserman carries on the family name and business, serving at the helm of Wasserman Media Group.

Herb Tobman never forgot his debt to Moe Dalitz. In 1990, launching an abortive bid to become Nevada's lieutenant governor, he told the press, "They always said I am an associate of Moe Dalitz, which I was and I'm proud to admit. They ought to name twenty schools after him." Tobman ran for mayor of Las Vegas in 1990 and lost. He died from a heart attack on March 14, 2006.

Bernie Rothkopf finished his illustrious gaming career at the MGM Grand. He died after a long battle with cancer, on August 15, 2007. Friends gathered for a "celebration of his life" at the Las Vegas Country Club on September 10.

* * *

There are survivors, too, as this work goes to press. As humans will, some prospered and some failed.

Merv Adelson sold his share of Paradise Developments to Irwin Molasky in 1999, devoting himself thereafter to a life that *Fortune* magazine described as "a show-business fantasy." When Hollywood became too hectic, Adelson retreated to the Lazy A, a ranch near Aspen, Colorado, that featured golf links, three hot tubs, and a horse barn so luxurious it rated a feature in *Architectural Digest*. By June 2003, Adelson faced divorce from his third wife and he was mired in debt. Creditors clamored for repayment of some $112.5 million, and the Lazy A was threatened with foreclosure. On June 8, while driving through Aspen with two-year-old daughter Ava, Adelson lost control of his car, striking two other vehicles, a street sign, and two trees. Police jailed him for driving while intoxicated; his lawyer blamed the crack-up on "a mini-stroke." September 2003 found Adelson bankrupt. Two years later, he staged a comeback, producing children's entertainment. "I'd like to end my career by doing something for kids," he told *Variety* in November 2005. "I love that idea."

After buying Adelson's share of Paradise Developments, Irwin Molasky built the Park Towers Las Vegas, described on its website as "one of the finest luxury condos in the world." He remains a Las Vegas icon.

Allard Roen leads a quieter life at Rancho La Costa. In August 2001 he celebrated fifty years of marriage to wife Evelyn, surrounded by various friends from Las Vegas.

Suzanne Dalitz Gollin received some unwelcome publicity from the *San Diego Reader* in February 2006. Reporters delved into her business dealings with James Waring, described in a feature story as a "real estate developer, attorney, high-tech investor, environmentalist, and close advisor to a Las Vegas mobster's wealthy daughter." Waring was a trustee for the M.B. Dalitz trust, established in Moe's will, doubling as Suzanne's partner in various real estate projects. Waring was also involved with Suzanne's charity, the Angelica Foundation, based in Rancho Santa Fe, five miles south of La Costa. Angelica's website describes it as "a small, California-based private family foundation that supports progressive activist organizations working for democratic change, environmental sustainability, and social justice." It also "continues its support for the Drug Policy Alliance, the leading organization working to overcome the drug war and promote new drug policies based on science, compassion, health, and human rights." Indeed, James Gollin — Suzanne's husband, the director of Angelica and chairman of the Rainforest Action Network — sits on the DPA's board of directors.

As revealed in the *Reader*, Angelica had purchased real estate in San Diego from the M.B. Dalitz Foundation in 1994, avoiding transfer tax by listing the sale as "intra-family." Fletcher Paddison, an ex-associate of Waring's at the law firm of Ross, Dixon and Bell, told the *Reader* that Moe's trust was initially handled "by former professionals who had worked for Mr. Dalitz" in Vegas and L.A., but that "the trust assets had been mismanaged. [Suzanne] had been struggling before [Waring's] involvement." In July 1994 Suzanne, Waring, Toni Lena Clark and others purchased real estate on L.A.'s Wilshire Boulevard. Captions on photographs filed in a special collection at the University of Nevada–Las Vegas indicate that Lena was the birth name of Wilbur Clark's widow Toni.

* * *

The face of Las Vegas has changed radically since Moe Dalitz died, but its greedy, grafting spirit remains untouched by passing time. After a brief and ultimately unsuccessful bid to make Vegas a "family town," Sin City has reverted to its early go-for-broke persona. Anything can happen there, and often does. For those who miss the point, bold advertisements boast, "What happens in Vegas stays in Vegas."

As for the Mob, local newspapers still deny its influence on legal gambling. A *Sun* headline from April 20, 1997, blared the same message repeated endlessly since 1946: "LV Mob Clout Doubtful." Wayne Newton, who has seen both sides of Vegas, seemed wistful when he told reporter Alan Richman, "The people I suspect might have been involved in organized crime, from Moe Dalitz down the line, I was never treated in any but a nice way by them. If anything, I miss them."

New developments along the Strip meant that the old joints had to change or disappear. ITT-Sheraton bought the Desert Inn from Kirk Kerkorian for $160 million, in 1993, and launched a four-year renovation project costing another $200 million. Starwood Hotels and Resorts Worldwide Inc. bought the DI, along with the rest of ITT, in 1998, then announced its sale to Sun International Hotels for $275 million in May 1999. On April 25, 2000, Steve Wynn paid $270 million for Moe's old resort, and closed it forever at 2 A.M. on August 28. Wynn demolished the DI's main tower on October 23, 2001, to make way for his new Wynn Las Vegas Resort and Country Club. The DI's second tower lingered as a museum for Wynn's art collection, but poor ticket sales prompted its implosion on November 16, 2004.

Moe's Stardust was the next to go. It had never quite recovered from the damage to its reputation suffered under Argent and Trans-Sterling, and promotion of annual "Lifestyles" conventions for swinging "play couples" did nothing to recoup the joint's lost glamour. Play ceased at the Stardust on November 1, 2006, and demolition charges flattened the resort on March 13, 2007, clearing the way for Boyd Gaming's new $4.4 billion "megaresort," the Echelon Place, scheduled to open in 2010. Boyd executives donated the Stardust's world-famous eighteen-story sign to the local Neon Museum.

* * *

And Las Vegas remembers. Those who matter in Sin City recognize the debt they owe Moe Dalitz and his fellow pioneers. They lionize him still, proud that he clawed his way up from the gutter to become "Mr. Las Vegas." And so what if the persistent critics are correct, and he kept one foot in the gutter to the bitter end? Which mega-millionaire can say his hands are clean?

Las Vegas, like Chicago, takes a certain pride in its grim origins, exulting in the muck that cakes its roots. In December 2007 Ellen Knowlton, FBI agent-in-charge of the Vegas field office during 2002–06, announced plans to open a $50 million Mob museum in 2010. The facility will be designed by Dennis Barrie, architect of Cleveland's Rock and Roll Hall of Fame and Washington's International Spy Museum. By late 2007, $15 million had been raised through sale of commemorative license plates.

Press reports announcing the museum's creation claimed that "organized crime was driven out of Las Vegas in the 1970s and '80s by the FBI, local police and prosecutors, state crackdowns and casino purchases by corporate interests." FBI headquarters is eager to promote that rosy vision, donating photographs, wiretap transcripts, and other proof of its "efforts to kneecap organized crime in the 1950s, '60s and '70s." As Bureau spokesman Dan McCarron put it, "This is a way to connect with the public and show the results of our work." It remains to be seen whether any display will note J. Edgar Hoover's friendship with gangsters or his decades of denial that the Mob existed.

As for Mayor Oscar Goodman, formerly paid to defend some of those whose mug shots will grace the museum, he celebrates the project for precisely what it is: another tourist draw. "Let's be brutally honest, warts and all," Goodman told reporter Ken Ritter. "This is more than legend. It's fact. This is something that differentiates us from other cities."

Cities like Detroit, Cleveland, Toledo, Buffalo, Newport, Covington, Miami, and Havana. All tolerated mobsters during their wide-open glory years, and all still harbor criminals today. But none rolled out the public welcome mat until Las Vegas showed them how. None worked so hard to make the Mob *respectable*.

Moe Dalitz gambled on Las Vegas, and he won. But in a larger sense he also gambled on America. He staked his life and reputation on a bet that money matters more than faith or family or honor.

Moe was, as Robbins Cahill once declared, a peerless judge of character.

America has yet to prove him wrong.

Bibliography

Books

Allsop, Kenneth. *The Bootleggers.* New Rochelle: Arlington House, 1961.

Anderson, Jack. *Peace, War, and Politics.* New York: Tom Doherty Associates, 1999.

Anson, Robert. *"They've Killed the President!"* New York: Bantam, 1975.

Asher, Court. *Sacred Cows.* The Author, 1931.

Asbury, Herbert. *The Great Illusion.* Westport: Greenwood Press, 1950.

Ashman, Charles, and Rebecca Sobel. *The Strange Disappearance of Jimmy Hoffa.* New York: Manor Books, 1976.

Balboni, Alan. *Beyond the Mafia.* Reno: University of Nevada Press, 1996.

_____. "Moe Dalitz," in *The Maverick Spirit*, ed. Richard Davies. Reno: University of Nevada Press, 1999.

Bald, F. Clever. *Michigan in Four Centuries.* New York: Harper & Brothers, 1954.

Barlett, Donald, and James Steele. *Empire.* New York: W. W. Norton, 1979.

Beaufait, Howard. "The Case of William Potter," in *Cleveland Murders*, ed. Oliver Bayer. New York: Duell, Sloan and Pearce, 1947.

Berman, Susan. *Easy Street.* New York: Dial Press, 1981.

_____. *Lady Las Vegas.* New York: TV Books, 1996

Biltz, Norman. *Memoirs of "The Duke of Nevada."* Reno: University of Nevada Press, 1967.

Bingay, Malcolm. *Detroit is My Own Home Town.* Indianapolis: Bobbs-Merrill, 1946.

Blakey, G. Robert, and Richard Billings. *The Plot to Kill the President.* New York: Times Books, 1981.

Block, Alan. *Masters of Paradise.* New Brunswick: Transaction, 1991.

Blumenthal, Sid, ed. *Government by Gunplay.* New York: Signet, 1976.

Bly, Nellie. *The Kennedy Men.* New York: Kensington, 1996.

Branch, Taylor. *At Canaan's Edge.* New York: Simon & Schuster, 2002.

Bruck, Connie. *When Hollywood Had a King.* New York: Random House, 2003.

Burbank, Jeff. *Las Vegas Babylon.* New York: M. Evans, 2005.

_____. *License to Steal.* Reno: University of Nevada Press, 2000.

Brashler, William. *The Don.* New York: Ballantine, 1977.

Brewton, Pete. *The Mafia, CIA & George Bush.* New York: S.P.I. Books, 1992.

Brill, Stephen. *The Teamsters.* New York: Simon & Schuster, 1978.

Browning, Frank, and John Gerassi. *The American Way of Crime.* New York: G. P. Putnam's Sons, 1980.

Cahill, Robbins. *Recollections of Work in State Politics, Government, Taxation, Gaming Control, Clark County Administration, and the Nevada Resort Association.* Reno: University of Nevada Press, 1972.

Canfield, Michael, and Alan Weberman. *Coup d'état in America.* New York: Third Press, 1975.

Carlisle, Rodney, and Dominic Monetta. *Brandy, Our Man in Acapulco.* Denton: University of North Texas Press, 1999.

Chandler, David. *Brothers in Blood.* New York: E. P. Dutton, 1975.

Cirules, Enrique. *The Mafia in Havana.* Melbourne: Ocean Press, 2004.

Cohen, Mickey. *Mickey Cohen — in My Own Words.* Englewood Cliffs: Prentice-Hall, 1975.

Cohn, Roy. *A Fool for a Client.* New York: Hawthorn, 1971.

Condon, George. *Cleveland: The Best Kept Secret.* Garden City: Doubleday, 1967.

Conot, Robert. *American Odyssey*. New York: William Morrow, 1974.

Cook, Fred. *Mafia!* Greenwich: Fawcett, 1973.

_____. *A Two-Dollar Bet Means Murder*. New York: Dial Press, 1961.

Demaris, Ovid. *The Last Mafioso*. New York: Times Books, 1981.

Denton, Sally, and Roger Morris. *The Money and the Power*. New York: Alfred A. Knopf, 2001.

Dinnerstein, Leonard. *Anti-Semitism in America*. New York: Oxford University Press, 1994.

Drosnin, Michael. *Citizen Hughes*. New York: Bantam, 1985.

Dunne, Dominick. *The Mansions of Limbo*. New York: Crown, 1991.

Edmonds, Andy. *Bugsy's Baby*. New York: Birch Lane Press, 1993.

Edwards, Jerome. *Pat McCarran*. Reno: University of Nevada Press, 1982.

Ehrenfried, Albert. *A Chronicle of Boston Jewry*. n.p.: n.d.

Eisenberg, Dennis, Uri Dan, and Eli Landay. *Meyer Lansky*. New York: Paddington Press, 1979.

Engelman, Larry. *Intemperance*. New York: Free Press, 1979.

English, T. J. *Paddy Whacked*. New York: Regan Books, 2005.

Evey, Stuard, and Irv Broughton. *ESPN*. Chicago: Triumph, 2004.

Evica, George. *And We Are All Mortal*. West Hartford: University of Hartford, 1978.

Exner, Judith. *My Story*. New York: Grove Press, 1977.

Facts on File Yearbooks. New York: Facts on File, 1948–1977.

Farrell, Ronald, and Carole Case. *The Black Book and the Mob*. Madison: University of Wisconsin Press, 1995.

Feder, Sid, and Joachim Joesten. *The Luciano Story*. New York: Popular Library, 1954.

Feldstein, Stanley. *The Land That I Show You*. Garden City: Anchor Press, 1978.

Fensterwald, Bernard. *Coincidence or Conspiracy?* New York: Zebra, 1977.

Fine, Sidney. *Frank Murphy: The Detroit Years*. Ann Arbor: University of Michigan Press, 1975.

Fischer, Steve. *When the Mob Ran Vegas*. Boys Town: Berkline Press, 2005.

Fisher, Eddie. *Been There, Done That*. New York: St. Martin's, 1999.

Fortenay, Charles. *Estes Kefauver*. Knoxville: University of Tennessee Press, 1980.

Fox, Stephen. *Blood and Power*. New York: Penguin, 1989.

Fraley, Oscar. *4 Against the Mob*. New York: Popular Library, 1961.

Fried, Albert. *The Rise and Fall of the Jewish Gangster in America*. New York: Holt, Rinehart & Winston, 1980.

Friedman, Allen, and Ted Schwarz. *Power and Greed*. New York: Franklin Watts, 1989.

Gage, Nicholas. *Greek Fire*. New York: Alfred A. Knopf, 2000.

_____. *The Mafia Is Not an Equal Opportunity Employer*. New York: McGraw-Hill, 1971.

Garrison, Omar. *Howard Hughes in Las Vegas*. New York: Lyle Stuart, 1970.

Gentry, Curt. *J. Edgar Hoover*. New York: W. W. Norton, 1991.

Giancana, Antoinette, and Thomas Renner. *Mafia Princess*. New York: Avon, 1984.

Glass, Mary. *Nevada's Turbulent '50s*. Reno: University of Nevada Press, 1981.

Gorman, Joseph. *Kefauver*. New York: Oxford University Press, 1971.

Gosch, Martin, and Richard Hammer. *The Last Testament of Lucky Luciano*. Boston: Little, Brown, 1975.

Greenspun, Hank, and Alex Pelle. *Where I Stand*. New York: David McKay, 1966.

Hammer, Richard. *Playboy's Illustrated History of Organized Crime*. Chicago: Playboy Press, 1975.

Haun, Charles. "Bloody July," in *Detroit Murders*, ed. Alvin Hamer. New York: Duell, Sloan and Pearce, 1948.

Headley, Lake, and William Hoffman. *Loud and Clear*. New York: Henry Holt, 1990.

Heimel, Paul. *Eliot Ness*. Nashville: Cumberland House, 2000.

Higham, Charles. *Howard Hughes*. New York: G. P. Putnam's Sons, 1993.

Hinckle, Warren, and William Turner. *Deadly Secrets*. New York: Thunder's Mouth Press, 1992.

Hoffa, James, and Oscar Fraley. *Hoffa: The Real Story*. New York: Stein & Day, 1975.

Hopkins, A. D. "Benny Binion," in *The Players*, ed. Jack Sheehan. Reno: University of Nevada Press, 1997.

Hougan, Jim. *Spooks*. New York: William Morrow, 1978.

Howe, Irving. *World of Our Fathers*. New York: Harcourt Brace Jovanovich, 1976.

Jackson, Kenneth. *The Ku Klux Klan in the City, 1915–1930*. New York: Oxford University Press, 1967.

James, Ralph, and Estelle James. *Hoffa and the Teamsters*. Princeton: D. Van Norstrand, 1965.

James, Robert. *The Informant Files*. New York: Electronic Media, 1994.

Jennings, Dean. *We Only Kill Each Other*. Englewood Cliffs: Prentice-Hall, 1967.

Johnston, David. *Temples of Chance*. New York: Doubleday, 1992.

Jordan, David. *Drug Politics*. Norman: University of Oklahoma Press, 1999.

Joseph, Samuel. *Jewish Immigration to the United States from 1881 to 1910*. New York: Arno Press, 1969.

Kaiser, Robert. *"RFK Must Die!"* New York: Grove Press, 1970.

Kalimtgis, Konstandinos, David Goldman and Jeffrey Steinberg. *Dope, Inc.* New York: New Benjamin Franklin House, 1978.

Kantor, Seth. *Who Was Jack Ruby?* New York: Everest House, 1978.

Karp, Alexander, ed. *The Jewish Experience in America. Volume IV: The Era of Immigration.* Waltham: American Jewish Historical Society, 1969.

Karpis, Alvin. *The Alvin Karpis Story.* New York: Coward, McCann & Geohegan, 1971.

Kavieff. Paul. *The Purple Gang.* Fort Lee: Barricade Books, 2000.

_____. *The Violent Years.* New York: Barricade Books, 2001.

Kefauver, Estes. *Crime in America.* New York: Greenwood Press, 1951.

Kelly, Kitty. *His Way.* New York: Bantam, 1986.

Kennedy, Robert. *The Enemy Within.* New York: Harper & Row, 1960.

Klaber, William, and Philip Melanson. *Shadow Play.* New York: St. Martin's, 1997.

Kobler, John. *Ardent Spirits.* New York: G. P. Putnam's Sons, 1973.

Konigsberg, Eric. *Blood Relation.* New York: HarperCollins, 2005.

Koskoff, David. *Joseph P. Kennedy.* Englewood Cliffs: Prentice-Hall, 1974.

Kunkin, Art. *The Breaking of a President.* City of Industry: Therapy Productions, 1974.

Kwitney, Jonathan. *Vicious Circles.* New York: Norton, 1979.

Lacey, Robert. *Little Man.* Boston: Little, Brown, 1991.

Lalli, Sergio. "Cliff Jones," in *The Players*, ed. Jack Sheehan. Reno: University of Nevada Press, 1997.

_____. "Howard Hughes in Vegas," in *The Players*, ed. Jack Sheehan. Reno: University of Nevada Press, 1997.

Lasky, Victor. *It Didn't Start with Watergate.* New York: Dell, 1977.

_____. *J.F.K.—The Man and the Myth.* New York: Dell, 1977.

Lee, Henry. *How Dry We Were.* Englewood Cliffs: Prentice-Hall, 1963.

Lewis, Oscar. *Sagebrush Casinos.* Garden City: Doubleday, 1953.

Louderback, Lew. *The Bad Ones.* Greenwich: Fawcett Gold Medal, 1968.

Lukas, J. Anthony. *Nightmare.* New York: Viking, 1976.

Lynch, Denis. *Criminals and Politicians.* New York: Macmillan, 1932.

Marrs, Jim. *Crossfire.* New York: Carroll & Graf, 1989.

McDougal, Dennis. *The Last Mogul.* New York: Crown, 1998.

_____. *Privileged Son.* Cambridge: Perseus, 2001.

Merz, Charles. *The Dry Decade.* Seattle: University of Washington Press, 1930.

Maclean, Don. *Pictorial History of the Mafia.* New York: Pyramid, 1974.

Maheu, Robert, and Richard Hack. *Next to Hughes.* New York: HarperCollins, 1993.

Mahon, Gigi. *The Company That Bought the Boardwalk.* New York: Random House, 1980.

Melanson, Philip. *The Robert F. Kennedy Assassination.* New York: S. P. I. Books, 1994,

Merz, Charles. *The Dry Decade.* Seattle: University of Washington Press, 1930.

Messick, Hank. *The Beauties and the Beasts.* New York: David McKay, 1973.

_____. *John Edgar Hoover.* New York: David McKay, 1972.

_____. *Lanksy.* New York: G. P. Putnam, 1971.

_____. *Razzle Dazzle.* Covington: For the Love of Books, 1995.

_____. *Secret File.* New York: G. P. Putnam's Sons, 1969.

_____. *The Silent Syndicate.* New York: Macmillan, 1967.

_____. *Syndicate Abroad.* New York: Macmillan, 1969.

_____. *Syndicate in the Sun.* New York: Macmillan, 1968.

_____. *Syndicate Wife.* New York: Macmillan, 1968.

Messick, Hank, and Burt Goldblatt. *The Mobs and the Mafia.* New York: Ballantine, 1972.

Messick, Hank, and Burt Goldblatt. *The Only Game in Town.* New York: Thomas Y. Crowell, 1976.

Messick, Hank, and Joseph Nellis. *The Private Lives of Public Enemies.* New York: Peter H. Wyden, 1973.

Moehring, Eugene. *Resort City in the Sunbelt.* Reno: University of Nevada Press, 1989.

Moldea, Dan. *Dark Victory.* New York: Viking, 1986.

_____. *The Hoffa Wars.* New York: Paddington Press, 1978.

_____. *Interference.* New York: William Morrow, 1989.

Moore, William. *The Kefauver Committee and the Politics of Crime.* Columbia: University of Missouri Press, 1974.

Morrow, Robert. *The Senator Must Die.* Santa Monica: Roundtable, 1988.

Nash, Jay. *Murder Among the Rich and Famous.* New York: Dell, 1984.

Neff, James. *Mobbed Up.* New York: Dell, 1989.

Newfield, Jack. *Only in America.* New York: William Morrow, 1995.

Newman, Peter. *Bronfman Dynasty.* Toronto: McClelland & Stewart, 1978.

Nickel, Steven. *Torso.* Winston-Salem: John F. Blair, 1989.

North, Mark. *Act of Treason.* New York: Carroll & Graf, 1991.

Oglesby, Carl. *The Yankee and Cowboy War.* Kansas City: Sheed Andrews & McNeel, 1976.

Olsen, Edward. *My Career as Journalist in Oregon, Idaho, and Nevada; in Nevada Gaming Control; and at the University of Nevada.* Reno: University of Nevada, 1969.

Oppenheimer, Jerry. *Barbara Walters.* New York: St. Martin's, 1990.

Ostrander, Gilman. *Nevada: The Great Rotten Borough.* New York: Alfred A. Knopf, 1966.

Pepper, William. *Orders to Kill.* New York: Warner, 1995.

Peterson, Virgil. *The Mob.* Ottawa: Green Hill, 1983.

Phelan, James. *Howard Hughes: The Hidden Years.* New York: Random House, 1976.

Pileggi, Nicholas. *Casino.* New York: Pocket Books, 1995.

Porello, Rick. *The Rise and Fall of the Cleveland Mafia.* New York: Barricade Books, 1995.

Raab, Selwyn. *Five Families.* New York: Thomas Dunne, 2005.

Rappleye, Charles, and Ed Becker. *All American Mafioso.* New York: Doubleday, 1991.

Redston, George, and Kendell Crossen. *The Conspiracy of Death.* New York: Bobbs-Merrill, 1965.

Reid, Ed. *The Grim Reapers.* New York: Bantam, 1969.

_____. *Las Vegas — City Without Clocks.* Englewood Cliffs: Prentice-Hall, 1961.

_____. *Mickey Cohen: Mobster.* New York: Pinnacle, 1973.

_____, and Ovid Demaris. *The Green Felt Jungle.* New York: Pocket Books, 1964.

Remnick, David. *King of the World.* New York: Random House, 1998.

Riis, Jacob. *The Battle with the Slum.* New York: Macmillan, 1902.

Rockaway, Robert. *But He Was Good to His Mother.* Jerusalem: Gefen Publishing House, 1993.

Roemer, William. *Accardo: The Genuine Godfather.* New York: Ivy Books, 1995.

_____. *The Enforcer.* New York: Ivy Books, 1994.

_____. *Roemer: Man Against the Mob.* New York: Ivy Books, 1989.

_____. *War of the Godfathers.* New York: Ivy Books, 1990.

Rothman, Hal. *Neon Metropolis.* New York: Routledge, 2002.

Rothman, Hal, and Mike Davis, eds. *The Grit Beneath the Glitter.* Berkeley: University of California Press, 2002.

Russo, Gus. *The Outfit.* New York: Bloomsbury, 2003.

_____. *Supermob.* New York: Bloomsbury, 2006.

Sann, Paul. *Kill the Dutchman!* New Rochelle: Arlington House, 1971.

Schaap, Dick. *Steinbrenner!* New York: G. P. Putnam's Sons, 1982.

Scheim, David. *Contract on America.* New York: S. P. I. Books, 1988.

Schlesinger, Arthur. *Robert Kennedy and His Times.* New York: Ballantine, 1978.

Schwartz, David. *Suburban Xanadu.* Routledge: New York, 2003.

Schwarz, Ted. *Joseph P. Kennedy.* New York: John Wiley & Sons, 2003.

Scott, Cathy. *Murder of a Mafia Daughter.* Fort Lee: Barricade Books, 2002.

Scott, Peter, ed. *The Assassinations: Dallas and Beyond.* New York: Vintage, 1976.

Sharp, Kathleen. *Mr. and Mrs. Hollywood.* New York: Carroll & Graf, 2003.

Sheehan, Jack, ed. *The Players.* Reno: University of Nevada Press, 1995.

Sheridan, Walter. *The Fall and Rise of Jimmy Hoffa.* New York: Saturday Review Press, 1972.

Shoumatoff, Alex. *Legends of the American Desert.* New York: Alfred A. Knopf, 1997.

Simich, Jerry, and Thomas Wright. *The Peoples of Las Vegas.* Reno: University of Nevada Press, 2005.

Skolnick, Jerome. *House of Cards.* Boston: Little, Brown, 1978.

Slater, Leonard. *The Pledge.* New York: Pocket, 1971.

Sloane, Arthur. *Hoffa.* Cambridge: MIT Press, 1991.

Smith, John. "Moe Dalitz in the Desert," in *The Players,* ed. Jack Sheehan. Reno: University of Nevada Press, 1997.

_____. *Running Scared.* New York: Barricade Books, 1995.

_____. *Sharks in the Desert.* Fort Lee: Barricade Books, 2005.

Special Report No. 13, Public Affairs Series: The Mafia Today. Los Angeles: Knight Publishing, 1977.

Starr, John. *The Purveyor.* New York: Holt, Rinehart & Winston, 1961.

Steinberg, Milton. *The Making of the Modern Jew.* New York: Behrfman House, 1948.

Steinke, Gord. *Mobsters & Rumrunners of Canada.* Edmonton: Folklore Publishing, 2003.

Sublette, Ned. *Cuba and Its Music.* Chicago: Chicago Review Press, 2004.

Summers, Anthony. *The Arrogance of Power.* New York: Viking, 2000.

_____. *Conspiracy.* New York: McGraw-Hill, 1980.

_____. *Official and Confidential.* New York: G. P. Putnam's Sons, 1993.

Sward, Keith. *The Legend of Henry Ford.* New York: Russell & Russell, 1968.

Tallberg, Martin. *Don Bolles.* New York: Popular Library, 1977.

Taylor, Dick, and Pat Howell. *Las Vegas, City of Sin?* San Antonio: The Naylor Co., 1963.

Thompson, Nelson. *The Dark Side of Camelot.* Chicago: Playboy Press, 1976.

Torgerson, Dial. *Kerkorian.* New York: Dial Press, 1974.

Tosches, Nick. *The Devil and Sonny Liston.* Boston: Little, Brown, 2000.

_____. *Dino.* New York: Dell, 1992.

Tronnes, Mike, ed. *Literary Las Vegas.* New York: Henry Holt, 1995.

Tuohy, John. *When Capone's Mob Murdered Roger Touhy.* Fort Lee, N.J.: Barricade Books, 2001.

Turkus, Burton, and Sid Feder. *Murder, Inc.* New York: Bantam, 1951.

Turner, Wallace. *Gamblers' Money.* Boston: Houghton Mifflin, 1965.

Turner, William, and John Christian. *The Assassination of Robert F. Kennedy.* New York: Random House, 1978.

Unger, Robert. *The Union Station Massacre.* Kansas City: Andrews, McNeel, 1997.

Van Meter, Jonathan. *The Last Good Time.* New York: Crown, 2003.

Velie, Lester. *Desperate Bargain.* New York: Reader's Digest Press, 1977.

Von Hoffman, Nicholas. *Citizen Cohn.* New York: Doubleday, 1988.

Wendland, Michael. *The Arizona Project.* Kansas City: Sheed Andrews & McMeel, 1977.

Whyte, William. *Cluster Development.* New York: American Conservation Assn., 1964.

Widick, B. J. *Detroit: City of Race and Class Violence.* Chicago: Quadrangle, 1972.

Wieder, Arnold. *The Early Jewish Community of Boston's North End.* Waltham: Brandeis University, 1962.

Wolfe, Donald. *The Black Dahlia Files.* New York: Regan, 2005.

Woodford, Frank, and Arthur Woodford. *All Our Yesterdays.* Detroit: Wayne State University Press, 1969.

Young, A. S. *Sonny Liston.* Chicago: Johnson, 1963.

Youngblood, Jack, and Robin Moore. *The Devil to Pay.* London: Anthony Gibbs & Phillips, 1961.

Zion, Sidney. *The Autobiography of Roy Cohn.* New York: St. Martin's, 1988.

Zuckerman, Michael. *Vengeance is Mine.* New York: Macmillan, 1987.

Articles

Alpern, David, et al. "Jimmy Hoffa vanishes." *Newsweek* (August 11, 1975): 19–21.

Bauder, Don, and Matt Potter. "Sanders man knows bootleg money game." *San Diego Reader* (February 9, 2006). www.sandiegoreader.com/news/2006/feb/09/sanders-man-knows-bootleg-money-game/.

Belknap, Tim. "Detroit's Purple Gang." *Detroit Free Press Magazine* (June 26, 1983): 6–10.

Bergman, Lowell, and Jeff Gerth. "La Costa." *Penthouse* (March 1975).

"Big Warm Blanket." *Time* (August 7, 1933): 14.

"Bootlegging and murder in Detroit." *Literary Digest* (September 29, 1923): 48–55.

Davidson, Bill. "The great Kentucky scandal." *Look* (October 24, 1961): 88–97.

Friedman, Robert. "Senator Paul Laxalt, the man who runs the Reagan campaign." *Mother Jones* (Aug.–Sept. 1984): 32–39.

"Hot potato." *Forbes* (December 1, 1971): 27–28.

Jedick, Peter. "Eliot Ness." *Cleveland Magazine* (April 1976): 48–57, 91–94.

Kasindorf, Jeanie. "The case against Evelle Younger." *New West* (October 23, 1978): 17–26.

Kelly, Bill. "Moe Dalitz: The Godfather of Las Vegas." *Detective Cases* 43 (August 1993): 36–41.

Kuznik, Frank. "The golden era of the mob." *Cleveland Magazine* (August 1978): 65–72, 155–156.

Lambert, William. "The hotshot one-man Roy Cohn lobby." *Life* (September 5, 1969): 26–30.

"Liquor runners keep police busy." *State Trooper* (July 1930): 15–16.

Lutz, Tom. "How Jim Brading got arrested and released." *Newsreal Series* No. 3 (July 1977).

Maxwell, James. "Kentucky's open city." *Saturday Evening Post* (March 26, 1960): 22–3, 82–85.

Messick, Hank. "The Schenley chapter." *Nation* (April 5, 1971): 428–431.

"Michigan troopers get rum-running plane loaded with much booze." *State Trooper* (September 1929): 28.

"Michigan's 'great booze rush' and its suppression by state and federal action." *Literary Digest* (March 15, 1919): 85–88.

Morton, Ira. "A legend in his time." *Jewish News of Greater Phoenix* (March 25, 2005).

"Notable Michigan 'spots' are raided." *State Trooper* (July 1932): 13.

Park, Kenneth. "Troopers aid in hunt for slayers of Buckley." *State Trooper* (September 1930): 9–10.

Peters, Pete, and Wade Cavanaugh. "Moe Dalitz." *Las Vegas Sun Magazine* (June 12, 1983): 8B–10B; (June 19, 1983): 7B–9B.

Potter, Matt. "Mob scene." *San Diego Reader* (November 18, 1999). www.sandiegoreader.com/news/ 1999/nov/18/mob-scene/.

Roberts, Michael. "Why they blew Shondor Birns away." *Cleveland Magazine* (July 1975): 48–57, 82–100.

"The rum war on the Detroit front." *Literary Digest* (July 6, 1929): 5–7.

St. George, Andrew. "The Mafia vs. the CIA." *True* (April 1970): 33–7, 79–87.

Seneker, Harold. "The Forbes Four Hundred." *Forbes* 130 (September 13, 1982): 100–172.

Silverman, Amy, and John Dougherty. "Haunted By Spirits." *Phoenix New Times* (February 17, 2000). http://www.phoenixnewtimes.com/2000–02–17/news/haunted-by-spirits/.

"Sin center." *Newsweek* (May 26, 1961): 19.

Stelzer, C. D. "Phoenix Rising." *Riverfront Times* (June 11, 1997). http://mediamayhem.blogspot.com/ 2004/08/phoenix-rising.html.

"Teamsters' Watergate connection." *Time* (August 8, 1977): 28.

Underwood, John, and Morton Sharnik. "Look what Louie wrought." *Sports Illustrated* (May 22, 1972): 40–54.

Vanderpool, Tim. "A good fella." *Tucson Weekly* (June 22, 1998). http://weeklywire.com/ww/06–22–98/ tw_curr4.html.

Waas, Murray. "Paul Laxalt's debt to the Mafia." *Rebel* (January 30, 1984): 26–35; (February 6, 1984): 46–51.

Wheeler, Keith, and William Lambert. "Roy Cohn: Is he a liar under oath?" *Life* (October 4, 1963): 24–30, 99–102.

Whelan, Edward. "The big split." *Cleveland Magazine* (June 1984): 63–65, 136–146.

_____. "The bombing business." *Cleveland Magazine* (April 1977): 57–63, 88–98.

_____. "How the Danny Greene bombing exploded the godfather myth." *Cleveland Magazine* (August 1978): 50–63, 95–96, 154–155.

Zehr, Edward. "John McCain, warts and all." *Washington Weekly* (February 14, 2000).

Newspapers

Arizona Republic, 1984–1997
Bakersfield Californian, 1971–1983
Boston Globe, 1951–1987
Buffalo Courier-Express, 1930
Buffalo Evening News, 1927–1930
Chicago Tribune, 1950–1987
Cleveland Plain Dealer, 1924–1980
Cleveland Press, 1931–1951
Detroit Evening Times, 1934
Detroit Free Press, 1920–1960
Detroit Labor News, 1925–1928
Detroit News, 1920–1977
Lansing State Journal, 1972
Las Vegas Free Press, 1950
Las Vegas Review-Journal, 1950–2000

Las Vegas Sun, 1954–2005
Las Vegas Valley Times, 1979–1980
Los Angeles Times, 1965–1980
Louisville Courier-Journal, 1944–1945
Maysfield (Ky.) Messenger, 1949
Miami Herald, 1965
Nevada State Journal, 1965–1966
New York Times, 1918–2000
Reno Gazette, 1966
St. Louis Riverfront Times, 1997
San Diego Union, 1976–1982
Tehachapi News, 1972–1978
USA Today, 1987
Wall Street Journal, 1980–1983

Official Sources

Affidavit of G. Robert Blakey in *Rancho La Costa v. Penthouse International* (February 4, 1976)
Akron city directories, 1926–1929
Ann Arbor city directories, 1925–1930
Applications for Social Security numbers, Andrew Dalitz and Moe Dalitz
Boston city directories, 1894–1903
Boston Marriage Registry Vol. 462, p. 186
Boston Registry of Births Vol. 468, p. 217
California Dept. of Justice, Organized Crime Control Commission. *First Report* (May 1978)
Campbell County (Ky.) Circuit Court records, 1935–1943

Certificate of death for Andrew Dalitz, Michigan Dept. of Health, File No. 48362
Certificate of death for Barnet Dalitz, Michigan Dept. of Health, File No. 1736
Clark County (Nev.) court records: Case Nos. 57300 and 71972
Clark County divorce file no. A4289
Clark County Secured Assessment Rolls, 1980–1985
Cleveland city directories, 1926–1930
Congressional Record, pp. 5887–5889, 6830–6832, 7423–7426, 22168–22169.
Cuyahoga County (Ohio) Court of Common Pleas, 1937–1950
Desert Showboat, Inc. list of officers (July 1962)
Detroit city directories, 1903–1918
U.S. District Court, Western New York, Case No. 11765-B
FBI files No. 62-HQ-47940, 92–3068, SU 94–284, 95–204, 183-HQ-912, 183-SD-57, 196–954, 197–2350
Florida Office of Vital Statistics, Marriage License No. 36390
Illinois Racing Board, Inquiry into License Nos. 402 and 409
Karat, Inc. articles of incorporation
Las Vegas Marriage Registry, Book 101, p. 333
Marion County (Ind.) Circuit Court, application for marriage no. 118–682
National Archives, World War I draft registration records
New Hotel Showboat articles of incorporation
New York Crime Commission, *Public Hearings, No. 5,* Vol. 4, (January 26, 1953): 2786–2791.
St. Louis Recorder of Deeds, marriage license for Moe Dalitz and Dorothy Brazzel
San Diego County Grand Jury, *Organized Crime in San Diego County* (July 7, 1976).
Social Security Death Index
Toronto Stock Exchange Listing Statement No. 1452, New Mylamaque Mines
U.S. Census records, 1900–1930
U.S. District Court — Boston, Mass., Vol. 222, pp. 28–28A, Naturalization certificate of Barnet Dalitz
U.S. House of Representatives. *Report of the Select Committee on Assassinations.* Washington: U.S. Government Printing Office, 1979.
_____. *Third Report by the Committee on Government Reform.* Washington: U.S. Government Printing Office, 2004.
U.S. Senate. *Hearings Before the Select Committee on Improper Activities in the Labor or Management Field.* Washington: U.S. Government Printing Office, 1957–1958.
_____. *Hearings Before the Special Committee to Investigate Organized Crime in Interstate Commerce.* Washington: U.S. Government Printing Office, 1950–1951.
_____. *Report of the Special Committee to Investigate Organized Crime in Interstate Commerce.* Washington: U.S. Government Printing Office, 1951.
U.S. v. Kleinman et al. 107 F. Supp. 407

Websites

AmericaMafia.com, www.americanmafia.com
Chequers Magazine, www.chequers.com
Crime Library, www.crimelibrary.com
Las Vegas Strip History, www.lvstriphistory.com
Nevada Online Encyclopedia, www.nevadahumanities.org
Wikipedia, en.wikipedia.org

Index